ESCAPE ON THE PEARL

The Heroic Bid

for

Freedom

on the

Underground Railroad

WILLIAM MORROW

An Imprint of HarperCollins*Publishers*

ESCAPE

on the

PEARL

———◆———

MARY KAY RICKS

Grateful acknowledgment is made to the following for the use of the illustrations and photographs that appear in the center insert: Collection of the author (pp. 1, 2, 3 top right, 4 top, 9 bottom left and right, 16 top right); Collection of Michael Winston (p. 3 top left); Library of Congress (pp. 3 bottom, 4 bottom, 5 bottom, 6 top, 7, 8 bottom, 10, 11, 12 top, 14 top right, 15); Washingtoniana Division, D.C. Public Library (pp. 5 top, 14 bottom); Corbis (p. 6 bottom); Historical Society of Washington, D.C. (pp. 8 top, 9 top); Virginia Historical Society (p. 12 middle); New Orleans Notarial Archives (p. 12 bottom); Madison County (New York) Historical Society (p. 13); National Archives (p. 14 top left); Dr. Marion Holmes (p. 16 top left); Rafael Crisostomo/*Washington Post* (p. 16 bottom).

Designed by Susan Yang

Map by Paul J. Pugliese

ISBN: 978-0-06-078659-5
ISBN-10: 0-06-078659-0

Book Club Edition

For my family

For the descendants of
Paul and Amelia Edmonson
and
For the many—whose names we may never know—
who were forcibly separated from families and loved ones
by the domestic slave trade

———◆———

If there is no struggle, there is no progress. Those who profess to favor freedom, and deprecate agitation, are men who want crops without plowing up the ground, they want rain without thunder and lightning.

FREDERICK DOUGLASS

Contents

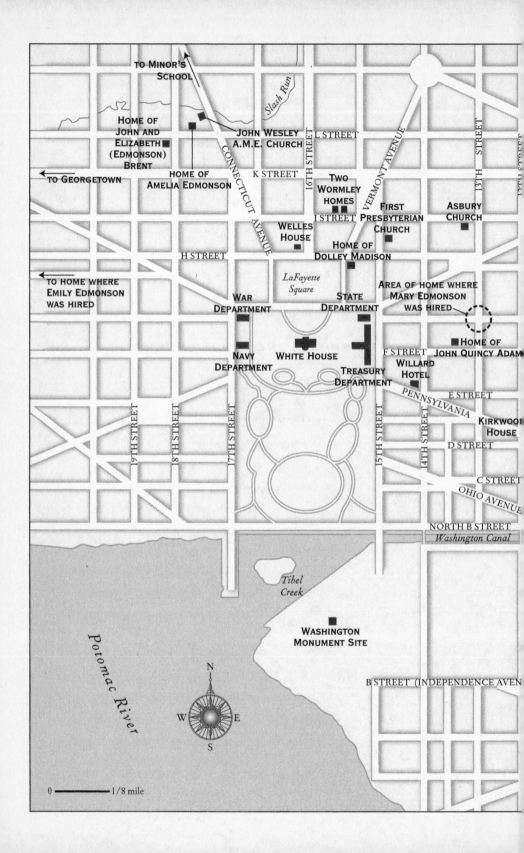

TO MINOR'S
SCHOOL

Slash Run

HOME OF
JOHN AND
ELIZABETH
(EDMONSON) BRENT

JOHN WESLEY
A.M.E. CHURCH

L STREET

16TH STREET

13TH STREET

VERMONT AVENUE

TO GEORGETOWN

HOME OF
AMELIA EDMONSON

CONNECTICUT AVENUE

K STREET

TWO
WORMLEY
HOMES

FIRST
PRESBYTERIAN
CHURCH

ASBURY
CHURCH

I STREET

WELLES
HOUSE

HOME OF
DOLLEY MADISON

H STREET

LaFayette
Square

TO HOME WHERE
EMILY EDMONSON
WAS HIRED

WAR
DEPARTMENT

STATE
DEPARTMENT

AREA OF HOME WHERE
MARY EDMONSON
WAS HIRED

NAVY
DEPARTMENT

WHITE HOUSE

F STREET

HOME OF
JOHN QUINCY ADAMS

19TH STREET

18TH STREET

17TH STREET

TREASURY
DEPARTMENT

WILLARD
HOTEL

PENNSYLVANIA

E STREET

15TH STREET

14TH STREET

D STREET

KIRKWOOD
HOUSE

C STREET

OHIO AVENUE

NORTH B STREET

Washington Canal

Tibel
Creek

Potomac River

WASHINGTON
MONUMENT SITE

N
W   E
S

B STREET (INDEPENDENCE AVENUE

0 ——— 1/8 mile

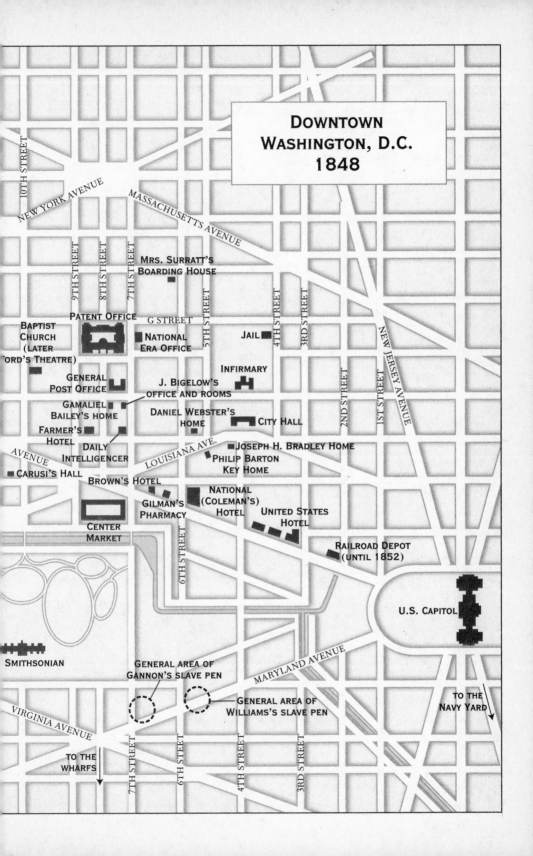

DOWNTOWN WASHINGTON, D.C. 1848

10TH STREET

NEW YORK AVENUE

MASSACHUSETTS AVENUE

9TH STREET

8TH STREET

7TH STREET

5TH STREET

4TH STREET

3RD STREET

NEW JERSEY AVENUE

MRS. SURRATT'S BOARDING HOUSE

PATENT OFFICE

G STREET

BAPTIST CHURCH (LATER FORD'S THEATRE)

NATIONAL ERA OFFICE

JAIL

2ND STREET

1ST STREET

GENERAL POST OFFICE

INFIRMARY

J. BIGELOW'S OFFICE AND ROOMS

GAMALIEL BAILEY'S HOME

DANIEL WEBSTER'S HOME

CITY HALL

FARMER'S HOTEL

DAILY INTELLIGENCER

LOUISIANA AVE.

JOSEPH H. BRADLEY HOME

PHILIP BARTON KEY HOME

AVENUE

CARUSI'S HALL

BROWN'S HOTEL

GILMAN'S PHARMACY

NATIONAL (COLEMAN'S) HOTEL

UNITED STATES HOTEL

6TH STREET

CENTER MARKET

RAILROAD DEPOT (UNTIL 1852)

U.S. CAPITOL

SMITHSONIAN

GENERAL AREA OF GANNON'S SLAVE PEN

GENERAL AREA OF WILLIAMS'S SLAVE PEN

MARYLAND AVENUE

TO THE NAVY YARD

VIRGINIA AVENUE

7TH STREET

6TH STREET

4TH STREET

3RD STREET

TO THE WHARFS

ESCAPE ON THE PEARL

Introduction

In April 1848 an audacious escape on the Underground Railroad involved more than seventy fugitives and a fifty-four-ton schooner named the *Pearl*. It took place in Washington, D.C., certainly not the first place most people envision when picturing American slavery. But the plan was not organized solely for the purpose of aiding enslaved people in the nation's capital to reach freedom. That could have been accomplished in the usual way, with smaller groups. This escape had evolved into a plan that would shock the country. For more than ten years, abolitionists had been lobbying for the end of slavery in the District of Columbia with no success. They now wanted to shine a light on the horrors of slavery and the slave trade—a good number of those fugitives were on the verge of being sold to the labor-hungry cotton fields of the Lower South—in the capital of the country that had successfully waged a revolution in the name of democracy and self-determination.

Political compromise after the American Revolution landed the capital near the North/South divide that would eventually lead to a war of terrible death and destruction. Slavery was legal because it came with the territory. On July 16, 1790, when Congress passed legislation to cut land from Maryland and Virginia, both slave states, to form the District of Columbia, it provided that the laws from both would carry over into the new federal enclave, at least initially. At the time the new capital was created, slavery still existed in the North. However, those states could be characterized as a society with slaves, while the South had already evolved into a slave society.

In the 1830s a growing and newly radicalized antislavery movement emerged in the North; one of its primary goals was to end slavery in the District of Columbia. Unlike the Southern states, where ending slavery was seen as far more problematic because of constitutional protection for states to regulate their own affairs, the capital was under the exclusive jurisdiction of the federal government. The United States Congress had the authority to pass a law that would abolish slavery and end the busy slave trade in Washington.

As local antislavery societies sprang up across the North, petitions began to flood Congress asking for the end of slavery in the federal enclave. But the rising heat of abolitionist rhetoric was met in kind with an adamant determination on the part of Southern legislators in Congress to hold tight to every inch of slave territory, no matter if it fell beneath the federal umbrella. The united front of the Southern legislators, who became widely known as the slave power, easily outmatched the handful of Northern legislators who were willing to support the end of slavery in the District of Columbia.

Even by 1800, significant changes had occurred in the Chesapeake region that impacted greatly on black people in and around the capital. During the last quarter of the eighteenth century, the labor-intensive tobacco crop that had formed the agricultural base of the area largely moved south, to be replaced by grains. Unlike tobacco, these crops required little maintenance and could easily be harvested by seasonal workers, leaving planters with a surfeit of slaves. Influenced by the same sentiments of the Revolutionary War period that led to the gradual emancipation of slaves in the North, a good number of slave owners freed their slaves, and the number of free blacks in the area, most particularly in Maryland, rose substantially. But that impulse did not last, especially after the invention of the cotton gin led to the Lower South's huge expansion of cotton plantations. After 1808, those in the market for slaves could no longer look to Africa, because the transatlantic slave trade had been outlawed by Congress (though a lessened illegal trade continued). Instead, they looked to the tobacco slave states to provide laborers, and the value of American slaves rose.

Thus began an internal slave trade that historian Ira Berlin has named the "Second Middle Passage." The first Middle Passage carried millions of slaves across the Atlantic from Africa to the New World. This new and wholly American Second Middle Passage forced an astonishingly large number of American slaves to migrate to the Lower South from the Upper South, an area that included Maryland, Virginia, and the District of Columbia. Owners sold their increasingly valuable slaves to local traders, often one by one or two by two, rending black families. Slave traders stowed their purchases in public jails, privately owned slave pens, the attics and basements of their own homes, and holding cells provided by small inns and hotels. They collected slaves until they had assembled a sufficient number to make the trek south overland or by water. Few black families would be untouched by it.

This massive transfer of slaves further south, which also included a significant number of planters who walked their slaves south to cut new plantations out of the Kentucky and Tennessee wilderness, became one of the largest forced migrations in American history. Historian Barbara Jeanne Fields states that Maryland saw a "steady hemorrhage" of slaves. Until recently, a number of scholars have minimized the number of slaves who were forcibly relocated, and the subject has received little attention in accounts of America's slave period. But recent definitive works by historians Robert H. Gudmestad, Steven Deyle, and Michael Tadman have established its magnitude. Between 1790 and 1860, at least one million slaves were transported from the Upper South to the Lower South; more than two-thirds of that total were removed by slave traders, while the others were marched farther south by their owners.

Not all area planters chose to sell excess slaves, at least not immediately. Instead, a significant number hired their slaves out to work for small farmers in the countryside and in the building and service trades in Washington, D.C. Many of the passengers who boarded the *Pearl* to seek new lives were hired slaves, including the six members of the Edmonson family who are profiled in this book. But hired slaves knew that they too were candidates for the slave trade, particularly when their owner died, or, all too often, for partition, when families were separated for distribution to heirs who often lived in disparate locales.

The high-volume sale of slaves led to increased activity on the Underground Railroad in the Upper South, and an organized cell had taken root in Washington by the early 1840s. But slaves had been fleeing their masters long before that, either to gain freedom in the North or to be with loved ones from whom they had been separated. Many were aided spontaneously along the way by free blacks, other slaves, and a small number of sympathetic whites, particularly members of the Society of Friends. But the more organized system of aid that sprang from the heightened antislavery fervor established a network to freedom that ensured help along the way.

Washington's cell was an anomaly. Most Underground Railroad operations were located in free territory that bordered slave land because it was very difficult for antislavery activists to operate within Southern cities or towns where outsiders were easily recognized and looked on with suspicion. But Washington, with a population of politicians, newspaper correspondents, and job seekers from the North, was unlike any other slave city. Underground Railroad activists could live and operate in the nation's capital with relative ease and form bonds with blacks to move slaves out of the area. Antislavery whites brought sources for money, links to safe houses operated by blacks and whites in the North, and, in some cases, support to get a new life started. And it was free blacks, and sometimes enslaved blacks, who operated safe houses in Washington, helped plan the escapes, and played principal roles in executing them.

The story of the escape on the *Pearl* and its aftermath, told largely through the eyes of one family, the Edmonsons, contains all these strands. Six siblings—two sisters and four brothers—who had been hired out to work as slaves in Washington by their owner in Maryland, joined a heroic escape that hoped to shake the conscience of the country at the same time that it delivered more refugees North. The sisters, Mary and Emily, became famous in abolitionist circles, and because of that brief prominence, there is an astonishing amount of information about their lives. In 1853 Harriet Beecher Stowe devoted a chapter to the sisters and their family in her *Key to Uncle Tom's Cabin*, a nonfiction account of slavery published to defend her blockbuster novel. That same year, the Philadelphia sea captain hired to lead the escape published the *Personal Memoir of Daniel Drayton*.

Even more information about the Edmonsons became available in 1916, when John Paynter, an Edmonson descendant and graduate of Lincoln University (AB 1883, Hon. D.Litt. 1941), revived the story with "The Fugitives of the Pearl" in the *Journal of Negro History*. In 1930 Paynter wrote an expanded and partly fictionalized book of the same title, which was published by G. Carter Woodson, the eminent scholar who was the founder of Black History Month. Paynter's work is particularly important because it was informed by interviews with family members close to the event, and, although it is missing some important facts and others were added for dramatic effect, much of Paynter's story has been corroborated.

But the story of the *Pearl*, which aroused heated debate in Congress, sparked a riot by proslavery white people, and contributed to the abolition of the slave trade in the District of Columbia, disappeared from the canon of America's history. It was lost for a number of reasons. After the Civil War, Jim Crow settled in Washington and remembrances of slave escapes were not considered appropriate matters to dwell on. By the early twentieth century, with the encouragement of President Woodrow Wilson, both the federal workforce and the city became increasingly more segregated. Many black parents were reluctant to pass down stories about slavery while they and their children were still suffering from its legacy.

Even some members of the Edmonson family were surprised to learn of their family's involvement in the *Pearl* escape when relatives shared Paynter's book with them in the 1970s. In 2002, when a profile of Mary and Emily Edmonson by this author appeared in the *Washington Post Sunday Magazine,* Dr. Dorothy Height, the legendary civil rights leader, reported that she was shocked that she had never heard of the story. Dr. Height wasted no time championing this extraordinary piece of history. At a gathering to celebrate her ninetieth birthday a few months later, she recounted the story of the largest known attempted escape on the Underground Railroad to her guests. When she finished, Dr. Height looked out over a star-studded crowd that included Oprah Winfrey, Danny Glover, and Paul C. Johnson III, an Edmonson family descendant, and told them that "we are all standing on the shoulders of the fugitives of the *Pearl*."

In addition to the accounts of Stowe, Drayton, and Paynter, this story relies on newly discovered private letters and papers, newspaper accounts, court records, city directories, wills, photographs, census materials, land deeds, Edmonson family records, and Civil War service records to flesh out the details. It charts more than an organized stab at freedom aboard a schooner in 1848. It traces one family's struggle to use every means possible to gain their family's freedom, including the fight for all to be free in the uniform of the U.S. Army.

This is their story.

ONE

Two Young Girls
Join an Audacious Escape

On the overcast evening of April 15, 1848, at around 9:00 P.M., a soft clump of dirt struck the window of a servant's small room above the kitchen in the home of Alexander Ray, a prominent businessman in Washington and Georgetown. The family's spacious and well-appointed house stood in the Foggy Bottom neighborhood, west of the President's House, tucked between Pennsylvania Avenue and the Potomac River, and just a few blocks from where a twenty-two-foot revolving dome cradled the Naval Observatory's telescope. Ray was a prosperous merchant who had the means and the connections to hire the very best of servants, and it was well known in their circle that a family by the name of Edmonson was uncommonly bright and talented help for the better class of people.

That evening, the noise at the upstairs window alerted thirteen-year-old Emily Edmonson, a still slightly plump girl with a warm brown complexion somewhere between her father's deeper color and her mother's much lighter skin tone. Emily's appealing features were set in a slightly rounded, gentle face that already showed the promise of the lovely young woman she was becoming. Lifting the window, she saw her older brother Samuel, about five feet, six inches tall and fair-skinned like his mother, standing at the side door of the house and looking up at her window. He had come from an elegant home some eighteen blocks to the east on Judiciary Square, not far from the Capitol. Samuel lived and worked as a butler in the home of Joseph Bradley, one of Washington's most successful and prominent lawyers.

Emily, neatly and modestly dressed as always, quickly picked up a small bag and quietly slipped through the house and out the door into the sleepy neighborhood. She and her brother began walking east near a factory at Seventeenth Street that produced ice cream, which could be delivered to a customer's door for $2.50 a quart, a hugely expensive treat at a time when an acre of nearby Maryland farmland cost about $15 and skilled workers earned around $1.25 a day. They walked steadily and quietly toward the other side of the Executive Mansion, which, as the Stranger's Guide in the most recent City Directory of Washington explained, was now commonly called the White House.

Emily and Samuel carefully made their way through the unlit and largely unpaved streets. The Washington Gas Light Company was in its formative stages with a bill of incorporation waiting to be reported in the House of Representatives from the Congressional Committee on the District of Columbia. Unlike New York, Boston, St. Louis, Louisville, Baltimore, or Newark, the city lacked any organized system of modern streetlights, and public lighting was limited to the whale oil that burned in a few dozen twelve-foot-tall iron streetlamps along Pennsylvania Avenue designed by Charles Bulfinch, the architect of the Capitol's low, copper-sheathed wooden dome. A year earlier, Congress had seen to its own needs by installing a self-contained gas lighting system that functioned only when Congress was in session. One of the city newspapers reported that the tall lighting apparatus had resulted in an alarmingly high death rate for swarms of birds drawn to its unusual light.

The darkness served brother and sister well as they made their way to another of the city's still few private homes near Thirteenth and G Streets, where their sister Mary worked, not far from where the recently deceased former president, John Quincy Adams, had lived. Though certainly not a radical abolitionist, Adams had endeared himself to enemies of slavery when he argued the appeal before the Supreme Court that freed the Africans who had revolted onboard the ship called *La Amistad* and when, as a member of Congress, he successfully campaigned against a congressional gag rule that had for eight years automatically tabled any slavery-related petition.

Mary was watching for her brother and sister. When Emily cautiously called up to her from the back of the house, Mary quickly opened the window above them and, to prevent alerting anyone, tossed out her shoes. At five feet, six inches tall, the slim, fifteen-year-old Mary stood four inches taller than Emily and carried herself with a more grave countenance over her lovely features. She was a sister to look up to in more ways than height: Mary had a particularly spiritual and winsome personality that immediately won over all she met.

Picking up her small bundle of belongings, Mary joined Emily and Samuel outside the house and quickly slipped on her shoes. The siblings stopped briefly to pick up food from a nearby bakery, where the late-night shift was preparing breakfast foods, and, in a trade where many blacks worked, found a trusted friend who was willing to discreetly supply them with rolls. With a half-hour walk ahead of them and time running short, the three Edmonsons set off at a brisk pace, but not so fast so that they drew untoward attention. This was not a night to answer awkward questions about where they might be going when they were so close to the 10:00 curfew bell that rang for all blacks, free or enslaved.

The three Edmonsons were slaves, and they were moving carefully toward the Potomac River, where a schooner from the North was waiting to take them on a journey to freedom. They were leaving behind an unusually close, highly spiritual, and even modestly prosperous family. Their parents, Paul and Amelia, lived on a forty-acre farm about fifteen miles north of the city in Norbeck, Maryland, a small rural crossroads in Montgomery County. Thirteen years earlier, shortly before Christmas

1835, Paul Edmonson, a free man of color, purchased his first twenty acres of farmland for $250. In 1847 he doubled the size of his farm with the purchase of an additional contiguous twenty acres of land for $280.*

The Edmonsons cultivated oats, corn, and Irish potatoes and harvested fruit from their orchards. They owned a few cows, pigs, and horses as well as a cart, which Paul and Amelia used to drive into the city to see their family, driving down the same Brookeville Road— today's six-lane Georgia Avenue—used by President Madison in 1814 when he briefly transferred the presidency to the safety of the small village of Brookeville, Maryland, less than ten miles north of the farm. In the summer and fall, the Edmonsons brought fruit and vegetables with them to sell in Washington, D.C.

The Edmonson farm, small when compared to most farms owned by whites, was astonishingly large relative to the holdings of other free blacks in the county who, if they owned any land at all, held far smaller lots. When the county's Society of Friends, centered in the town of Sandy Spring just a few miles north of the Edmonson farm, answered the call to free their slaves in the late eighteenth century, many gave each family a half acre of land to go along with their freedom. But as large as Paul Edmonson's farm was, its value did not equal what just one of his attractive daughters could fetch in a New Orleans slave market.

Even though Paul Edmonson was free, all of his children were born enslaved because his wife, Amelia Edmonson, was enslaved when she gave birth to them. The law was clear in all slave jurisdictions: a child's legal status flowed directly from the mother. The earliest reference to Amelia that has been found is in a will drafted in 1796, the same year that John Adams won election as America's second president. Henry Culver, a substantial landowner in Montgomery County, bequeathed a feather bed, a small sum of money, and a young slave named Amelia to his daughter Rebecca. Of the three bequests, the most valu-

---

* See Appendix A for a more detailed description of the Edmonson farm.

able by far was Amelia. After she married Paul Edmonson, each child
born to the couple was enslaved, significantly increasing the value of
Rebecca Culver's holdings.

Amelia Edmonson's unmarried owner lived with a married sister in
Colesville, Maryland, which was less of a town than a collection of
landowners, not far from the Edmonson farm. According to papers
filed in the Montgomery County courthouse in 1827, Rebecca Culver
had been showing signs of mental deficiency since she was two years
old. Culver's oldest brother, Henry Culver Jr., petitioned the Montgomery County court for a writ *de idiota inquirendo* to determine his
sister's mental competency. As part of that legal proceeding, a list of all
of Rebecca Culver's property was submitted to the court. Her possessions consisted of furniture worth $5.00 and eleven human beings,
Amelia Edmonson and the ten children she had borne by that time,
who were worth $1,595.00.

The court concluded that Rebecca Culver was incapable of taking
care of herself, and Francis Valdenar, her brother-in-law, was soon appointed to manage her affairs, including the supervision of her slaves.*
Valdenar had purchased land from the Culver family and would eventually own a total of 450 acres and twenty-nine slaves. He was a man of
high profile in the county, serving, at various times, as vice president of
the Montgomery County Agricultural Society, a commissioner for the
Montgomery County Silk Company, and a representative of the county
to settle a border dispute with Prince George's County to the east. But
he apparently did not put as high a premium on looking after his mentally deficient sister-in-law as he did on overseeing her valuable property. Amelia Edmonson would later report to Harriet Beecher Stowe,

---

* Valdenar was also reputed to have been a tobacco inspector and, though there are no
records to prove it, the son of a French officer who had come to fight in the Revolutionary War and then remained. A Francis Valdonous, who may have been that father, was
fined for keeping a "publick house" without a license in 1788. Valdonous operated Mud's
Tavern, just north of Tennallytown (now Tenleytown), which later became part of the
northwest quadrant of the District of Columbia.

the author of *Uncle Tom's Cabin*, that she had witnessed a barefoot Rebecca Culver performing menial jobs and sleeping in a room exposed to the elements.

Amelia was allowed to live with her free husband, where she continued to sew and perform other tasks for her mistress. By 1848 she had given birth to at least fourteen children, and thirteen were still living. She and her husband kept their children with them, but only until each became old enough to be hired out to work. Thirteen was the common age when young slaves were sent out to earn a living for their masters, though some enslaved children were hired out at an even younger age. Emily Edmonson could not have been away from her parents' home for very long.

Amelia's four oldest girls—Elizabeth, Martha, Eliza, and Eveline—had been allowed to purchase their freedom with the help of husbands and other supporters, and a fifth grown daughter, likely named Henrietta, may have been the daughter who was reported to have been on her deathbed when the money to purchase her freedom had finally been raised. There are few details about her in any of the family accounts, which suggests that she died young. At some point, Valdenar decided that he would allow no more Edmonsons to purchase their own freedom. By 1848 he had six of the younger siblings—Mary, Emily, Samuel, Ephraim, Richard, and John—hired out to work in some of the best homes in Washington, and the wages they earned contributed to the upkeep and care of Rebecca Culver. It was an arrangement that many slave owners found comfortable. Two more siblings, Josiah and Louisa, were still in Montgomery County, and they too would soon be hired out.

There was one more Edmonson brother, whom Emily and Mary had never known. Fifteen years earlier, Hamilton Edmonson, in the company of another slave, named Charles Brisco, ran away. Caught before they left Maryland, both men's names were logged onto the runaway slave ledger at the Baltimore jail on July 1, 1833, where Hamilton was described as an escapee from the Culver estate. They may have been trying to blend in with the large number of free blacks and hired slaves in Baltimore—the latter of whom included Frederick Douglass at one time—who lived in the busy port on the Chesapeake Bay, or they may have been attempting to find a ship that would smuggle them north. Hamilton Edmonson was sold to a slave trader and taken farther south.

On their way to the Potomac River that night, the Edmonson sisters and their brother Samuel approached Pennsylvania Avenue, the 160-foot-wide expanse that links the Capitol to the White House and beyond in both directions, which most residents referred to simply as "the Avenue." It was the spine that gave structure and life to the city with shops, hotels, and boardinghouses scattered along its expanse. There was more choice than expected in a city that was so often called a backwater. Magruder & Co. touted three hundred pairs of Moroccan walking "slips," while Mr. Kahl offered an assortment of superior pianofortes and a "splendid" grand piano with all the modern improvements. Fancy grocers set out an array of Arabian dates, Turkish candy, jalea de guayaba (guava jelly), African ground nuts, and Bordeaux prunes in glass jars. Those in need of a cure could visit Samuel DeVaughan's shop, which was well stocked with Swedish leeches. And book merchants offered the last installments of Charles Dickens's *Dombey and Son* and Emily Brontë's *Wuthering Heights*, published the year before in England, though one American critic, surprisingly, found it "written much more nearly to the life than it should be, to be either gratifying or useful."

———◇◆◇———

A day that had started sunny and delightfully warm had turned into a much cooler evening. As a light rain began to fall, with still a mile's walk ahead of them, the Edmonsons crossed the Avenue, passing the dark hulk of the city's usually bustling but now silent Center Market. In daylight, the market's crowded stalls, with a good number of black vendors, served city residents of different colors and incomes. All of Washington rubbed shoulders while browsing through the market, including the hawk-faced Supreme Court Chief Justice Roger Taney and the easily recognized massive head of Senator Daniel Webster, one of the city's more serious gourmands, who knew the value of selecting his own terrapin.

In the quiet of the evening, the Edmonsons crossed over one of the bridges spanning the Washington City Canal that ran along the north side of the National Mall—filled in as today's Constitution Avenue. Smells lingered in the air from the tepid canal, where fishmongers stored their catch in containers suspended in the same water where vendors tossed fish remains, meat trimmings, and decaying fruits and vegetables. The darkened Capitol loomed to their left. To their right, a section of land was marked for Monday's scheduled excavation to begin laying the foundation for the Washington Monument. The Monument Society's ambitious memorial—designed by Robert Mills to show an obelisk arising out of a multicolumned Greek Pantheon that supported a bare-chested, chariot-riding George Washington—was to be financed by the American people, dollar by dollar.

On the south side of the Mall, Mary, Emily, and Samuel passed the construction site for the Smithsonian Institution, where red Seneca sandstone, hauled down the Chesapeake and Ohio Canal by barges from a waterside quarry twenty miles up the Potomac River, was rising in Gothic splendor. Behind and east of the Smithsonian, the notorious slave trader William H. Williams operated Washington's most infamous slave pen at that time, which differed little from the other houses nearby save for the high wall that rimmed its backyard, the fierce bark of his dogs, and the shackles and whips inside. If this escape failed, the Edmonsons knew, they stood a good chance of ending up inside those walls or in another pen like it. They knew too that they would then be taken away from their loved ones in the Washington area for sale to the Southern market, where slave traders were again making huge profits as the country recovered from a financial depression. Cotton plantations had sprouted across the South and into the Southwest after Texas entered the Union in 1845. The demand for slave labor had increased dramatically.

Knowing the dangers involved in an escape attempt all too well, the Edmonsons still decided that it was worth the risk to join other fugitives on a schooner that was leaving from Washington that night. They were not running away because they had been hired out to work in oppressive conditions. Samuel served the wines and set the table for a gracious and powerful lawyer who sometimes used his courtroom skills to win the freedom of other slaves, and Mary and Emily were respected and liked by the families for whom they worked. When slaves like the Edmonsons, surrounded by loving family, made the decision to run away, it was almost always because they had learned that their owner was on the verge either of selling them south or dying, which often meant separation or sale. It is very possible that their aging and mentally deficient owner was ill and the Culvers were making preparations to divide up or sell her assets, the Edmonsons. William Culver, one of Rebecca Culver's nephews, had already sold his future share of the family to his brother two years earlier.

Seventh Street Wharf

The Edmonsons continued walking toward the river, and houses soon gave way to open fields as they neared the waterfront. The main wharf predated the founding of the capital and had only become known as the Seventh Street wharf after Peter L'Enfant (as the French-born engineer signed his maps) assigned numbers to the streets running north-south, letters to streets running east-west, and state names to the expansive diagonal streets that cut through the grid. A few years before John Adams arrived with a federal workforce of just over 180 employees in 1800, that same wharf had served the needs of a fifteen-hundred-acre estate owned by Notley Young, a prominent Catholic and one of the founders of nearby Georgetown College. A map of that time shows a scattering of buildings along the river that appear to be cabins for some of his two hundred slaves, while a nearby larger structure is marked "overseer." While there were certainly pockets of marshland around the city, much of it, as Young's large plantation attests, was eminently suitable for crops and orchards.

Thomas Law, a wealthy and eccentric Englishman who married Eliza Custis, one of George Washington's more unpredictable step-granddaughters, had invested heavily in land around the wharf area in the steadfast belief that it would spring forth as the city center of the new capital. Law was an early arrival in Washington and settled in quickly with extensive land and slaves, some of whom he hired out to the federal government. Neither the marriage nor his commercial inter-ests worked out as planned. The couple divorced, and the wharf area, though busy, became just another of Washington's outflung neighbor-hoods that had erupted like gopher holes around the city. Most of the commercial activity centered on the Avenue.

Before they reached the river at the bottom of Seventh Street, Samuel carefully detoured his sisters to the more secluded and "rather lonely" White-house wharf, named for its nearby solitary white house, a good deal distant and certainly less impressive than the home designed by James Hoban for the president of the United States. No source has clearly pinpointed the small wharf's exact location on the river. A few days later, the *Alexandria Gazette* reported that they had gone to a landing east of Seventh Street, where the shore-line dipped sharply south along a spit of land called Buzzard's Point. The city's Democratic Party newspaper, the *Daily Union*, thought the runaway slaves had left from the "the steamboat wharf below the Long Bridge," which was located at the foot of Fourteenth Street. Drayton reported that after they unloaded the wood they had brought to Washington, they had moved the *Pearl* downriver, which would have taken it east of Seventh Street. The wharf's location was likely somewhere along the stretch of land leading to Buzzard's Point.

Anchored at the small landing in front of them, below a high bluff that ran along the river and obscured the goings-on below from the open fields above, was a gray-hulled, fifty-four-ton schooner called the *Pearl*, with a single light at either end. The small, two-masted vessel, likely sixty-five to eighty feet in length, was commonly called a bay-craft; it was designed for the currents and winds of the semiprotected waters of the Delaware and Chesapeake Bays. Caleb Aaronson, the *Pearl*'s owner, would later issue a statement through his lawyer that he had had no knowledge of any plan to use his vessel to carry fugitive slaves out of the nation's capital. He stated that he thought Edward Sayres—the captain he hired for his ship—was leaving New York around March 30 to pick up a load of wood at Fort Deposit on the Susquehanna River at the north end of the Chesapeake Bay.

Since nightfall, individuals and small groups had been steadily and quietly making their way to the secluded wharf to find that same schooner. Lucinda Bush, a free woman of color, is reported to have gone to a number of homes in Washington "to retrieve the slaves under some ruse and to have taken them to the *Pearl*." She would have proved an invaluable operative. Not only were she and her husband, William, well versed in the cautionary ways of the Underground Railroad in Washington, but Lucinda could easily pass for a white woman and therefore could move unquestioned through the streets of the city in the company of black people, who would be presumed to be her slaves.

At the wharf, the fugitives silently boarded the *Pearl* to come face-to-face with a nervous young white man dressed in a navy coat with two rows of brass buttons. Chester English held up a lantern to scan their faces, though it wasn't clear what he was expecting to see. When the Edmonsons came aboard, English opened the hatch for them to enter the hold and, just as he had been instructed, quickly closed it after them.

Samuel carefully helped his sisters belowdecks, where they joined an increasingly large crowd in a hold with less than six feet of head room. A baycraft was built to "draw but little water," making for a shallow storage area below. Waiting for them among the other passengers, as expected, were three more Edmonson siblings who had also been hired out by Valdenar to work in Washington: Ephraim, the oldest; Richard, married, with children; and John, of whom the least is known. They had managed to commandeer a few boxes to make Mary and Emily a small sitting area for the arduous journey ahead.

A few small lanterns softly illuminated the faces of the passengers around them. Along with the Edmonsons, these worried would-be émigrés from slavery, bearing the surnames of Bell, Brent, Calvert, Dodson, Marshall, Pope, Queen, Ricks, and Smallwood—names that still resonate today in Washington and Maryland's thriving black middle class—knew that, if caught, most would be exchanging a servant job for that of a field hand, or even worse for the more attractive women among them. They also knew that, if caught, they would probably never see their families again. But a good number faced those consequences anyway. At least four of them had escaped from slave traders who were preparing to take them south, and others knew that their chances of being sold south were high. They had watched enough of their neighbors, friends, and family members disappear suddenly.

The Edmonsons would have recognized a good number of the other passengers around them. With four free married sisters in Washington, D.C., to whom Mary and Emily had bid a teary good-bye earlier that day, the Edmonsons were part of a prominent and extensive family, with close ties to at least two black churches. John Brent, the husband of their oldest sister, Elizabeth, was a long-standing leader at Mt. Zion Church in Georgetown, formed in 1816, just two years after the British burned much of official Washington. It was the first African-American congregation established in the District of Columbia, and while the church remained under the control of the white Methodist ministers, it maintained its own spiritual leaders. But many perceived them to be independent. The City Directory of 1830 described it as "the African Church" located in a small brick building on Mill Street just north of today's P Street near Twenty-seventh. The directory added that they were "Methodists and have a minister of their own."

At the time of the escape, Brent was a preacher at Mt. Zion and led one of its religious classes, an essential part of Methodism, in which church members met together weekly in small groups to study their religion. Brent's group met every Sunday in his home at the corner of Eighteenth and L Streets in a neighborhood near Georgetown, which served Mt. Zion's members who lived in Ward 1 of the city of Washington. Several other members of the Edmonson and Brent families belonged to Mt. Zion at various times, including Martha Edmonson; Dennis Orme, who was married to Eliza Edmonson; and John Brent's brother, Elton. As the first black church in the area, Mt. Zion would have naturally drawn Methodists from across Washington.

Brent is also credited with being one of the founders of the Asbury Methodist Church, established in 1836 at the corner of Eleventh and K Streets, where Mary and Emily and other members of the family worshipped. In light of the restrictive laws known as the black code—which prevented blacks from meeting in groups larger than seven without a permit, denied them the right to hold certain jobs, and even proscribed them from flying kites—the churches were more than houses of worship; they were essential community organizations for Washington's blacks, both free and enslaved. And the churches' black preachers, exhorters, and class leaders, including Brent, played an important leadership role in that community. Brent and other black religious leaders would have provided the most reliable means of disseminating information to those looking for passage out of the city when the schooner arrived.

———

As the passengers continued to fill the hold of the *Pearl*, Daniel Drayton, the forty-six-year-old ship captain from Philadelphia, was away from the vessel making final preparations for the journey. The weathered and lean-faced seaman who was in charge of the journey was born in Cumberland County, New Jersey, to a devout Methodist woman who bore nine children and died when he was twelve. After Drayton's father remarried, he ended what little schooling he had received and became apprenticed at various trades. He put in a stint as a shoemaker, while struggling both with his faith and the temptations of drink and gambling, before finally turning to the sea. Drayton had often sailed ships between Philadelphia and Washington, D.C., transporting wood, oysters, and anything else he could carry and later sell. He was very familiar with baycraft schooners, though he had mainly worked on larger coastal vessels that went up and down the Atlantic seaboard. The journey itself didn't concern Drayton. But the vagaries of the weather, complicated by the logistics of secreting a large number of people who, when missed, would bring the authorities running, made it that much more difficult. Because Sunday was the only day when slaves were often left alone to see to family concerns and spiritual needs as they attended church to worship the same God as their owners, Saturday evening logically offered the best chance for them to get some distance from Washington before their absences would be missed. He was stuck in a very narrow time frame over which he had little control.

Drayton needed a really good piece of luck to make it all work and, unfortunately, his track record swung wildly between success and utter failure. At least five vessels had the misfortune to sink under his command. He lost one as far south as Ocracoke, North Carolina, and another up near New York's Long Island. He now had a hold filled with somewhere between seventy-four and seventy-seven slaves who, all together, were worth close to a 1.5 million dollars in today's money.*

This wasn't Daniel Drayton's first foray in assisting slaves to escape

---

* We may never know exactly how many fugitives were on board the *Pearl*. See Appendix B for details on the passengers.

from Washington. Just the summer before, he had been trading up and down the Chesapeake in a hired vessel with only a small black boy to assist him. After docking at Washington's Seventh Street wharf with a cargo of oysters, Drayton was approached by a "colored" man who quietly asked him if he would be willing, for a fee, to provide passage north for the wife and children of a free man. If the man's family did not leave the jurisdiction as soon as possible, he told Drayton, they would be sold to slave traders and sent south. It is unclear whether the man was speaking about his own family but shielding his identity, or if he was an operative from Washington's Underground Railroad network making contact on the family's behalf. He was never named.

Drayton agreed to take the job on. The family's bedding and other belongings were loaded in open daylight as black men loading furniture and other goods would not have looked unusual to anyone ashore. But after nightfall, Drayton moved his vessel to a more se-cluded spot along the river, where the woman with five children and a niece could board without raising suspicion. It was the very same White-house landing where he would anchor the *Pearl* nearly a year later. Drayton said that he took the family to a place called French-town, where they were met by the woman's husband. As Drayton tells the story, he never saw any of them again but later heard that they had safely reached freedom.

There is another account of that incident. Dr. Charles Cleveland, a former college professor teaching at a girl's seminary in Philadelphia and the president of the Philadelphia Anti-Slavery Society, said that a black man named Stevenson arrived at his door looking for help in the summer of 1847. Stevenson explained that he had hired an "oysterman" (a term generally used for fishermen, crabbers, clammers, and oyster dredgers—and not one to which Drayton would have answered) to transport his enslaved family from Washington, D.C., to Philadelphia by boat. But now his wife and children were stuck in Frenchtown, be-cause the oysterman refused to transport them any farther until he was paid the twenty dollars still owed to him. Cleveland had very likely been working in concert with Underground Railroad people in Washington who were helping the Stevenson family escape; otherwise the husband would never have known to go to him for help.

The Frenchtown where the family was stranded was a landing near a single tavern on Maryland's Elk River, which branched off to the east at the northernmost reach of the Chesapeake Bay. It is one of the few places in the northern section of the bay with sufficiently deep water for vessels to dock and, for that reason, had once been a well-used hub for travelers going back and forth across the bay by either turnpike or the railroad that linked the Chesapeake Bay with the Delaware River. But after the Chesapeake and Delaware Canal was cut through the DelMarVa peninsula four miles to the south of Frenchtown, allowing vessels to turn into the canal to cross the peninsula and then continue on to Philadelphia and other points north, traffic had decreased at the landing. It was, in many ways, an ideal spot for the Underground Railroad to operate.

Charles Cleveland gave Stevenson the money he needed and Drayton returned to Frenchtown to take the family through the canal and then up to Philadelphia. The job appeared to be concluded and successful. But a week or so later, Stevenson returned to Cleveland's house and, this time, brought Drayton with him, because the captain was demanding payment for outstanding escape-related expenses. Cleveland said that he settled the outstanding accounts with Daniel Drayton.

Sometime later, Drayton returned to Cleveland's home to talk with him alone. He proposed that the Philadelphia abolitionists purchase a vessel and appoint him as its captain. Drayton explained, according to Cleveland, that this would enable him to "sail between Philadelphia and Washington, and that if any cases occurred similar to the Stevenson family, he would run the risk & bring them off." Cleveland rejected the proposal out of hand. But a determined Drayton returned again to press his cause, and this time Cleveland agreed to pass Drayton's idea on to other antislavery activists. But no one took him up on his offer—at first.

In February 1848 Cleveland received a letter from a "gentleman of Washington" who said there were "two or three slave cases there of great distress—females who had for months been concealed by humane families to prevent them being sold; that it was exceedingly desirous that they should soon be got off." The gentleman asked Cleveland to contact Daniel Drayton, or someone like him, to say that he would be paid liberally for the job.

The professor contacted Drayton, who, even though he had no ship of his own, decided to make his way to Washington to "see what could be done." If the abolitionists weren't willing to purchase a vessel for him, they were at least willing to provide funds for him to hire one. Drayton agreed to take on the job and quickly returned to the Philadelphia area to find a vessel. Time was of the essence, because some of the intended fugitives were on the verge of either sale or discovery in the hideouts where they were being sheltered as runaways. But the first constraint the planners faced was that Drayton needed to travel through the canal to reach Washington, and it would be another month before the water that fed the canal was sufficiently high to take a ship through.

At some point, possibly when Drayton was in Washington to discuss the plans, the organizers had decided to significantly expand the number of fugitives to be transported. On March 25 William L. Chaplin, the agent of the New York Anti-Slavery Society working for the Underground Railroad cell in Washington, alerted Gerrit Smith, the enormously wealthy New York radical who contributed generously to many antislavery causes and was the likely financier for the escape venture, that "there are not less than 75" enslaved Washingtonians who were ready to escape and that he was "expecting the arrival of a vessel from Philadelphia" that could hold fifty or more runaways. Drayton set about to find a vessel large enough to hold a substantial number of runaways. The initial idea had evolved into a plan that would make a stunning political statement.

The first few men Drayton approached declined the job because of the danger involved. But when he proposed his plan to Edward

Sayres, he agreed to use the schooner to carry runaway slaves some hundred miles down the Potomac River from Washington, D.C., and then up to the Frenchtown landing at the top of the Chesapeake Bay for the fee of one hundred dollars. Sayres had been running the *Pearl* for six months on trips that occasionally took him down the Chesapeake Bay, so he was familiar with a part of the journey he had been contracted to carry out. Business was slow, which made Drayton's offer all the more attractive. The fact that Sayres would most likely pocket the entire fee without his employer's knowing a thing about it made the offer all the more tempting. It was a journey that would take anywhere between three and five days depending on the winds and Sayres could be back about his regular business on the *Pearl* before his employer would suspect a thing.

Both seamen knew the consequences if caught. In a well-publicized case four years earlier, Captain Jonathan Walker was convicted of attempting to transport fugitive slaves from Florida to the Bahamas. In what would be immortalized in a John Greenleaf Whittier poem, "The Branded Hand," a judge ordered that the initials "SS"—for slave stealer—be branded on the palm of Walker's right hand at the base of the thumb.

Drayton and Sayres's responsibility would end at the Frenchtown landing. Later, Drayton would state that "according to the arrangement with the friends of the passengers, they were to be met and carried to Philadelphia," likely using a mix of travel across the sixteen-mile-long New Castle and Frenchtown Turnpike road after dividing into smaller groups, or going due north the twelve miles to the Pennsylvania border. Groups could be transported in wagons, small vessels, closed carriages, or led by foot. Frenchtown offered a variety of ways to head north.

The captains agreed that Sayres would have control of the ship's operation and would have no dealings with any of the people involved in organizing the escape, while Drayton would be in charge of the passengers he "chose to receive on board." In the face of Drayton's strong objections, a young man named Chester English would be joining them on the voyage. Sayres had hired English to serve as cook and deckhand for one year and insisted on bringing him along. English, though married and a father, was viewed by Drayton as "inexperienced as a child." But the young man was eager to go on what he thought was a trip to pick up timber. And he had never seen Washington.

William Chaplin, an antislavery activist and correspondent for the *Albany Patriot*, an abolitionist newspaper published in New York, was the gentleman from Washington who had contacted Cleveland, met with Drayton, and then relayed information to Gerrit Smith. It had grown into a bold plan, one that had Chaplin's fingerprints on it. If it succeeded, they hoped, the escape of more than seventy slaves on a schooner out of Washington would reignite the slackened passion of abolitionists in the North to end slavery in the nation's capital and would also gain the political support in Congress they needed to do it.

The *Pearl* Leaves Philadelphia and Arrives/Freedom in France

On the journey to Washington, the *Pearl* made her way through the Chesapeake and Delaware Canal to the Chesapeake Bay, then sailed down to the mouth of the Potomac River and turned north toward the capital. After two years of hauling goods on the mid-Atlantic waterways, Drayton knew the river far better than Sayres and took the wheel to navigate the vessel up the Potomac. On the way, they stopped at a landing in Machudock, Virginia, to pick up twenty cords of firewood to mask the schooner's real purpose.

Charles Cleveland—who was obviously involved in the planning of the escape beyond sending Drayton to Washington—provided money to purchase the wood, and the proceeds from its sale would secure supplies for the fugitives. Drayton, a veteran of the wood shipping trade, reported that it was a business dominated by baycraft vessels of thirty to sixty tons that could carry between twenty-five and fifty cords of wood. Given those figures, the fifty-four-ton *Pearl* was carrying a load of wood into Washington that filled about half of the hold.

Chester English, the young ship's mate, later said that shortly before they reached Washington, Sayres and Drayton quarreled. Sayres had asked Drayton to get the wood ready, to which Drayton sharply replied that if he did Sayres would forfeit the one hundred dollars he was being paid for the journey. It would not be their last disagreement.

The schooner arrived on Thursday, April 13, leaving two days for both crew and fugitives to prepare for a Saturday evening departure. English discovered that there was more to see in Washington than he could have ever wished for in his first visit. Their arrival coincided with a series of celebrations to mark the recent restoration of democracy to France. In February 1848 Karl Marx and Friedrich Engels, working with Communists from a number of countries, published a pamphlet called *The Communist Manifesto*, a tract that predicted the collapse of the capitalist economic system and coincided with an outbreak of revolutions across Europe. Most were squashed just as quickly as they had erupted.

But the democratic revolution in France looked promising, and, given the special relationship between that country and the United States growing out of the Revolutionary War, there was intense excitement in Washington. The Democratic Party of Washington was sponsoring a number of celebratory events including a torch-lit procession, a citywide candle illumination, and a program of open-air speeches in front of the *Daily Union* newspaper, which was scheduled for that day.

While Drayton was finalizing details with his contacts in the city, Sayres and English were free to listen to first-term Senator Henry S. Foote, a proud slave owner from Mississippi, give one of the most rousing speeches of the evening, later printed in full by the *Daily Union*. William Chaplin had recently described him for readers of the *Albany Patriot* as being "in possession of those elements of character peculiar to the Southron—consisting of a species of Roman dignity . . . having written one of the ablest works extant upon Mexico. . . ." That night, the forty-five-year-old Foote excitedly proclaimed to the crowd that the events in France held out "to the whole family of man so bright a promise of the universal establishment of civil and religious liberty" and added that "the age of tyrants and slavery was rapidly drawing to a close." White Washington was delighted by the coming of freedom to white Europeans.

The rival newspaper, the *National Daily Intelligencer,* scornfully reported a few days later that the illumination was hardly a citywide affair when only 58 out of the city's 5,893 dwellings were "elegantly il-luminated." The *Georgetown Advocate* had qualms about how the French would be conducting this new revolution, wondering if they might go so far as to precipitously grant immediate emancipation to the blacks of the French West Indies. The paper grudgingly allowed that "given the character of [the French] . . . the revolution has been accompanied with less of excess than was to have been anticipated." No one had forgotten the violent slave uprising in Haiti that had followed the last French revolution.

Washington was astir with activity that Thursday night beyond the political demonstrations. For an entrance fee of fifty cents, vocal enthu-siasts could attend the first in a series of three concerts by the Hutchin-son Family Singers at Carusi's Saloon, at Eleventh and C Streets, a large and elegant hall that had hosted inaugural balls for Presidents John Quincy Adams and William Henry Harrison. Three months earlier, Rep. Abraham Lincoln, in his first and only term in Congress, had been at Carusi's with his wife to attend a performance of the Ethiopian Sere-naders, the black-faced white minstrels whose repertoire included "De Color'd Fancy Ball."

The antislavery Hutchinsons—the Peter, Paul, and Mary of their day—appeared before a crowd of fourteen hundred people. All went well until they began singing "There's a Good Time Coming," which de-scribed war and slavery as "the monsters of iniquity." At that point, slave-holders in the audience began to hiss "like so many venomous serpents," but "a cry of 'order' put a stop to such contemptible demonstrations," and they won the whole crowd over with their new song, "The Revolution in Europe." The concert ended to thunderous applause. It was a heady moment for the small number of antislavery activists in the audience, a few of whom might have been aware that the *Pearl* had just arrived at the Seventh Street wharf, a mile south of the Avenue.

The Hutchinsons were used to ruffling feathers with their songs and may have been surprised that there wasn't far more hostility from an audience in slave territory. The year before, they were booed in New York when they sang their antislavery pieces, and in Philadelphia officials chased the singers away after telling them that the city could not protect them from assault if they persisted in singing such songs.

On Friday, after the three men had unloaded the twenty cords of inferior wood, Drayton went about the business of selling it. He ended up with a promissory note, which he exchanged for half cash and half provisions. Drayton took three bushels of meal, two hundred and six pounds of pork, and fifteen gallons of molasses, certainly more than enough food for a journey that was expected to last about four days. But he took the deal he was offered and could always sell what was left over at the end of the trip. Later that evening, while both Drayton and Sayres were away from the ship to watch more celebrations for the French Revolution, and English was alone, two black men boarded the *Pearl*. They said they were looking for Drayton but, not finding him, went away.

On Saturday, after a visit to the tavern and Drayton's many comings and goings from the schooner, everything seemed to be in place and it was time to clue Chester English into the nature of their coming cargo. At supper that evening, Drayton explained to English that some Negroes had hired them to transport the group down to the bay and would be boarding this evening. English innocently asked if that was more profitable than hauling ship timber. Drayton replied that it was. And, because of the "unusual nature of the business," he promised the young man a bonus of ten dollars.

Drayton then instructed Sayres to move the *Pearl* down the river and tie up at the "other" wharf, the same one where Drayton had successfully loaded the Stevenson family for their earlier trip north. He told them that he would make his own way to the new site and see them there. As English prepared to raise the sail, Sayres brushed him aside saying that they could as easily drift there. But in a short while Sayres called out to English to put the sail up as they caught what seemed to be the last gasp of air before the wind faded.

After they had relocated the *Pearl*, Sayres disappeared from the schooner. Around 8:00 P.M., with Drayton also away, three visitors arrived at the *Pearl*—two "negro men and a woman." When Drayton returned, English told him that the visitors were in his cabin. They were either the first arrivals of the evening or three of the organizers of the escape coming to speak with Drayton. The woman may have been Underground Railroad operative Lucinda Bush, who is believed to have helped transport fugitives to the vessel from across the city. After Drayton glanced in his cabin quickly, he left again, but it is unclear whether the three people went with him or remained.

When Drayton returned later that evening, Sayres was still gone and English was loading the passengers into the hold. To his alarm, he saw that another small vessel had anchored nearby. Drayton approached the ship and, even though he saw that it had an all-black crew, bluntly informed the skipper that he would be in grave danger if he were to report anything he saw that night. He knew that the possibility of a money reward was incentive enough to turn people of any color into informers.

Another source of worry for Drayton was the public path running along the shoreline tucked underneath the high bank. Drayton tensed at the sight of two unknown white men walking on the path and coming toward them. But thanks to the cover of darkness and the still-falling unpleasant rain, the men seemed to take little notice of the small baycraft and the dark figures quietly moving near the entrance of its hold.

With precious little time before the river tide would turn against them, Sayres had returned to the vessel and then slipped off again. An annoyed Drayton asked English if he had told the other captain, as he had asked, that he wanted him to remain onboard the *Pearl*. English replied that he had certainly told him but that Sayres left anyway. Drayton instructed English to "get ready to make sail" because it was already 11:00 P.M. and they needed to leave. At that point, Sayres appeared and Drayton sharply chastised him. "I don't mind a man drinking liquor," he said, but added that he didn't want it to interfere with his duties. Sayres angrily chafed at Drayton's rebuke but settled back in and they cast off.

After drifting a mere half mile, the tide turned and they were forced to drop anchor just to keep from being pulled back up the river. The captains were used to unpredictable wind and weather, but on this run, time was critical. The longer they waited, the more likely they would be caught. The *Pearl* remained motionless with slack sails until the sun began to rise and a small breeze finally picked up over the water. They quickly lifted the anchor and, as they slowly made their way down the Potomac, Drayton turned to English and, referring to the more than seventy black people in the hold below, told him that "this is the load of ship timber we were after."

As daylight increased, they found themselves in clear view of Alexandria, another eighteenth-century tobacco port about ten miles downriver on the Virginia side. The town had been a part of the District of Columbia until two years earlier, when all of the land that had been cut from Virginia was retroceded back to that state. Fortunately it was Sunday, and the wharves were quiet. The Sabbath—if not the rest of the week—was taken seriously in the Washington area, and working, gambling, dancing, and drinking ceased for twenty-four hours.

Several Alexandria residents owned passengers on the *Pearl*, and had any of them been awake and looked out to the river at that moment, they might have idly wondered where the little schooner was heading. They would have been struck dumb to learn that the vessel was carrying nearly eighty slaves fleeing the nation's capital—and that some of them were theirs.

TWO

Washington's Underground Railroad

The more recent organized system of aiding slaves to escape from Washington, D.C., with links to supporters in the North, had been in place for about seven years at the time the escape on the *Pearl* was devised. William Chaplin—a still handsome fifty-two-year-old—who hired Daniel Drayton to take a shipload of fugitives to freedom was born into a distinguished Congregationalist family in Massachusetts in 1796. His grandfather Col. William Prescott had been a commander at the Battle of Bunker Hill; his father, a venerable Puritan minister; and his older brother, Dr. James Chaplin, a physician renowned for his innovative treatment of mental illness.

Chaplin attended Harvard and practiced law, but then became swept up in the growing antislavery movement. In 1836 he became an agent for the New York State Anti-Slavery Society and put his writing talents to use in antislavery publications. By 1841 he was the editor of the *Rochester American* and was urging his readers to assist runaway slaves who were making their way to Canada. The Northern states were never a completely safe territory for runaways. Under the authority of the federally enacted Fugitive Slave Act of 1793, slave catchers still came north and, when successful, returned the runaways to their owners for a sizeable reward.

But the eighteenth-century law was increasingly ignored by Northern authorities. In New York, Governor William Seward ordered that all alleged runaways be afforded a jury trial. While Northerners generally had little use for the free blacks and runaways living in their midst, they did have a growing distaste for watching slave catchers wrench them away and returning them to slavery.

Chaplin joined Gerrit Smith's Liberty Party, formed in 1840 on the central issue of abolitionism, and then replaced Charles Torrey as editor of the party's *Albany Patriot* when Torrey left for Washington in 1841 to set up an Underground Railroad cell and send reports on Congress and the abolitionists' campaign to end slavery back to the newspaper.

Of course, enslaved blacks had never waited for the involvement of sympathetic whites to escape from slavery. As evidenced by advertisements placed in local newspapers, slaves had been running away from their owners since the city was founded.

Those advertisements did more than just announce that another slave was on the run from Washington: they provide miniature portraits of urban slavery. In 1826 Edgar Patterson, a prominent Georgetown resident who owned several mills in the area and had secreted the Declaration of Independence in one of them as the British were burning the city in 1814, placed lengthy advertisements for a runaway family in both Washington and Pennsylvania newspapers. It read in part:

⤙⤜•⚬•⤚⤘ $150 REWARD   ⤙⤜•⚬•⤚⤘

RAN AWAY . . . A SLAVE NAMED Bill but calls his name William Sutherland Bowman. He is about 27 years of age, 5 feet 6 or 8 inches high, a little stooped shouldered and bandy legged. . . . His clothing was numerous amongst which were a new fine blue cloth coat and pantaloons, a suit of fine black cloth, half worn. His working clothes, twilled undressed cloth, the color he may alter as he knows something of the dying business, having worked in a wool factory for eleven years past. He is an excellent spinner, scourer and fuller and understands something in each branch of the woolen business. He is also a good hand in a paper mill, having been employed eight years. . . .

Patterson added that Bowman's skills included carpentry, gardening, and stonemasonry and that he had taken his wife and child with him, who were fair enough that they might attempt to pass for white. The mill owner added that the Bowmans were likely accompanied by an indentured white boy going by the nickname of "Rat," who disappeared at the same time and were likely heading to Pennsylvania where they had once lived. An angry Patterson concluded in his advertisement that the Bowmans were "artful, deceitful, and ungrateful." He may well have lost one of his most able workers, who quite possibly managed one of his mills. To be sure, not all slaves performed such a variety of highly skilled tasks as William Bowman, but there were a fair number who were master chefs, bricklayers, and talented seamstresses—or, like the Edmonsons, highly polished houseservants.

When Charles Torrey arrived in Washington in late 1841, it took him little time to find a partner in the black community. The Yale-educated minister turned passionate abolitionist forged a formidable partnership with Thomas Smallwood, a tenacious free black man who worked at the Navy Yard in southeast Washington; together, they enlisted help from other members of the black community.

Smallwood was soon leading groups of fugitives north and then he too began sending reports to the *Albany Patriot*, writing under the pseudonym of Samivel Weller Jr., a name plucked out of Dickens's *Pickwick Papers*. Not only were Washington's free blacks working in the Underground Railroad cell, but at least one of them had become a correspondent for a Northern newspaper.

Some details of Smallwood's work were provided by Rep. Seth Gates, after he met a Washington runaway in his home state of Ohio six years later. In a letter to colleague Joshua Giddings, Gates reported that John Douglass, a Washington runaway who had waited table at the boardinghouse in Washington that Gates and Giddings shared with a small band of antislavery congressmen, told him that he left Washington in a group of eighteen who made their way on foot to Philadelphia where they were "boldly taken on board the [railroad] carrs [*sic*]," and delivered safely to Canada. Gates reported that Douglass had moved to Rochester, New York, after eighteen months in Canada and was employed in the "*Rochester Democrat* office."

The congressman also reported that three weeks after John Douglass ran away, his owner arrived with a carriage at the Washington place of business where his enslaved brother worked and told him that he was taking him home. The brother saw a rope inside the carriage and, suspecting that he was to be tied up and taken to a slave trader, told his owner that he had two months worth of wages for him but it was with his mother. When the owner stopped the carriage in front of where his mother either lived or was employed, Douglass's brother went in, continued directly out the back door, and then made his way to "Smallwood of the Navy Yard." The Underground Railroad agent put him under the care of a man who was either a close friend, or possibly a brother, employed by attorney Joseph Bradley, who would also hire Samuel Edmonson. According to Gates's letter, the lawyer was away from home and Douglass's brother was safely secreted in his garret for three weeks until "another gang" could be led north by Smallwood.

Torrey made strong contacts with the leaders of the black community by attending services in their churches, and made it abundantly clear that he much preferred their services to the white ones. He became close enough with Mr. Cartwright, the "colored minister" from Mt. Zion in Georgetown, that when Cartwright traveled north to raise money to free two enslaved members of his family, he stayed at the Torrey home in Salem, Massachusetts.

In November 1842 Smallwood reported in the newspaper that they had aided 150 escapes in eight months. While there may have been some exaggeration in both Chaplin's and Smallwood's reports—not by any means uncommon in the abolitionist press—they were clearly operating a lively line that was steadily moving people to freedom in the North. But the work was extremely dangerous, and a year later a frustrated Smallwood sensed that his identity had been compromised. He bitterly reported that he strongly suspected a turncoat in the black community. He decided to relocate his family to Canada but agreed to do one more escape before he left.

On November 24, 1843, Smallwood and Torrey stored a wagon and horses in the stables behind the home of John Bush, a free man of color who may have been related to William and Lucinda Bush.* When the fugitives were brought to the stable, a waiting Captain John H. Goddard of Washington's auxiliary guard broke in, seized the runaways, and confiscated the wagon. Torrey and Smallwood managed to escape, but Bush was arrested. Goddard and other members of Washington's guard were specifically trained to be on the lookout for runaway slaves.

Smallwood made it safely to Canada with his family, and Bush was eventually acquitted. But Torrey, showing an alarming lack of judgment, filed a claim against the city to retrieve the confiscated wagon and horses. He further compromised himself when he surfaced in Baltimore to negotiate the release of a free black man who was being held as a slave by Hope Slatter, one of the city's more notorious slave traders. Torrey was captured and easily convicted. Two years later, at the age of thirty-three, he died of tuberculosis in a Baltimore jail. To the end, he conspired with enslaved prisoners to plan future escapes.

---

* This was an unusually active family. William Bush was related to Leonard Grimes, who drove runaway slaves out of Virginia in his hack. He was arrested in the District of Columbia and sent to Virginia, where he spent two years in the penitentiary. When freed, Grimes became a minister in Boston but that did not end his involvement in the Underground Railroad. His congregation became known as the "Church of the Fugitive Slave."

William Chaplin arrived in Washington to pick up where Torrey had left off. Like his predecessor, he developed contacts in the black community and, on Sundays, attended black churches. He may well have met John Brent and other members of the Edmonson family at Mt. Zion in Georgetown or at Asbury Methodist Church, which had grown to become the largest black congregation in Washington. These churches had their own direct links to the liberty line. A report in William Lloyd Garrison's newspaper, the *Liberator*, states that a runaway had once hidden in the attic of a Methodist church in Washington while waiting to escape, and it's believed that the holding cell in Mt. Zion's Georgetown cemetery, where remains were stored when the ground was too frozen to dig, was used to hide runaways.

Chaplin also established the Bureau of Humanity to raise money to finance Underground Railroad activities and, on occasion, to purchase the freedom of a number of enslaved Washingtonians, particularly members of families who were already involved in the Underground Railroad. The latter was not a practical solution to ending slavery, and many abolitionists strongly disapproved of buying slaves on the grounds that it legitimized the sale of human beings and at the same time gave money to slave traders who would then use it to purchase more slaves. But Chaplin strongly believed that such activities, coupled with his descriptions of slavery in Washington for the *Albany Patriot*, would help to increase the level of national revulsion for slavery in the nation's capital.

One of the people assisted by Chaplin's Bureau was Mary Baker, the woman who had been captured almost three years earlier by the auxiliary guard in John Bush's stable while preparing to join her husband in Canada. In Washington City's Register of Free Blacks, where all emancipations, also called manumissions, were recorded, Baker and her son were entered as number 2,226. That record states that her owner, who also owned nearly forty other slaves in nearby Prince George's County, Maryland, freed her "in consideration of good will, justice &

humanity." His goodwill was sweetened with a payment of $300 from "W. L. Chaplin of Utica, New York."

In January 1848 an impatient Chaplin strongly hinted in the *Albany Patriot* that the Underground Railroad cell in Washington would be stepping up its activities. He reported that "[I]f we cannot summon virtue and manliness enough among our people to cleanse this District from the foul practices of oppression, nature is likely to take the work into her own hands at last." Chaplin reported that some four hundred enslaved "servants," mostly from Washington and Georgetown, had been sold to traders during the previous year. He added that another two hundred had "fallen in love with the *voluntary* principle, and gone to the North," presumably with help from the Washington Underground Railroad cell. There is no way to confirm these numbers, and it is possible that they were inflated. Nonetheless, Chaplin was giving clear notice that something big was in the works. The next month, he wrote to Dr. Charles Cleveland in Philadelphia to ask where he could find a vessel and a man to sail it.

In Chaplin's March letter to the wealthy Gerrit Smith, keeping him abreast of their plans, he described a number of the soon-to-be fugitives, including three women who had been sold to a slave trader by a wealthy Georgetown shipping merchant. The women had successfully slipped away and were hidden by the Carters, a black couple deeply involved in the network, whose home had been used for such purposes before. He also mentioned a young servant girl, who belonged to former first lady Dolley Madison, who was also waiting in a safe house. And there was a family "of great interest" who consisted of two sisters and their three brothers. He didn't name the family, but he was undoubtedly referring to the Edmonsons. Either he had the number of brothers wrong, or another decided to join them after that letter was written.

In John Paynter's account, Samuel Edmonson was named as one of three black men who planned the escape. A plot that involved some seventy-five enslaved escapees, a fifty-four-ton schooner, several safe houses in the city, and a complicated journey would hardly have been possible without the aid of black partners, and there is no reason to doubt that Samuel was one of them. It isn't clear why Paynter made no mention of the white men who were involved in the plan, though it is possible that he didn't know any of those details.

The other two black men credited with involvement in the escape plan—Paul Jennings and Daniel Bell—were both free. All three men had extensive contacts in Washington's unusually cohesive black community, and they would have been able to command the trust of fugitives waiting for the schooner to arrive.

These three men also had ample opportunity to communicate with one another and with other organizers of the escape in the months before the *Pearl* arrived in Washington. Jennings worked as a butler in the home of the powerful Daniel Webster near City Hall, which was close to attorney Joseph Bradley's elegant, marble-stepped home, where Samuel Edmonson worked in the same capacity. Both men would have had a good deal of opportunity to meet with Chaplin and any others involved at the Washington end of the plan. In addition to the Sunday time they had on their own, Jennings and Edmonson would have been free to roam the Center Market and make their way to other shops on the Avenue and on Seventh Street, which would have easily allowed them to meet with other operatives.

The third man, Daniel Bell, was employed as a blacksmith at the Navy Yard at the bottom of Eighth Street in southeast Washington, on the northern bank of the Anacostia River. He put in a regular ten-hour, six-day week and earned a decent wage of $1.20 per day. Bell had hired attorney Bradley to represent his family, who were being claimed as slaves by the widow of the owner who had freed them, but they had lost their case in multiple trials. By March, Bell was in communication with

Chaplin. In an article under the headline "Bureau of Humanity," Chaplin wrote of a desperate case within his own knowledge, clearly referring to the Bells, where "a husband and father is kept constantly for weeks or months in succession, in terrible agony, in expectation that his wife and children will be torn from him and sent to the far South." Drayton later said that the "expedition had principally originated in the desire to help off a certain family, consisting of a woman, nine children [the correct number was eight] and two grand-children, who were believed to be legally entitled to their liberty." He was describing the Bell family.

The Underground Railroad cell in Washington that began with Torrey and Smallwood had now mushroomed into a well-organized group capable of planning an escape that would eclipse anything that had come before. But their dangerous scheme of sailing a large number of fugitives to freedom was off to a frightening start. After the *Pearl* had finally begun to pick up more speed after passing Alexandria, Drayton went down into the hold, where he saw nearly equal numbers of men and women, some boys and girls, and two small children. To make them more comfortable, Drayton took down the bulkhead that separated the cabin and small galley from the ship's cargo hold, giving them more space and a place to cook and prepare food. Drayton next called Samuel Edmonson and a few other men into his cabin. He told them candidly that the trip had not begun well but assured them that he would be able to make up their lost time.

The Journey Begins: Paul Jennings

As the sun began to rise in the sky, the wind increased even more and the schooner finally took off. Sunday looked to be shaping up as one of Washington's spectacularly beautiful spring days. Early bulbs had flowered and some fruit trees were in full bloom with pale new leaves beginning to sprout. But the lovely day would soon be spoiled for a sizable number of slave owners when they learned that some of their valuable property was missing. Once discovered, the news would travel quickly through the city's churches and streets before the sun rose too high in the sky.

Both Drayton and Edward Sayres were relieved that they were finally beginning to make up the lost time as Drayton had promised. If anyone, even someone in the black community, acting out of self-interest—because there was always money to be made or a favor to be gained in information—had given an early warning that the fugitives were heading downriver in the schooner that had mysteriously left Washington without a word to anyone, trouble could already be on its way. While Drayton was watching the fugitives board the *Pearl*, he had seen a black man he didn't know standing next to one of Washington's ubiquitous brick kilns near the wharf. The man reassured Drayton that he had no reason to fear him and likely did so by revealing that he knew Chaplin and was intimate with the escape plan and knew some of the principals involved.

That man may have been forty-nine-year-old Paul Jennings, one of the three black men reported by Paynter to be involved in planning the escape. Jennings was certainly known to Chaplin, because he had profiled his unusual story in the *Albany Patriot*. Jennings, who had only recently been freed, was a highly respected figure in Washington's black community and was also well known in Washington's circle of powerful politicians.

Until 1846, Jennings had been owned by former first lady Dolley Madison, one of the most admired women in the country. He knew Madison's household well and may have been at the dock to ensure the safe deliver of Mary Ellen Stewart, who had run away from Madison's home. While he was still a young boy, Jennings had accompanied the Madisons to Washington to serve in the household of the fourth president of the United States in the President's House. Mary Cutts, Dolley Madison's niece, remembered young Jennings. She described him as a "handsome mulatto" who had been one of Aunt Dolley's favorite pages. His mother was almost certainly a Madison slave, and his father was reported to have been a white man named Benjamin Jennings, an English trader in Virginia. The U.S. Census of 1820 lists a white man of that name living in Chesterfield, Virginia, just south of Richmond.

Jennings would later produce the first memoir of a servant's life in the White House, which included his eyewitness account of the chaotic events surrounding the brief but fiery British occupation of the capital in 1814. He reported that before President Madison rode out to Bladensburg, Maryland, where the militias and a contingent of white and black seamen were attempting to hold back the advancing British, Madison asked Commodore Joshua Barney if his "negroes would not run on the approach of the British." Barney replied, "No sir, they don't know how to run; they will die by their guns first."

Margaret Bayard Smith, the wife of the editor and founder of the *National Daily Intelligencer*, the first newspaper to be published in the capital, was less sanguine about the black community's loyalty. "As for our enemy at home," as she referred to the black community in a letter, "I have no doubt that they will if possible join the British," doubtless remembering that thousands of slaves fought for the British in return for their freedom—though many were betrayed in the end—during the American Revolution. Smith's relieved husband later reported that the "free people of color of this city, acted as became patriots." But enslaved blacks did slip off to join the British just as so many had done during the Revolutionary War.

As Jennings and the other servants were preparing the meal for President Madison's return from Bladensburg, a free black man named James Smith galloped up to White House shouting, "Clear out! Clear out!" Jennings reported that Mrs. Madison left the White House with as much silver as she could "crowd into her old-fashioned reticle" and ordered that the Gilbert Stuart portrait of George Washington be rescued. Jennings said that the French doorkeeper and the president's gardener removed the painting from the White House wall, still in its frame, and laid it flat in a wagon, contrary to the legend that has Dolley Madison rolling it up. Then they all fled.

After they returned to Washington and news reached them that the Treaty of Ghent had ended the war, the butler was instructed to "serve out wine liberally to the servants and others." Jennings played the President's March on the violin as they all celebrated. The doorkeeper remained drunk for two days.

When James Madison left office, Jennings returned to Virginia with his owners and served as the former president's personal attendant until his death in 1836. Dolley Madison returned to Washington's Lafayette Square, bringing Jennings and a few other servants with her. By 1846, Madison's financial outlook was grim and, thanks largely to her profligate son from her first marriage, Montpelier and all its slaves were sold and the nearly penniless Madison began to sell off her Washington slaves. Two years before the *Pearl* arrived in the city, Madison sold Paul Jennings to an insurance agent named Pollard Webb for the surprising low price of two hundred dollars.* She at least had the decency not to sell Jennings to a slave trader specializing in the internal slave trade to the Lower South. Some owners who preferred to keep their former slaves in the area would publicly advertise a slave sale but add that they would only entertain local buyers.

The relatively small sum of two hundred dollars suggests that Jennings had already been making payments toward his own freedom and that Webb had paid only the balance to the cash-strapped Dolley. Ten months later, Webb sold Jennings to the powerful senator Daniel Webster for the even lower figure of one hundred and twenty dollars.

---

* The bill of sale was found inside the wall of a house undergoing renovation in Georgetown. At the top of the document were the words "Paul's Bill [of] Sale." Historian Michael Winston noticed the document in an auction catalogue and immediately recognized that "DP Madison" was the former first lady. He then discovered the identity of "Paul" and, with G. Franklin Edwards, published Paul Jennings's 1865 memoir together with a commentary that includes a recounting of the *Pearl* story.

Although Webster immediately freed Jennings, it was not a generous gesture that his pocketbook was willing to absorb. On March 19, 1847, Webster signed the following document:

I have paid $120 for the freedom of Paul Jennings. He agrees to work out the sum at $8.00 a month, to be [furnished] with board, clothes and washing—to begin when we return from the South. His freedom papers I give to him; they are recorded in this District.

Signed:
Daniel Webster

Jennings may very well have been hired out to Webster while he was owned by Pollard Webb and had managed to continue making payments for his freedom at that same eight dollars per month. It would account exactly for the eighty-dollar reduction in Jennings's purchase price when he was sold to Webster. Webster, likely finding Jennings's services much to his liking, purchased his freedom to make sure that no one else would buy Jennings and put him to work elsewhere. At the time of the *Pearl* escape, Jennings, while technically free, still had a few months left to complete the payments on his debt.

A month before the *Pearl* arrived in Washington, William Chaplin wrote a slightly different account of an unnamed man whose description neatly fits Paul Jennings. Chaplin reported in the *Albany Patriot* that Mrs. Madison had promised to set her husband's "attendant" free but instead hired him out in the city for nearly two years and then kept his wages to the "last red cent." Fearing that Madison was on the verge of selling him, the attendant—undoubtedly Jennings—gave her two hundred dollars toward his freedom to stave her off. Chaplin abruptly ended his report with the news that Mrs. Madison had sold him. In an interesting but not unusual twist, Jennings's later account of Mrs. Madison in his memoirs was far kinder than Chaplin's. It was common for those who worked for, or were owned by, the powerful and the famous to make note of that prestige and take pride in their connections—which, interestingly, could coincide with aiding other slaves, like Mary Ellen Stewart, escape from those very same people.

Chaplin also filed a report in the *Albany Patriot* about Stewart. He said she had been sent to the public water pump in Lafayette Square, in front of Madison's home, where slave traders were waiting to seize her as arranged with the former first lady. Her transfer to the traders outside of the home was planned to cause the least amount of commotion in the Madison household, where Stewart's mother was still enslaved and would have grievously objected. Fortunately, the traders bungled their part, and Stewart "made tracts down the street." Paul Jennings would have been one of the first people to turn to for help—he already knew William Chaplin, who was happy to add another passenger to the list of those waiting for a vessel from Philadelphia.

John Paynter, the Edmonson family descendant who wrote the 1916 article and the 1930 novel on the fugitives of the *Pearl*, said that Jennings was planning to join the fugitives onboard the vessel and had left a letter addressed to Senator Webster to explain that a "deep desire to be of help to my poor people" had led him to leave the city. That same account states that Jennings had a change of heart when he realized that he would be leaving before he had repaid his debt to Webster in full, which would have been a dishonorable thing to do. However, it is far more plausible that his going on the *Pearl* with the fugitives was an unnecessary risk that would expose a free man to criminal charges if captured. Drayton and Sayres, and to a lesser degree English, were facing that danger out of necessity. Jennings, or any other of the other agents involved in the plan, could do no more for the cause by endangering themselves. In the end, Jennings remained on dry land to await the fate of the *Pearl*.

By Sunday afternoon, the *Pearl* was making her way downriver with a speed that would quicken any sailor's heart. If it continued, they would easily be able to make the turn north up into the Chesapeake Bay before anyone discovered they were gone. Back in Washington, an excited and anxious William Chaplin made his way to the Willard Hotel to spend the day with the Hutchinson Family Singers, accompanied by Gamaliel Bailey, the editor of Washington's moderate abolitionist newspaper, the *National Era*. While the two clearly had their differences, they were both Liberty Party men, and each served his own antislavery purpose in Washington.

Over the last couple of days, the singers had managed to see some of the sights around Washington. At the Capitol, they had visited with a good friend of abolition, Senator John Hale of New Hampshire, who would soon be the presidential nominee for the Liberty Party in the 1848 election. A leading antislavery voice in Congress, Hale had recently attempted to read a petition on the floor of the Senate proposing the immediate dissolution of the Union. Echoing a view strongly held by leading abolitionist William Lloyd Garrison, the petitioners wished to separate themselves from the slaveholding South. Even though the gag rule against antislavery petitions had been lifted, Hale's petition was tabled without being read or even discussed.

Now on this Sunday morning, Chaplin told the Hutchinsons that the *Pearl* was on its way to freedom with a cargo of Washington slaves. It is unknown whether Bailey was hearing of the escape for the first time or whether he had been privy to the plan all along. There is no evidence that the newspaper editor had played any role in planning the escape, and it is unlikely that he would have endangered his precarious position as the editor of an antislavery newspaper in slave territory, even if it was the nation's capital. But he would have seen the merit in such a venture for the antislavery cause. The singers were told to keep silent about the escape—and they could be trusted to do so—though it wouldn't be very long before everyone in the city would learn of the disappearance of an astounding number of the city's servants.

On Sunday afternoon, the families and friends of the enslaved passengers on the *Pearl* were nervously waiting to hear news of their loved ones. At that point, no news was good news, because the fugitives would still be in the middle of their journey. Daniel Bell, the blacksmith from the Navy Yard, may have been making his way to Frenchtown, Maryland, to meet the fugitives, where they would most likely converge with activists from Pennsylvania and possibly Delaware who were waiting to lead them to Philadelphia.

Paul and Amelia Edmonson remained at Elizabeth and John Brent's home, where they had been able to spend some time on Saturday with their six children who would be leaving on the *Pearl*. All of the family in Washington would have come together that Sunday after church at the Brent home to continue to pray for the success of the *Pearl*'s journey.

The Beginnings of Chattel Slavery in America

The Montgomery County where Mary and Emily Edmondson grew up was not settled to any extent until tobacco plantations spread north from southern Maryland in the early 1700s. Tobacco had already become the cash crop of Virginia before Lord Baltimore—the titled name of George Calvert and his heirs, who were given a colony of their own by King Charles I—sent a mix of Catholics and Protestants to settle Maryland in 1634. Some twenty-five years earlier, when the first Jamestown settlers arrived in 1607 expecting to find precious metals, the only glint of gold they ever saw was in a leaf of *Nicotiana latissima* from South America, more commonly known as the Orinoco strain of tobacco.

Plantations in Maryland and Virginia revolved around the fourteen-month cycle of the labor-intensive tobacco plant. Workers prepared the fields, transplanted the seedlings, picked green tobacco hornworms from the plants' leaves—a job which many planters believed was ideally suited for a child's fingers—and trimmed the tops off every plant to encourage thicker growth. At harvest time, laborers cut the heavy stalks of tobacco and threaded them onto spear-headed sticks, which they then hung to dry over the winter in tobacco barns with slatted walls. In March, after the next crop's seedlings had already been started in shelters, they stripped the leaves from the dried stalks, sorted them by quality, hand-tied them in fanlike bundles, and packed them into huge hogshead barrels for shipment to England from ports such as Georgetown and Alexandria.

Initially, the bulk of the workforce for the tobacco fields in the Chesapeake area consisted of indentured servants, mainly from England. Planters purchased those servants, often from the ship captains who had transported them across the ocean, and after they completed a limited form of slavery that ran anywhere between five and ten years, those fortunate enough to survive the hard labor and diseases were freed and, in the early days, given land of their own, on which to begin their own tobacco farms.

Africans were introduced in English-speaking North America as early as 1619, when British pirates arrived at Jamestown with a cargo of slaves stolen from a Portuguese slave ship. Historians now believe the slaves were Christians from the coastal regions of Angola, seized directly by the Europeans. The pirates bartered some twenty "negars" in exchange for provisions. By that time, slavery had existed in Brazil and a few other parts of the Americas for more than one hundred years.

Much of Europe was clamoring to join the highly profitable African slave trade. Whatever qualms some might have had over consigning human beings to a life of chattel slavery, a condition that passed on directly to their children, were largely quelled by a rationalization that consigned blacks to a different species of human beings who were fit only for slavery. Any discomfort over the appalling conditions of the Atlantic slave trade was soothed by the enormous wealth that flowed from a commercial enterprise that had far more economic significance in Europe than has been widely acknowledged. When the English received the coveted *Asiento*—the contract to transport slaves from Africa—there were torch-lit celebrations in the streets of London, and Liverpool was soon transformed from a small fishing village into a prosperous city.

But unlike the colonies where slave-run sugar and tobacco plantations fueled the economy, the Virginia Company that settled Jamestown had never anticipated a need for slavery and had no provisions at hand to regulate it. While a rapidly increasing reliance on tobacco plantations would soon change that, the lack of laws in the early days may have led to the first Africans' being treated more like indentured servants than slaves for life. At the very least, it left more room to maneuver. Slaves sometimes owned their own cattle, became skilled artisans, and cut their own deals on time they could claim as their own, even eventually winning their freedom.

There was another way that freedom may have come to Africans in the early days. In 1622, after both Pocahontas and her father, Powhatan, were dead and the peace partly brokered by her marriage to an Englishman ended, the natives launched an attempt to finally wipe out the settlements in and around Jamestown, which resulted in the deaths of more than three hundred settlers out of a total of some twelve hundred. The Africans in Jamestown at the time undoubtedly fought side by side with the English for survival. That too could have led to freedom, as it would in future American conflicts from the Revolutionary War—primarily from the British side but in Northern states and in Virginia as well—to the Civil War. A black man named Antonio was sold in Jamestown in 1621, the year before the Indian attack, and was later commended for his "hard work and service." Antonio, who became Anthony Johnson, would go on to appear in Virginia records as a free man of color who owned 250 acres of land; he had indentured servants and even owned his own slaves.

The first Maryland colonists brought indentured servants with them to the New World, and at least one free black man, Mathias de Sousa, who is believed to have voted at a Maryland General Assembly meeting. They also appear to have brought slaves. The first Lord Baltimore, who never set foot in his colony, instructed his agent to purchase forty cattle, ten sow, forty hens, and ten Negroes to take to the new colony. Before the 1630s ended, slaves had been imported into all of the North American colonies, and the first American slave ship had been built in Marblehead, Massachusetts. America was not to let so prosperous a trade pass it by.

But Maryland planters, for far longer than those in Virginia, continued to rely predominantly on indentured servants but it might not have been because of any disdain they held for slavery. In 1662 Maryland Governor Charles Calvert wrote to his father in London to explain that they were "naturally inclin'd to love neigros" [*sic*]" but their purses could not "endure it." Slaves for life were far more expensive than indentured servants.

By the 1690s, as changes in the economy brought about better opportunities in England, fewer people were willing to sell themselves into a limited form of slavery that many knew they would never survive. Consequently, Maryland planters began to purchase a steadily increasing number of Africans, some directly from Africa and others from the West Indies. Stockholders in the Royal Africa Company, which at one time included political philosopher John Locke, saw profits rise as the company delivered seventy-five thousand slaves to British North America between 1673 and 1725. Those numbers would swell until the transatlantic slave trade was outlawed in 1808.

The expansion of slave labor helped spur the annual American tobacco export of 20 million pounds in the 1670s to 220 million pounds by the 1770s, though harvests could be erratic and prices suffered when the market became saturated. By 1780, most of the white indentured servants had been replaced in the Chesapeake area alone by upward of one hundred thousand slaves. But in that transitional time, white indentured servants and black slaves commonly lived and worked side by side, a portrait of early America that is little known. In the beginning, there was no clear prohibition against unions between blacks and whites, and some voluntary interracial liaisons ensued. Consequently, laws were gradually implemented to fix the legal status of interracial children produced by these unions. In the end, the fate of a mixed-race child would turn completely on the status of the mother. An enslaved woman's children were enslaved and an indentured woman's children were required to serve out the same term as the mother had begun. Occasionally, an enslaved person who managed to trace his or her ancestry back to a free white woman was able to win freedom in a court of law. But laws were soon passed in both Virginia and Maryland forbidding interracial unions and marriage. Other laws fixed a system of chattel slavery for life, passed on to the children, based on race.

Tobacco was exceedingly harsh on the land, stripping the natural nutrients from the soil in short time. In the early days, when land holdings were vast and still largely unsettled, planters often found it easy to abandon their spent fields and move westward to cultivate new ones in virgin soil. But as Maryland became more settled, it became impractical to do so, and planters increasingly turned away from tobacco and began planting increasingly profitable grains. By the end of the Revolutionary War period, most Maryland farmers had abandoned tobacco; others purchased land in Kentucky and Tennessee and walked their slaves south to carve out new tobacco plantations on more hospitable soil. Landowners who stayed behind slowly nursed the land back to health, first with plaster of Paris and then with guano—bird feces— shipped from South America.

The end of tobacco as the lifeblood of Maryland's economy recast the fate of the state's enslaved population. Grains could be planted and largely ignored until harvest time, leaving slave owners with a surplus of laborers who needed to be fed, clothed, and housed, however minimally. In that short-lived spurt of idealism stemming from the American Revolution, some planters in Maryland freed their slaves outright. Others agreed to allow them to earn wages, commonly known as "free trading," with which they could purchase their own and their family's freedom. The population of free blacks in

Maryland rose from 2.5 percent of the entire population in 1790 to 12.8 percent in 1850, and the state had the highest number of free blacks in the Union. The number of free blacks in all of the slave territories rose as well, from 100,000 in 1810 to more than 228,000 in 1850.

In the District of Columbia, the free black population increased dramatically in the early years, in part due to the city's attractiveness for free blacks living in Virginia and Maryland: work was often available in the constantly expanding capital; there were no legal prohibitions against schools for free black children; and black churches, such as Mt. Zion in Georgetown, were being established as early as 1816. By 1830, free blacks slightly outnumbered enslaved blacks. At the time of the *Pearl,* nearly three times as many free blacks as enslaved were living in the nation's capital.

As Washington grew more populated, slaves were hired out to work as servants in the city's private homes, hotels, and boardinghouses. Some of those hired slaves were children. One woman's memoir of life in Washington during the mid—nineteenth century described the small black chimney sweeps who were hired out by their masters. She said that one "little fellow went about clad in one garment only—a blanket which fastened close around their necks and their poor eyes were always inflamed and red and weeping from the soot and their elbows and knees raw and bleeding." This practice became so common that an English visitor staying at the Willard Hotel remarked that there was not one servant in the hotel who was not a slave hired from some distant owner. His account, if accurate at the time, would not remain so: the Northern-born Willard brothers became slave owners.

Slave owners who lived in the area now commonly referred to as the Upper South—Maryland, Virginia, Delaware, Kentucky, Tennessee, and sometimes North Carolina—had another increasingly profitable way to dispense with slaves they no longer found useful. They sold them to local slave traders for transportation to the Lower South, where they were resold at a substantial profit to the owners of labor-hungry plantations. Spurred on by Northerner Eli Whitney's cotton gin, which revolutionized the production of cotton, new plantations exploded across the Deep South. With the African slave market technically closed to planters, those plantations looked to the former tobacco states to supply the slaves they needed for their fields.*

Slave traders eager to meet the increasingly profitable labor demands of cotton plantations fanned out across the Tidewater around the Chesapeake Bay, the Eastern Shore of Maryland, and Virginia, staying at inns in small towns, and in hotels in cities like Washington. The traders advertised for "likely Negroes," meaning healthy and young. They housed their purchases in local jails, slave pens, and even hotels that had fitted out their basements as holding pens. The newly purchased slaves, abruptly separated from their families, were transported south by foot, ship, and even train, mainly to New Orleans, where they were sold to work on the cotton and sugar plantations and in the sugar refineries of Louisiana, the last of which had a particularly low life expectancy. Occasionally, planters would bypass the slave trader and travel to the Washington area and Richmond to purchase their own slaves.

Initially, Baltimore was the epicenter for the domestic slave trade in the area but soon the District of Columbia began to rival it, at least while Alexandria was still a part of the capital. While visiting a slave pen in Baltimore in 1835, a correspondent of an antislavery group said that he was told by a slave trader that there were a dozen or so traders in

---

* Congress could not abolish the Atlantic slave trade until 1808. Article I, Section 9, of the Constitution protected the slave trade for twenty years in order to accommodate slave owners in still growing states like South Carolina and Georgia. Without such a constitutional protection, these Lower South states would have refused to join the United States. Many prominent slave owners in the Upper South eagerly supported the end of the Africa slave trade. The significance of the potential profits that would accrue to slave owners in their area was not lost to them.

his city but that Negroes were scarce. He added that there was a good deal of business in the nation's capital, citing the Alexandria firm of Franklin & Armfield.

The expansion of slavery across the Lower South had not been universally anticipated. Many had expected slavery to simply fade away when Congress abolished the Atlantic slave trade but the increasing profits in cotton and slaves proved them wrong. Cotton plantation fever struck, and many who had never farmed bought new land, purchased a few slaves, and set off to make their fortunes. From sunup to sundown, slaves worked the cotton fields as the valuable harvest was shipped off to the rapidly growing mills of England, France, and other European countries. The mills of Pennsylvania and Massachusetts bought cotton, too, often purchasing it from smaller cotton growers, some of whom did not own slaves or were themselves free blacks.

A substantial number of fugitives who successfully fled from their owners had made the critical decision to run away when they learned they were to be sold away from their families. Many could readily see the signs that they were in danger—an owner's economic downturn or an imminent death—even before the slave trader arrived. And with husband and wife often owned by different people, they knew that one could be sold while the other was left behind. Many felt they had little to lose by running: their punishment if caught was usually sale to a trader—the same fate they were attempting to avoid. And if they succeeded in reaching freedom in the North and could begin to make a living there, they had some hope that they might be able to help free other family members after they were settled, although this was an enormously expensive proposition.

Some runaways, like an ancestor of Rep. Eleanor Holmes Norton of the District of Columbia, found refuge within the black community in the slave territory of Washington. Richard John Holmes slipped away from a plantation in Virginia when "[m]ost of those he'd known since childhood" had been sold further south—a striking statement that speaks to the magnitude of the internal slave trade. With the aid of a compass and the kindness of other slaves he met along the way, Holmes made his way as far as the shore of the Potomac River, where he could see the Capitol on the other side. Standing tall and exuding self-confidence, Holmes struck out across the Long Bridge near Fourteenth Street and slipped into the relative safety of the large black community in the nation's capital. Fugitives like Holmes could survive in the capital as long as they were not challenged by the authorities and ordered to show their free papers. Some surely obtained fake papers. It is impossible to know how many may have lived in the city under these circumstances. They certainly did not step forward to be counted when the census takers came around.

The *Pearl* headed down the steadily widening Potomac, past George Washington's Mt. Vernon, set high on a bluff over the river. They passed small towns with Algonquian-sounding names like Nanjemoy and Piscataway, the latter for the Indians who lived on both sides of the river more than two hundred years earlier when Capt. John Smith recorded his journey up the "Patawomeck." To the delight of all onboard, the wind kicked up an even higher notch, and the little schooner was racing. With their journey finally well under way, the passengers asked if they could hold a religious service in their cramped quarters to thank God for the journey so far and pray for safe deliverance. A few of the younger passengers read Bible passages out loud and they all softly sang together. Mary and Emily added their lovely voices to the singing but couldn't contribute to the readings because both were illiterate.

It was a relief to everyone on the *Pearl* that they were finally moving farther away from Washington, but they knew they were not out of danger. By late Sunday morning many of the owners would have discovered them missing and sounded the alarm to the authorities. All hoped that whatever search party had formed would look first to the roads leading north out of the city, which were the most common routes of escape.

When the sun went down Sunday evening, the fugitives could finally come up to the deck for fresh air. While they were forced to stay below out of sight, the *Pearl* had tacked across the river twice as Sayres pushed the small schooner to its limits, leaving a few of the passengers, including the more fragile Mary, seasick. A worried Samuel carried his sister up through the hatchway to the deck and placed her where she could lean on the foremast under the care of Emily and their brother Richard, known to his family as the quiet sibling. Richard—with a wife and children, who were most likely free, left behind in Washington— looked after his sisters while Samuel went back to the hold to retrieve provisions they had brought with them: a flask of brandy, some potted meats, and tea and rolls. Mary revived, and everyone relaxed a little.

According to Harriet Beecher Stowe's later account, Richard had been trying for years to buy his freedom from Francis Valdenar, Rebecca Culver's guardian. But whenever he came close to meeting the purchase price, Valdenar would raise it. After allowing older sisters Elizabeth, Eveline, Eliza, Martha, and, apparently, Henrietta to purchase their freedom, Valdenar had become more reluctant to let any more Edmonsons go. Like many, he was finding the system of hiring out his slaves to be a profitable and reliable one. At the time of the *Pearl* escape, Richard had been hired out to work as a coachman for Robert John Walker, the secretary of the treasury under President James Polk. The Pennsylvania-born Walker had migrated south and first appeared in Washington as a senator from his adopted state of Mississippi. Richard was not the first Edmonson to work for Walker. In 1844 Valdenar had allowed Senator Walker to purchase Richard's sister Eliza for three hundred dollars. Two years later, after Eliza had married a free man of color named Dennis Orme, Walker freed both Eliza and Samuel Isaiah, the couple's fourteen-month-old son. The manumission records for the city indicate only that Eliza and Samuel were freed by Walker. It is likely that Dennis Orme made payments to Walker for his wife's freedom, but that was not recorded in the manumission record.

The Bell Family

The six Edmonsons were not the largest family unit among the fugitives onboard the schooner racing down the river. That distinction belonged to the eleven members of Daniel Bell's family: his wife, Mary Bell; their eight children; and two grandchildren. Bell, the forty-five-year-old free man employed as a blacksmith at the Navy Yard, did not board the *Pearl* that night. Though some reports state that he was with his family on the schooner, only one Daniel Bell ever appeared in any of the documents related to the escape, and that was his fifteen-year-old son. As with Paul Jennings, it would have been a needless danger for a free black to board the vessel, because it could have led to criminal charges, just as John Bush and others had been criminally charged for abetting escapes. Bell was likely making preparations to meet his family when they arrived at Frenchtown and then help them make it safely to the free state of Pennsylvania.

Bell's family had been owned by Robert Armistead, a master caulker who had also worked at the Navy Yard until he became gravely ill. In 1835, shortly before his death, Armistead signed manumission papers that freed Mary Bell outright and then reduced the term of slavery for their six children born at that time, as follows:

ANDREW, 16	FREE AT AGE 40 (1859)
GEORGE W., 4	FREE AT AGE 35 (1866)
MARY ELEANORA, 8	FREE AT AGE 30 (1857)
DANIEL, 2	FREE AT AGE 35 (1868)
HARRIET, 3 MONTHS	FREE AT AGE 30 (1865)
CAROLINE, 6	FREE AT AGE 30 (1859)

The Bell family presented the manumission papers at city hall, where they were recorded in the District of Columbia Free Negro Register. Mary Bell was free, and the children, with their status changed to a limited term of slavery, were less likely to be sold.

But now Daniel Bell was in trouble. An account in the *New York True Wesleyan*, an abolitionist organ of the breakaway Methodists who had remained steadfast against slavery, stated that Daniel Bell, a "robust, worthy, industrious man" originally from Prince George's County, Maryland, was still enslaved at that time and, because he had played a pivotal role in persuading Robert Armistead to sign the manumission papers, he had been sold to a slave trader.

In retaliation for his efforts on behalf of his family, Bell's owner, very likely related to Armistead, sold him.* He was seized at the Navy Yard and hauled off to a slave pen, "then kept in Seventh Street on the Avenue." Bell's friends enlisted help from a marine officer at the Navy Yard, who agreed to buy Bell from the trader on the condition that he would be repaid the purchase price in installments. Bell dutifully made his payments through a "trusty friend" named Thomas Blagden, a wealthy white Washingtonian who owned a wide swath of land across the Anacostia River, including a tract called St. Elizabeth's. However, when the full amount—thought to be one thousand dollars—was nearly paid, the officer died. It then came to light that the deceased had mortgaged Bell to a relative, who was claiming the full amount. Blagden negotiated the amount down to six hundred dollars, which Bell was only able to pay after a number of years.†

---

* Susannah Armistead, Robert's widow, was referred to in the article as the "widow Greenfield," which was very likely her maiden name. There are strong connections between the Bells, the Armisteads, and the Greenfields. In 1836, about the same time that Daniel Bell was securing better conditions for his family, an Ann Bell filed a petition for freedom on behalf of herself and her two sons against Gerald T. Greenfield, who was a member of a prominent Prince George's family with an ancestor who had sworn his oath of allegiance to the American Revolutionary cause and fought admirably in the war. Gerald Greenfield had inherited Ann Bell, who was very likely related to Daniel Bell; as an adult she was listed living in his home in later census records. Ann Bell, with the help of attorney Joseph Bradley, won her suit for freedom against Greenfield. Susannah Armistead's daughter, Mary Jane O'Brien, testified on behalf of Greenfield at the trial.

† There is no record of Bell's freedom in the city records but that does not mean he wasn't freed as this account details. A good number of free blacks chose not to pay the recordation fee. If well known or employed at a place such as the Navy Yard, they were usually safe from harassment. When Bell's minor daughter filed a petition for freedom in 1844, a free black man named William Simms took on the required role as her "next friend," or adult representative. It is very doubtful that a slave would have

Susannah Armistead, the executor of her husband's estate, had no intention of recognizing the manumission records her husband had signed. Three years after his death, she filed an inventory of his property with the orphans' court—the precursor of today's probate court—describing the children as slaves for life, a far more valuable holding than slaves for a limited term, and placed their value at $1,225.00. She made no reference to their mother. The remainder of her husband's personal property was valued at $74.25 and consisted of a few bureaus, a mahogany table with twelve chairs, a candle stand, three school benches and desks (at one time they had set up a small school in their home), and one bed. Like Rebecca Culver, Susannah Armistead's only significant assets were human beings.

A year later, Armistead submitted a final accounting of her husband's estate to the court. Andrew Bell's earnings had averaged $2.00 per month over three years; Mary Eleanora had brought in $1.50 per month for one year and $2.00 per month for the next two. Armistead had even put ten-year-old Caroline to work for five months, for which she received $1.50 per month. The accounting also listed the expenses their owner had incurred in board and clothing expenses, including the hefty—and undoubtedly padded—sum of $20.00 to feed and clothe seven-year-old George and $30.00 to do the same for three-year-old Harriet.

The Bells may not have immediately known that Armistead was claiming the children as slaves for life, but it soon became apparent that they were in danger. In 1843 Susannah Armistead applied to Judge Nathaniel P. Causin of the orphans' court for an appraisal of the Bells, describing them as slaves for life, so that she could have them "divided" among her children.

Daniel Bell turned to James Mandeville Carlisle, a highly capable

---

been allowed to act in that capacity. However, two years later, when his daughter Harriet filed a similar suit, Daniel Bell was named as her representative, indicating that he was free by that time.

young Washington lawyer, to block the intended division of his family. With a good number of white Marylanders heading out to take advantage of better opportunities in the new lands to the south and west, it was highly likely that Armistead was attempting to send the Bell children well out of the reach of their parents. As a precaution, Mary Bell returned to city hall on October 18, 1843, to obtain another copy of her certificate of freedom. The Registrar of the City of Washington certified that he had seen "satisfactory evidence of the legality of her title to freedom," which allowed her to "reside in the said city of Washington."

Carlisle did more. On September 13, 1844, he filed petitions for freedom for two Bell daughters: Mary and Eleanor. The petitions dragged on for a few years with no final resolution. Again, the Bells got on with their lives. But in 1846 the family learned that Armistead was planning to send Harriet, now eleven years old, out of the city. Carlisle filed a petition with the court for Harriet's freedom and then filed a request for an injunction that would prevent Armistead from removing the child from the jurisdiction. He submitted evidence (unfortunately lost) and argued that his client "fears that by such removal she may be lost in irredeemable slavery." Judge William Cranch, the well-respected jurist and nephew of John and Abigail Adams, granted the injunction against Armistead. Harriet was safe, but only for a while.

In October 1847 the Bells' petitions for freedom finally went to trial. The widow Armistead argued that her husband had been mentally enfeebled prior to his death and that Daniel Bell had tricked him into signing papers that granted outright freedom to Mary Bell and allowed the Bell children a gradual schedule of freedom. She testified that Bell had waited until she was away from the family home and then managed to get her husband, as well as the family Bible listing all of the birthdays of the Bell children, into a cart that took the sick man to the poorhouse. Once there, she continued, Bell was joined by Edward W. Clarke, the city's guardian of the poor for their ward, and the two men forced her husband to sign the manumission papers. Armistead's claims may have been true, and it shows to what incredible lengths Daniel Bell, in collusion with a sympathetic white man, had gone in order to protect his family. Carlisle argued that Armistead had gone to the poorhouse to get proper food and care.

But Edward Clarke's death signaled the end to whatever protection he had been able to afford the Bells, not only as a city official but also as a witness to Robert Armistead's lucidity at the time he signed the papers. Daniel Bell, a black man, could not testify against a white woman in court. Four depositions were entered into evidence, three of which were illiterate and signed their statements by making their marks, stating that Robert Armistead was not in his right mind when he signed the manumissions. A Dr. Williams, who had been treating Robert Armistead for chronic rheumatism, also submitted a signed statement, in which he stated that the rheumatism had not impaired his patient's mind, and that he was certainly capable of understanding the effect and operation of a deed of manumission. But in the end, the jury sided with Susannah Armistead. It was not very difficult for an all-white jury in slave territory to conclude that any man who would sign away his only real wealth had to be mentally incapacitated.

The family appealed the court's decision and also hired the talented Joseph Bradley to request a new trial. On his oath, Bradley submitted to the court that new evidence—unfortunately unknown—had materialized, and the request for a new trial was granted. In March 1848, before the new proceedings began, the appellate court upheld the original jury verdict in favor of Armistead. By then the family's funds were exhausted along with any hope of reaching a successful outcome in another trial. After Bell made arrangements with Washington's Underground Railroad cell to take their chances on the Underground Railroad, they withdrew the request for a new trial. A month later, his family boarded the *Pearl*.

Other fugitives on the schooner were owned by men with connections to the same legal system that had just let down the Bells. Jane Brent belonged to Dr. Nathaniel Causin, the namesake relative of Judge

Nathaniel Causin of the orphans' court, who had approved Susannah Armistead's request to have the Bell family appraised in advance of dividing them among her children. Daphne Paine belonged to General Alexander Hunter, the U.S. marshal for the District of Columbia, who had summoned Mrs. Armistead to answer the petitions of freedom filed by the Bells. Hunter's responsibilities as the U.S. marshal also included the seizure and sale of property to satisfy legal judgments. Nine months before his own slave slipped away to board the *Pearl*, Hunter had auctioned off two slaves in a public sale. William Williams, the slave trader who operated the pen behind the Smithsonian that was visible from the windows of the Capitol, placed the winning bid for both slaves. Fortunately, Washington antislavery operatives were able to enlist the aid of a "warm-hearted" Washington resident to purchase their freedom and redeem them from the slave pen where Williams had taken them to await shipment south. Such gestures were usually expected to be paid back in full.

Cornfield Harbor

Later on Sunday evening, shortly before the *Pearl* reached Point Lookout, where a lighthouse marked the end of the Maryland peninsula and the Potomac meets the Chesapeake Bay, the wind increased again—but this time to dangerous levels. As whitecaps rose on the river and the fugitives hastened to secure themselves belowdecks, some became ill from the rough water. It was soon clear that the small baycraft would not be able to turn north with "the wind being dead in our teeth, and too strong to allow any attempt to ascend the bay." Drayton, knowing that the longer they stayed on the river, the greater the risk that they would be caught, pleaded with Sayres to take the schooner across the bay and then turn it slightly south into the Atlantic Ocean, where, he argued, they would be less likely to be found.

Sayres refused, arguing that not only was the vessel not fit to sail the ocean, but also that such a move was not part of their deal. They had agreed that the *Pearl* would go only as far as the Frenchtown landing on the Elk River at the north end of the bay. They had no choice but to remain where they were.

About 9:00 P.M. on Sunday, Sayres dropped anchor in Cornfield Harbor, a crescent-shaped deepwater shelter on the river side of the Point Lookout peninsula, a spot ships commonly used to wait out a storm. They would resume their journey as planned on Monday morning if the wind calmed down. A weary Drayton, who had not slept since the Friday night before they disembarked, collapsed into sleep. So did Sayres and young Chester English. The fugitives below had had little sleep in the uncomfortable hold, and they too tried to rest. They had to get through this one last night on the river, and then face the still dangerous journey of sailing up the Chesapeake Bay to Frenchtown, all the while surrounded by slave territory.

THREE

Slavery in the Washington Area

Earlier that Sunday in Washington, news of the escape spread quickly through the city's well-attended churches, where some residents, as one wag put it, recovered from a "habit of frequenting the ball-room, the billiard and bowling saloons, the pistol galleries, the card table, the theatre, the batteries, the race course, and the fandangoes" of Saturday night by gathering around the "sacrament table, with sanctimonious faces." This Sunday, churchgoers learned that something much more exciting than a Spanish fandango dance had taken place the night before. Some found out when they woke that morning. So unexpected was "this hegira of the servants," as one newspaper breathlessly reported, "that one lady, on coming down to breakfast on Sunday morning, was surprised to find the fireplace cold and no breakfast prepared." More owners discovered similar inconveniences; others, when they learned of the escape, looked for their slaves and found them missing from their quarters, the homes where they had been hired, or from the homes where they lived with free members of their own families.

In the Washington of 1848, it would have been difficult to find anyone in the white community willing to speak out publicly against slavery. But in earlier days, there was some organized sentiment against slavery. As late as 1828, just as the antislavery movement in the North was beginning to heat up, a surprising display of moderate opinion manifested itself in a petition in which nearly eleven hundred Washingtonians, many of them prominent residents, prayed to Congress "for the gradual abolition of slavery in the District of Columbia." In the "monster petition," as it was dubbed, the signers stated that "[w]e have no hesitation in believing your honorable body never intended that this odious law [the Maryland laws sanctioning slavery] should be enforced." Acknowledging that a sudden emancipation of the city's slaves would be rash, the petitioners proposed that Congress enact a law of gradual emancipation, whereby any child born to a slave after July 4, 1828, "shall be free at the age of twenty-five years."

Signers included William Cranch, the chief judge of the District of Columbia circuit, who would later issue an injunction to prevent young Harriet Bell's removal from the city; shoe manufacturer Andrew Hoover and grocer Samuel Brereton, both of whom had fugitives aboard the *Pearl;* and, surprisingly, B. O. Shekell, a city slave trader. The name of Robert Armistead, the man who had tried to manumit the Bells, is also on the petition. Many of the signers were strong supporters of the American Colonization Society, which had established the African colony of Liberia. A few noted next to their names that they supported emancipation only on the condition that the slaves be removed there. Judge Cranch did not add such a stipulation, but he too strongly supported colonization. He briefly served as president of the Alexandria Colonization Society, whose rolls included members of Robert E. Lee's family. However, Congress wasn't receptive to the petition. A congressional committee concluded that the gradual emancipation of slaves in the District of Columbia was not expedient at that time.

Even more surprising, a year later the American Convention for Promoting the Abolition of Slavery and Improving the Condition of the African Race was convened in Washington's city hall on December 8, 1829. Seven delegates from the Washington City Abolition Society were among the twenty men who came together, while two came from a similar organization in Alexandria, and four from Baltimore.

Quaker Benjamin Lundy, the editor of an antislavery newspaper in Baltimore with the upbeat name of the *Genius of Universal Emancipation*, who was said to have had a hand in the monster petition, was also the force behind the convention. The attendees spent several days discussing slavery-related issues with particular attention to the situation in Washington, D.C. During the convention, they prepared a memorial to Congress which deplored that "[m]any of the African race, purchased for a distant market, are concentrated here, where the sounds of the clanking fetters mingle with the voice of the American statesmen, legislating for a free people."

Such a convention would never meet again in Washington. New and far more radical antislavery voices, black and white, were beginning to rise across the North, which would have a decided impact on antislavery activities in the more moderate slave states of the Upper South. In September 1829 a free black man named David Walker published an *Appeal to the Coloured Citizens of the World* in which he called for black revolution. Then, on January 1, 1831, William Lloyd Garrison broke new ground in white abolitionist circles by calling for the immediate end of slavery—as opposed to its gradual abolition—in the inaugural issue of the *Liberator*, published in Boston.

Garrison had attracted a great deal of attention in Washington just the year before he began his newspaper when his stint on Benjamin Lundy's antislavery newspaper landed him in jail for articles attacking the slave traders of Baltimore. He was released on the condition that he quit Maryland and never return. Garrison explained in the first issue of the *Liberator* that he had initially planned to publish his newspaper in Washington, D.C., and had sent out public notice to that effect. He attributed the move to Boston to the fact that Washington "was palsied by public indifference"—a stunning understatement. It is doubtful that the first issue of the *Liberator* would ever have reached the streets of Washington. When William Wormley, a free black man whose father operated a public hack business in the city and owned a substantial home near Lafayette Square, agreed to act as an agent to distribute the Boston-printed *Liberator* in the city, he was promptly arrested.

Nearly all moderate antislavery voices in slave territory were silenced in August 1831, when a slave named Nathaniel Turner, a self-proclaimed visionary, led a bloody insurrection in Southampton County, Virginia, 190 miles south of Washington. Turner and his supporters killed some sixty white men, women, and children before they were stopped by a mix of state militia, volunteers, and federal forces. Vigilantes retaliated by killing more than one hundred and fifty blacks, most of whom had had nothing to do with the insurrection.

Turner's uprising hardened hearts, intensified whites' fear of more insurrections, and deepened Southern distrust of the North. In Washington, D.C., Virginia, and Maryland, harsher laws were passed to further hamstring the black community, viewed as culprits whenever there was slave trouble. Georgetown, the former tobacco port in the District of Columbia, passed a black code that included a provision that made it unlawful to read or possess antislavery publications, specifically singling out the *Liberator*. Virtually all slave jurisdictions would ban such incendiary materials.

The newly radicalized William Lloyd Garrison came up with more ways to cause trouble. In 1832 he led an attack on the American Colonization Society, an organization he had once supported. In 1816, in Washington, D.C., well-known figures such as Senator Henry Clay, Gen. Andrew Jackson, Supreme Court Justice Bushrod Washington, and national anthem author Francis Scott Key—all slave owners—joined together with moderate antislavery activists and missionaries to form an organization that would resettle free blacks to Liberia. One of the signers of the organization's constitution was John Stull, a prominent Georgetowner who owned three of the fugitives aboard the *Pearl*.

Garrison, Benjamin Lundy, and Gerrit Smith originally believed that colonization was the only way to convince slave owners to give up their slaves. But others agreed with Henry Clay, who lauded colonization as a way to "rid our country of a useless and pernicious, if not dangerous portion of its population": free blacks. Suspicions that the society cared more for eliminating free blacks than it did for freeing slaves were further bolstered when founder Bushrod Washington, who had inherited Mt. Vernon from his uncle, the first president, sold fifty-four of his slaves for ten thousand dollars. When an observer recognized his slaves being forcibly marched through Leesburg, Virginia, likely on their way to Wheeling, where slaves were shipped down the river, the Supreme Court justice came under fire for duplicity. He responded angrily that no one had the right to question how he disposed of his property, and added that it was the slaves' own "insubordination and disregard of authority that rendered them useless" and therefore gave him no choice but to sell them.

Notwithstanding that unfortunate incident, many state colonization organizations were formed in the North and, a few months before the *Pearl* arrived in Washington, the Massachusetts Colonization Society advertised for funds to aid thirty-seven slaves on a Louisiana plantation, who would be freed only if they were sent to Liberia.

Maryland had set up its own colony, Maryland in Africa, adjacent to Liberia. In 1831, largely in reaction to Nat Turner's rebellion, the state legislature passed a law requiring that all slaves freed after the passage of that act leave Maryland, and provided financial assistance for their transportation to Africa. To establish which blacks would be allowed to stay, though they still would be encouraged to go to Africa, the state authorized a special census whereby every county sheriff was to record the name and age of every free person of color. On September 14, 1832, Sheriff William O'Neale Jr., of Montgomery County, submitted his list, which included the name of Paul Edmonson, Mary and Emily's father, giving his age as forty-five. Sheriff O'Neale noted on his submission that not one of the free blacks he visited "is willing to go to Liberia."*

---

* After that law was passed, Maryland slaves continued to buy or win their freedom, but there is evidence of only one freed slave being forcibly removed from the state. When the

That census establishes that Paul Edmonson was a free man by 1832 but does not reveal when he gained that freedom. The county deed book may. On April 1, 1820, a widow named Margaret Lazenby recorded a document in which she stated that at the time of her death she wished to set free "a negro man named Paul," aged thirty-five. Lazenby, who lived on the Brookeville Road in Montgomery County, Maryland, not far from where Paul Edmonson's farm would soon be located, died the next year. There are enough links between the Lazenby, Culver, and Edmonson families to safely assume that Paul Edmonson, age forty-five in 1832 and the only free black man named Paul in the county census, was the same thirty-five-year-old Paul who became free in 1821. The legal detritus of the nineteenth century—marriage records, slave names, property deeds, inventories, and wills—reveal an interrelated mesh of lives, property, and fortunes that crossed color lines. One of the men who witnessed the document that freed Paul was the brother of Rebecca Culver, who owned Amelia Edmonson. Years earlier, Culver's father had purchased land in Montgomery County from a wealthy white land-holder named Edmonson, who may well have had slaves who took his surname, a practice that had less to do with any fondness of their owners than with the protection and benefits that flowed from connections with a prominent family, which were extremely important to free blacks. Paul or earlier members of his family were likely Edmonson slaves at one time.

The increased hostility toward free blacks and abolitionists failed to dampen the rising tide of abolitionism. In 1833—the same year that Britain passed legislation to end slavery in all of her colonies by compensating slave owners—impassioned Protestant evangelicals joined together with steadfast Quakers and, with the support of leaders in the free black community, established the American Anti-Slavery Society

---

fears raised by the Turner uprising had calmed down, farmers turned once again to the free black community to harvest their fields, with little more said about the mandatory emigration program.

in Philadelphia. In one of the first public gatherings to see a large number of female participants, their convention called for the immediate emancipation of all slaves, an end to the internal slave trade, and a complete rejection of the colonization movement.

A more sharply focused and far more militant faze of antislavery activity had begun. The American Anti-Slavery Society sponsored a campaign specifically targeting slavery in the District of Columbia and encouraged local societies to exercise their constitutional right to petition the federal government. A swelling number of sympathizers showered the House of Representatives with petitions praying for an end to both slavery and the slave trade in the District of Columbia. Many of those petitions were organized and signed by women: they constituted the sole means in which they were allowed to participate in the political process.

As part of that campaign, the American Anti-Slavery Society produced a provocative broadside called "Slave Market of America," which featured nine scenes related to slavery in the nation's capital. One image showed a slave coffle (from an Arabic word meaning caravan) exiting a slave pen belonging to a J. Neal, on Seventh Street. In the image, the slaves were chained together two by two, with another long chain threaded through to link the pairs together. These coffles were frequently led by fiddlers or banjo players, both to set the pace and to mask the sorrow. Neal's slave pen was very likely the same pen at Seventh Street and Maryland Avenue, just below the Mall, that was later operated by William Williams. It was also likely the same pen that Daniel Bell had been taken to after he was seized at the Navy Yard.

The broadside also featured the infamous Franklin & Armfield slave pen of Alexandria, then still a part of the District of Columbia. That partnership was one of the first in the capital to solicit for area slaves to resell to the cotton-growing South, and their business was so successful that they were soon transporting slaves out of Alexandria in several of their own vessels, one of which was named the *Isaac Franklin*.

Southerners were outraged by these assaults from the North. In addition to increasing the antislavery ranks in their own region, the radicals woke a sleeping giant of passionate and particularly cohesive proslavery sentiment. In 1836, the slave power, as the united and vocal senators and congressmen from the South came to be known, was strong enough to corral a sufficient number of Northern votes in Congress to pass a gag rule that automatically tabled any petition raising the slavery issue in any way, thereby blocking the constitutional right to petition the government. Even after the gag rule was finally lifted eight years later due to the relentless efforts of Rep. John Quincy Adams, Southerners still managed to marshal enough votes to table nearly every antislavery petition that was submitted.

Abolitionists refused to back down. Committed to changing the hearts and minds of slaveholders through moral suasion, they organized a drive to send antislavery pamphlets and newspapers directly to the South. Howls of protests rose in Congress and the slave power charged that the U.S. mail was being used to deliver incendiary and dangerous materials. An angry Rep. James Hammond, who as a senator in 1858 would declare that "Cotton is king" on the floor of Congress, condemned materials showing graphic illustrations of floggings and slave auctions. He complained bitterly that such tracts, as though they were a form of pornography, were inappropriately being targeted to young people.* Outraged citizens of Charleston, South Carolina, broke into the city post office, confiscated the antislavery materials, and burned them in a public bonfire on the town square. An alarmed Amos Kendall, Andrew Jackson's Massachusetts-born postmaster general, proclaimed that because those materials violated the spirit of the law, Southern postmasters could intercept them at will. The postmaster for New York City

---

* In 1839, Hammond purchased a young female slave with an infant daughter. He took the woman as his mistress and fathered several of her children before replacing her with her twelve-year-old daughter. His sexual proclivities did not get him in trouble until he turned his attentions to his sister-in-law.

simplified that process by seizing materials offensive to the South before they left their point of origin.

Many Northerners also viewed this spike in antislavery activity with barely veiled hostility that sometimes escalated into physical assaults. In September 1835, anti-abolitionist forces erected a makeshift gallows in front of William Lloyd Garrison's door in Boston, and a few months later a tense abolitionist rally ended with Garrison's being snatched from a lynch mob with a noose laced around his neck.

The Snow Riot

The fallout from the new radicalism of the mid-1830s increased tensions in Washington, where a trio of racial incidents exploded. In August 1835 a seemingly disturbed or inebriated eighteen-year-old slave named Arthur Bowen was charged with the attempted murder of his owner, sixty-year-old Anna Thornton, who was the well-respected widow of the architect of the Capitol. He had entered her bedroom holding an axe. His own mother hustled him away before any harm was done, although it is unclear whether he really intended to kill anyone.

It was quickly made known that Bowen had participated in a debating society organized by Presbyterian minister John F. Cook, the founder and director of the Union Seminary, a school for free black children in Washington. Bowen may well have been "adversely" influenced by the debating society. On one occasion before the incident, Cook, a noted leader in the black community, organized a benefit for the purpose of aiding "A young man, about to disenthrall himself from slavery." The evening opened and closed with a prayer and included discourses on "Slavery & Freedom" and "Indignant sentiments on National Prejudices, Hatred and Slavery."

Bowen was taken to the Washington jail, where an angry white crowd surrounding the building threatened to lynch him. With the situation clearly well beyond the control of the small crew of constables headquartered in the Center Market on Pennsylvania Avenue, District

Attorney Francis Scott Key asked the government to send in the marines to control the mob.

A few days later, with emotions still running high over the Thornton affair, abolitionist pamphlets turned up on the counter of a busy Georgetown hardware store. Scrawled across their tops was the name of Reuben Crandall, a nonpracticing physician from Connecticut who had come to the District of Columbia to be a tutor in a family who had recently relocated to the area. Much preferring the study of botany, he had taken an office to pursue his avocation.

Crandall faced a near lynching before he was whisked to the same jail where Bowen was being held, and charged with sedition. The authorities searched his Georgetown rooms and found copies of Garrison's *Liberator*, which Crandall claimed he had used only to wrap plants for his botany studies. It didn't help that two years earlier Crandall's sister, Prudence, had become a heroine of the abolitionist movement when she went to jail for refusing to close down her Connecticut school for young women of color.

The marines remained at the jail to ensure that the still-roiled crowd would be unable to reach either Bowen or Crandall. But the rowdies were still looking for trouble when word reached them that Beverly Snow, a free man of color who owned the Epicurean Eating House at Sixth Street and Pennsylvania Avenue, had made disparaging remarks about the wives of the city mechanics, as skilled workers were called, some of whom were among the troublemakers. The mob of white men immediately moved on to the restaurant and—as a few of Snow's affluent white patrons quickly removed him to safety—destroyed most of what they could get their hands on.

The white mob next turned its wrath on the black community, seeking out black schools in particular. The District of Columbia had no prohibition against free blacks educating their children, but public money was provided only for white schools: black parents paid so that their children could learn to read and write. As John Cook's school burned, he fled to Pennsylvania in fear of his life and remained away for a year. He taught school there and participated in the annual Philadelphia convention of the Free People of Color. While Cook was clearly one of the progressive black leaders in Washington, when he returned to the city he did not turn his back on those who either chose or were forced to go to Liberia. When the *Liberia Packet* left from Baltimore in April 1848, he was there to pray with the emigrants before they sailed.

Before turning to black homes, the mob burned down two more schools. One was operated by Dr. James Fleet, a talented musician and dedicated educator, who had been trained as a physician by the American Colonization Society a few years earlier to go to Liberia. But he too had joined other blacks in rejecting colonization and refused to go. The other school was run by Maria Wormley, a free young woman of color much given to poetry who was from one of Washington's most prominent black families. She was the niece of William Wormley, who had been arrested for attempting to distribute the *Liberator*. Until the mob was brought under control, fires lit up the skies over Washington.*

When calm returned, the city reacted as it usually did: it passed more laws to further restrict the free black community. As a result of what came to be known as the Snow Riot, blacks were prohibited from obtaining city licenses to operate restaurants or perform any other city-licensed activity except for driving a public hack.

---

* U.S. Attorney Key zealously prosecuted Arthur Bowen, who was convicted of attempted murder and sentenced to hang. However, Mrs. Thornton was not happy with that outcome and successfully appealed to President Jackson to postpone his death sentence, and later to pardon him. The young man had been raised in her home, and he was a particular favorite of her aging mother, a woman who had seen her own husband hanged in England after being convicted of fraud. Mrs. Thornton then sold him for $750 to a friend of President Jackson's. Reuben Crandall's attorneys, who included Joseph Bradley, succeeded in having all charges dropped against him. But his stay in prison contributed to his bad health and he soon died of tuberculosis. That same year, Bradley represented Beverly Snow in a civil suit filed by David Crockett against the black restaurateur but, unfortunately, no details of that lawsuit exist. It may have been abandoned when Snow fled Washington or when Congressman Crockett headed west to the Alamo.

The black community replaced and repaired their schools and supported their families the best they could. As usual, when things quieted down, they found ways to circumvent the more restrictive laws—Beverly Snow's restaurant was discreetly reopened by another black entrepreneur. But it was not a good time to be black in Washington, either enslaved or free.

In that tumultuous year of 1835, Paul Edmonson quietly bought his first twenty acres in Montgomery County, Maryland, and Amelia gave birth to Emily. The following year, black members of the Foundry Methodist Church in Washington broke away to found the Asbury Methodist Church, where many of the Edmonsons would worship. But the views of many citizens had dramatically altered in regard to slavery. There would be no more monster petitions proffering what was then considered a more than reasonable proposition for gradual emancipation. In 1837, and then again two years later, petitions were submitted from the District of Columbia that made clear that the majority of its citizens had no interest in abolition in any form. In December of 1841, Charles Torrey arrived, teamed up with Thomas Smallwood, and opened an active hub on the Underground Railroad in Washington. If the radical abolitionists could not end slavery in Congress, they would attempt to remove it from the city by stealth.

Some ten years after District residents asked Congress to maintain slavery in the nation's capital, the correspondent for Horace Greeley's antislavery *New York Tribune* reported that the shockingly large slave escape on a schooner was the talk of the town that Sabbath. The irony that the escape had occurred soon after a torch-lit parade to herald freedom in France was not lost on the *Tribune* reporter, who noted that a strong contingent of the black community had turned out to view that parade. Samuel Edmonson, Daniel Bell, and Paul Jennings were said to have been among them, and there is no reason to doubt that. But those events did not inspire these men to plot the escape. The escape plan was already well laid and the *Pearl* was waiting for her passengers at the dock. "Whether France will sustain a Republic," the correspondent continued, "and whether these colored fugitives will escape their pursuers, appear to be equally problematical."

It did not take long before a posse was assembled and learned that the slaves had left the city in a schooner. Some sources claim that the posse was tipped off by a free man of color named Judson Diggs, a hack driver who had reputedly transported a fugitive's belongings to the wharf and, to his annoyance, was told that he would be sent his fare of twenty-five cents after his passenger had reached freedom.

A second motive plays prominently in the 1930 novelized account of the event. John Paynter claimed that Diggs, "short, stout and stubborn"—much like his mule, Caesar—had proposed marriage to Emily Edmonson. When she rejected his offer, an angry and vengeful Diggs, who was always willing to do the bidding of the white community for a fee, pointed the posse toward the river. There are a number of problems with this scenario, beginning with the fact that Diggs, freed in 1844 at the age of forty-five, was more than thirty years older than Emily and lived with a wife and three children. There was always profit to be made in giving information to a posse seeking valuable runaway slaves, regardless of whether Diggs had been bilked out of a fare or rejected by a very young woman.

That Sunday Diggs reportedly drove by John and Elizabeth Brent's home in his cart, and a worried John Brent asked him if he had any news about the *Pearl*. A nervous Diggs replied that the fugitives had better not lose any time because a large group of men had "gone tearin' down" to the wharf. Church records of Mt. Zion in Georgetown reveal that Brent was still both a preacher and a class leader at the Mt. Zion Methodist Church in Georgetown and his class met in Washington's Ward 1 every Sunday. That class included four people with the surname of Diggs, though Judson was not one of them. But Diggs may well have occasionally joined the Sunday class. If he did indeed point the posse to the river, he betrayed the very people who had accepted him into their home.

There are a few other accounts of how the authorities may have found that the escape was by river. Ezra L. Stevens, the correspondent for the *Cleveland Daily True Democrat* and an activist increasingly involved in the Underground Railroad, reported that a slave owned by a city constable was questioned on Sunday "forenoon" and flogged until he confessed that he had considered joining the escape but had changed his mind at the last minute. Stevens reported that he then revealed that the fugitives were headed down the river where they were to be transferred to a larger vessel and then taken to the "gulph." The largely inaccurate and improbable report indicates either that the man had little real knowledge of the escape plan or was being deliberately misleading. But his information would have sent the posse in the right direction. According to Stevens, he also told his interrogators that Drayton was to be paid four dollars for each person he transported.

There is another report of a man's being questioned about the escape, although it may well be the same man described by Stevens. William Still, a black abolitionist in Philadelphia deeply involved in the Underground Railroad, recorded the story of every runaway who came through his station. In 1854, an escapee from Washington named Anthony Blow told Still that he had been apprehended by the authorities at the time of the *Pearl* escape and questioned in a "Georgia Pen," as slave pens were still called from the days when slaves were sold to till the fields of Georgia. Later, some called them "Texas pens." Blow told Still that he had been hired out by his owner to work on an anchor weighing about ten thousand pounds. The only place in Washington where such anchors were constructed was in the blacksmith's shop at the Navy Yard where Daniel Bell also worked. Blow may well have known Bell and might have known of the plan to escape from Washington.

At the Seventh Street wharf authorities learned that a small baycraft named the *Pearl* had unloaded a cargo of wood and then mysteriously disappeared without a word. If the fugitives were onboard that vessel, they would be well on their way downriver heading to the Chesapeake Bay. The wealthy Dodge family of Georgetown, who were missing three slaves belonging to Francis Dodge Jr., offered up their steamboat, the *Salem*, to pursue the fugitives. In his March letter to Gerrit Smith, Chaplin was very likely writing about Dodge when he said that three of the people waiting for the vessel from Philadelphia had run away from a wealthy Georgetowner while he was in the process of selling them to a slave trader.

Major Hampton C. Williams, a justice of the peace who had been chosen to lead the posse, later reported that he had walked to Georgetown, likely with a few other men from Washington City, to join others in Georgetown waiting to take off in the *Salem*. The armed and angry posse clambered aboard the steamboat and, powered by a potent engine under the command of Captain Samuel Baker, set out downriver to look for the *Pearl*.

When the posse on the *Salem* realized that the brisk wind and the schooner's substantial head start had put it at a significant advantage, their hopes for catching the fugitives dimmed. But after Captain Baker signaled to the passing *Columbia* passenger steamboat that they wished to talk to its captain, their prospects looked better. The captain of the *Columbia* told them that he had passed a vessel fitting the description of the *Pearl* just above the point in the river where the Potomac takes a sharp turn near the Nanjemoy Reach in Charles County, Maryland. When the posse realized that the distance between them and the *Pearl* was less than they thought, Baker pushed the *Salem*'s engine to the fullest and sped off, hoping to overtake the schooner.

But by the time the *Salem* reached the mouth of the river near the Chesapeake Bay in the dark of the very early hours of Monday morning, they had seen no sign of their prey, and it looked like the *Pearl* had successfully made its way up into the bay before the heavy winds had kicked in. The *Salem* was stymied. The steamboat was only insured to operate on the river, and they would have to abandon the chase. But just as Captain Baker was preparing to head back up to Georgetown, a sharp eye spotted a large dark shadow in the marshes on the edge of the cove. It looked to be a small schooner.

The jarring sound of a steamboat blowing off its steam woke the sleeping passengers and the three crew members of the *Pearl*, and immediately they knew they had been found. Mary and Emily's four brothers joined a hurriedly formed committee of fugitives in Drayton's cabin. Samuel and a few others argued that they should resist capture with whatever means they could find. But Samuel's three older brothers sided with those who opposed fighting, and Emily and Mary quickly added their plea that the group surrender to avoid bloodshed. Drayton counseled caution, too. He knew that the posse would be fully armed and that any attempt to resist would be futile.

The *Salem* aligned itself directly alongside the *Pearl* while members of the posse jumped onto the schooner's deck. The now fully awake crew and passengers listened to the crash of heavy footsteps above, followed by the sound of men's voices. One called out for a lantern so he could read the name painted on the vessel. When it was confirmed that they had just boarded the *Pearl*, the men gave three cheers. One of them immediately lifted the hatch and looked down to see the faces of a number of the fugitives. "Niggers, by God," he called out.

The posse knew from the visit to the Seventh Street wharf that they were looking for Daniel Drayton, and they immediately called out his name. When he did not readily appear, Thomas Orme, the twenty-nine-year-old captain of the Georgetown police watch, set out to find him. Orme entered Drayton's cabin, saw the captain "groping around," and quickly trained his carbine on him. Drayton readily acknowledged that he was their prisoner and began to dress slowly—much to Orme's annoyance.

The Thomas Orme who kept Drayton carefully trained in his gun's sights bore a family name with deep roots in Maryland. In 1774 Archibald Orme, a Georgetown innkeeper, gathered with other property owners from the area in a tavern at a crossroads now called Rockville, Maryland, to discuss the rising political tensions between Great Britain and her colonies. Orme was chosen as clerk to record and then read out loud the agreed-upon resolutions. The gathering of old-line families, most of whom were slave owners, stood hushed together alongside Sandy Spring Quakers and German-born farmers, the former of whom—along with all of Maryland's Quakers—would formally renounce slaveholding three years later, and the latter of whom had little use for it. After first commending Boston for the suffering they had incurred in their common cause, Orme told the county residents who had gathered that they had resolved that "the most effectual means for the securing of American freedom will be to break off all commerce with Great Britain and the West Indies."

Twenty-six years and a revolution later, another Thomas Orme played a role in the volatile election between John Adams and Thomas Jefferson in 1800. Residents of Georgetown in the newly created District of Columbia were still entitled to vote as Marylanders, and Orme rode the circuit in support of Federalist Adams. In an interesting and counterintuitive twist of early political mudslinging, Federalists who were supporting John Adams alleged that Thomas Jefferson would free the slaves if he were elected. The Federalists handily won every seat in the legislature except, to the chagrin of that Thomas Orme, the district of Georgetown.

Orme may well have had a connection to the Edmonsons. One of the Edmonson siblings, Eliza, was married to a free man of color named Dennis Orme, who was very possibly related to the white Thomas Orme who was training his gun on Captain Drayton onboard the captured *Pearl*.

As Thomas Orme hurried Drayton along, other members of the posse secured Edward Sayres and Chester English. The three white men were brought on deck in preparation of their being transferred to the steamboat. Drayton was right; the posse was "armed to the teeth with guns, pistols, bowie-knives, etc., and well provided with brandy and other liquors." The fugitives would never have stood a chance against them. According to Orme's later testimony, the sole weapon on board the *Pearl* was a double-barrel gun.

One of the Edmonson brothers, to show the posse that they would be taken peacefully, led a number of the fugitives up on deck to surrender. When he reached the deck, he loudly shouted, "Do yourselves no harm, we are all here." The significance of his words, borrowed from the apostle Paul—who had also spoken them to reassure his captors—was lost on the tense men who had captured the *Pearl*.* As more of the fugitives stepped up onto the still-darkened deck, a jittery man struck a blow to the side of Samuel's head, but it glanced off him and landed with full force on John's back. When the posse appeared to be on the verge of launching into a full-scale attack, the physically restrained captains protested that the fugitives were unarmed and would not resist. The men argued among themselves, but calmer heads prevailed, and the tense moment passed.

The two captains and the young mate were retained on the *Salem* while the fugitives were kept aboard the *Pearl*. A second Georgetown constable, twenty-five-year-old William Craig, later said that he was left alone with the three men before they were separated from one another for questioning. He reported that both Sayres and English broke down crying but that Drayton remained composed and quiet. Drayton admitted that he and Sayres knew exactly what they were involved in but adamantly maintained that English had known nothing of the plan in advance.

Interrogation began in earnest, and Drayton was questioned the most intensely. Posse leader Williams, interviewed shortly after his return to Washington by a correspondent from the *Daily Union* newspaper, reported that Drayton admitted that he was guilty of receiving and concealing the slaves and that Northern abolitionists had helped plan the escape. But he refused to give up their names. According to the

---

* Drayton's account of the capture makes only one reference to the fugitives' actions in which he confirmed that they had considered resistance. Paynter's account makes few references to Drayton and focuses on the actions of the fugitives. This incident is detailed in Paynter's 1916 article. However, his later 1930 account included the same incident but attributed the apostle Paul quote to Ephraim. It is unclear why he switched brothers.

newspaper report, Drayton explained that if he named names, his family would lose all financial support.

Thomas Orme later said that Drayton claimed to be "only a mite, or one of the smaller fry" in the affair and that he had just been hired to take the fugitives to the top of the bay. Drayton told him that he had done it for money. He added that he had once been a religious man but that he had "backslidden." The captain later admitted to having shared his life's story with the men, but claimed that Orme had given a confused and incorrect recounting of their conversation.

Another member of the posse, John Dewdney, said that Drayton had told them he had no sympathy for the slaves and was doing it only for the money. He added that when someone told Drayton that there was a steamboat waiting to capture them on the other side of the Chesapeake and Delaware Canal, Drayton replied that they would have failed because he wasn't going that way.

At one point, Williams and Orme left Drayton alone with a few of the more inebriated and angry members of the posse. One raised the possibility of an immediate lynching. Posse member Andrew Hoover, who owned two of the captured fugitives (and whose name appeared on the 1828 monster petition to gradually end slavery in the District of Columbia), began to interrogate Drayton in a "very insolent tone," and the prisoner refused to answer any more questions.

Another captor flashed a dagger and proclaimed that if he were in Hoover's place, he'd surely put the blade right through Drayton. Orme returned to the room and put a stop to their threatening behavior, telling the belligerent men that it was "unmanly to treat a prisoner in that way." Inebriated members of the posse were not the only ones to suggest that kind of summary justice. A report in the *New York Tribune* said that when a senior member of President Polk's administration, who hailed from New York, was asked what laws should apply to the slave stealers, he replied, "The first volume of Lynch."

William Craig told Drayton that he had "committed the highest crime, next to murder, known in their laws" and that trouble was already building in the city over the affair. Fearing an attack—or worse, a lynching—by an angry mob when they returned to Washington, Drayton suggested that it might be better if one of the constables just took him up on deck and shot him then and there. Drayton told his captors that he felt much like the Methodist minister who declared that he was not afraid to die, but still ran from an attacking bull. The chagrined minister later explained that while he did not fear death, "he did not like to be torn in pieces by a mad bull." Craig assured Drayton that he and the other two men would be protected.

With the fugitives secured belowdecks, the *Pearl* was taken in tow by the steamboat. As the sun came up, the *Salem* moved north a short distance to the Piney Point Lighthouse, located across from St. George Island, where the first Maryland settlers had landed in 1634. At Piney Point they left the *Pearl* under the watchful eyes of a few of the posse while the others took the steamboat up the Coan River in search of a good supply of wood to power it back to Washington. By noon on Monday, the *Salem* was steaming north pulling the *Pearl* behind it with a guard posted near the female slaves to ensure that none of them attempted suicide by jumping from the schooner.

In Washington that Monday, an auction at the home of the ambassador from France, Alphonse Pageot, managed to distract residents eagerly awaiting news on the fugitives. He had been recalled to France after the recent revolution but, because he wasn't expecting a warm welcome there, he chose to sell most of his household goods and resettle in England. William Chaplin tartly remarked in the *Albany Patriot* that Pageot was "so much attached to the Bourbons, that he cannot sanction the new order of things in France." Up for auction were rosewood armchairs à la Pompadour, velvet sofas, Turkish and Belgian carpets, a table of bois d'Afrique, a sixteen-light chandelier, a yellow embroidered satin divan, a complete set of silver, and two carriages with a handsome pair of bay horses.

This was only a temporary distraction at best. Washington's residents, both white and black, were far more interested in learning the fate of the little schooner and the shockingly large number of highly valuable slaves who were running away from what most white people considered an exceedingly gentle form of slavery.

By Monday evening, Captain Baker had towed the *Pearl* to Fort Washington, which sat high on a bluff in Prince George's County, some thirty miles south of Washington, D.C. They stopped for the night and would complete the short journey into Washington the next morning. All that night, Drayton and Sayres, tied together arm-in-arm with one arm free, were carefully watched over by a changing team of two armed guards. Drayton reported that the captured black men were tied with both their arms bound behind their backs.

On Tuesday morning, residents learned that the fugitives had been captured, and "much excitement" was generated in the city. First reports that had seven fugitives dead after intense resistance were soon disavowed. The magnetic telegraph saw to it that the news reached newspapers in cities other than Washington, including Baltimore, where the *Baltimore Sun* had reported earlier in the day that it looked like the escape "has been entirely successful."

An excited crowd gathered around the bulletin board outside the office of the *Baltimore Sun* to wait for more breaking news. The Baltimore correspondent for the *Washington Daily Union* reported that some in the crowd rejoiced at the *Pearl*'s capture, but a few, most likely some of the city's free black population, seemed disappointed. He added that it was "a bold stroke, and there can be no doubt but that many white persons were cognizant of and assisted the adventurers." Later, a correspondent of the *Baltimore Sun* described the abolitionists behind the escape as "a horde of idle, unprincipled, soulless fanatics, who have seduced [the fugitives] from the comfort and privileges of the old homestead."

Around 7:00 A.M. on Tuesday, Captain Baker ordered the engines fired, and the steamboat continued the journey upriver to return to Washington. As the steamer passed the Alexandria wharf, a festive crowd was waiting to see it pass. To gratify them, Drayton, Sayres, and English, along with a number of the fugitives, were brought up on deck and displayed to the cheering crowd. Drayton believed the real reason the posse had stopped Monday night was to give them an opportunity to show off their prisoners in the best of circumstances and to the greatest number of people.

Below the crammed deck of the *Pearl*, the fugitives were fed from the store of food onboard. One posse member later reported that many of the slaves were eating and happily singing on the journey back to the city. In his book *My Bondage and My Freedom*, written eight years after the *Pearl* was captured, Frederick Douglass wrote about how the singing of slaves was so wrongly interpreted. He explained that "the songs of the slave represent the sorrows, rather than the joys, of his heart." To make his point, he quoted one of the young women among the despondent slaves in the hold of the vessel. "As Emily Edmunson [*sic*] tells us," Douglass continued, "when the slaves on board of the *Pearl* were overtaken, arrested, and carried to prison—their hopes for freedom blasted—they found . . . a melancholy relief in singing."

Friends and loved ones of the fugitives, including a disheartened Paul and Amelia Edmonson, were devastated to learn of the capture of the *Pearl*. All of the Edmonsons, the Bells, and relatives of other fugitives immediately began working to see what they could do to help their loved ones. William Chaplin couldn't help on this occasion because he had quickly disappeared from Washington, as had his byline in the *Albany Patriot*, leaving an uninspired and unnamed correspondent to fill in for him. But Jacob Bigelow, a forty-eight-year-old Massachusetts lawyer involved in the Underground Railroad, was in Washington, and so was newspaper correspondent Ezra Stevens. They would help where they could.

Paul Jennings and Daniel Bell may have gone into hiding along with any others who could be implicated in the escape plan. It is also possible that they had already left Washington to make their way to Frenchtown, Maryland, to meet the runaways. All of Washington's black community tensed. Thirteen years earlier, a white mob had burned their homes and schools in retaliation for far less. They waited to find out what would happen to them and their property this time.

When the *Salem* reached the jurisdictional waters of Washington on Tuesday, Major Williams summoned the three white men to a proceeding before him to determine whether they had committed a crime for which they could be detained. Williams, a justice of the peace as well as the leader of the posse, took testimony, though it is not known who testified or whether the captured men were permitted to speak on their own behalf. Williams committed Daniel Drayton and Edward Sayres to jail for further examination. Apparently, the two captains had convinced their captors that Chester English was innocent, and he was not charged. The fugitives did not need an official proceeding. They would be committed as runaways to the city jail, and, after identification, most of their owners would choose to sell them to eagerly waiting slave traders.

After they docked in Washington, Williams led the men off the *Pearl*, still tied together two by two, with the women and children unfettered, much like the slave traders' coffles that regularly marched south. The posse members, unarmed because Williams was confident that his group of volunteers could keep order, were strung out alongside the procession to keep order. As the captured fugitives, the two captains, and their confused shipmate began to walk north, an excited crowd steadily grew alongside the procession. Gangs of street rowdies added to the increasing tension, and the crowds jeered and cursed the loudest when the three white men who had aided the fugitives came into view.

Emily and Mary walked tightly together with their arms around each other's waists. One observer shouted out from the crowd to ask them if they were ashamed of themselves for causing all this trouble. Emily replied that she was not ashamed and would do the same again. The questioner turned to a neighbor and asked, "Hasn't she got good spunk?"

Members of Washington's black community were watching, too. A journalist reported that "the colored population are in anguish. They know that the runaways will be separated from friends and kindred and scattered over the land to see each other's faces no more." He reported that many of the black observers were in tears, and one mother cried out for her son as he passed, asking if she would ever see him again. John Brent, Mary and Emily's brother-in-law, was in the crowd. When he saw the Edmonson sisters marching behind the coffle of men, he fainted.

The slave owners who had fugitives onboard the *Pearl* were generally content to let Major Williams take his charges to jail and let the law deal with the scoundrels who had stolen their property. But slave trader Joseph Gannon, even though he had no known connection to any of the fugitives, was not so disciplined. As the procession neared his slave pen, a block north of William Williams's slave pen behind the Smithsonian, an angry Gannon waited for the men who had attempted to sail the slaves to freedom. When the line of prisoners reached him, the aggrieved slave trader lunged into the coffle with a knife and nearly took off Drayton's ear. Emily later said that the assault left him bleeding.

Gannon and his partner, B. O. Shekell, who, surprisingly, had signed the 1828 monster petition in support of the gradual end of slavery in the city, placed advertisements for their business in Washington's newspapers. One said:

☞   NEGROES WANTED   ☜

WE WANT TO PURCHASE
A LOT OF NEGROES, IN FAMILIES.
For such the highest cash price will be paid.
Apply at the Farmers' Hotel,
corner of D and 8th Streets, Washington city, D.C.
Negroes taken to board by the day, at 25 cnets [*sic*] per day.

SHEKELL & GANNON

The Farmer's Hotel was located just a block north of Pennsylvania Avenue in the heart of Washington's commercial district. Gannon and his partner kept their office in the hotel, but took purchased slaves to their pen on the south side of the Mall, where Gannon owned land and where he and his family likely lived. Like most slave traders who owned pens, they also offered boarding facilities for slaves belonging to owners who were visiting or traveling through Washington, as well as for slaves freshly purchased by traders with no pens of their own.

In the early days of the new capital, as the domestic slave trade was beginning to thrive, traders relied on taverns, hotels, and even local jails to house slaves. In 1815, Dr. Jesse Torrey of Philadelphia traveled to Washington to observe the state of slavery in the capital. He learned that an enslaved woman detained in the attic of Miller's Tavern at Thirteenth and F Streets, NW, one of the city's better neighborhoods, had attempted suicide by leaping out of the third-story window to the pavement below. Torrey went to the tavern and found her recovering from two broken arms and other injuries. She told him she had become so distraught when she and her children—since sent south without her—had been separated from her husband that she wanted to die. George Miller, the tavern keeper, made it publicly known that he was only trying to keep slaves out of the more oppressive conditions in the D.C. jail, but he would desist in trying to be so helpful in the future. As the traffic in slaves continued to increase, slave traders established their own private slave jails.

While Torrey was in Washington, he witnessed a slave coffle being brought into the city from an outlying Maryland region. As he was leaving his boardinghouse near today's Supreme Court, a young boy came through the door yelling that the Georgia traders were passing by with a drove of slaves. Torrey hurried outside to see a covered wagon followed by "a procession of men, women and children, resembling that of a funeral." He reported that some were bound together by ropes and some by chains. Torrey asked the man who was leading the coffle where he was taking the slaves.

"To Georgia," the man replied.

"Have you not . . . enough such people in that country yet?" Torrey asked.

"Not quite enough," the trader replied.

It is unknown how many slave pens operated in the city. The City Directory discreetly carried no listing for such businesses, and it only took a secure space and a guard to create a pen in a basement or small building in an alley anywhere in the city. But the more well-known slave traders—Williams and Shekell & Gannon—kept their pens located just south of the Mall. In an article reprinted in the *Albany Patriot,* an antislavery activist who was a "long resident of Washington" (likely William Chaplin or Jacob Bigelow) described the city's pens as, "next to the copy of the Declaration of Independence also preserved here, the greatest curiosity to be seen at the Federal City." The writer suggested that interested visitors should find a "proper person for a chaperone and go over to the 'island,' " as that part of the city was known because it was cut off by the Washington Canal on the Mall. If the traders were making up gangs to head south, he explained, a visitor "will see the heavy shutters thrown back, and he will perceive that the substantial iron bars which secure the prison house are lined with dark, sweat-begrimed faces, panting for air." If a gang had just left, a visitor would instead find "the premises as silent and gloomy as the despair and agony which weigh to the earth the spirits they are used to cage."

It is rare to find a firsthand account of what life was like inside those pens for the men, women, and children who were consigned in them, but one such account describes the pen of William Williams in Washington, D.C. In 1841 Solomon Northup, a free black man from New York, was lured to Washington with the promise of a job as a violinist in the circus, drugged, and sold to slave trader James H. Birch, who lodged him in the Williams slave pen. He was taken to New Orleans and sold. After twelve years of slavery in the South, Northup was freed with the help of the governor of New York, and then wrote an account of his kidnapping and enslavement. He described the Williams pen as

> two stories high, fronting on one of the public streets of Washington. Its outside presented only the appearance of a quiet private residence. A stranger looking at it, would never have dreamed of its execrable uses. Strange as it may seem, within plain sight of this same house, looking down from its commanding height upon it, was the Capitol. . . . A slave pen within the very shadow of the Capitol!

Until he was led out of the pen for the journey south, Northup was kept with the other slaves in the yard that extended to the rear of the property thirty feet and was rimmed by a ten- or twelve-foot-tall wall. He said:

> [t]he top of the wall supported one end of a roof, which ascended inwards, forming a kind of open shed. Underneath the roof there was a crazy loft all round, where slaves, if so disposed, might sleep at night, or in inclement weather seek shelter from the storm. It was like a farmer's barnyard in most respects, save it was so constructed that the outside world could never see the human cattle that were herded there.

Slave auctions were not common in the city but they certainly happened. It was against the law for slaves from outside of the District of Columbia to be brought into the city for the purpose of selling them (a similar law prevented slaves being brought into Maryland for sale there), but no such constraints operated against the District's own residents. What auctions took place, accordingly, were for slaves owned by city residents who, for a variety of reasons, were put up for auction. Most auctions were held pursuant to a forced sale caused by the legal resolution of a debt or an estate sale caused by their owner's death. Slave traders attended those auctions, and many of those slaves ended up in the slave pens awaiting transportation south.

As members of the posse disentangled Drayton from Gannon's attack, they assured the slave trader that the captured captain was in the hands of the law and would be dealt with accordingly. "Damn the law!" Gannon retorted. He offered to give up three of his own slaves for the right to have just one solid knife thrust at Drayton.

The procession of fugitives continued walking northeast toward the jail at Fourth and G Streets, two blocks north of city hall. Unlike their journey three days ago, they now crossed the Mall in the morning light as captives. As they reached Pennsylvania Avenue near the United States Hotel, an immense mob began coming toward them. Drayton could hear loud voices—directed at the captains—shouting "Lynch them!" Attorney Jacob Bigelow, who also functioned as a correspondent for the *Boston Whig,* reported that the growing crowd was increasingly excited and poised to rush the captains. He heard cries from the crowd, directed at Drayton, shouting out "Shoot him! Knock his damned brains out! Shoot the hell-hound! Hang the damned villain!" Any hope of reaching the jail without trouble vanished. In desperation, the posse threw the two captains into a hack to extricate them from the mob and drive them quickly to the safety of the prison.

In the excitement of removing the captains from the mob scene near Pennsylvania Avenue, Chester English was left behind. The bewildered mate made his way back to the wharf, where he revealed his predicament. Someone put him in a hack and sent him to the jail, where he was charged with the other two men and held for trial. Drayton later noted wryly that if English had had the sense to just get out of the city, he would never have been imprisoned.

The fugitives completed their walk to the three-story jail, known locally as the Blue Jug for its garish hue, which was "anything but attractive." The jail was surrounded by a high wall and, for further security, the windows on the third floor were covered both by iron bars and "shutters built of heavy board slats." An early account of the jail reported that the "only pleasant thing about it was the singing of the prisoners which could be heard on the side streets, especially on Sunday." In addition to the run-of-the-mill criminals, runaway slaves were detained in the basement cells until their owners could come and make an oath of ownership. If a black person claimed to be free but had no papers to prove it, he or she would remain in the jail until evidence of such freedom was produced and a fee paid for board and lodging. Black skin was a presumption of slavery. If papers weren't produced and no owner came forward to claim the alleged runaway, the marshal of the District of Columbia was authorized to sell the slave for a term of years to pay the jail fees. It was also not uncommon for slaves who were suing for their freedom in the District of Columbia courts to be jailed in the Blue Jug during the course of their litigation.

The jail's first floor housed the administrative offices and the kitchen. A middle staircase led to the second floor. At the top of the stairs there was a locked iron grating. Two rows of cells with tightly shuttered windows were set back from the passageway. The women's cells lined the wall along the front of the jail on that same floor; and the third floor was reserved for debtors.

The four Edmonson brothers were placed in the damp crowded basement cells with the other men, while Mary and Emily were incarcerated above them with the other women, likely in cells usually reserved for white women. As a cold rain moved into the city to make their quarters even more uncomfortable, the sisters managed to send the one blanket they were given down to their brothers, who had nothing to ward off the harsher chill in the basement.

Drayton and Sayres were each allotted two thin blankets to make a bed on the stone floor, a bucket for night waste, and a can for water, which

Drayton used as a pillow. Initially, they were lodged in the same cell on the second floor, but they were soon separated and placed in cells on opposite sides of the staircase, effectively blocking all communication.

More questioning of the captains soon took place, this time by John Goddard, the captain of the auxiliary guard, who began with Sayres. When he turned his attention to Drayton, the captain refused to answer his questions on the grounds that Sayres had already given him a full account. Of course Sayres knew very little about the people who were behind the escape plan. Only Drayton knew the name of his Washington and Philadelphia contacts, and the revelation of their names would endanger more than just those two men. It would be enormously damaging for the entire abolitionist movement to be associated with a criminal event; no one knew whether Drayton would be able to remain silent.

The escape on the *Pearl* was never meant to be a local affair. It was designed—if only because of its size—as a provocative political protest against slavery in the District of Columbia. At least that part of the plan succeeded. The news of the *Pearl*'s capture was being broadcast along the telegraph wires to out-of-town newspapers, and the political debate surrounding the morality of slavery in the nation's capital would soon erupt in Congress.

Nor had Judson Diggs's suspected role in betraying the runaways on the *Pearl* been forgotten. John Paynter wrote that a group of young black men found Diggs near the "bank of a small stream, at a point midway [of] the square bounded by L and M Streets, Connecticut Avenue and Eighteenth, which in those days was a tributary of the old Rock Creek and flowed eastward through the city."* Diggs struggled as he was pulled from his cart and then forcibly rolled down the bank into the water, where he was pelted with stones from the banks. Paynter added that he had spoken with older members of the black community, who reported that Judson Diggs was "despised and avoided" for the rest of his life.

---

* Connecticut Avenue was unpaved at that time and remained so for many years. That tributary, known as "Slash Run," runs beneath today's paved Connecticut Avenue.

FOUR

Waves in Congress

On April 18, the Tuesday that the *Pearl* arrived back in Washington, fifty-three-year-old Rep. Joshua Giddings, from Ohio, who would soon interject himself personally in the events surrounding the *Pearl* affair, rose on the floor of the House of Representatives to introduce a resolution, a courtesy usually granted without a vote. But after the recent death of John Quincy Adams, Giddings had become the most vexing antislavery voice in Congress, so his request was greeted with shouts of "Object!" Just knowing that the resolution was coming from Giddings, the large and rather unkempt ten-year veteran congressman, on the very day that the slave fugitives had been returned to the city, was enough to propel several apoplectic Southern congressmen to their feet. Giddings had already been accused of involvement with the Underground Railroad by one of his Southern colleagues. Three years earlier, Rep. Edward Black, from Georgia, accused him of working directly with Charles Torrey in organizing slave escapes from Washington, but Black was never able to produce any credible evidence showing that Giddings was involved.

Rep. Richard Meade, of Virginia, allowed that he would agree to its being read if it had nothing to do with slavery, but other voices shouted out, "Oh! Let it be read." The Speaker of the House halted all proceedings until the congressmen took their seats and came to order. Giddings then read out loud: "Whereas more than eighty men, women, and children are said to be now confined in the prison . . . without being charged with [a] crime," Congress should appoint a select committee to investigate these circumstances. In particular, Giddings wanted the committee to examine why a prison that had been erected and was sustained by federal funds—generated from free as well as slave states—was being used to hold slaves. He added that these fugitives were doing no more than attempting "to enjoy that liberty for which our fathers encountered toil, suffering, and death itself."

Southern congressmen were enraged, and Isaac Holmes, of South Carolina, immediately rose to respond. He said that if the Giddings resolution was considered, he would move to amend it by adding an inquiry to ask "whether the scoundrels who caused the slaves to be there ought not to be hung." The resolution was rejected, but the debate had only just begun.

Giddings was a curious radical. He was first elected to Congress in 1838 and developed into one of the most tireless of the small handful of antislavery representatives. But Giddings also managed to infuriate radical abolitionists like William Lloyd Garrison and Wendell Phillips by restricting his legislative and public attacks on slavery to its manifestation in the District of Columbia and the territories. Giddings publicly acknowledged that the Constitution protected the right of states to legislate slavery, and he conceded that Congress could not interfere with those rights.

But there were abolitionists who believed that the Constitution did not support slavery. In 1845 noted legal theorist and fervent abolitionist Lysander Spooner published *The Unconstitutionality of Slavery*, a treatise that was touted in William Chaplin's *Albany Patriot* and other abolitionist papers. However, Spooner's theories were not held in much regard by William Lloyd Garrison, who condemned the Constitution, one of the most sacrosanct of the founding documents, as passionately as he condemned slavery. He made his contempt clear when he publicly burned a copy of it to protest slavery.

Giddings was a Whig, a party formed in the 1830s largely in opposition to Andrew Jackson's Democratic Party. It favored government support for improvements in roads, canals, railroads, and infrastructure that were much needed in the still underdeveloped parts of the country. Whigs crossed the North/South divide, and the same party that claimed Giddings also embraced Senator John C. Calhoun, of South Carolina, the leading voice in defense of slavery, as well as Henry Clay, of Kentucky, a slave owner considered a moderate on the subject. Clay had crafted the Missouri Compromise of 1820, neatly dividing the land acquired by the Louisiana Purchase, which extended as far north as the Canadian border, into free and slave segments. Abraham Lincoln, also a Whig, avidly shared Giddings's support for Henry Clay.

Antislavery Whigs like Giddings were called "Conscience Whigs." Their counterparts in the Democratic Party were called "Barnburners," after the farmer who once said he would burn down his own barn, if he had to, to rid it of rats. In the colorful lexicon of the day, Northern Democrats who sided with their Southern counterparts on the slavery issue were called "doughfaces" for being so easy to manipulate, and the most radical of the proslavery politicians and theorists were called "fire-eaters." As the growing intensity of the name-calling indicates, the North-South alliances in both parties were cracking over the expansion of slavery into the territories.

The growing sectarian tension was further pushed to crisis by Democratic congressman David Wilmot, of Pennsylvania. In 1846 Wilmot crafted an amendment to a funding bill for the Mexican War that would outlaw slavery in any newly acquired land that was sure to be acquired at the end of hostilities. The Wilmot Proviso would dog Congress for years, eventually passing the House of Representatives, but always blocked in the Senate, and remained a burr under the saddle of slavery expansionists. It was a stark reminder to the slave power that they were a few votes shy of a containment policy whereby the number of slave states would remain static while the number of free states would grow—and so would their voting clout. The slave power was increasingly worried by the fact that many Northerners who cared little about whether slavery existed in the South cared very much about protecting jobs and wages in the new territories that would one day become new states. Senator Calhoun argued that slaveholders had the constitutional right to take their slave property into all new territory. The conflict over the extension of slavery continued to stoke the fire of secession and would later explode in "Bleeding Kansas."

Giddings lived at Mrs. Sprigg's boardinghouse in Duff Green Row across from the Capitol on first street. Dubbed "Abolition House" by antislavery activists, Mrs. Sprigg's attracted congressmen of varying degrees of radicalism. Her house was also host to Joshua Leavitt and Theodore Weld, leading abolitionist theoreticians who had provided research for John Quincy Adams in his attack on the gag rule.

In 1846 a newly elected lanky congressman from Illinois booked rooms in Mrs. Sprigg's boardinghouse. He was an antislavery man, but no one would have called Abraham Lincoln an abolitionist. He supported a gradual end to slavery rather than an immediate one, and would continue to do so after he was elected president. But he was appalled by the sight of slave pens in the nation's capital. In a later speech attacking slavery, Lincoln described a slave pen—very likely the Williams pen—as

a peculiar species of slave trade in the District of
Columbia, in connection with which in full view from
the windows of the capitol, a sort of negro-livery stable,
where droves of negroes were collected, temporarily
kept, and finally taken to Southern markets, precisely

like droves of horses, had been openly maintained for
fifty years.

Even if Joshua Giddings also fell short of the radical abolitionists'
ideal, no one doubted his personal hatred for the "peculiar" institution.
Not long after he arrived in Washington in 1839, Giddings came face-
to-face with a slave coffle of about sixty-five men, women, and children
being driven along a city street. The sight of that coffle sparked Giddings to dedicate himself to campaign for the end of slavery in the capital and if he did not aid Charles Torrey and others involved in the
Underground Railroad, as he was charged in the U.S. Congress, he
certainly wished them well.

A few months before the *Pearl* incident, Giddings became directly
involved in a dispute with a slave trader. On the evening of January 14,
1848, Giddings and a few companions from Mrs. Sprigg's returned
from an after-dinner stroll to learn that in their absence three men with
drawn pistols had seized Henry Wilson, an enslaved servant who had
been hired out to work for Mrs. Sprigg, and taken him to Williams's
slave pen. Wilson had been making installment payments to his owner
to purchase his freedom, and he and his wife, a free woman who also
worked at the boardinghouse, were expecting him to become a free
man shortly. Instead, he was carried off in handcuffs to a slave pen.

After learning what had happened, the Ohio congressman quickly
enlisted two of his colleagues from Pennsylvania to accompany him to
the slave pen. Entering the front yard, they encountered a man who led
them around a chained guard dog and then down a dark passage to a
more comfortable room.

Giddings and his companions were told they were too late; Wilson
had already been removed from the Williams pen, sent to Alexandria
for shipment, and was now on his way to New Orleans. When a furious
Giddings returned to Congress, he offered a resolution calling for an
inquiry into laws that enabled a slave to be abducted in that manner,
but a majority of congressmen voted to block it. Yet it came closer to

success than any previous attack on slavery in the District of Columbia. William Chaplin, writing in the *Albany Patriot*, said "[t]here never has been, I suspect, so close a vote on any question that comes so directly home to the apprehensions and fears of slaveholders." Chaplin blamed the Northern "jacks" whose votes prevented the resolution from passing. There were three from New York, three from Pennsylvania, three from Maine, four from Ohio, and three from Illinois—"all bastard Democrats." But there were also a few Northern Whigs who voted against it.

Giddings then learned that Henry Wilson had not been sold south. He turned for help to Duff Green, the strident proslavery activist who owned the building that Mrs. Sprigg rented, and he agreed to intercede on behalf of Wilson. The woman who owned Wilson consented to free him if she received the remainder of his purchase price and was reimbursed for the expenses she incurred with the slave trader, a sum of $195. Giddings quickly raised the money by appealing for donations from the Whig members of Congress, and Wilson was freed.

Giddings became a trusted friend to Washington's black community. Ezra Stevens, the correspondent for the *Cleveland Daily True Democrat*, reported that a few weeks after the Wilson affair he was in Giddings's room when two free men of color arrived separately to ask Giddings to help save their loved ones from being sold south. Giddings knew the antislavery men in the city and thus knew where to send the two men for help—a journey that most likely led to Chaplin, Bigelow, and other members of the Washington cell. Giddings may not have been actively involved in planning the escape on the *Pearl*, but he may have unwittingly increased the number of passengers awaiting a vessel from Philadelphia.

On Tuesday evening, after Captain Goddard had secured the jail with a reinforced guard, the angry crowd regrouped on Seventh Street in front of the abolitionist newspaper the *National Era*. The newspaper's office, with a printing press in a building attached at the rear, faced the still unfinished eastern façade of the Patent Office on Seventh Street, between F and G Streets, and was readily identified by the twelve-inch-tall gold letters that spelled out *National Era* across the front.

Gamaliel Bailey, the paper's editor, had arrived in Washington in December 1846, along with his wife, their six children, and the editor's aging parents. He was a charming and well-dressed man—slim and neat, with dark wavy hair swept back from a high forehead and a full curly beard below a clean-shaven, thin upper lip. The Baileys soon established an amiable relationship with their next-door neighbor William Seaton, the mayor of the city and coeditor of the *National Intelligencer*. They also established a weekly salon in their E Street home across from the General Post Office, where attractive young women, powerful politicians, and antislavery visitors from out of town gathered for lively conversation and parlor games of blind man's bluff. Sixteen months after the newspaper began printing in Washington, Bailey and his gracious, Virginia-born wife had settled in surprisingly well, with little overt hostility—at least until the *Pearl* took off carrying a large number of the city's slaves.

The belligerent crowd attempted an assault on the premises of the *National Era*, which, they charged, had either participated in the *Pearl* escape plan or, by its very presence, encouraged the kind of grand theft that Washington had just experienced. The crowd was further riled that, while the captured ship captains would surely be made to pay the price for their crimes, men like Bailey would likely go unpunished.

Before Captain Goddard arrived with a small contingent of the auxiliary guard, a number of bricks had crashed through the newspaper's windows, followed by an attack on the front door. According to the *Baltimore Sun*, as Goddard and a number of men placed themselves in front of the building, the crowd was told "that no man should enter the door unless he first killed those who were bound to protect it." Giddings later reported that a number of respectable people who were observing the mob that night warned him that hostile forces were looking to do him harm and were asking where he lived. Some had suggested that he be lynched. Giddings's friends advised him to arm himself for protection.

Fortunately, Goddard and his guards were able to hold back the crowd, whose anger the weather had already begun to put a damper on. As so often happens in Washington, April delivered a cold northern blast that evening, one that dropped snow in Baltimore and freezing rain in Washington. As the crowd broke apart and headed for home, angry voices vowed that they would return the next evening. The three-day Washington Riot of 1848 had just begun.

The Blue Jug

On Wednesday morning, cold rain continued to fall as Mary, Emily, and their brothers woke—if they had been able to sleep at all—in the uncomfortably crowded jail. Residents throughout the city read the details of the escape in the local newspapers and an announcement stating that the owners of captured slaves should go to the jail that same morning to identify their slaves. The *Alexandria Gazette* reported the details of the affair and suggested that it would be wise to bar all of Washington's free blacks from entering Alexandria. Newspapers in slave territory weren't the only publications to disapprove of the escape. The *New York Herald* claimed it had "never heard of a more outrageous or audacious violation of constitutional and personal rights than that perpetrated by a gang of Abolitionists and kidnappers in Washington, D.C.," adding that "the abolitionists may be safely charged with the transaction."

The *National Daily Intelligencer* had had little to say about the escape on Monday or Tuesday, when newspapers as disparate as the *Baltimore Sun* and the *New York Tribune* reported it. William Seaton, the editor of the *National Daily Intelligencer,* had more at stake over the affair than other newspaper editors: he was the city's mayor. But during this crisis, Seaton was ill and confined to his substantial home on E Street, just west of Seventh Street, next door to the Baileys. On

Wednesday, with the fugitives and captains safely locked up, the *Intelligencer* finally reported:

CAPTURE OF RUNAWAY SLAVES

DURING THE WHOLE OF SUNDAY, Monday, and yesterday, very great excitement has prevailed in the city and Georgetown, arising out of the fact that many citizens of the two places had been deprived of their servants, and its being ascertained that they had been taken on board a suspicious vessel which had brought wood to this city . . .

The story described the schooner's capture in Cornfield Harbor and noted that "all on board the *Pearl* were thus made prisoner without bloodshed, although it was evident that the slaves would have resisted if there had been any chance of escape." The account added a congratulatory nod to the posse, noting that it was "to the credit of the pursuing party that they succeeded in capturing the fugitives and their aiders and abettors without bloodshed, and in so expeditious and effectual a manner." The main point was clear: all is well and calm in Washington.

Wednesday's democratic newspaper, the *Daily Union*, was clearly pleased that the affair was nearly over, adding that "[t]oo much credit cannot be given to Captain Baker [of the *Salem*] and the volunteers for their energy and discretion in the whole proceeding." Discretion and order were the themes upon which the rival newspapers could agree. The *Georgetown Advocate* included a report on the attempted escape from the *Baltimore Clipper*, which stated that "the negroes were deluded through the influence of those who, with all their profession of philanthropy, are the very worst enemies of the blacks." It was the standard line in defense of the benevolent slave owner, who was the real friend to the slave.

The Washington reporter for the *Baltimore Sun* had more to say along those lines. He described the runaways as "men, women, and children born and raised in our very best families; colored it is true, but between whom and their owners feelings of regard, almost amounting to affection, have ever existed." He neglected to say that the vast majority of these "very best families" would never have let their near affectionate feelings interfere with the business of buying and selling human property.

Nor did public officials hesitate to break up such felicitous relationships. That same day, the *Daily Union* carried a routine notice announcing the sale of a slave in front of the jail. "General Hunter," as the U.S. marshal was known, stated that he would be exposing "to public sale . . . one negro boy named Andrew, aged about 24 years, seized and levied upon as property" to satisfy a judgment against his owner. Andrew was owned by Francis Lowndes, a member of one of the area's oldest families and another signatory of the 1828 petition to end slavery in the District, who had fallen into financial difficulties. At the time that he was preparing to sell young Andrew to pay his owner's debts, Hunter's own slave, Daphne Paine, was locked up in the same jail with the other fugitives captured on the *Pearl*.*

That Wednesday morning, the jail keeper at the Blue Jug looked to a full schedule. Major Williams and Captain Goddard, both justices of the peace, would be examining Drayton, Sayres, and English in preparation for filing formal charges, and the owners would be arriving before noon to identify their property. A number of those owners allegedly paid Francis Dodge Jr., the owner of the *Salem*, $50 per slave for returning the fugitives to their custody. That amount cannot be accurate. According to historian Josephine Pacheco, court records reveal that

---

* The position of U.S. marshal for the District of Columbia was a presidential appointment of much prestige that would some years later be held by the renowned abolitionist and former slave, Frederick Douglass. Hunter clearly had links to some of the more powerful families in the area. He owned an estate named "Arlington" in northern Virginia, and his brother was named Bushrod Washington Hunter.

Susannah Armistead paid Dodge $282 for retrieving eleven members of the Bell family, which is far less than $50 per fugitive. Dodge then paid each posse member $27 in compensation for the role they played in salvaging the runaway cargo. But some members of the posse were dissatisfied and later sued him for more money. Pacheco reports that the court records are unclear as to whether the men received any additional compensation but that, in his defense to their suit, Dodge belittled them, claiming that the men had joined the posse "in anticipation [of] an agreeable excursion."

The growing crowd in and around the jail included newspaper reporters, lookers-on drawn to the excitement, and slave traders who knew there would be business for them. A correspondent for the *Baltimore Sun* reported that "[t]he jail and surrounding premises are crowded—'the slaves' form a theme for every tongue."

To add to the tension, Congressman Giddings arrived at the jail in the morning, accompanied by Edwin Hamlin, the coeditor of the *Cleveland Daily True Democrat*, a newspaper that advocated civil, religious, and political equal rights for all without distinction of "Color, Birth or Property." Hamlin, a former Conscience Whig congressman from Ohio, had once boarded with Giddings at "Abolition House" but then returned to Ohio to practice law and publish his newspaper. He usually relied on his coeditor, Ezra Stevens, to report on Washington events, but since he was in Washington when the *Pearl* was captured, and he might prove useful as a lawyer, he accompanied Giddings and then prepared the report for his newspaper.

At the jail, Giddings and Hamlin entered a ground-floor room where they found themselves in the midst of slave owners arriving to claim their slaves. Giddings told the jailer that they wished to speak with the men charged with carrying away the slaves, and shrewdly asked the jailer to accompany them to the cells to avoid any hint of conspiracy. However much Giddings was distrusted by proslavery forces in Washington, he was still a member of Congress, and his position would be respected. It is quite possible that William Chaplin had asked the congressman to go to the jail in the event the *Pearl* was captured, to tell the captains that they and their families would be looked after—a reassurance they hoped would guarantee Drayton's silence in regard to the people who had hired him and planned the escape. Drayton had it within his power to implicate Charles Cleveland, in Philadelphia; William Chaplin; and possibly Paul Jennings and others. Some years later, Giddings wrote that he had been informed of the escape by "a friend" shortly after the *Pearl* sailed on Saturday night.

Ignoring loud protests from some of the men in the entrance area, the jailer unlocked the gated door to lead Giddings and Hamlin to the upstairs cells. He relocked it from the other side and passed the key to a guard, instructing him to let no one up. At the top of the stairs, he opened another gated door and then took them to the captains' cells. The two men immediately assured the captains that "they had friends who would see that they had a legal trial." While Giddings was present, one of the three jailed men, undoubtedly English, burst into tears. Hamlin assured the men that he would be with them at the hearing before a magistrate later that same day.

Giddings needed to return to Congress. But as they were preparing to leave, a fierce-looking man found the key to the gate at the bottom of the stairs, opened it, and came up as far as the locked gate at the top. While he was admonishing the jailer for letting Giddings and Hamlin in to talk with the prisoners, he was joined by many from the crowd below who clamored for the two men to leave the jail. The jailer, still with Giddings and Hamlin but becoming increasingly alarmed by the threatening men on the staircase, advised the two visitors to remain behind in the secured passage, because he could not guarantee their safety. But Giddings and Hamlin insisted on leaving. The mob somehow parted and the two men made their way out, shaken but unharmed. The next day, the *Baltimore Sun*'s correspondent felt compelled to say a few words in defense of the men who had menaced Giddings and Hamlin. He reported that the mob were really "the respectable, quiet, unoffending injured citizens, who were present, pursuant to a public call, for the purpose of identifying their property." Giddings later claimed in a statement introduced into the record of the House that he had been informed by a gentleman that the slave dealer Hope Slatter had proposed to "lay violent hands upon me" when he exited the jail.

As Giddings was leaving, he looked inside a room where he saw the fugitives being examined by slave dealers. He might have recognized one of them. Giddings later recalled that he had met Richard Edmonson, who had worked as a coachman for Robert Walker, the secretary of the treasury. He described Richard as a man whose "phrenological development bespoke a high order of talent."

Edwin Hamlin needed to prepare for the hearing he would be attending later, and set out to find a member of the Washington bar to join him in representing Drayton, Sayres, and English. He returned with David A. Hall, the Vermont-born Washington lawyer who had successfully represented John Bush five years earlier when he was caught working with Charles Torrey and Thomas Smallwood in an Underground Railroad escape. Hall and Hamlin squeezed their way through the hostile crowd that continued to surround the jail and made their way back up the stairs to the cells. In the meantime, Philip Barton Key, the United States attorney for the District of Columbia (and the son of Francis Scott Key, who had held the same position ten years earlier), had arrived at the jail for the same hearing. When Barton Key, as the prosecutor was known, saw Hall, he urged him to leave immediately, because his life was in danger from the angry crowd. Hall replied that "things had come to a pretty pass" if a lawyer was not permitted to talk with his client. Drayton heard Key reply, "Poor Devils! I pity them—they are to be scape-goats for others!"

The owners were admitted to the temporary courtroom equipped with two tables, one reserved for justices of the peace Major Williams and Captain Goddard, and the other for Key, the prosecutor. Hamlin and Hall were left to stand with the prisoners. After the general facts of the escape were laid out, the men—including the unfortunate English—were bound over for trial on charges of stealing slaves and illegally transporting them out of the city.

An exorbitant bail was set for each man at $76,000, a sum that represented $1,000 for each fugitive on the *Pearl*. Given that figure, the initial number of seventy-seven slaves—thirty-eight men, twenty-six women, and thirteen children—had been reduced by one possibly over some confusion related to Daphne Paine, the woman who was owned by U.S. Marshal Alexander Hunter. In Major Williams's first accounting of the slaves onboard the *Pearl*, Paine had been listed with a child. Thereafter, Paine was listed as the sole fugitive owned by Hunter, and there was no further mention of a child.

Next, the slaves were brought into the room to be identified by their owners. Hamlin reported that a number of women had infant children in their arms, and they were asked the name of each child. One enslaved woman was asked how she could leave such a good home and replied, "I wanted *liberty*, wouldn't you, sir?" When the name of another fugitive was called out, she responded, "Here I am, sir; once *free*, again a *slave*." A seventeen-year-old "fine-looking, intelligent mulatto girl," who may have been Mary Edmonson, turned to address Drayton, Sayres, and English. While shaking each of their hands, she said, "God bless you sirs, you did all you could; it is not your fault that we are not free." Everyone understood that the vast majority of the fugitives would never see their owners again. Once they had identified their property, those few who decided not to sell their captured slaves took them home, while the rest began making arrangements with the waiting slave traders.

Pleas for funds to buy some of the fugitives went out to Northern contacts of the Underground Railroad activists in Washington, but it would take too long to assemble to do much good—and it had never been easy to raise money for their operation. They would have to look to more local sources for money.

Elizabeth Edmonson's husband, John Brent, arrived at the jail with his wife and several of the girls' other married sisters, to attempt to stave off the sale of the six siblings. While Brent spoke with Francis Valdenar, who represented their owner, the Edmonson sisters attempted unsuccessfully to enter the jail to see their family. Through the bars of their cell, Mary and Emily could only look down and see their sisters crying.

The Brents had taken on the role of surrogate parents to the younger siblings who were hired out to work in the city, and according to John Paynter, John Brent was trusted to collect the wages of the Edmonson siblings for delivery to Valdenar. It was an arrangement that gave him some control over the Edmonsons' employment. Now he hoped he could rely on that business relationship to buy enough time to raise money for the six jailed brothers and sisters. But all he could extract out of Valdenar was a promise to give him one more day to assemble a good-faith deposit. That might buy enough time for Chaplin and other supporters to collect the rest of the purchase money.

While Mary and Emily's sisters set out to spread the appeal to friends in their communities and churches, Brent likely turned to Dr. Harvey Lindsly, a member of the Board of Health for Ward 3, who had had a hand in securing Brent's own freedom. Lindsly had purchased Brent from the estate of Richard Wallach, the scion of a prominent Washington family whose two sons would become, respectively, a leading newspaper publisher and a mayor. Lindsly's purchase had prevented slave traders from buying Brent for the Southern market, but he would not free him until he had been reimbursed for the amount he had paid for him. That sum was paid, and John Brent's freedom was registered at city hall on April 21, 1840. Lindsly may have done the same thing for Mary and Emily's twenty-two-year-old sister Eveline. In 1846 he sold Eveline to her husband, William Ingraham, and then recorded her freedom.

Daniel Bell faced the same quandary with his family. He turned again to Thomas Blagden, who had helped the family in the past, and he agreed to advance enough money for Daniel Bell to purchase his wife, Mary, and the couple's youngest son, Thomas. Blagden, too, fully expected to be reimbursed.

Members of the black community were also contributing to the Bell fund. Blagden signed a receipt acknowledging that Alexander Taverns, a free man of color, had paid the astonishingly high sum of seventy-five dollars, clearly noting that the money he received was for "for Daniel Bell." It is possible that Taverns was connected to the Bell family by marriage. Two years earlier, he had invited contributors to a select tea party at the Assembly Rooms located on Louisiana Avenue, where sacred music was played, to raise money to purchase the freedom of his sister, E. H. Bell, of Alexandria.

Jacob Bigelow, the sometime correspondent for the *Boston Whig* and increasingly busy Underground Railroad operative, was desperately looking for other sources of local money, but there were so many fugitives that it was simply impossible to raise enough money to save them all from the slave traders. Bigelow had an interestingly high profile in Washington's small business community. He served on the founding board of the Washington Gas Light Company and actively pursued a patent law practice in the city. He would continue his work aiding runaways for many years to come.

Unfortunately, no ledger lists the fate of all the *Pearl* fugitives. But details of what happened to the following fugitives have been pieced together from reports in the *Albany Patriot* and other antislavery newspapers as well as other sources.

A young woman named Grace Russell was sold by her owner, a Dr. Triplett, and sent to a Richmond slave pen that functioned as a clearinghouse for slave traders dealing with the Southern slave market. Fortunately, with the aid of family and antislavery activists in the North, her mother, a free woman living in New York City, was able to redeem her before she was sold again. William Chaplin described Russell as a "beautiful girl of eighteen, of slender constitution, intelligent and capable," and reported in the *Albany Patriot* that her uncle had put up $300 and a "generous friend in New York" contributed the balance of $650 or $700. Dr. Triplett still owned at least one other member of Grace's immediate family, her equally beautiful sister Emily.

Hannibal Rosier was owned by the wealthy Ariana Lyles who owned extensive rural land just north of Georgetown, part of which she sold after the Civil War to the highly successful black hotel owner James Wormley, the brother of schoolteacher Mary Wormley. Rosier was not sold south because his name, along with Lyles, appears in the emancipation records when slavery was ended in the District of Columbia in 1862.

Former fugitive Alfred Pope also avoided the slave traders. The light-skinned, twenty-four-year-old Pope returned to the elegant mansion on Georgetown Heights that he had run away from. His owner, John Carter, a South Carolinian who had served four terms in the House of Representatives and remained in the area after marrying into the well-known Marbury family, had purchased Pope from his brother in the South. The young Alfred Pope was said to bear such a strong resemblance to Carter's brother that it caused great discomfort to his wife, and Pope needed to be removed from the household.

Fifteen-year-old Mary Ellen Stewart, who had gone into hiding after eluding the slave traders sent by Dolley Madison to hover near the public water pump in Lafayette Square, was sold to a slave trader and taken to Baltimore. Madison had finally succeeded in what she had set out to do. But efforts were being made to free Stewart.

Two fugitives identified only as William and Kitty remained in the area. They were owned by Elizabeth Dick and her niece Margaret Laird, who lived together in an impressive brick mansion on the southwest corner of today's N and Thirtieth Streets in Georgetown built in the late 1790s by Margaret Laird's father, a leading tobacco merchant.*

---

* At that time the streets were named, respectively, Gay Street and Washington Street. Those names were later changed when Georgetown was incorporated into the city of Washington.

Her sister, Barbara, was married to Judge James Dunlop, who sat on the District of Columbia Circuit Court. While Dunlop did not own any of these slaves (he did own others), his wife stood to inherit all or a portion of them along with the impressive house, which was later purchased by Robert Todd Lincoln, President Lincoln's eldest son. When Elizabeth Dick died eleven years later, she bequeathed freedom to her "servants William and Kitty."

Jane Brent, owned by Dr. Nathaniel Causin, was not sold south. But eighteen months later, she was on the run again. Justice of the Peace J. H. Goddard placed an advertisement in the November 27, 1849, edition of the *National Daily Intelligencer,* which indicates that Brent was in police custody when she escaped. He was offering a fifty-dollar reward for anyone who caught Jane Brent, who "was of the number who ran off some time back and were captured aboard the *Pearl.*" Daniel Drayton may have been describing Brent when he later wrote that one of the fugitives from the *Pearl* returned to the jail to bring him a Bible. He didn't give her name, but he did add that she made another attempt to escape to freedom and on that second try she succeeded.

There is some information about the fugitives who were sold south. John Calvert, who was owned by the Baptist minister Obadiah Brown, had the distinction of being the only runaway from the *Pearl* who is recorded in the ledger of runaway slaves that was just recently discovered. The D.C. Department of Corrections Runaway Slave Book, with entries beginning in June of 1848, was lost until 1991, when an employee of the D.C. Corrections Department found it propping up another book in a display case in the now defunct district prison in Lorton, Virginia. That ledger states that Calvert was committed to the jail in April 1848 by order of Justice of the Peace Hampton C. Williams; he was released to slave trader William Williams on June 22, 1848. No other runaway slave ledger for the D.C. jail has been found. There is no explanation as to why Calvert was incarcerated for two months before he was sold to Williams, but it might have been because his owner was out of town.

Obadiah Brown, one of Washington's most influential clerics, may have been descended from Obadiah Brown, of Rhode Island, a prosperous Baptist slave trader whose descendants split over the slavery issue and contributed to the founding of Brown University. In 1821 the Washington Obadiah Brown served as the founding president of the board of trustees for a new multidenominational college that is today's George Washington University. He was instrumental in moving his church to Tenth Street, where black members worshipped in the balcony. In 1839 black members of the church broke away to form their own congregation on the previous church property at Nineteenth and I Streets, though it was said that Reverand Brown "did not believe in distinction on account of color." Among the founders of the first black Baptist church in the city of Washington were William Bush and his wife, both of whom were already, or were about to become, operatives on the Underground Railroad.* A few years later, Brown would sell the Baptist church on Tenth Street to a man named Ford, who opened a theater on the site.

According to Harriet Beecher Stowe's *Key to Uncle Tom's Cabin*, the nonfiction account of slavery written when her famous novel was attacked as unfairly exaggerating the horrors of slavery, one of the captured women who was sold was the wife of an enslaved man named Thomas Ducket, who did not himself board the *Pearl*. It is unknown whether they were owned by the same master or by different men, a common circumstance in the Upper South, where slaveholdings were small and slaves needed to look outside their own quarters for a spouse. Stowe states that when Ducket's owner learned he had known about the escape in advance, he brought him into Washington from Maryland to sell him to a slave trader. Stowe reported that the Washington antislavery committee filed a lawsuit in an attempt to block the sale on the grounds that it was against the law for an owner to bring a slave from Maryland into the District for that purpose. Few slave traders ran into

---

* William Bush and his wife joined a group that broke away to form the Second Negro Baptist Church.

this problem because they or their agents purchased slaves in Maryland, and only brought them into the capital to temporarily house them before their journey south.

According to Stowe, Ducket withdrew the lawsuit because he decided that he wished to be sold south to be closer to his wife and children. This scenario seems improbable. The chance of a slave ending up near a loved one, after being sold at different times, was a near impossibility. Their wishes almost always counted for nothing among the traders or buyers. But there is no doubt that Ducket knew the names of some of the most active antislavery men in Washington. He managed to send a number of letters addressed to Jacob Bigelow, the attorney involved in the city's Underground Railroad cell. In the only surviving letter, dated February 18, 1850, he pleaded for help. "Mr. Begelow," Ducket wrote, "I hop yu will not for[get] me. . . . You no et was not my falt that I am hear. . . . I hop you will nam me to Mr. Geden Mr. Chaplen Mr. Baly to healp me out of it."

But that same letter casts doubt on Stowe's claim that his wife was sold south. Two years after the *Pearl* escape, Ducket was not asking the men in Washington to help find and then free his wife and children; he was asking only that they help free him and let him know how his family was doing. Ducket's letter strongly indicates that he was involved in Washington's Underground Railroad cell, but it does not as clearly establish that he was connected to the *Pearl* escape.

More is known about many of the other owners than about the fugitives they owned because details of their lives are more readily available through city directories, wills, and newspapers. Owner Ignatius Mudd was at various times, the deputy collector of customs in Washington and the commissioner of public buildings, and John M. Young was a coach maker. William Upperman and Samuel Brereton were grocers near the Center Market. Emily Corcoran was the widow of Thomas Corcoran and the sister-in-law of the wealthy banker William W. Corcoran, who had recently made his fortune by selling bonds in Europe to support the Mexican War.

A number of slave owners professed shock that any of their slaves could have taken part in the escape. A letter signed "A Volunteer" sent to the *Albany Patriot* reported that he knew a master and mistress who had aboard the *Pearl* a mother and her daughter. When the owners went to the jail, they told the mother they would forgive her and take them both back, but first they wanted to know why she had run away from their pleasant home. The woman answered that she did it because she wanted freedom for herself and her daughter. For reasons unknown, according to that same report, only the daughter was sold south.

Some of the owners were wealthy, some were small-business men, and some depended almost exclusively on the income generated by their slaves. Had the escape succeeded, at least two of the slave owners, Susannah Armistead and Rebecca Culver, would have lost the only income-producing assets they possessed. Both women would have stood a good chance of slipping into poverty.

On the same day the bulk of the fugitives were sold, Congressman John Palfrey of Massachusetts rose to the House floor and presented a resolution concerning Giddings's disturbing visit to the jail. Palfrey, who stayed in room 56 at Coleman's Hotel, may have arrived at Congress less groomed than usual. The *New York Tribune* reported that one of the men—"a very faithful man"—who had slipped away to board the *Pearl* worked as a bootblack at Coleman's. Palfrey asked that a committee be established to determine whether or not Giddings had been threatened in violation of a member of Congress's right to privilege.

To make sure that everyone had all the facts at hand, Giddings joined the debate and refused to back down in face of the slave power's outrage. He maintained that the slaves of the District of Columbia "possessed before the universal world and before God himself the right to free themselves by any means God has put into their power." But Giddings did acknowledge that Drayton and Sayres had broken the law by their actions and had to be punished. But, he said, these were legal, not moral, crimes. Giddings had reached a new level of irritation to the Southern members of Congress who, for so long, had succeeded in preventing slavery's being discussed in any length. Now, conflict over slavery had erupted in the streets of Washington and seeped right into the House of Representatives with Giddings in the middle of it all. A few weeks later, he would be violently pushed on the floor of the House by a Southern congressman said to be intoxicated and carrying a "bowie-knife."

As Wednesday evening approached, authorities braced for trouble. Word had quickly spread through the city that Joshua Giddings had visited the three prisoners, further incensing those who were planning to reassemble in front of the *National Era* that evening. The Democratic and proslavery *Daily Union* complained that "public indignation had been increased by the mischievous resolution" that Giddings had presented in Congress the day before.

No one was more apprehensive than Gamaliel Bailey, the forty-year-old diminutive editor of the *National Era*, who usually exhibited "an almost boyish brightness of manner and lightness of spirit." He remained in his home at the corner of Eighth and E Streets, right across from the main entrance to the Robert Mills–designed General Post Office, described as "one of the most splendid buildings in the United States," where a center portico of Corinthian columns fronted the Greek Revival structure, which also housed Samuel Morris's telegraph office. Just on the other side of the General Post Office to the north was the equally beautiful and still unfinished Patent Building, which had become the closest thing the city had to a museum before the Smithsonian began to take shape on the south side of the Mall. Models of patent applications were on display and the building was a leading tourist attraction.

Bailey had had a taste of trouble the night before, and he knew that he would continue to be pulled into the unrest swirling around the escape attempt. He had been through this before. Bailey, the son of a dissident itinerant Methodist preacher, was born in the small New Jersey town of Mount Holly. New Jersey was far from a hotbed of abolitionist activity. Although the state passed a law in 1808 that would bring about the gradual abolition of slavery, the U.S. Census for 1850 listed 235 people still enslaved in New Jersey, a number of whom were, inexplicably, under the age of ten. After a stint as an editor for the *Methodist Protestant* in Baltimore, and a course of study in medical school followed by an increasing disinterest in the practice of medicine, Bailey followed his parents to Cincinnati, Ohio. There, he was exposed to some of the most gifted and committed of the emerging young antislavery activists, including Theodore Weld, who would later stay at Mrs. Sprigg's boardinghouse in Washington. Weld combined dramatic oratorical cadences with the new call for the immediate end of slavery. He organized the legendary 1834 debates at Lane Seminary, where slavery was passionately discussed for eighteen days, which ended with declarations supporting immediate abolitionism and condemning colonization. When the Lane Seminary administrators ordered the students to cease their abolitionist activities, the radicals decamped for the more hospitable two-year-old Oberlin College.

In 1835 the newly committed Bailey helped found the Cincinnati Anti-Slavery Society and became one of its officers. About that same time, James Birney, an abolitionist and former slave owner from Alabama, moved his antislavery newspaper, the *Philanthropist*, to Cincinnati, and Bailey became an assistant editor of the paper. But the paper was not well received. Even though Ohio was a free state, Cincinnati had a history of Southern sympathy that grew out of its proximity to the slave state of Kentucky and its long-standing business dealings with the South. The city was known for its repressive black code. Just as proslavery forces were becoming louder in their attacks against abolitionists in other parts of the country, mobs were repeatedly threatening to lynch Birney and destroy his printing press. True to their word, a white mob tore down the press. But instead of lynching either of the white men, they took their rage out on the black community, burning property and physically assaulting its residents before city authorities dispersed the mob.*

---

* The *Philanthropist* wasn't the only antislavery newspaper to be attacked. In November 1837, Elijah Lovejoy, who had already had three presses destroyed, had just received

Bailey raised the money needed to replace the printing press but in 1841, when the Ohio Supreme Court ruled that any slaves brought into the state would automatically become free, antiblack rioters attacked black businesses and homes, and then dumped Bailey's printing press into the Ohio River. He again raised the money to replace the press.

Bailey's unyielding stand in Cincinnati raised his stature in the eyes of the abolitionist movement and made him an ideal candidate to begin an antislavery newspaper in Washington, which was initially being funded by Lewis Tappan, a wealthy New York merchant and abolitionist. Bailey made it clear from the beginning that this newspaper would not condone illegal acts in its stand against slavery, a necessary assurance for any antislavery newspaper operating in slave territory. But he disappointed radical abolitionists when he publicly agreed with Giddings that, while slavery was patently wrong, it was legal under the Constitution and came within the regulatory powers of the states.

In February 1848 Bailey became the sole proprietor of the *National Era*, announcing that "no change, of course, will be made in the character of the paper." The *Era* enjoyed modest success, largely through mail subscriptions, and was particularly popular for its interesting literary content under the direction of Quaker poet John Greenleaf Whittier, in Massachusetts. Whittier, for whom Richard Nixon's California hometown was named by its founding Quakers, recruited Nathaniel Hawthorne and other respected writers to produce serialized stories for the paper, much of which was unrelated to slavery.

But the poetry and stories were accompanied by Bailey's cogent arguments against slavery and vivid descriptions of the slave trade in the nation's capital. Seven months before the attempted escape on the *Pearl*, Bailey reported that "a coffle of slaves, to the number of eighty-

---

delivery of yet another press in a warehouse in Alton, Illinois, on the eastern bank of the Mississippi River. He chose to take delivery fully armed. A mob surrounded the warehouse and stone throwing escalated into shots from firearms. When the mob attempted to set the roof afire, Lovejoy exited the warehouse to try to put out the fire and was shot and killed.

five, was marched from this city, across the Long Bridge over the Potomac, for the South. They consisted of men, women, and children; the men chained together; some of the women carrying children, walking with them; other women and children riding in two wagons which accompanied the train. Some were weeping; many were ragged; nearly all were barefoot; one was playing a fiddle—a not unfrequent accompaniment of such scenes!"

Now, on Wednesday night, as Bailey faced the return of an even larger and angrier mob, his neighbor Mayor William Seaton offered a suggestion from his sickbed. He advised the editor to distribute a handbill throughout the city disclaiming any knowledge of the escape attempt, which would also be published in Seaton's own newspaper, the *National Daily Intelligencer.* Bailey quickly produced a handbill in which he pledged that he would never "take part in any movement that would involve strategy or trickery of any kind."

At dusk, the crowd began to assemble in front of the *National Era* offices and it steadily grew. Newspaper reports of its size varied greatly, ranging from the *Alexandria Gazette*'s estimate of no more than four to five hundred people to the *Boston Whig*'s report of three thousand people. The correspondent for the *Baltimore Sun* was on Seventh Street watching the crowd gather and at 9:30 P.M. sent a telegraphic message of the evening's events from the telegraph office in the Post Office on the next block. He reported that "not less than three thousand persons had assembled in front of the *National Era* office."

No matter which report was more accurate, it was clear that Captain Goddard's auxiliary guard would not be able to disperse this group. With the mayor in his sickbed, Walter Lenox, a thirty-one-year-old lawyer and president of the Board of Aldermen, stepped into the breach. With a number of prominent Washingtonians by his side, the Yale-educated lawyer persuaded the crowd to relocate around the corner to the southern façade of the Patent Building, which was visible from the corner where Gamaliel Bailey and his family lived.

When the crowd had reassembled, the Washington-born Lenox

stepped forward to address the crowd. He pleaded with them not "to accomplish by force what could be effected by law" and pointed out that the city would likely have to pay for any damages incurred. But his pleas were shouted down by some with clubs in their hands with cries of "It's too late! Down with the *Era*! [and] Damn the Expense!" Lenox tried to end the standoff by assuring the crowd that the city would listen to their complaints about the abolitionist newspaper at a meeting at city hall on Friday.

But the crowd didn't budge. They were finished listening to Lenox and called out to hear from a man named E. B. ("Bull") Robinson, a man they knew would be more to their liking. Robinson immediately stepped forward and demanded to know why the city had not asked a grand jury to indict the *National Era* on public nuisance charges and run Gamaliel Bailey out of the city just as they had run William Lloyd Garrison and his newspaper out. The crowd shouted with glee. Then Robinson added, referring to Bailey, that these "moderate scoundrels are the worst kind of scoundrels . . . [and] the press should not be suffered to exist." He proposed that they give Bailey "till tomorrow to decamp . . . and if the law will not protect us, we must take the remedy into our own hands."

"Give it to them, Bull," someone in the crowd yelled out.

Some voices called out for attorney Joseph Bradley, described by the correspondent of the *New York Herald* as one of Washington's "most influential and intelligent citizens," but he did not appear. Then they called for Daniel Radcliffe, another prominent Washington lawyer. The thirty-eight-year-old attorney, who owned a ten-year-old mulatto slave, tried to calm the crowd. He told them that everyone knew he stood with the South but that he really couldn't do anything. Someone in the crowd suggested that they could tear down the *National Era*.

"Under the darkness of the night?" Radcliffe asked.

"No," they replied, laughing, "the moon is shining."

Radcliffe acknowledged that the escape attempt was "mad schemes of deluded people," but urged the crowd to disperse and then reassemble in a day or two to discuss the situation. Voices in the crowd yelled back, "Now! Now! Now!" When Radcliffe realized that the mob could not be stopped, he changed his approach. If the mob could not wait for an organized town meeting to take place on another day, he would bring the meeting to the mob. He proposed they form a committee to call on Dr. Bailey that same night.

The crowd readily accepted his suggestion. After some haggling over committee members, they assembled five "respectable" men from each of Washington's city wards, five from Georgetown, and another five from Tenleytown, which had grown up around Mud's Tavern. With Radcliffe at its lead, the committee set off for Bailey's nearby home to inform him that he had become a public nuisance that must be removed from the city. The rest of the crowd milled around in front of the Patent Office, waiting for the committee to return with a report.

Bailey opened his door and stepped out to meet the committee. Radcliffe informed him that his newspaper was a great threat to the public peace and that he would have until 10:00 A.M. the next day to remove it from the city. "You are demanding from me," Bailey responded calmly, "the surrender of a great constitutional right—a right which I have used, but not abused." He said that he could not agree to remove his own press. Bailey told the committee that he would rather die than abandon the newspaper and become "a party to my own degradation."

Radcliffe conceded that the removal of his printing press surrendered a great constitutional right and that their request was unreasonable. But even so, he told Bailey, it was necessary in order to calm the mob. Another committee member described himself to Bailey "as one of the oldest citizens" of the group and assured him that "it is in all kindness we make this request." That same man told Bailey that the prisoners captured on the *Pearl* were in his hands for a time, but he would not allow his men to harm them.

At that point, Bailey's elderly father appeared at the door with choice words for the committee. Bailey gently chided his father and told him that the committee was composed of gentlemen and that he should not talk to them that way. Finally, the newspaper editor told the committee to go "tell those who sent you hither that my press and my house are undefended—they must do as they see proper. I maintain my rights, and make no resistance."

Radcliffe returned to the Patent Office and told the crowd that Bailey had been respectful and had talked of constitutional rights. The news was greeted with hisses and cries of "Down with the *Era!*" As people ran toward the *National Era* office around the corner on Seventh Street, a number of Bailey's friends, including Congressmen John Palfrey and John Wentworth, dashed into his home. They carried the Bailey children from their beds to Mayor Seaton's house next door, fearing that the crowd might return and attack the house.

The correspondent for the *New York Herald* hurried back to the *National Era* office in time see a stone thrown ("ting-el-ling went the glass") and a brickbat flung at the door while others yelled, "Fight!, Fight!" But then Captain Goddard's increased guard began to "roll back the human tide . . . like the 'Spartans at the pass of Thermopylae.'" Goddard quickly arrested one of the brick throwers as someone urged the crowd to move the assault to the rear door.

At that point, Barton Key, the district attorney, jumped up on a horse trough in front of a nearby grocery store to address the crowd. The prosecutor shouted out to the mob that he was no friend of the abolitionists.* But Key called on the crowd to rely on the law for justice and told them that he did not believe that the instigators of the mob were the least interested in protecting slave property. Bull Robinson, the printer who had earlier addressed the crowd, supported Key's call for legal action against the newspaper. Finally, a man named Honeykont, reported to be a clerk in the Treasury Department, mounted the horse trough

---

* Indeed, he wasn't. The slave schedule of the 1850 U.S. Census shows that Philip Barton Key owned two women, twenty-four and twenty-five years old, and a thirty-year-old man.

and promised to lead an assault against the *National Era* the following morning if they would disperse. As Captain Goddard and his deputies stood between the crowd and the newspaper, the rearguard assault fizzled, and the crowd began to leave. By midnight the streets were clear.

Thursday, April 20

The mob did not materialize the next morning but, remarkably, the usual weekly edition of the *National Era* did. Bailey described the attacks of the night before, calling them an outrage against freedom of the press at the same time that he denied any involvement in the *Pearl* escape. He said that "we cherish an instinctive abhorrence of any movement which would involve us in the necessity of concealment, strategy, or trickery of any kind." He added that the outrage was said to continue.

The potential for more trouble that night was indeed high, and city officials and other notables were increasingly alarmed. Mayor Seaton's *National Daily Intelligencer* printed Bailey's handbill denying all knowledge of the escape plan in that day's paper, and the *Daily Union* called for an end to violence—but made sure to note that it wanted strict enforcement of the law against the kidnappers.

City authorities produced their own handbill by late morning stating that "fearful acts of lawless and irresponsible violence can only aggravate the evil." Signed by Walter Lenox and John Goddard, it asked Washington's citizens to "sustain them in their further efforts to maintain the peace and preserve the honor of the city." There were many reasons the city wanted to maintain the peace. The correspondent of the *New York Express* offered one self-serving explanation, writing that such unrest could be used to agitate for the removal of the seat of government out of the District of Columbia, and talk of such a possibility would depreciate real estate value.

Even leaders of national organizations were becoming increasingly alarmed by the tense and uncertain situation. Elisha Whittlesey, the director of the Washington Monument Society, was worried that their campaign to raise money would be compromised if the city appeared lawless. With the cornerstone for the monument scheduled to be laid on July 4 after a parade featuring Dolley Madison, Whittlesey took his concerns directly to President Polk. This turmoil could ruin their plans.

There was no question where Polk stood on the slavery issue. In 1830, as the House of Representatives was debating a bill that would provide for penitentiary punishment of criminals in the District of Columbia, the future president argued that penitentiary time would not be appropriate for slaves—he maintained that they were far better suited to flogging. He spoke as a slave owner who had entrusted his new plantation in southwestern Tennessee to an overseer. The following year, Polk voted against an ultimately successful bill to increase America's vigilance in enforcing the 1808 ban on the African slave trade. With slavery spreading rapidly across the Lower South, some Southerners were calling for the repeal of the federal ban on the transatlantic trade. Polk would soon purchase land in Mississippi and have his slaves walked there to clear land and construct a new plantation.

Now President Polk was being asked to help prevent a mob from attacking an abolitionist newspaper in the nation's capital, and he knew that his visitors were right. Such disorder in the nation's capital was a disturbing local event that could escalate the debate on slavery at a national level and reflect badly on him. But, as Polk noted sympathetically in his diary, the mob was rightfully provoked by the grand theft of so many valuable slaves.

The president called his cabinet together and instructed them to forbid their department employees from engaging in any violence and to act instead as peacekeepers. Robert Walker, the secretary of the treasury, gathered his clerks together when he returned from the meeting to ask for their help. Even though one of the men who had offered himself up as a leader for an attack on the *National Era* was reported to be a Treasury clerk, the clerks cheered the plea from the stooped and diminutive secretary. Walker, of course, had an unusual personal link to the affair.

His coachman, Richard Edmonson, was incarcerated in the Blue Jug.

Captain Goddard and Walter Lenox, along with a few other officials from the city government, also met directly with the president at the White House to discuss security. Polk decided against calling out the militia, but he ordered the U.S. marshal's office to help suppress further disturbances in front of the *National Era*. Even the *Baltimore Sun* took a conciliatory stand on the attempted attack on the *National Era*. It asked "but what if the proprietor of the *Era* were entirely innocent? What if he had no knowledge of the preparation and progress of the late abortive exodus of slaves from the District?" Apparently, if Bailey had had any prior knowledge of the escape plan, the mob action and destruction of property would have been warranted.

Talk of the attempted escape would not go away on Capitol Hill. On Thursday, Rep. John Palfrey, of Massachusetts, who had helped carry the Bailey children out of their home the night before, pursued the question of whether Joshua Giddings's right of privilege as a U.S. congressman had been violated by the physical threats hurled against him. Proslavery congressmen were put in the awkward position of defending a mob's rampant disregard for law in the attack on Bailey's property, while at the same time demanding that the rights of slave owners be protected to the letter of the law.

White Southerners were adamant that antislavery members of Congress had had a hand in the *Pearl* affair. Rep. Robert Toombs, of Georgia, charged that Giddings was clearly trying to protect himself from prosecution for aiding the illegal escape, and Rep. William T. Haskell, of Tennessee, proposed an investigation to determine if antislavery members of the House had been involved. Haskell cut very close to the truth when he alleged that the abolitionists, unable to convince Congress to pass legislation to end slavery in the District of Columbia, were now undermining slavery by conspiring with slaves to run away from their masters.

Giddings stood to respond to his attackers. He acknowledged that while slaves had a moral right to attempt to escape from slavery, it was against the law to do so in the District of Columbia, and he again reaffirmed that those laws must be obeyed. In answer to Haskell's charge, Giddings denied knowing Drayton and Sayres before visiting them in the D.C. jail.

In the Senate that same day, before a full gallery that included Gamaliel Bailey, Senator John Hale, of New Hampshire, launched a new offensive. With the attack on the *National Era* clearly in mind, he asked leave to introduce a bill, similar to one already in existence in Maryland, which would hold the city of Washington responsible for any damages to property caused by mob attacks. The *Congressional Globe*, the official record of Congress, reported that Hale's proposal produced "a debate of a most exciting and personal character," and because a "subject of such delicacy" needed to be presented in full, it was reported in an appendix, where more attention could be given to it. After the capture of a schooner full of runaway slaves, the subject of slavery was finally off the table and exploding in Congress.

A furious Senator John C. Calhoun, the silver-haired, commanding leader of the slave power and former vice president of the country, rose to speak. "[T]here is but one question that can destroy this Union and our institutions, and that is this very slave question," his impressive voice rang out.

William Chaplin had once listened to Calhoun in awe as the elder statesman raised his concerns over the Mexican War, but he knew they seldom would be on the same side. Now Calhoun condemned any bill that would thwart the "just indignation of our people from wreaking their vengeance" on the perpetrators of the attempted slave escape. He warned the Senate that the country was approaching a crisis. Instead of the bill that Hale was introducing, they needed laws to "prevent these atrocities, these piratical attempts . . . these robberies of seventy-odd of our slaves at a single grasp." Calhoun defended the "great" institution of slavery, "upon which not only [the South's] prosperity, but its very existence depends."

Senator Jefferson Davis suggested that a federal law was clearly needed to punish anyone who would come into the District of Columbia "to steal a portion of that property which is recognized as such by the Constitution of the United States." Both Davis and Calhoun had converted the unruly acts of a lawless mob into an act of just indignation.

But it was left to Senator Henry Foote, of Mississippi, the same man who had spoken so eloquently for freedom in Europe, to propose a punishment that went beyond the law. After accusing Hale of direct involvement in a "covert and insidious" attempt to discourage anyone from holding slaves in the District of Columbia, Foote suggested that there would be ample opportunity for the senator from New Hampshire to shed his own blood for his crusade to end slavery in the District. But should he survive that crusade, Foote welcomed him to come to Mississippi, where he could not go more than ten miles before his body, with a rope around his neck, would "grace one of the tallest trees of the forest." Foote, later known as the "Hangman of Mississippi," assured Hale that he would join in the effort along with the patriotic citizens of his state.

Like Giddings, Hale insisted he had no involvement with the *Pearl* escape but acknowledged that the fugitives would not have been able to organize the escape without some aid. He admitted that he was in league with other antislavery activists, including Joshua Giddings, John Palfrey, and Gamaliel Bailey, but he solidly maintained their purpose was to change the law, not thwart it. While most papers in the South heartily approved of the threats leveled by Foote and the outrage voiced by other Southern politicians in Congress, there was at least one pragmatic dissent. The correspondent of the *Times Picayune* of New Orleans regretted that "Honorable Senators talked of lynching Mr. Hale." He observed that the "denunciations of Messrs. Calhoun, Foote and Davis, of Mississippi, will only serve to rally the abolitionists to a man and to strengthen and confirm that bigoted party."

The *Times Picayune* was right. One abolitionist newspaper remarked that before the escape, "the District was forgotten" and the old agitation of years before, when slavery in the nation's capital was "the battleground," had died away. Now the extensive debate caused by the attempted escape on the *Pearl* had again riveted attention "upon slavery in the ten-mile square." The escape on the *Pearl* had succeeded in that goal.

FIVE

The Fate of the Edmonsons

On Thursday, as authorities prepared for more trouble later that evening, John Brent returned to the Blue Jug to continue negotiating with Francis Valdenar. John Paynter stated that the woman who had hired Mary Edmonson, likely responding to the family's call for help, also arrived at the jail to pledge $1,000 to prevent Mary's being sold south. But there was nothing left to negotiate. Valdenar had already sold all six of the Edmonsons for $4,500 to Joseph Bruin, a slave trader from Alexandria, Virginia. Any further negotiations in regard to the Edmonsons would have to be with him.

The thirty-nine-year-old Bruin prided himself on a Christian bearing and deportment, which he believed put him in a class well above the average slave trader. An abolitionist who bargained with him face-to-face two years later in Alexandria reported that Bruin was all smiles and politeness, and he had manners that would "eclipse even Lord Chesterfield himself."

But Bruin seldom veered from his primary purpose: the buying and selling of slaves at the highest possible profit. When John Brent approached and asked him if he would accept a deposit to hold the

Edmonsons until they could raise the money to free them, Bruin refused, adding that they couldn't possibly match the money he would be able to get in New Orleans, where he hoped to double the money he had just paid. That evening, under cover of darkness, Bruin returned to the Blue Jug and removed the six Edmonsons from the jail. He placed Mary and Emily and their handcuffed brothers in a carriage for the relatively short drive to his slave pen in Alexandria, Virginia. With abolitionists in Congress railing against slavery in the city and the potential for further mob scenes, Bruin wanted them out of Washington quickly.

⊰•◦•⊱

That same evening, a crowd began to gather on Seventh Street for the third straight night. Some observers, including Gamaliel Bailey, estimated that Thursday's crowd was the largest yet. With support from President Polk and the cabinet secretaries, Captain Goddard had substantially reinforced his guard. By nightfall, nearly one hundred enforcement personnel were on the street, a daunting and unprecedented presence in Washington.

With Captain Goddard and an intimidating array of deputies barring the door of the *National Era*, the crowd did little more than mill about for some time before losing steam. By 10:00 P.M. the mob had largely dispersed, and a good number of Goddard's men began drifting away. But the mob had one more angry gasp left. A contingent of some two hundred rowdies took off for Bailey's house and informed him that they planned to throw his press into the canal that ran along the Mall. Bailey asked to address them first, and spoke for ten or fifteen minutes. He later reported that "they became comparatively quiet, and at the close of my remarks Mr. Radcliffe jumped on the steps before me, made a short but earnest appeal to them, moved adjournment, put it to a vote, and the crowd resolved to adjourn with but one dissenting voice. In ten minutes not a man was to be seen about my dwelling. The crowd gradually melted away from the office, and by 12 o'clock everything was quiet."

When calm had returned to Seventh Street, Bailey wrote in his newspaper that "[i]n a certain sense, all's well that ends well" and added a profuse tribute to Captain Goddard for how he handled the disturbance that left the paper's printing press intact. But while calm may have returned to the streets of the city and freedom of the press had been protected, all did not end well for the fugitives who, six of them, Mary and Emily and their brothers, were already beginning a journey that would take them far beyond the world they knew.

The Slave Pen

The carriage taking the Edmonsons to Virginia crossed a bridge spanning the Potomac River, made its way to Alexandria, and stopped at a two-story house in a neighborhood known as the West End. At their destination, the young women were separated from their brothers and placed alone in a damp, dark room. Men and women were kept in separate quarters; small children were allowed to stay with the women.

The abolitionist who would later visit Bruin's slave pen in a failed attempt to purchase Emily Russell, the sister of *Pearl* fugitive Grace Russell, described the West End neighborhood as a "dreary" place, "marked by the frowns of Omnipotence: a fit theater for piratical operations." The area was predominantly used to process meat and other agricultural products for export by ship and railroad. But the neighborhood's export business wasn't limited to agricultural products. It was host to two of the largest exporters of slaves in the Washington area.

One of those merchants was Virginia-born Bruin. As early as 1831, at the age of twenty-two, Bruin was described as a "trader in Negroes." In 1832 he paid $1,500 for a two-acre lot at 1707 Duke Street and opened his slave pen for business. Like most slave traders who owned a pen, Bruin provided boarding facilities.

Bruin had entered into a number of partnerships with other traders, but, as the owner of the slave pen, he always remained the senior partner. Such a partnership was particularly helpful when a coffle was heading south and someone was needed to look after the ongoing business of buying yet more slaves and supervising them at the pen. Some coffles were walked to Wheeling, Virginia, to be shipped down the Ohio and then the Mississippi rivers. Others were walked as far as Natchez, Mississippi, and were either sold there or shipped by steamboat to New Orleans. Coffles still took off for the auction houses of Richmond and the slave pens of Charleston, South Carolina, which was once the leading site for the importation of slaves from Africa.

In August 1843 Bruin was in a partnership with a man named Jones and they placed many advertisements in the *Alexandria Gazette* offering "cash for negroes." One advertisement stated that they were looking for "fifty to seventy-five likely young Negroes of both sexes." But that partnership ended, and in 1845 an advertisement asked all "persons having Negroes to sell" to call at the new establishment of "Bruin and Hill, West End, Alexandria." Henry Hill was Bruin's partner when the Edmonsons arrived at the slave pen.

Bruin made an excellent living. The slave schedule of the 1850 U.S. Census recorded that he owned twenty-eight slaves, thirteen of whom were under the age of sixteen. In 1860 the slave schedule showed that Bruin owned fifteen slaves, of whom five were under the age of fifteen. Of course, these figures represent only those slaves who were on his property when the census was taken. Many more had left in the coffles heading south, and many more would arrive. The U.S. Census for that same year listed Bruin as a "trader in negroes," who reported real estate valued at $10,000 and personal property in the sum of $100,000. Bruin was the equivalent of a multimillionaire today.

The number of enslaved enumerated in a particular area was an important tabulation for the purpose of congressional representation in slave territory. Article 1, Section 2 of the Constitution provided that "those bound to Service for a term of years" would be counted as three-fifths of a person. The word *slave* does not appear anywhere in the Constitution.

At the other end of Duke Street in Alexandria, the partnership of Franklin & Armfield, which had once run the most profitable slave pen in the area, had moved on, but George Kephart, a slave trader who had worked with Bruin in Virginia and also operated in Maryland and Washington, D.C., had purchased the property and continued the slave trade. The District of Columbia's reputation as a major slave-trading site was owed in large part to these Alexandria slave traders. When the portion of Virginia that was part of the District of Columbia was returned to the state in 1846, the volume of the slave trade in the nation's capital sharply decreased.

After a sleepless night, the terrified sisters were relieved to see their brothers at breakfast in the morning in a nearby building where communal meals were served. Bruin actually owned four buildings stretched across the front of one block. The "Negro Jail," where Mary and Emily spent the night, was at the western corner and was the largest of Bruin's four structures. It extended forty-two by thirty-four feet, with a walled outdoor yard in the back. A one-and-a-half-story washhouse about half the size of the larger building was set back from the street and attached to one side of the jail. The building on the opposite corner was Bruin's family residence.

Samuel Edmonson was distraught. He had had a hand in the escape and now blamed himself for putting his siblings, particularly his sisters, into the unimaginably bleak situation they were now facing. Mary and Emily had exchanged two comfortable homes in Washington, near family and friends, for a Virginia slave pen; and their future looked even worse. After breakfast, the girls were put to work emptying night waste and washing clothes for the dozen or so men in the pen.

Bruin was likely anxious to gather together enough slaves to make up a decent shipment and send them south as soon as possible, as the New Orleans slave market was nearing the end of its selling season. Most of the wealthy residents of New Orleans, including that class of slave buyers looking for attractive young women, abandoned the city during the summer season, when tropical diseases broke out. Traders had their investments to protect. Come May, the danger of losing valuable slaves to disease virtually suspended the trade. The quickest way possible to get the Edmonsons to New Orleans was to ship them down the Atlantic Coast.

In Washington on Friday, fifty or so of the *Pearl* fugitives were readied to leave the jail. They had been purchased by Hope Slatter, the Baltimore trader who had been spotted a few days earlier in the angry crowd around the jail and on Seventh Street. After thirteen years of dominating the trade in Baltimore, Slatter was winding down his career, and this purchase may have been one of his last. In all, Slatter had completed sixty shipments, taking a total of 2,533 slaves to the Lower South from the Baltimore wharves. It is not known how many more were walked south in coffles.

Slatter was in the process of selling his slave pen at 244 West Pratt Street to brothers Bernard and Walter Campbell. He may have already begun working with the Campbells when he purchased the fugitives at the D.C. jail because John G. Campbell, who was likely a Campbell brother, was also at the jail. In one of the few jail documents that have survived, Justice of the Peace Hampton Williams signed an order authorizing the jailer at the Blue Jug to deliver Harriet Queen, one of the *Pearl* fugitives, to her owner, William H. Upperman. On that same document, Upperman then directed the jailer to "deliver the above named slave to Mr. J. G. Campbell."

Slatter put iron shackles on the men and the older boys and assembled them in a line; the unfettered women carried young children. They were marched about three blocks through the public streets of Washington to the railroad depot, near the grounds of the U.S. Capitol on New Jersey Avenue. At the depot, Slatter loaded the fugitives into a railroad car for the two-and-a-half-hour journey to Baltimore.

Observers, including several of Washington's antislavery journalists, watched as family and friends surrounded the car to say sorrowful good-byes to loved ones they knew they would likely never see or touch again. John I. Slingerland, from Albany, New York, who was serving his first term in Congress, was also on the scene and witnessed a harrowing picture of misery and grief in the shadow of the U.S. Capitol. In a letter addressed to "Friend [Thurlow] Weed," publisher of the *Albany Evening Journal* and respected political advisor, Congressman Slingerland described the visibly upset people of color struggling to say good-bye to their loved ones who had been captured on the *Pearl*. That letter was later published in a number of newspapers, including Horace Greeley's *New York Tribune,* and it was clearly written with the help of abolitionist journalist Ezra Stevens, because he published virtually the same letter under his own name in the *Cleveland Daily True Democrat*. Jacob Bigelow also may have had a hand in this important letter. When William Lloyd Garrison's *Liberator* printed it, the paper said that it came from the "Washington Correspondent of the *Boston Whig*," a position associated with Bigelow. But as a relatively new member of Congress—one who was not known as a rabble-rouser—Slingerland's signature would have given the letter more credibility with less radical publications.

The letter reported that "wives were there to take leave of their husbands, and husbands of their wives; children of their parents, and parents of their children." Inside the car, four rough-looking guards stood, two at each end, armed with clubs, while Slatter—the "old grey headed villain"—stood in the middle of the car. It said that one man, who claimed to have papers to prove his wife was free "clambered up to one of the windows of the car to see his wife, and, as she was reaching forward her hand to him, the black-hearted slave-dealer ordered him down." When he refused, one of the guards used his club to knock him off the car. One report later said that the Bells were the family referred to "with so much affect by Mr. Slingerland." The freedom of Mary Bell and her youngest son was purchased, but other members of the family were sold south.

Slingerland's letter emphasized, as was so frequently done by sympathetic Northern whites, that many of the women had but a "slight tinge of African blood in their veins—they were finely formed and beautiful." One of the women he described might have been fifteen-year-old Mary Ellen Stewart, the daughter of Dolley Madison's cook, or Grace Russell, who would later be freed from a Richmond auction house.

While they waited to leave Washington, the forty-six-year-old Reverand Henry Slicer, the chaplain of the U.S. Senate, arrived on the scene. The well-known Methodist minister, who preached with a style that was once described as "Southern in every respect" with none of that "go-to-sleep-quick sort of operation," walked up to the railroad car and entered it. As Slingerland and others watched, Slicer offered his hand to Hope Slatter, and the slave trader shook it. The two men then chatted. Slingerland accused Slicer of appearing "to view the heart-rending scene before him with as little concern as we should look upon cattle."

In addition to meeting the spiritual needs of the Senate, Slicer was beginning his second assignment at the Montgomery Street Methodist Church in Georgetown. Part of his responsibility was the oversight of the spiritual needs of Mt. Zion, the black Methodist church in Georgetown that had broken from the Montgomery Street Methodist Church in 1816. When he was in Georgetown in 1836, Slicer sometimes preached three times a week at Mt. Zion. However, when he became the Senate chaplain during that time, his attendance at the black church dropped off precipitously. Ezra Stevens's account of this incident in the *Cleveland Daily True Democrat* stated that many of the slaves in the railroad car were members of the African Methodist Church in the city, likely meaning Asbury, at the corner of

Eleventh and K Streets. Slicer had served that congregation as well between 1838 and 1840. In fact, it had been Henry Slicer who was the presiding elder at the 1836 quarterly conference that approved the founding of Asbury.

In the earlier decades of the nineteenth century, the Methodist Church had enforced its prohibitions against owning slaves for life and against trading in the sale of human beings. Records from the Georgetown church show that the congregation, with some exceptions, had tried to follow those strictures. But times changed. With a growing number of Southerners in the church, many with slaves, the enforcement of those prohibitions slipped substantially—even for its ministers.

In 1831 Richard Whitehead, a slave-owning Methodist minister, was working in a field with his slaves in Southampton County, Virginia, when Nat Turner and his supporters approached. One of Turner's men called out to him as "Dick," reversing the demeaning practice whereby whites called blacks only by their first name. Then they killed him in front of his slaves.

By 1844, the Methodist Church was still trying to prohibit bishops from owning slaves, but it was becoming more and more difficult to enforce. That year the Baltimore Annual Conference, which included the District of Columbia, considered the issue of whether a bishop in Georgia who had become a slave owner by marriage should be removed from his position. The conference voted 110–68 to suspend him while he remained a slaveholder, leading the Southern conference members to intensify discussions about formally separating from the Northern-dominated church. Maryland-born Henry Slicer voted to retain the slaveholding bishop.

Slingerland's letter was published in a number of Northern newspapers, and a shocked and hurt Slicer wrote a letter to the *Daily Union*, Washington's Democratic newspaper, in protest. Slicer protested the "wonton and unprovoked attack" on him. He explained that the moment he saw the railroad car of colored people, he realized they were fugitives from the *Pearl*, and because one of the fugitives had been under his "pastoral care," he immediately made his way into the car. Subtly chiding Slingerland for his reference to the attractive, light-skinned women among the captured fugitives, the minister said that he had sought out a "very dark Methodist brother" and, when he found him, had shook his hand as, he said, he would have done with anyone, black or white, even if slightly known.

Slicer added that this man's former owner was his neighbor, and that he had learned that the former fugitive had been so "mortified at being brought back in the *Pearl* that he refused to remain with his owner in Georgetown; and was, therefore, reluctantly sold." This rueful tale of a forgiving and benevolent owner and a shamed slave follows a well-used template, whereby the prodigal runaway realizes he was better off with his white owner and had lost all dignity by betraying him.

A strong supporter of the American Colonization Society, Slicer advised Slingerland that he would better serve humanity by giving as much money as he had to purchase the freedom of colored people—presumably on the condition that they emigrated to Liberia—instead of attacking an "unoffending minister of the Gospel." For good measure, he added that " 'busybodies in other men's matters' have never been, since the days of St. Peter, an envied class."

Slingerland, or one of the Underground Railroad operatives using his name, published a reply to Slicer's letter that is particularly significant because it names the *Pearl* fugitive whose hand Slicer shook. The letter writer wondered what "Henry" thought when he saw the hand from which he had received "the emblems of Christ's body and blood" reaching out to him. It is doubtful that a sympathetic congressman simply passing the railroad depot would have known the name of one of the captured fugitives from the *Pearl*.

There were only two men named Henry on the *Pearl*. Henry Graham's owner was a grocer living in Washington, D.C. Henry

Smallwood, who had been a faithful member of the Mt. Zion Church in Georgetown since 1830, was undoubtedly the same Henry referred to in the letter. In 1848 Henry Smallwood suddenly disappeared from Mt. Zion's records. The last notation next to his name simply states "sold."

Joseph Bruin soon removed the Edmonsons from the slave pen and marched them to the Alexandria waterfront. The four brothers and the other men being transported were put in irons for the journey, then all were placed aboard a steamboat headed for Baltimore from where they were to be shipped to New Orleans.

When they arrived in what was the South's second-largest city (after New Orleans), they were walked the fifty yards from the busy steamboat landing to Joseph Donovan's slave pen at 11 Camden Street, conveniently located next to the railroad station. The men working on Baltimore's waterfront—whites, free blacks, and hired-out slaves—were used to seeing slaves arrive at the wharf.

Donovan's pen, like Bruin's, was a crude jail used to house slaves temporarily. But the two slave traders were different in demeanor and habit. Joseph Bruin cultivated the appearance and manner of a gentleman, someone of religion and culture, and believed he was a slave trader by profession, not definition. In contrast, Donovan was a coarse and profane man who addressed obscenities to the women in the pen. He forbade Mary, Emily, and the other women in the pen from praying together. In defiance, the sisters rose early in the morning to lead a group of women in secret prayer.

Faith was essential to the Edmonsons. They were not a family that attended church on Sunday and then gave little thought to their religion for the rest of the week. They lived their faith every day and became leaders in the black Methodist community. John and Elizabeth Brent were not the only family members who had helped to establish new churches. Mary and Emily's sister Eveline and her husband,

William Ingraham, are listed as founders of Asbury Methodist Church. Another older married sister, Martha Young, helped raise funds to build the new John Wesley Methodist Church that John Brent and others were forming at the time of the *Pearl* escape.

The same faith that sustained Mary and Emily and their brothers sustained their parents after six more of their children were sold to slave traders. It had helped them fifteen years earlier when Hamilton was sold south. Amelia had always lived with the fear that Francis Valdenar could sell her children at any time. She later said that whenever she saw a strange white man anywhere near their cabin in Maryland, she always hid the children, just in case he was a trader coming to look them over. But she had never expected this—six gone at once, waiting to be shipped to a New Orleans slave market from Baltimore.

By the time Mary, Emily, and their brothers arrived at Donovan's pen, he had shipped more than thirteen hundred slaves from the wharves of Baltimore. Donovan had been in the Camden Street location for just two years though he had been in the business since 1843. In his early days, Donovan operated out of the former pen of Baltimore's most notorious slave trader, Austin Woolfolk, who was the architect of the city's slave trade when the business exploded in the 1820s. Woolfolk and his family worked the Eastern Shore of Maryland, just across the Chesapeake Bay from Baltimore, so extensively that "Woolfolk" became the generic name for a slave trader used by the slaves. Woolfolk, like Donovan and Slatter after him, used slave coffles to walk the slaves from their pens to one of Baltimore's many wharves. Slatter would later use omnibuses to transport them to New Orleans–bound vessels.

Coffles bound for ships docked at Fell's Point, an early shipbuilding center, were led through the streets of Baltimore past a house on Philpot Street, where a young slave named Frederick Bailey once lived. Bailey, who would later take the surname of Douglass and become one of the era's most prominent and influential abolitionists, could hear the rattle of the coffle's chains as it passed. The sound was all the more chilling because several members of the young man's family from the Eastern Shore had been sold to Woolfolk and likely walked that same path. Douglass nearly did himself. When he later returned to the Eastern Shore, his first attempt to escape failed, and he came close to being sold. Instead, Douglass's owner sent him back to Baltimore, where, as a hired-out slave, he worked as a caulker for a shipbuilder. At the age of twenty, with the borrowed papers of a free black sailor tucked in his pocket, Douglass boarded a railroad car with his soon-to-be-wife, Anna, a free woman of color who is said to have suggested the ploy. The couple rode the train to freedom in the North.

Frederick Douglass wasn't the only influential abolitionist who once lived in Baltimore. In 1829, when Douglass was a twelve-year-old slave in the city, a young man named William Lloyd Garrison arrived in Baltimore to work for the *Genius of Universal Emancipation,* owned by Quaker Benjamin Lundy. Garrison was already an antislavery man on his way to becoming an abolitionist firebrand. Woolfolk and the Baltimore slave trade hastened the process.

Lundy's newspaper was initially tolerated in Baltimore, and the paper listed distribution as far south as North Carolina, Kentucky, Arkansas, and South Carolina. Jacob Janney, a member of a well-known Quaker family from Waterford, Virginia, acted as its agent in Washington, D.C. But a slave trader like Woolfolk would tolerate only so much criticism, and he viciously attacked Lundy on a Baltimore street after the editor had turned a sharply critical eye on the slave trader's business. Lundy sued Woolfolk for physical assault and won. But the judge made it perfectly clear where his sympathies lay by awarding Lundy damages in the amount of one dollar.

Garrison followed suit by profiling a ship captain from Newburyport, Massachusetts, his own hometown, who was profiting in the slave trade. When the captain complained to authorities that Garrison was interfering with his business, they decided that they had had enough and successfully filed charges against him for criminal libel. After a short stint in a Baltimore jail, they agreed to free Garrison if he and Lundy would just leave.

Radicalized both by the slave trade he had observed firsthand and by the time he had spent with activists in Baltimore's free black community, Garrison moved to Boston and began publishing the *Liberator*, the abolitionist newspaper that mobilized a spirited new antislavery movement. The *Liberator* called for immediate and complete emancipation. It was the nineteenth-century rendition of the twentieth-century civil rights movement's cry for "Freedom Now."*

In addition to the Edmonsons, Donovan had approximately forty other enslaved people waiting to be shipped to New Orleans, but he could always use more. On April 26, he placed the following advertisement in the *Baltimore Sun*:

☞   NEGROES WANTED   ☜

the subscriber being permanently located and has a strong
and comfortable House and Yard to keep Negroes takes this
method to inform the public that he is always ready to pay
them the very highest cash prices for their NEGROES, and
will also receive and keep Negroes at the usual rates. Joseph S.
Donovan, Office in Camden street adjoining Railroad Depot.

---

* Both men considered moving to Washington to establish an antislavery newspaper in the nation's capital but, in the end, neither did. The city filed criminal charges against both Garrison and Lundy. They were charged with the illegal publication of a "scandalous and mischievous newspaper, the *Liberator*, for the purpose of enflaming and exciting the free negroes and slaves to insurrection." The charges against the two went no further as both stayed out of Washington. Presumably they could have been imprisoned and tried if either set foot there. Lundy was not involved with the *Liberator* but he did continue to publish antislavery newspapers from the North and became an agent on the Underground Railroad.

Donovan made arrangements to ship his slaves to New Orleans on a 180-ton "fast sailing coppered" ship named the *Union*. The ship was a brig with two masts and a square rig, docked at O'Donnell's wharf in Baltimore's Inner Harbor. On May 4, the *Union*'s master, Edward Hooper, advertised that his vessel, "having part of her cargo engaged," was ready for a quick dispatch. A portion of that cargo was lodged in Donovan's slave pen. Hooper boasted of the vessel's excellent accommodations for passengers and added that he still had room for additional freight.

The *Union* was described in Hooper's advertisement as a packet, which indicates that it regularly plied the route from Baltimore to New Orleans with a mixed load of passengers and freight and may have also carried some U.S. mail. That particular vessel transported its first shipment of slaves from Baltimore to New Orleans in 1847, when Hooper took on fifty slaves owned by Hope Slatter. Hooper certainly had no objection to slavery. At the time of the U.S. Census of 1850, he owned five slaves himself.

Nearly a month after the *Pearl* was captured, Mary, Emily, and their brothers were forcibly marched to the *Union* docked at O'Donnell's wharf—the site of today's Marine Mammal Pavilion of the National Aquarium—and secured in the hold along with the other slaves being transported that day.

As required by law, Captain Hooper and Joseph Donovan signed the required "Manifest of Negroes, Mulattos, and Persons of Color" that listed all of the slaves being shipped south. In so doing, Hooper and Donovan were attesting that the listed Negroes had not been imported from Africa after January 1, 1808, the date when the transatlantic slave trade was outlawed. Unfortunately, that law did not stop slave traders from using the Atlantic Ocean forty years later to transport slaves from the Upper South to the slave markets of the Lower South.

Of the forty passengers listed on the slave manifest, the following people were also on the list of fugitives who were captured on the *Pearl*:

NO.	NAMES	AGE	HEIGHT		COLOR*
			FEET	INCHES	
3	JOHN EDMONSON	26	5	10	BLACK
4	ISAAC TURNER	21	5	8	BLACK
5	PHILIP CROWLEY	24	5	9	"
6	SAM TURNER	24	5	10	"
7	MATHIAS MARSHALL	24	5	7	"
8	SAMUEL EDMONSON	21	5	8	BROWN
9	EPHRAIM EDMONSON	30	5	8	"
10	RICHARD EDMONSON	24	5	8	"
11	PERRY GROSS	23	5	8	BLACK
12	MADISON PITTS	22	5	7	BROWN
13	MADISON MARSHALL	24	5	1	MULATTO
16	AUGUSTUS CHASE	23	5	8	BLACK
24	PETER RICKS	20	5	9	"
28	GEORGE SHANKLIN	23	5	8	"
33	MARY EDMONSON	17	5	6	BROWN
34	EMILY EDMONSON	15	5	1	BROWN

All of the former fugitives were shipped by Donovan, Joseph Bruin's partner, except for George Shanklin, who was shipped by William Williams of Washington, D.C., as evidenced by the signatures on the manifest. This list appears not to include any of the fugitives who had been purchased by Hope Slatter and sent to Baltimore in the railroad car.

Emily Edmonson, among the youngest of the forty slaves onboard, was listed as fifteen years old while Mary was listed as seventeen. In the nineteenth century, record keepers weren't scrupulous about listing

---

* The colors that follow are often arbitrary and subjective, as was also true of census takers who made the decision whether a free black was black or a mulatto, and that designation could change from census to census. While census categories were commonly limited to those two choices, Donovan used three: Black, Brown, and Mulatto.

ages correctly or spelling names consistently. The manifest stated that Ephraim Edmonson was thirty years old, John was twenty-six years old, and Richard was twenty-four years old. However, the dates provided during Rebecca Culver's mental competency hearing in 1827 indicate that the brothers were several years older. But, of course, traders had a reason to underreport ages on a slave manifest. Men close to forty had fewer years of work left in them than younger men and were therefore less profitable. On the other hand, a thirteen-year-old girl was still on the young side for men looking for attractive young women. In the case of Mary and Emily, the ages may have been slightly increased.

William Chaplin wisely stayed out of Washington until he could be reasonably sure that he would not be implicated in the escape attempt. The *Albany Patriot* explained that Chaplin had been prevented from writing for the paper recently because of "ill health and circumstances entirely beyond his control." Chaplin had returned to upstate New York, where he had many friends. In May he surfaced in Utica, New York, where he and Frederick Douglass spoke at a meeting of the New York State Vigilance Committee. Such committees had risen up in many Northern states for the purpose of aiding runaway slaves. The members of vigilance committees and antislavery societies often overlapped, but it was necessary that the organizations be distinct. The work of the vigilance committees was technically illegal.

That same newspaper account, undoubtedly referring to Chaplin, said that "an agent" for the vigilance committee reported at the meeting that he had helped more than a hundred fugitives reach the North. It would have been dangerous to name him because the acts he was describing were illegal.

Chaplin's fund-raising appeals for the fugitives on the *Pearl*, together with Gerrit Smith's long-standing relationship with the wealthy Astor family of New York, produced a substantial contribution. A descendant of the recently deceased John Jacob Astor sent $900 specifically for the Edmonsons. Joshua Giddings later said that he had personally received the donation. That money wasn't enough to free either Mary or Emily, who were each worth closer to $1,200. But that money could free one of the brothers. The family decided that it would be Richard, whose wife and children were reportedly ill in Washington.

But by the time the money arrived in Baltimore, the inspector for the Port of Baltimore had already inspected the Negroes on the *Union*, and the ship had moved away from the wharf. While Joseph Donovan was more than willing to accept the money for the purchase of Richard Edmonson, he refused to return the ship to the wharf to take him off the vessel. The manifest was signed and certified, the vessel was ready to depart, and Richard Edmonson would stay onboard, even if he was a free man. The *Union* began to make its way down the Chesapeake, heading for the Atlantic Ocean.

After their journey had begun, Chaplin published a fund-raising appeal in the *Albany Patriot* under the heading of "Humanity . . . Fraternity . . . Pity." In his appeal for money to redeem some of the fugitives, Chaplin described the Edmonsons as the "most interesting family-group, consisting of four brothers and two sisters by the name of Edmeston [*sic*]." He described the sisters as "beautiful girls" and reported that Richard was the highly esteemed coachman of Secretary of the Treasury Robert Walker. According to Chaplin, Secretary Walker had made his way to the D.C. jail after the fugitives had been towed back to Washington in an attempt to free Richard. Congressman Giddings also reported that Walker had attempted to negotiate a price for his coachman. Either Valdenar or Bruin had assured Walker that he would sell Richard to him the next morning but then changed his mind.

Chaplin wrote that the total sum needed to free the entire family was about $5,800 and that a "noble man" from New York, "with rare disinterestedness and liberality," had already sent $900. He stated that the Edmonson family—the siblings and the sons-in-law—had collected every penny they could find, but they needed help.

In that same appeal, Chaplin made a special bid for fifteen-year-old Mary Ellen Stewart, the young woman who had been owned by Dolley Madison and was now jailed in Campbell's Baltimore slave pen, recently purchased from Hope Slatter. Stewart, described by Chaplin as the "sprightly, active" fifth child of a grieving mother, whose other four children had been sold away, would be one of the fortunate ones. Dr. Joseph Evans Snodgrass, Baltimore physician, antislavery publisher, ally of the Washington activists, and good friend of Edgar Allan Poe, went to the Campbell slave pen and paid $475 for Stewart's freedom. The *Rochester North Star* of August 25, 1848, confirmed that "Dr. Snodgrass, of Baltimore, with the aid of some kind friends, has purchased Mrs. Madison's slave who attempted to escape on board the *Pearl*, and set her at liberty."

As the *Union*'s sails picked up wind, the ship began making its way south, taking Mary and Emily even farther from home. At night, the sisters were confined in a small, crowded compartment with the other women, and their brothers were put in a similar compartment with the men. During the day, they were allowed out of those rooms to spread out on the deck, because there was little threat of escape.

The *Union* passed through the mouth of the Chesapeake Bay not far from where they had been captured on the *Pearl* almost a month earlier and sailed out onto the Atlantic Ocean. Emily's spirit, bolstered by her faith in God, was strong enough to get her through a slave escape, a gauntlet of insults in Washington, and two slave pens, but even with calm waters, seasickness hit her so hard that her brothers and sister feared she might die. Mary also suffered, as did many of the others. Few, if any, had ever seen the ocean or expected to be on a sea voyage that would take more than two weeks. The four Edmonson brothers, though sick as well, managed to look after their sisters.

Mary and Emily soon became accustomed to the rhythmic rolling of the brig, and their sickness eased. For brief periods, they even managed to push thoughts of their circumstances out of their minds and look out in awe at the vastness of the ocean and the seemingly infinite horizon, a view of God's magnificent work. Those early days on the brig during the calm afforded Mary and Emily and their brothers a time to take comfort in one another. They still hoped to be greeted in New Orleans with the news that Richard would not be the only one of them to be freed. Surely, by then, the supporters in the North who had helped organize the escape would have raised enough money to supplement what their family was still raising. They just hoped it would come through before they, like so many others, were lost to "irredeemable slavery." They prayed, of course, because that was what sustained them.

On one particularly beautiful day, after the noonday meal had been served, the sisters settled under the foresail on the upper deck with their older brothers. Peter Ricks, Madison Pitts, Isaac Turner, Augustus Chase, George Shanklin, and the other *Pearl* veterans were there, too, as were other men and women who hadn't been on the *Pearl* but were their companions on this voyage. Captain Hooper and the crew, save the one left behind to tend the wheel, were resting below in their quarters. Under the wide open sky, on what could have looked like a pleasure cruise, Mary and Emily talked quietly with their brothers and some of the others gathered together under a sail that cast a cooling shadow over them. It was the middle of May, and the sun was becoming increasingly warmer the farther south they went.

But that peaceful mood quickly turned somber when Emily confessed that she couldn't stop thinking of their mother and the terrible pain she must be suffering with six of her children taken from her all at once. She told them she could see their mother on her knees praying for their safe return. The youngest of the Edmonson siblings then asked them all to kneel and pray. In pairs and small groups under the huge square sail, they joined Emily in silent prayer, each remembering his or her loved ones left behind, and eyes all around filled with tears.

Emily's voice broke the quiet as she began to sing softly about the captive Jews of long ago who had also been taken away from their homes and forced to live in a strange land. Her sweet, lone voice rose out to sing, "By the rivers of Babylon, there we sat down," and then Mary, her closest companion in the world, added her voice to sing, "yea, we wept, when we remembered Zion." Soon most were singing and the voices grew stronger, near thunderous, as the pain from an ancient time cut directly into their hearts. "For they carried us away captive and required of us a song," they continued, conjuring coffles of slaves forced to sing as they set out on the arduous walk to a land of unfamiliar cotton fields and sugar cane plantations. Mary and Emily cried out in song—"How shall we sing the Lord's song in a strange land"—a cry for everyone who had been clamped into a coffle or herded onto a vessel to be transported to distant slave markets.

Emily, Mary, and the others were so intent on their song that they barely noticed that nearly all the crew had been drawn up to the deck by their singing. The sight of enslaved human beings onboard was not new to them. Any sailor who worked ships out of Baltimore or farther points south was familiar with the trade. But those voices cut through whatever calluses had grown over those seamen's hearts until the entire crew encircled the kneeling slaves with their caps in their hands. When they finished the song, the man in charge of the slaves asked them to sing another song. They declined.

After the *Union* reached the Carolinas, strong winds began to blow them far off course and away from Key West. Mary, Emily, and their brothers, along with many of their companions, prayed that the winds would turn the vessel north instead of steadily steering them closer to the markets of New Orleans. According to the family's account, a few of the seamen had by then become sympathetic to the enslaved passengers. One promised Samuel Edmonson that if the winds drove them within a hundred miles of a Northern port and the slaves would help him, he would lead a mutiny against Captain Hooper.

That didn't happen. A pilot boat approached the *Union* to see if Hooper wished to pay to have the ship guided around the treacherous reefs along the Florida Keys, made even more dangerous by the winds. Even with the new forty-six-foot-tall lighthouse topped with fifteen oil lamps at Key West, the *Union* would have found it impossible to take the shortcuts around the Keys without help.

But the arrival of the pilot boat worsened conditions for the slaves. For whatever reason, perhaps thinking he would be charged more if the pilot saw his valuable cargo, Hooper hid all the slaves belowdecks while he and the pilot negotiated the fee. Mary and Emily were now tightly locked up with the others in the cramped, suffocating hold, blocked from air and light by a heavy canvas hood placed over the gated hatchway. While the captains endlessly bickered over the fee, some of the men managed to punch holes in the canvas to allow air in for the increasingly desperate people locked below. Some had the strength to push themselves close to the air holes for relief, but others fell behind, fainting in the heat.

Finally, the captain of the pilot boat rejected Hooper's best offer and left him to his own devices. At least that lifted the lockdown, and the Edmonson brothers, who were also weakened by the horribly hot conditions below, were able to carry Emily and Mary up to the deck for air. But with no pilot boat to guide them, Hooper was forced to take a wide course around the Keys, which added days to the trip. Food and water soon began to run low, and the captain began to ration supplies. The slaves were each issued a "gill" of water—about four ounces—for the whole day, while the sailors received a quart each. A few of the sailors passed some of their water to the Edmonson brothers to give to Mary and Emily, and likely helped others, too.

After the *Union* cut across the Bay of Mexico and approached the mouth of the Mississippi River, they encountered a violent storm that alarmed the crew as much as it did the enslaved passengers. But it passed without damage, and the brig continued on its way. A towboat took the *Union* on tow and began the ninety-mile ascent upriver to New Orleans.

The busy and prosperous city of New Orleans already had a history rich in language, food, and trade. First claimed by the French in

1699, the original territory extended east to Spanish-held Florida, stretched north to south between the Gulf of Mexico and Canada, and then spread to the west all the way to the Rio Grande. In 1718, the Company of the Indies, chartered by Louis XIV, sent some twenty-five convicts and the same number of semiskilled workers to begin a settlement on a Native American trading site ninety miles north of the mouth of the Mississippi River. The trading site had been well chosen by the natives. Inside the curve of an upside-down U-shaped patch of the river, where alluvial deposits had accumulated next to deep water suitable for shipping, the ground was firm enough to build a new city.

In 1719 about two hundred slaves from the West Indies were brought to the site, since named for the Duke of Orlean, to speed construction. More slaves followed, with many arriving directly from Africa. In 1723, a year after New Orleans was named the capital of the territory, there were more than two thousand slaves in the city.

As the city grew haphazardly, so did its black community, both free and enslaved. Some slaves were freed for performing militia service in skirmishes with Native Americans. Others worked to purchase their own freedom, and some were freed by an owner's will. A *code noir*—the ubiquitous black code that followed free blacks like night follows day—was soon established. But the French code included some protections for enslaved blacks. It granted them the right to a Catholic education, access to the courts for mistreatment, and a family protection clause that prevented families from being separated by sale. While free blacks could not vote, they could participate freely in the business of the city except for serving alcohol. They were permitted to attend theater and opera, open schools, and even buy and sell slaves. They had become the *les gens de couleur libre*—free men of color.

In the early days, slaves established a Sunday market on a field beyond the ramparts of the city where they could sell their own produce, fish, and other products. At first it was called *Place des Negres* and later Congo Square. It was a place where slaves could congregate with others from their particular area of Africa and perform tribal dances, with musicians and singers retaining the sounds and rhythms of their home. It was a rare preservation of African custom and culture outside of the sea islands of South Carolina and Georgia.

Liaisons between the French white male Creoles and attractive young black women, both free and enslaved, became a part of New Orleans life and produced a large number of fair-skinned blacks. In a system known as "placage," French and Spanish Creole men would take a woman of color as a second wife and live between two homes, one public and the other private. Some of the attractive young daughters of these liaisons became the women who attended the legendary quadroon balls in the city.

In 1802 France sold Louisiana to the United States for $15 million. After the upheaval and bloodshed in their former colony of Haiti and years of costly war in Europe, Napoleon was happy to be rid of it. The New Orleans that would soon receive Mary, Emily, and the other slaves had become considerably more American, though French Creole culture remained predominant. And it became increasingly American in the restrictive laws it passed to govern both slaves and free blacks.

By 1830, free blacks were required to carry papers proving they were not slaves. That same year, Louisiana passed a law requiring recently freed slaves to leave the state. It was similar to the law Maryland passed but differed in that Louisiana was far more likely to enforce its law. By 1842, Louisiana had outlawed free blacks from entering the state, cutting off many well-off black Creoles from contact with extended family and friends in the West Indies. Many free blacks took that as a signal to leave the state and sold their homes, businesses, and other assets. The free black population of nineteen thousand in 1840 had decreased to ten thousand by 1850. But no laws were passed to limit the importation of slaves from the Upper South into New Orleans. By the 1840s, the hunger for slaves in the Lower South had turned the city into the most important distribution point for slave traders in the country.

The slaves traveling from Baltimore on the *Union* were approaching New Orleans for just that purpose. While the brig was being towed upriver, they were allowed to remain on deck. Mary and Emily's first sightings of land just south of New Orleans were the uncultivated mud flats and swamps that reached out from either shore. Then fields of sugar cane and cotton, the cash crops of Louisiana, began to appear. In the distance, they could see figures—plantation slaves—dotted across the landscape.

The sisters were entering another world, one where a large number of planters owned a far greater number of slaves than they had ever seen in either Maryland or Washington. In the Berry Division of Montgomery County—Mary and Emily's own father's census division—two of the major slave owners were Francis Valdenar and Francis Blair. In the U.S. Census of 1850, Valdenar owned twenty-nine slaves, a figure that included Amelia Edmonson and her younger two children. Francis Blair, a major political power brought to Washington by Andrew Jackson, owned a home directly across from the White House—much later sold to the government and called "Blair House"—and a country estate named Silver Spring. He owned twenty slaves. However, it was not unusual for Louisiana slave owners to own more than one hundred slaves. In New Orleans, where there were no fields to tend, owners had far fewer slaves. Of course, a number of wealthy planters had both plantations and a house in the city.

The *Union* docked at the city wharf opposite the beef market, but the slaves were kept onboard overnight. The *Daily Picayune,* which reported all vessel arrivals and departures, announced the arrival of the *Union,* captained by Edward Hooper, on June 14, and stated that it had been in transit for twenty days with a cargo of assorted merchandise.

The Edmonsons arrived in a city with a resident population of 79,998, according to a census taken in December 1847, but those who could afford to leave the city when the hot weather arrived had done so after seeing to it that their woolen garments were carefully wrapped in tobacco leaves to protect them from summer infestations. They fled the area to wait out the various tropical diseases that arrived regularly at this time of year. The wealthy went to Europe or New England, while less-moneyed whites headed north to resorts in the mountains of North Carolina and Virginia. A resort in Warm Springs, Virginia, advertised widely in New Orleans touting its healthy air and comfortable accommodations.

Early the next morning, the slaves disembarked onto the wharf in preparation for their delivery to a slave pen. Although June was far from the busiest time for shipping—that would come after the cotton and sugar harvests—the port around them was still busy. In addition to the *Union,* other arrivals included three barks, one schooner, a steamship yacht, and three other brigs. Goods needed to be unloaded, including 210 baskets of champagne from Havre and 12,936 bushels of salt from the Turks Islands. Just recently, 1,396 bales of cotton, likely the last of the previous year's crop, had left for Liverpool on the *Jenny Lind,* and three other vessels, carrying more cotton, set sail to the same destination, one of New Orleans's prime trade routes. The northwestern English town built on the profits from the slave trade now controlled the worldwide cotton market and set its price.

Steamboats arrived in the city on regular runs from Cincinnati, Natchez, Mobile, or Nashville, often delivering more slaves and then leaving with New Orleans residents eager to escape the heat and tropical diseases. Their routes included the West Indies and across the bay to Mexico. When the Edmonsons arrived, government supplies had just left on a steamboat headed to American forces in Vera Cruz under the charge of General Winfield Scott, who was due to arrive in New Orleans any day. A ladies' hat shop had advertised that women planning to join the public celebration to greet him should do so in a new hat, an accessory that, in a particularly mean-spirited law, black women were banned from wearing. The more prosperous women of color retaliated by creating particularly beautiful silk turbans.

The voices that Mary and Emily heard on the wharf reflected another change in the city. In the 1840s an increasing number of Europeans had joined the waves of immigrants to America and were drawn to New Orleans. Driven by revolution, poverty, and famine, German, French, and—in the highest numbers—Irish immigrants jostled for a place to work. Many of the city's free blacks working on the waterfront struggled to hold on to their positions in the face of an onslaught of desperate white job seekers.

New Orleans still retained much of its French flair and some aspects of Spanish traditions as well. A few months earlier, a visitor to the city described the New Year celebrations. He reported that over the course of two days, the whole city was in motion. Dancing was everywhere, with the less refined doing a "double shuffle time" in one of the city's four ballrooms that catered to that group. Six theaters flourished on Sunday evenings, a night when many in the North refrained from public entertainment. Admission to the bullfights in Washington Square cost fifty cents on January 1 and 2, with proceeds from one of those fights marked for the poor. The regular Sunday French market thronged with "[y]outh and age—all colors, nationals and tongues were there, commingled in one heterogeneous mass of delightful confusion."

Less delightful were the slave markets that thrived in the mélange that was midcentury New Orleans. As early as 1828, with the demand for domestic slaves from the Upper South extremely high, the traffic in slaves was so busy that one visitor compared the harbor of New Orleans to that of Río de Janeiro, where the importation of slaves directly from Africa was still legal.

Mary and Emily, along with their brothers and the thirty-four other passengers, were marched about six blocks east to a slave pen on Esplanade Avenue near the corner of Chartres Street on the eastern border of the French Quarter. On the other side of the avenue was the Faubourg Marigny, a suburb where many prosperous men kept their families of color. A block south of the slave pen, the "Louisiana Ballroom—American Style" was holding "White" balls on Sunday, Tuesday, Wednesday, Friday, and Saturday evenings. Thursdays were reserved for the quadroon or, as an English-language newspaper put it, the "Quarter-oon" balls, where only the men would be white. The term *quadroon*, which means one-quarter black, had evolved into a general term for fair-skinned black women. Some of the attendees at the ball may well have been octoroons, or one-eighth black.

The structure of the New Orleans slave pen was similar to those the Edmonsons had already experienced in Alexandria and Baltimore—a large, wall-enclosed yard with cramped sleeping quarters inside. But the pen they were in now had a feature that few pens in the Upper South had need for, except for Richmond: a showroom for buyers.

By the mid–nineteenth century, the New Orleans slave markets were moving more slaves than "Richmond and Charleston combined." Labor on the Louisiana sugar plantations was hard and cried out for strong men; more were always needed. And the whole world was hungry for cotton. At the time that Mary and Emily arrived in New Orleans, slave traders were selling to Texas planters and gearing up for what they hoped would be a substantial increase in traffic and a rise in prices once the new southwest territory won from Mexico became slave land.

By 1848, the slave trade was such an accepted part of the New Orleans culture and economy that little attempt was made to hide it from the general public. City authorities did try to contain the business within certain areas, but auctions were held all too visibly in two of the city's most prominent French Quarter hotels: the St. Charles and the St. Louis. For a brief time immediately after Nat Turner's bloody uprising, the state discouraged bringing in slaves from Virginia for fear of contaminating slaves in Louisiana with ideas of insurrection. But the trade continued and slaves from Virginia, after a modest wait, returned to the New Orleans markets in droves.

The slave markets supplied the Lower South with more than field hands. Both the residents of New Orleans and plantation owners needed house slaves and skilled mechanics. In his seminal work, *Slave Trading in the Old South*, Frederic Bancroft describes the range of skilled slaves available for sale in New Orleans as follows:

calkers, masons, butlers, coopers, coachmen, lady's-maids, nurses either wet or dry, waiters, waitresses, accomplished seamstresses, highly expert engineers . . . "a first-rate wheelwright and whitesmith," a "No. 1 confectioner and candymaker;" baker either French or American . . . a horse-doctor, a spinner, a tiger-man, an ox-driver; a valet that spoke English, French, Spanish and German and "would suit any gentleman for traveling;" highly skilful gardeners . . . Maryland cooks who thought they could not be equalled in the preparation of terrapin or the frying of chicken; better still, Creole cooks, such masters of the French cuisine with Louisiana variations as to make every repast a delight; little children from jet black to blond, with or without mothers . . . butchers, carpenters, blacksmiths, plasterers . . . and now and then a foreman capable of managing a rice, a sugar or a cotton plantation. . . .

And then there was the trade in "fancy girls," young women who were usually fair-skinned, attractive, and generally well-spoken. The name comes less from the common adjectival use of the word and more from the transformation of the verb "to fancy" into an adjective. Traders were able to demand a high price from Southern gentlemen who sought enslaved women for sexual purposes—sometimes, but not always, under the pretense that they were seeking household servants. The two were not mutually exclusive. Bruin had publicly bragged that the New Orleans market would give him back twice what he had paid for Mary and Emily, and it was already clear that he was planning to market the sisters for sexual purposes.

Fancy girls were sold directly from slave pens and at the public auctions held in the rotundas of the French Quarter hotels. Bidding often instigated intense rivalries among the men. Solomon Northup, the free New Yorker who had been kidnapped in Washington by slave trader

James Birch, kept in the Williams slave pen, and then taken to Theophilus Freeman's slave pen in New Orleans, observed such auctions. He reported that men in New Orleans would sometimes pay as much as $5,000 for a fancy girl if only to prevent a rival from buying her.

Many traders were not disinterested figures in the mix of slavery and sex. In *Soul by Soul: Life Inside the Antebellum Slave Market*, Walter Johnson states that "[t]he slave market was suffused with sexuality [including] the traders' light-skinned mistresses, the buyers' foul-mouthed banter, the curtained inspection rooms that surrounded the pens." Such practices were not limited to New Orleans. Johnson added that Theophilus Freeman, who also operated in Fredericksburg, Virginia, sometimes received visitors while in bed with a woman he had once owned.

Many of the traders utilized the picturesque balconies along the Esplanade to display slaves who were for sale. Some used the public sidewalks outside the pens until banned by the city from doing so in 1853. Visitors with any antipathy to slavery described these scenes with dismay and horror, but there was little outcry in Congress. It was a state issue.

A number of traders from the Upper South operated in New Orleans or formed partnerships with traders who did. Joseph Bruin was a well-known figure in the busy and crowded world of the New Orleans slave trade, and he advertised that interested buyers could find him "at his old stand, corner of Esplanade and Chartres Street, near the mint." He helpfully added that the "omnibuses running on Royal and Chartres all pass my house." The Campbell brothers of Baltimore also kept a pen in the city—and ran a plantation outside the city as well, where slaves could be seasoned.*

There is no evidence that Bruin was in New Orleans when the Edmonson sisters arrived with their brothers. The family story told by

---

* Seasoning helped newly arrived slaves become accustomed to the infections and diseases they had not been exposed to in the Upper South. It is an expression that goes back to the earliest days of the American colonies, when many immigrants failed to survive their first year.

John Paynter in *The Fugitives of the Pearl*—the only detail we have about the family through much of their journey—states that they were delivered into the custody of a man named Wilson. Undoubtedly, this was Jonathan Wilson, also of Baltimore, who was Joseph Donovan's partner, as well as an associate of Bruin's. Wilson was listed in the city directory of New Orleans as a slave trader at 15 Esplanade. Two years later, the U.S. Census of 1850 listed Wilson as a "negro trader" with forty slaves at hand.

When Mary and Emily arrived at Wilson's slave pen with the others, they were put in the walled yard. They saw men, women, and children scattered about, standing dejectedly in small groups or alone, awaiting their turn in the showroom. Unless money arrived soon from Washington, that same fate awaited the Edmonsons.

The siblings watched as slaves, picked for exhibition in the showrooms, were dressed in clean clothing and groomed to look presentable. Some traders in the city adopted the fashion of dressing male slaves in well-tailored black dress suits with tall beaver hats and white gloves. The women were given nice clothes and a silk kerchief to wear over their hair. Traders often divided the slaves into two lines, with males on one side and females on the other, lined up in order of height.

Solomon Northup, who had described the inside of the Williams pen in Washington, also produced one of the most detailed observations of the New Orleans slave market. He wrote that Theophilus Freeman, the slave trader who owned him, ordered them to hold their heads high and walk briskly while potential buyers reached out to feel their arms and legs. On some occasions, Freeman demanded that Northup play a violin while the slaves danced. Those who refused were disciplined with paddles with holes drilled through them, which left fewer of the telltale welt marks of a whip that would signal a troublesome slave to a potential buyer. Nonetheless, truly rebellious slaves were still whipped.

As slaves left with new owners, the traders plucked new candidates from the yard for exhibition inside. That first day, a still tearful Emily was summoned to the showroom. An overdressed and showy young man had arrived seeking a housekeeper. He was willing to spend $1,500 for the right young woman, and he selected Emily. But when the young dandy saw Emily's tearstained face, he told the trader that he had someone more cheerful in mind. When the man left, Wilson slapped Emily across the face, warning her that she would receive a whipping if he ever caught her crying again in the showroom. An older woman in the yard took Emily aside and gently explained that it would do her no good in the end to do anything but smile. Otherwise, she told her, she would suffer all the worse for it. The Edmonson brothers, fearing what could happen if their sisters appeared uncooperative, advised Emily to take the woman's advice.

That night, Samuel, Ephraim, and John were prepared for the showroom. Wilson saw to it that their hair was cropped and their mustaches, a mark of a "genteel" family, were shaved; he also made them exchange their own clothes for "suits of coarse blue jean." Their sisters barely recognized them. The day's ordeal was followed by an uncomfortable night, as Mary and Emily slept on the floor of the women's crowded and hot indoor quarters with just a blanket under them.

The Edmonson sisters were not spared the humiliation of standing on the balcony of the slave pen for all passersby to see, including the passengers on the horse-drawn omnibus route. Paynter reported that the Edmonsons were "subjected to examination in much the same way as if they were a horse or cow." If a potential buyer was interested in a particular slave, he could request a more detailed inspection. In smaller rooms, men were usually stripped naked and women undressed down to the waist. Mary and Emily were mortified when "[t]heir persons were handled rudely to the accompaniment of indecent or vulgar jests."

Samuel and his brothers approached Wilson to explain that their sisters would not be able to stand up to the indignities they were being forced to undergo. Wilson understood that it was not in his interest to have Mary and Emily collapse in tears in front of buyers. Thereafter, he made sure they were treated less roughly.

The nominally free Richard was allowed to leave the pen, and he immediately set out to find their thirty-three-year-old brother, Hamilton. After Hamilton had been captured as a runaway and sold south, the family had somehow learned that he was living in New Orleans. Richard located him at 121 Girard Street and quickly led his older brother back to Wilson's slave pen, where he was joyfully reunited with his siblings. He had left when Mary was still a baby and had never seen Emily. But the sisters knew all about him. They grew up in the log cabin off the Brookeville Road in Norbeck, Maryland, listening to endless stories about Hamilton, the second oldest of the Edmonson children. Now, even if surrounded by horrendous circumstances, Mary and Emily were overjoyed to see him. Soon after their happy reunion, Hamilton told them his story.

After his capture in Baltimore, Hamilton had been taken to a slave pen in New Orleans, where he was purchased by a man named Taylor who lived in the city. Hamilton learned the skills of a cooper, or barrel maker, a good trade to have in a busy port where barrels were always in high demand for shipping. At some point, his owner allowed him to keep a percentage of his earnings. After many long days making barrels out of staves and metal bands, Hamilton had finally saved enough money to buy his freedom, only to have the money stolen. He started again and had just recently purchased his freedom. He now owned his own cooperage business.

Hamilton's story gave the Edmonsons hope. Their brother had also been captured after a run for freedom and then succeeded in becoming free. He had taken on the same surname as his owner and was known as Hamilton Taylor. It is likely that the man who had owned him was a prominent figure, and, as in other parts of the South, a free black man could gain some leverage and even protection by using a former owner's surname. At the very least it implied contacts with powerful people.

Possibly using those connections, Hamilton managed to negotiate an arrangement with Jonathan Wilson that allowed his sisters to stay in his home at night, where they would be more comfortable.

From that point on, Mary and Emily left the slave pen every evening and slept in clean beds with good food. But every morning they had to return. The arrangement was not that startling, as there was a surprising amount of elasticity in the walls surrounding the pens. A number of traders hired out slaves to work around the city and expected them to return at night, sometimes allowing them to keep a portion of the wage they earned. Traders often used favored slaves as stewards and, in that capacity, a slave could pass in and out of the pen on errands. Sometimes, an enslaved steward would even deliver purchased slaves to their new owners.

Mary and Emily's situation had improved, but they were still subject to the pain and discomfort of standing daily in the showroom, constantly prepped for inspection by prospective buyers while always under the watchful eye of the slave trader and his assistants. Even if Wilson had agreed to keep the usual indignities to a minimum for the sisters, they were witnesses to the daily cruelties in the pen. Slaves caught sleeping during the tediously long day in the showroom were beaten. Mary and Emily kept watch over the little ones so they could wake them when a trader was near.

Louisiana law provided a consumer protection for buyers that allowed them to demand a refund if, within a certain period of time, a slave was found to be defective. Slaves who were returned as unacceptable were usually beaten for ruining the sale. While the Edmonsons were in Wilson's pen, a man and woman who hoped to marry were purchased by different owners. The young man was returned within a week, and the slave trader was forced to refund the money he had been paid. Wilson ordered that the male slaves in the pen flog him nightly for a week. If any of the slaves balked, then they too would be flogged. The young woman was also sent back to the pen, but not because her owner wished to rescind the sale: he had returned her to have her whipped.

One day, Samuel Edmonson was taken away from the slave pen in a carriage and did not return. He was the first of the Edmonsons to be sold, and Mary and Emily were heartbroken to see their brother leave. Samuel was purchased by Horace Cammack, a wealthy forty-five-year-old English cotton merchant who lived at the corner of St. Louis and Bourbon Street in the heart of the French Quarter. At least Samuel stayed in the city and would be working as a house slave instead of in a plantation field. Hamilton may have even helped arrange the sale so that Samuel would be with an owner who would not be abusive.

Sales remained slow at Wilson's pen and the city was again under threat from yellow fever, one of the most dreaded of New Orleans scourges. Initially, the disease caused backaches, high fever, chills, nausea, and jaundice; then, after those symptoms subsided, it returned to fatally attack the kidneys and the liver. No one knew then that it was caused by a bite from an infected female mosquito; all they knew was that it could either devastate the city or pass it by. In 1846, yellow fever caused between 100 and 160 deaths; in 1847, the toll reached epidemic proportions, with closer to 3,000 deaths.

Although epidemics rarely struck in consecutive years, Wilson took any report of the fever very seriously, and Joseph Bruin would have been watching the situation in New Orleans closely. He had a significant financial investment in the Edmonsons and he didn't want to lose it through the misfortune of illness.

Bruin had another reason to return the sisters to the Washington area. He later stated that he had been given a "positive assurance" that the money needed to free them would be raised when they were returned. Some months later, Jacob Bigelow wrote that the girls were returned to the Washington area because of the "importunities of their brother, who was then with them." William Chaplin, who was back in Washington, also likely had a hand in pressuring Bruin, making the argument that if the family and their supporters could match what he could get for them in New Orleans, Bruin would still be in a very good position.

Captain Hooper was getting ready to sail the *Union* back to Baltimore, and Wilson marched Mary and Emily back to the ship they knew only too well. The *New Orleans Commercial Bulletin* of July 3 reported that the *Union* would sail on Wednesday, July 5. The nominally free Richard and his two sisters began their journey back to Baltimore.

SIX

Trials and Tribulations

While the Edmonsons were facing the horrors of a New Orleans slave pen, Daniel Drayton, Edward Sayres, and Chester English remained in the D.C. jail awaiting trial. Unlike other prisoners, Drayton was confined to his cell and not allowed into the passage that ran the length of the cells secured by a locked gate. No visitors were allowed except attorney David Hall and Congressman Giddings, and even then the jailer was present for all their discussions. English was still in jail, but they were still hoping that the charges against him would be dropped.

It had become clear to the authorities that Drayton was the one in charge of the escape, and they continued to pressure him to reveal who else was behind the plan. He later reported that a jailer told him he had been authorized to offer Drayton a thousand dollars for the names of the organizers. But Drayton remained quiet and took comfort in the kindness of Washington's black community. In addition to the woman who had brought him a Bible, another black woman, who cooked at the jail, took special care of him, making sure he received decent food.

In Boston, spearheaded by many of that city's leading figures in the antislavery movement, a support committee was formed to raise money for the men's legal expenses and to locate counsel. Samuel May, a Unitarian minister and uncle to Louisa May Alcott, had been an early and indefatigable convert to the cause of immediate emancipation. Richard Hildreth, a lawyer who had lived for a time in the South and returned to Boston in 1836 to write *The Slave, or Memoirs of a Fugitive,* one of the earliest antislavery novels, would soon be directly involved in the legal defense of Drayton and Sayres. Dr. Henry Bowditch, a pioneer in the treatment of pulmonary disease and the founder of the first Massachusetts board of health, was dispatched to Washington to interview Drayton.

Not all members of the committee were seen as committed abolitionists, who were still viewed as wild-eyed fanatics in much of the North. Samuel Gridley Howe, the founder of the Perkins School for the Blind (where Anne Sullivan would later study before taking on the assignment to teach a girl named Helen Keller), did not fall into that category. Although he had gone to Greece in 1824 to volunteer his medical services to the army fighting for Greek independence, Howe was then on the fringes of the abolitionist movement and his presence made the committee appear more rounded. That would change later, but at the time of the *Pearl* escape Howe considered many of the radicals to be too rigid—and they probably thought him too pliant. Yet it was Howe who would soon provide them with a lead defense attorney.

The committee distributed a hundred posters throughout Boston announcing the committee's meeting at Faneuil Hall on April 25, 1848. They also released a circular addressed "To the Friends of Liberty throughout the United States," which appeared in abolitionist newspapers in the North. It proclaimed that "whatever may be the case in the States, slavery in the District of Columbia is a national affair—our affair," and made it clear that a considerable amount of money was needed to defend the jailed men. They held out hope that the case would go to the Supreme Court, where they could challenge the legality of slavery in the District of Columbia and in the new territories that had just been acquired from Mexico. The debate over the extension of slavery into those vast new lands was becoming the pivotal antislavery struggle of the time, even eclipsing the issue of slavery in the nation's capital. They had learned from their frustrating efforts in the District of Columbia that slavery was difficult to eliminate once it had become rooted. Now they hoped that the legal case growing out of the escape on the *Pearl* would end with a ruling that slavery was illegal in all federal jurisdictions.

Putting aside their differences, the various factions of the abolitionist movement came together to garner support for the legal proceedings. The circular announced that donations could be sent to Charles Cleveland, the Philadelphia professor who connected Drayton to the organizers of the *Pearl* escape, and also to William Harned, who was running the office of the Foreign and American Anti-Slavery Society, at 61 John Street in New York City. Harned's organization had broken away from William Lloyd Garrison's American Anti-Slavery Society in large part because Lewis and Arthur Tappan and many other antislavery stalwarts objected to women serving in prominent positions in the movement. The splinter group also supported political action to end slavery, which the Garrisonians eschewed.

Gerrit Smith responded to the plea for financial support by sending five hundred dollars. Not only were the trials politically crucial, but his friend William Chaplin, who was both an agent for the New York Anti-Slavery Society and a Liberty Party man, was at risk of exposure. Two hundred dollars of Smith's contribution was immediately dispatched to Washington with committee member Richard Hildreth to secure local counsel. Smith's contribution was the largest the committee ever received, and they would remain bedeviled by money problems. Contrary to what many Southerners claimed, Northerners were reluctant to reach into their pockets to aid the antislavery campaign.

In Philadelphia, Professor Cleveland took on the responsibility for raising funds for the support of the men's families, a crucial part of the defense program and a commitment that had to be honored. He located

Mrs. Drayton and her family at 120 Oak Street in Philadelphia near the Delaware River and reported that he found her in a good deal of distress. Cleveland comforted her, assured her that they would take care of her, and gave her five dollars. Good to his word, he returned four days later with twenty dollars. While he was still at Mrs. Drayton's home, a Boston committee member arrived after his visit in Washington and informed them that Drayton was in "good health and good spirits."

Cleveland contacted Chester English's family in Burlington, New Jersey, to offer help, but was told they were in no need of financial assistance. He also located Captain Sayres's wife, who boarded on Perry Street in the home of her employer, where she worked as a dressmaker. Cleveland gave her five dollars.

The committee began looking for high-profile antislavery activists to represent the captains. They wanted men who could argue passionately that slavery was illegal in the District of Columbia and take that argument all the way to the Supreme Court. Samuel Gridley Howe proposed his good friend Horace Mann, who had just been elected to fill the congressional seat left empty by the death of John Quincy Adams. Howe and Mann were both bold and progressive visionaries in the field of education and were such fast friends that Howe and his poetry-writing wife, Julia Ward Howe, had accompanied Mann and his wife, Mary, on their honeymoon. Even though Mann had not practiced law in years, Howe was convinced that his sobriety and perceived neutrality were exactly what the committee needed.

In a letter dated April 26, just ten days after the capture of the little schooner, Samuel E. Sewell wrote to Mann on behalf of the committee to ask him to serve as defense counsel for the *Pearl* defendants. He told him that he would be taking the case to the Supreme Court and suggested that a local attorney would be needed to help him navigate the local court customs.

While Mann's sympathies were clearly antislavery, his passion was education reform, and he had assiduously avoided any political cause that might alienate his supporters in Massachusetts. No one, including Mann, would have described him as a radical abolitionist. But the convention of Whigs meeting in Newton, Massachusetts, decided that Mann could meet the standards set by his predecessor—and so did the voters. Mann took his seat in Congress on April 13, the same day the *Pearl* docked at the Seventh Street wharf to await her cargo.

The committee did not want to settle on one attorney. Sewell told Mann that other lawyers as Mann "may think desirable" would be added to the defense team, though in truth the committee clearly wanted to retain a say in the matter. Sewell suggested they approach either Congressman Giddings or Senator Hale, the two politicians in Washington most deeply enmeshed in the affair.

Mann was hesitant to accept the position. In early May, he wrote Howe to suggest that his friend's bid to appoint him counsel was "dictated more by a love for me than by a regard for them. . . . I have been too long a stranger to the courts." Howe urged his friend to take the case, telling him that "[n]o man in the country will make more out of a bad case than you can." On May 8, 1848, Howe traveled to Washington to discuss the matter with the new congressman and stayed with his close friend at Gordon's boardinghouse on Capitol Hill. If the primary purpose of Howe's visit was to convince Mann to accept the offer, he succeeded. Mann and Howe went to the Blue Jug the next day to meet the three men charged in the escape attempt. The following day Mann wrote to his wife that two of the men "bear it very well" but the third (certainly English) is a "deep mourner." On May 12, the afternoon that Howe left Washington, Mann wrote his wife to tell her that he was "engaged" by the committee and cautioned her "that the less said about it the better. This, we deem very important." As the lead defense lawyer for the captured captains of the *Pearl*, Mann was coming very close to filling the shoes of John Quincy Adams, and he was doing it without charging a fee.

Howe used that jail visit for propaganda purposes, returning to draft a pamphlet in which he described Drayton as "a bold, stern, determined man, ready to do battle unto the death in the cause of right. He has in him much of the stuff of which martyrs are made, and he will, I trust, bear unflinchingly to the end, all the moral and bodily suffering which he is doomed to endure." That pamphlet would later be expanded and sent to England to enlist support from abolitionists there.

The Boston Committee still wanted another high-profile attorney to work with Mann. The names of Joshua Giddings and John Hale were dropped. Professor Cleveland thought Daniel Webster would be ideal, but others immediately rejected that idea, because Webster was far from the strong abolitionist they were looking for—and he was also too expensive. The committee looked most favorably on Salmon P. Chase, a lawyer from Cincinnati and a powerful force behind the new Free-Soil Party formed to fight the extension of slavery into the territories.

Chase, who had come to be called the "defender of the fugitive" in Cincinnati, was receptive to the idea. He excitedly wrote back to Sewell and told him that his "first antislavery impressions were received in the District of Columbia." When he was eighteen years old, Chase wrote, he had moved to Washington to study law under William Wirt, the attorney general of the United States. During that time, he became involved "in drawing up the celebrated petition for District Emancipation presented to Congress in 1828." While he may have played a role in distributing the monster petition, his name was not included among the signatories, perhaps because he was only a temporary resident.

The captains and the mate remained in jail, unable to meet the enormous bail. In June, Charles Cleveland wrote to Mann to tell him that he could not help with the daunting task of raising the $76,000 bail as "we have no Gerrit Smiths in Philadelphia." He was still responsible for raising the ongoing financial commitment to the Drayton and Sayres families. But Cleveland had more disturbing news to pass on to Mann. He reported that both Captain Drayton and his wife were upset over a missing sum of money that the prisoner had sent to her from jail. Drayton was so angry that he "said that if the money is not paid he will 'blow up' the abolitionists." While Cleveland told Mann that the money must be made up, he asked, rather disingenuously, "[w]hat he has to blow up I know not." Cleveland seemed unwilling to acknowledge that his name was among those that Drayton could reveal. He then added that "[w]ere it not for injuring him in his present state, I would be glad to make a statement of the whole as far as I know." This incident served as a portent of what was to become an increasingly antagonistic relationship between Cleveland and the Draytons.

Shortly before Mary, Emily, and Richard Edmonson left New Orleans to return to the Washington area, the June session of the District court opened in city hall under the gavel of the Honorable Thomas Hartley Crawford, described as "dry as dust" by one observer. On June 19, an oppressively hot day, Alexander Hunter, the U.S. marshal for the District of Columbia, assembled grand jurors to consider the charges of larceny and illegal transportation of seventy-six fugitives on the *Pearl*. But the jury did no more than answer to their names that morning, because the heat was so intense that Judge Crawford excused the jurors until 10:00 A.M. the next day.

Washington's summer weather could easily rival that of New Orleans. On the worst days, the heat ripened and magnified the smells of the Center Market, the horse droppings on the Avenue, the piles of oyster shells behind city taverns and hotels, and the garbage scattered on empty lots. Pigs, ducks, and even goats rambled loose through the city, answerable to no one, though both Washington City and Georgetown passed law after law to try to keep them under control.

Fortunately, Washington's heat could break. The next day, when the grand jury returned to the courtroom, the temperature had eased and the more pleasing aspects of the city stood out. Horace Mann wrote to his wife, Mary, that day and told her that he could "hardly conceive how beautiful" the west front of the Capitol was, with its "lawns and cultivated trees and flowers below." Mann described to her "the city stretched out to Georgetown in the west . . . the Potomac in the distance and the loveliest of all skies above, mak[ing] one of the most beautiful scenes I ever beheld."

The first case the grand jury heard was the charges against the three white men captured on board the *Pearl,* clearly the most important case on the court's docket. The jury was made up of a fair number of prominent men from the District of Columbia. Peter Force, a journalist, publisher, and former mayor of the city (and serious collector of historical documents and memorabilia that are now stored in the Library of Congress), was selected as the jury foreman. His signature had appeared on the petition submitted to Congress ten years earlier asking that no effort be made to end slavery in the District of Columbia.

Still another former mayor, Thomas Carberry, considered a progressive in his time, was on the grand jury. In 1822 he had been elected mayor of Washington, running as the poor man's candidate during a brief window when the pool of white men entitled to vote was widened to include those whose only property consisted of the clothes on his back. But Carberry wasn't so progressive that he did not own slaves.

Thomas Blagden, the wealthy landowner in Anacostia who had advanced money so that Daniel Bell could redeem his wife and his youngest son, also served. So did Hamilton Loughborough, who lived on a lovely large estate in Tenleytown, just north of Georgetown, with seventeen slaves. They were joined by Evan Lyons, who operated a mill on Rock Creek that sat below a rise of land that reached up to Georgetown Heights. (Today's Rock Creek Parkway runs over the site of Lyons's mill.)

On June 28, the grand jury handed down a total of 330 indictments. Prosecutor Barton Key had fashioned the presentments to the jury so that each man was charged with thirty-six indictments for larceny, one for each of the thirty-six slave owners with passengers aboard the *Pearl*. Additionally, each of the three men was charged with seventy-four indictments for the illegal transportation of the *Pearl* fugitives, indicating that the number of fugitives had changed again. David Hall, the local attorney assisting the defense, had already alerted Mann that Key would be paid ten dollars for each indictment, the implication being that Key was fashioning the indictments to reap the largest possible fee. The defense now faced an impossible number of trials; they would make Key's financial interests in the indictments an ongoing issue in the trial.

The newspapers in the Baltimore and Washington area, with the exception of the antislavery *National Era,* expressed strong support for the prosecution. At the same time that the *Baltimore Sun* was praising the work of prosecutor Key, it published a shocking report from a missionary in Sierra Leone who had boarded a slave ship that had been captured in the illegal African trade. Sierra Leone, established in 1787 for the resettlement of free blacks from London and Nova Scotia— many of whom had sided with the British during the American Revolution on the promise of freedom—was used to resettle slaves taken from captured slave ships. Under the heading of "Horrors of the Slave Trade, etc.," the missionary reported that the "deck was literally covered with men, women and children, some lying down, some sitting, some standing. . . . Below were crowded two or three hundred, between floors not exceeding 2½ feet apart." Readers learned in startling detail how they were "crowded in as close as they can be jammed; the first row sitting on the floor with their backs against the side or end of the vessel, then another row sitting in the same way crowded close in between their legs. . . ."

The newspaper apparently saw no hypocrisy in American slave owners' breaking up families and selling human beings to the lucrative Southern market. That same issue of the *Baltimore Sun* carried the regular advertisements from slave traders Donovan and Campbell soliciting slaves. While the conditions on the ships leaving Baltimore for New Orleans were less abhorrent than those on the illegal African traders, loved ones were still wrenched from their families, young women were set up for exploitation, and human beings were bought and sold.

On July 3, 1848, the day the prisoners were arraigned, David Hall was guiding Mann through the intricacies and customs of the Washington court. Both men were expecting a continuance until the spring term, but Judge Crawford, the Pennsylvania-born judge who presided over all criminal trials, denied their request. The trial would begin in three weeks. The immediacy of the trial played hard on Drayton's nerves. The day of the arraignment, Hall sent an urgent note to Mann to tell him that Drayton "insists on seeing you this afternoon—his mind is much excited."

Mann soon had other serious problems. David Hall had withdrawn as counsel for the defense, and Salmon Chase was unable to extricate himself from legal commitments elsewhere. On July 20, Mann wrote to Howe in a panic. "Here I am alone, no one to help me investigate the case—a case of the greatest difficulty, range and complexity. I am nearly worn down." He told his friend that he was so desperate that he would "employ somebody here, at my own expense."

Mann complained to his wife that all of the Boston Committee, except Howe, are "abolitionists and they will not consent to have a lawyer employed in the case whom they do not like—abolitionially." He knew that a radical cocounsel would only hurt his clients and refused to allow it. Two days before the trial was to begin, a nervous Mann hired a carriage for one dollar and drove out to the country home of James Mandeville Carlisle, the highly respected local attorney who had represented the Bell family in their petitions for freedom. He found Carlisle bedridden with a colic, but the lawyer was willing to join the defense team. More help was on its way. On Sunday, July 23, the day before the trial was scheduled to begin, Richard Hildreth arrived in Washington to aid the defense and take careful notes on the proceedings with an eye to publishing a report on the case. Things were beginning to look up.

On July 27, in what would be the first of multiple trials, Drayton was charged with stealing two slaves with a value of one thousand dollars, belonging to Andrew Hoover. Mann immediately moved to consolidate the considerable number of indictments into one trial, and questioned why the prosecutor was receiving ten dollars for each indictment. An outraged Key denied that he had acted in any way to line his own pockets and informed Mann that there was a ceiling on the fees he could receive. Key maintained that the multiple indictments were warranted because this was a case of the "most horrid atrocity." Judge Crawford denied Mann's motion, even though he admitted it made sense. He told the defense attorneys that he lacked authority to order Key to consolidate the cases.

Barton Key had already played a personal role in the events following the capture of the *Pearl*. He had helped quell the mob in front of the *National Era* by reminding them that he, the city prosecutor, was no friend of the abolitionists. Key had been raised with slaves in the family. His father, Francis Scott Key, did free a family slave outright and allowed several others to purchase their freedom. In the U.S. Census for 1850, Barton Key is listed as owning three slaves and, unlike his father, there is no evidence that he ever manumitted any of them.*

In a hot, crowded courtroom, a jury was sworn in to try the case against Drayton for stealing Andrew Hoover's two slaves. It had been pulled together from the crowd around the courthouse and included men clearly hostile toward the captains. Many from that same crowd filed into the courtroom to watch the trial. Horace Mann noted that many of the very same men who had drawn a "dirk" on Drayton and cocked their pistols when the men had been paraded through the streets of Washington on their way to jail were right there in the courtroom, commenting loudly on the guilt of the defendants. Richard Hildreth reported that during breaks in the trial, the jury freely talked back and forth with the spectators.

Key opened the case against Drayton by arguing that the property rights of certain residents had been violated in a way that differed dramatically from most larcenies. In a unique and interesting analysis of the difficulty of protecting slave property, Key argued that "other

---

* Key was connected to another luminary in Washington's legal community. His uncle was Roger Brooke Taney, appointed to the Supreme Court in 1835, the same year his father was prosecuting the cases related to the Snow Riot. Taney was married to Francis Scott Key's sister.

kinds of property were protected by their want of intelligence; but the intelligence of this kind of property greatly diminished the security of its possession." Because slaves were human beings with intellects, the prosecutor seemed to be arguing, the theft was all the more grave, and he asked the jury to give the defendant the "most serious consequences."

Key called Andrew Hoover to take the stand as his first witness. The forty-seven-year-old shoe factory owner, worth a considerable $30,000 in real property, testified that as of 8:00 P.M. the two slaves in question, brothers named Joe and Frank, were in his possession and must have then left on their own, because there was no sign that the house had been broken into. He said that the brothers later told him that they had left the house about 10:00 P.M.

Joe and Frank were brought into the courtroom so that Hoover could identify them for the jury. Their owner testified that one drove a cart while the other served in the house. He had purchased their mother when the brothers were but one and two years old and said that he had raised them in his home.

Hoover also told the court that he had been offered $1,400 for his two servants but that he would not sell them for twice that amount. Drayton relates a different account. He said that Hoover did sell the men to the traders. But when his wife found out what he had done, she demanded that he buy them back, as they had been raised in their home and she did not want to part with them. With some relish, Drayton reported that Hoover did so at a financial loss.

The trial continued with testimony from justice of the peace and posse leader Hampton Williams, who recounted the details of the capture and added that he suspected that Drayton was "an agent of the 'underground railroad to freedom.'" Thomas Orme, the captain of the police guard in Georgetown, testified that Drayton had once been offered $400 by a Negro to take him north but that he had refused to do it. Orme gave testimony in regard to Drayton's naming the abolitionists that was somewhat conflicting. He first said that Drayton had told him that, if the slave owners would let him go or sign a petition for his release, he could give information that would lead them to the principals behind the escape. But Orme also testified that Drayton had told him that if his employers let his family suffer, then he might be willing to talk.

William Craig, another Georgetown constable, reported that when he asked Drayton if he would have been well paid had he succeeded, the captain replied yes and then Drayton asked Craig if he would be well paid for catching him.

Key argued that Drayton was planning to take the fugitives farther south to sell them for his own profit, pointing to the substantial provisions found onboard the schooner as evidence. But Drayton couldn't have taken the slaves farther south on an ocean route. Captain Baker of the *Salem* had testified that the captured schooner was "in a condition to go up the bay, and nowhere else." Key then maintained that a brig had been seen some two or three miles from where they found the *Pearl* in Cornfield Harbor, and it might have been waiting to take the slaves to Cuba. But that theory too fell apart when several members of the posse confirmed that the harbor was a common place of anchorage.

Key next attempted to paint Drayton as a slave trader. He brought in a witness from Baltimore who would testify that he had seen Drayton in the Camden Street slave pen of Joseph Donovan a year earlier. Key wanted that testimony to support his argument that Drayton had suggested to Donovan that he could pick up slaves who appeared to be runaways and, after a makeshift search for the true owners, the slaves could then be sold south to the profit of both. Key said that Donovan refused his dishonorable proposition. However, Judge Crawford ruled that the testimony was inadmissible.

Now it was Horace Mann's turn. He introduced himself to the jury as an "utter stranger" to them and wondered if there was any man in the "vast assembly who has any sympathy for my client or for me." He told them that the "fierce excitement" that had blazed at the time of the *Pearl*'s capture was still "hot" and that the "thronged spectators . . . [show] what their feelings are towards the prisoner and his defenders."

Mann held out the Boston Massacre to them as an example of American fairness. The British redcoats who had killed five Americans were defended by John Adams and Josiah Quincy. The Massachusetts jury, whose sympathies were with the men who were fired upon, acquitted the British because it was the right thing to do. Surely, a Washington jury could act just as fairly.

Mann argued that the prosecution had failed to prove the requisite elements of larceny. Without knowing that he was voicing a strongly held belief by slave owners, Mann pointed out that Joe and Frank could just as easily have been influenced to run away by free blacks, or even other slaves, who knew of the plan. Mann noted that a number of black Washingtonians could read. "[W]ho knows but some of them have read the Declaration of American Independence" and, he added slyly, "in their blindness and simplicity of mind, applied its immortal truths to themselves?" Coming dangerously close to the truth, he added that even white people who were hostile to slavery could have informed Joe and Frank that a schooner was down at the wharf; then the two men could have made their own decision to board the ship.

Mann began reading a document to the jury to which Judge Crawford objected only when he heard him read that "the age of tyrants and slavery is rapidly drawing to a close. . . ." While the spectators began shouting loudly in protest, an angry Crawford broke in to chastise Mann for bringing such inflammatory language into the courtroom. As James Carlisle, the local attorney, rose to support his co-counsel, the spectators fell "hushed to a grave-like silence." Carlisle called on "heaven to preserve American tribunals of justice from following the examples of the worst times of English judicial tyranny, when the basest minion of the crown were elevated to the bench. . . ."

A visibly upset Judge Crawford replied, somewhat confusingly, that he understood that Mann's argument was perfectly legitimate, but the inflammatory language was not. Key, as though cued by the defense, demanded that Mann identify the document he was reading. Mann happily replied that it was the speech given by the Honorable Henry Foote, of Mississippi, in honor of the democratic revolution in France that had been reprinted in the *Daily Union*, a proslavery newspaper. Crawford had to silence an outburst of laughter from the spectators before he could explain to Mann that Senator Foote had not meant for those words to apply to "our" slaves.

After arguments that cited the school days of Sir Walter Scott and Laurence Sterne's *Sentimental Journey*, written in 1768, Mann informed the jury that he would confess the worst of Drayton's crime. He admitted that Daniel Bell had requested Drayton's help because the heirs of the man who had freed his family were attempting to reenslave them. The heirs had rejected their emancipation, Mann explained to the jury, because "the living and dead have very different views on the subject of slavery." Mann explained that the Bells had told some of their friends who then told some of their friends and so on. As a result, while Drayton was away from the schooner, far more fugitives than were expected made their way into the ship's hold. Mann added that when the "slaves were ordered to come on deck after their capture, the prisoner was as much astonished as anybody at the number of fishes that had got into his net." It may have been a good defense but it was far off from the truth.

Mann's report of the trial does not mention that he might very well have created a dangerous situation for Daniel Bell. Fortunately, no attempt was made to charge Bell with aiding in the escape. Bell's employment records at the Navy Yard show that he missed work only for a short period in April, when he was making preparations to send his family on the risky journey to freedom. By May, Daniel Bell had returned to his normal schedule at the Navy Yard but for one change: his wages had been reduced from $1.20 to $1.12 per day.

Mann offered to put several of the *Pearl* fugitives on the stand for the purpose of showing that Drayton had not stolen them, but the offer was rejected. Judge Crawford explained that slaves could not be called as witnesses against whites in the District of Columbia. Drayton did not testify, but several character witnesses were called to the stand to speak on his behalf. Samuel Nelson, of Philadelphia, the keeper of a ship chandlery selling anchors and chains, testified that he had known Drayton for eighteen years, during the last two of which he had lived just 150 yards from the captain's home. Nelson stated that he had never heard anything against Drayton's moral character. On cross-examination, he was asked if he had ever heard people talk of Drayton's being involved in carrying away slaves from the South or stealing slaves. Nelson replied that they used to laugh about Drayton one day running away with a Negro, but, he quickly added, he had never heard that Drayton had done it.

In his closing argument, Key argued that it made no difference whether Drayton was stealing Hoover's slaves to liberate them or to sell them. He said the evidence established that Drayton knew they were slaves and had admitted that if he had succeeded he would have realized an independent fortune.

Horace Mann rose and pointed out that Drayton could well be a dead man before all of the trials would be finished. He stated that the prosecutor had spoken rudely both to him and about his client, when he referred to Drayton as "a liar, a thief, a felon, a wretch, [and] a rogue." He cautioned the jury to remember that the so-called confessions that Drayton made concerning the money he was to receive were made when he was surrounded by armed men and in perceived peril. He further cautioned them that the evidence failed to show that Drayton had enticed the slaves to go aboard the *Pearl*.

James Carlisle spoke next, and he also chastised Key for the language he used toward the defendant. Key heatedly replied that he had only used those words when addressing the jury, which is certainly allowed. It may be allowed, Carlisle acknowledged, but it was not in good taste. Carlisle argued that Judge Crawford's broad definition of slave stealing could cause unexpected results. He told the jury that he had found out that the best servant he had ever hired turned out to be a runaway slave. Under the definition of stealing before the jury, the lawyer pointed out, when he took his servant to Baltimore with him, he could have been charged with larceny.

At 10:00 A.M. on August 4, the jury reported that they still had not reached a verdict. After they were sent back to resume deliberations, Barton Key began Drayton's second trial, with a new jury, on the charge of stealing Harriet Queen and her fifteen- and nine-year-old daughters from grocer William H. Upperman. Unlike Hoover's two slaves, Queen and her daughters had been sold to slave dealer John Campbell and would not be brought into court.

While Major Williams, the leader of the posse, was testifying that he couldn't really remember if Drayton said that he would have made a fortune if the escape succeeded, the jury from the first trial returned with a verdict of guilty. After twenty-one hours, Mann explained to his wife the next day, the jurors who believed that Drayton was innocent of larceny had been convinced by the others that if they didn't agree to convict, they would lose all "patronage and custom in the city." But Mann believed that they had made a good record for appeal. For now, they had to continue with the second trial. Mann was becoming more and more dependent on the courtroom skills of the young and eloquent Carlisle.

As the second trial continued, Washington's sluggish heat again broke to give them a respite of a few cooler days. Bolstering Key's allegation that Drayton had seduced the slaves into leaving their masters, Upperman testified that on the evening of the escape, he had seen a man who looked like Drayton standing on the sidewalk opposite his house on Pennsylvania Avenue. He said that after he had retired to bed, he then heard Harriet Queen coming down the stairs in the house—she likely slept in slave quarters in the attic—but didn't suspect that she was about to run away. On August 8, Mann delivered a closing argument that lasted two and a half hours. The next day the verdict came in: guilty.

Satisfied with Drayton's two convictions, Barton Key scheduled his first case against Edward Sayres for August 10, on the same charge of slave stealing. Shortly before the trial began, Key announced that he had entered a *nolle prosequi* on all indictments against Chester English, which dismissed the charges against the emotional crewmate. But Key wasn't quite finished with him. English was called as a witness for the prosecution. He described the role he had unwillingly played in the escape and added that Sayres had been drinking before they had cast off to begin their journey down the Potomac River.

Sayres's trial went better than Drayton's. After complaints that some of the jurors in the earlier prosecutions had been drawn from "a class of loafers who frequent the courts for the sake of the fees," the U.S. marshal was instructed to expand the jury pool. After a three-day trial, it took only fifteen minutes for the jury to acquit Sayres on the charge of stealing Hoover's slaves.

Key next tried Sayres on the charge of stealing Upperman's slaves. The prosecutor, surprised that the first jury had acquitted Sayres, delivered a three-and-a-half-hour-long closing argument in the second trial. The correspondent for the *New York Tribune*—no more objective than the correspondent for the *Baltimore Sun*—described it as a "tissue of misrepresentation of law and facts from beginning to end, proving the District Attorney to be either a blockhead [or] stupid beyond any hope of redemption." He may have been right, however; the jury took only ten minutes this time to acquit Sayres.

A discouraged Key agreed to a deal where an impaneled jury would be presented with a summary of all the facts and would then dispose of the remaining larceny charges. After a short deliberation, it acquitted Sayres. A second jury was impaneled, but this time the jury considered the lesser charges of illegally transporting seventy-four slaves. With a charge that was virtually impossible to defend against, Sayres was quickly found guilty.

But the prosecutor refused to offer the same deal to Drayton. Crawford sentenced Drayton to ten years in jail for each of his two convictions of theft. A hearing on the appeal of those convictions was scheduled for the end of November before a three-judge panel made up of the civil judges on the court. There would be a respite from trial work while Mann and Carlisle, with the able aid of Richard Hildreth, prepared their arguments.

A Panic of Sympathy

When Mary, Emily, and Richard returned to Baltimore on the *Union*, attorney Jacob Bigelow was waiting to meet them to make sure that no mistake was made regarding Richard Edmonson's freedom. Unfortunately, there was nothing he could do for Mary and Emily. After Richard said his good-byes to his sisters, he set off with Bigelow to make his way back to Washington, and the sisters retraced their steps from the wharf to Joseph Donovan's slave pen under the watchful eye of a guard, now with only each other for comfort. They and the other fugitives of the *Pearl* hadn't been completely forgotten in Washington. On July 10, Senator John Hale introduced a petition from Winnebago County, Illinois, that prayed Congress would restore the brief freedom the fugitives had experienced during their escape. The petition was tabled, and nothing more came of it.

Unexpected solace appeared when their father and oldest sister, Elizabeth Brent, arrived. A small family reunion inside the cold and barren slave pen brought tears, solace, food, and news of family back in Washington and Maryland. Their father had to report that even with the help of William Chaplin and their good friend Paul Jennings, they had not been able to collect the extraordinarily high price demanded by the traders, and Joseph Bruin had no intention of selling

Mary and Emily for anything less than he could get on the New Orleans market.

Paul and Elizabeth spent the night in the slave pen. Elizabeth stayed with her sisters in the women's quarters, and their father was given a small, uncomfortable room directly above them. While it gave him comfort to see his daughters again, the visit brought home the horrors of what they had been through. The despair, discomfort, noise, and smell of the slave pen enveloped him. All night, through the floor in his room, he could hear his three daughters crying below. According to John Paynter's family history, Mary and Emily's father described that night in Donovan's pen to his family as "the most miserable of all his life."

Shortly after Paul Edmonson and Elizabeth left Baltimore, Joseph Donovan and Joseph Bruin ended their partnership, and Mary and Emily were abruptly returned to Bruin's pen in Alexandria. More than four months after they were captured, Mary and Emily were still enslaved and the threat of their being taken south again hung over them and their family. As before, the sisters washed clothes, cleaned the slave pen, performed other unpleasant tasks, and waited for help.

But at least one thing changed to relieve some of their misery. Bruin brought the sisters into his own comfortable home on the same block, where he lived with his wife, Martha; their two young daughters, seven-year-old Mary and four-year-old Martha; and his seventy-eight-year-old mother. Bruin made a very comfortable living in the slave trade, and his home would have reflected that. On the 1850 U.S. Census, Bruin reported owning real estate valued at $5,400. In the Bruin home, Mary and Emily performed household chores and looked after the two young girls. As always seemed to happen, Mary and Martha Bruin quickly became firmly attached to Mary and Emily.

But time was running out. The Edmonson family had done all they could do in their Washington community, and what sources for money that could be tapped by William Chaplin's appeals were exhausted.

They desperately needed a new approach and decided that Paul Edmonson would go to New York City with William Chaplin to help make a direct public appeal for the money.

Before they left for New York, they collected a number of statements to bolster their campaign. In a letter dated September 5, 1848, Joseph Bruin wrote that the sisters had been brought back from New Orleans only because he had been promised that the money to purchase them was forthcoming. Now that the father wished to appeal to the "liberality of the humane and the good" for help, and even though he was "on the very eve of sending them South the second time," Bruin stated that he would give them another chance. He would retain the girls for another twenty-five days, but only if Paul Edmonson could pay him $1,200 within fifteen days; at the end of the twenty-five days, the remaining $1,050 would be due. Bruin added that his patience was wearing thin. If the deadlines were not met, he told them, "we shall be compelled to send them along with our other servants." Bruin, who considered himself a man of culture, preferred the word *servant* to *slave*, as did the better class of people in the area.

Jacob Bigelow, who had escorted Richard from Baltimore to Washington to make sure he returned a free man, also wrote a letter to help the campaign. He said the letter's bearer, Paul Edmonson, has two daughters of "uncommon promise" with a "fine appearance," and that only the payment of $2,250 would save them from "a fate which the father and his family so much dread." Strongly implied, but not yet explicitly stated, was the suggestion that the girls would be sold for sexual purposes as "fancy girls." Bigelow added that the family was willing to sacrifice what little property and savings they had but even that was not enough. He was right. The proceeds from the sale of both the Edmonson farm and the Brent home in the city would fail to net enough money to purchase the girls.

Paul Edmonson also obtained a letter from the Reverend John Cook, the educator and minister who had been run out of Washington during the Snow Riot and was known to antislavery activists in the North from his year in exile. Cook appealed to "a humane and Christian public" to help the family. Dr. Harvey Lindsly, a respected white man in Washington who had signed off on John Brent's freedom some years before and Eveline Edmonson Ingraham's freedom just two years earlier, confirmed that Paul had two daughters held at Bruin & Hill. He wrote that of the sum needed to free the girls only a part had been raised in Washington, and they were now "compelled to appeal to the charitable elsewhere."

Paul Edmonson took the twelve-hour train ride to New York, where he was met by friends who took him directly to the New York office of the Foreign and American Anti-Slavery Society. While the antislavery activists began to circulate an appeal for money throughout New York, Edmonson was sent to meet with a number of ministers in the city.

On the recommendation of William Harned at the Anti-Slavery Society, Edmonson approached the Reverend James Pennington of the Shiloh Presbyterian Church. There was little doubt that Edmonson would be received sympathetically in this church: Pennington was a runaway slave from western Maryland. A year later Pennington published his own story, *The Fugitive Blacksmith*, in which he gave an account of his meeting with Paul Edmonson. He said that an "aged coloured man of tall and slender" form approached him with a face that revealed "anxiety bordering on despair." Even though the members of Pennington's church struggled to support themselves and many were attempting to collect money to free their own loved ones, the black Presbyterians of New York City were sufficiently moved by the older man's story that a collection brought in the significant amount of $50.

Many of the wealthier residents of the city were sympathetic but hesitated to contribute because of the unbelievably large sum of $2,250 that was being asked of them to free two young girls. The New York abolitionists realized that they had a problem and enlisted a "highly respectable lawyer" in Washington—surely Jacob Bigelow—to try to negotiate a lower price with Bruin. On September 12, 1848, the lawyer wrote to say that he had been trying to negotiate Bruin down to a more reasonable price from the very first but, after several interviews and an exchange of letters, the trader would not budge on his asking price. However, the lawyer added that he thought if $2,000 in cash could be quickly raised in New York, Bruin might accept it.

Before he closed, the lawyer added a more graphic assessment of what would happen to Mary and Emily if they were sent south again— a description he hoped would aid their cause and explain the high price Bruin demanded. "The truth is *their destination is prostitution!*" He added that anyone would be certain of this if they were to see Mary and Emily, because "they are of elegant form, and have very fine faces."

But the New York committee continued to meet resistance because of the high ransom. On September 25, 1848, William Chaplin wrote to tell the committee that Bruin refused to budge on the price he was asking for the sisters; but the Underground Railroad operative had come up with another idea. He suggested that they target the many churches of New York to help raise the money, emphasizing that they would be asking these churches to contribute money not just to save the lives of the two girls but to save them from being defiled. "If my suggestion meets with approbation," he wrote, the story of the Edmonson sisters would be the "best *missionary text* for New York ever put into the mouth of a moral man, who has a heart and tongue to denounce slavery." He advised the New York committee to pursue the plan with "cool determination" and tell "every church and congregation" that two Methodist girls are to be "sold for prostitution."

Next, they asked the New York Methodists to form a committee for what was becoming a religious campaign. The widely distributed stories that a Methodist church pew owner, Hope Slatter, had bought fugitives from the *Pearl* and that a Methodist minister, Henry Slicer, was friendlier to the slave trader than to the enslaved had embarrassed the

Methodists. Now they were being given an opportunity to show their better side.

The abolitionists felt they needed still more documentation to present to the Methodist ministers who were to meet on October 14, 1848, and Chaplin set out to enlist Methodist leaders in Washington to corroborate Mary and Emily's devotion to God, virginal purity, and good standing in the Methodist church. But on September 30, while he was still collecting letters, Bruin's deadline for receiving the complete payment of $2,250 expired, and he was now at liberty to send the girls with the next shipment. Chaplin wrote that he didn't think the girls would be sent south immediately, but he knew that there was no certainty as to when a shipment would leave. He pleaded with the committee to come up with at least $2,000 while he tried to find the remaining $250 in Washington. If needed, Paul Edmonson's farm could be encumbered with a loan for that amount. Chaplin again urged them to let every minister and church member in New York and Brooklyn know the importance of their campaign.

Chaplin collected a number of important letters in support of the sisters. On October 5, 1848, the Reverand Mathew Turner, the white minister who oversaw the Asbury Church at Eleventh and K Streets where the Edmonsons had worshipped (just as the Reverend Henry Slicer had done on an earlier occasion), wrote that Mary and Emily were "exemplary members of the Methodist Episcopal Church." He added that "up to the time of their leaving in the schooner *Pearl*, they bore irreproachable characters, and, as far as I can learn, have continued to do so up to the present date." He prayed "that the efforts of their friends may be crowned with success in securing their freedom"—and, he implied, maintaining their virginity.

Chaplin transmitted Turner's letter with one of his own. He reported that Eli Nugent, one of the leaders of Asbury, who had earlier preached with John Brent at Georgetown's Mt. Zion, could speak to the spiritual life of Mary and Emily because he had been the leader of their

Methodist study class at the church for nearly two years. He spoke in the "highest forms of their capacity, and of their uniform Christian deportment. All their friends and acquaintances bear the same uniform testimony."

Clearly, it was not enough that Mary and Emily were Methodists. Countless numbers of Methodist men and women were enslaved. Since the first Great Awakening in the late eighteenth century, Methodism had appealed to American's blacks, both free and enslaved. By the mid–nineteenth century, American black Methodists outnumbered European Methodists. But Mary and Emily Edmonson were two particularly devout young Methodists in imminent danger of being forced into a life of sin, and the New York ministers were being told that they had the power to prevent it. It was a rare opportunity, and New York activists hoped to make the most of it.

At a meeting of Methodist Episcopal Church leaders, a committee was formed to organize a public meeting "for the purpose of laying the matter of the Edmondson [*sic*] girls before the public" and book the Broadway Tabernacle for the sum of $50 for such a public rally on October 23, 1848. They also decided to publish "The Case of the Edmondson [*sic*] Sisters," a pamphlet that included a brief history of the family as well as copies of all the letters that had been collected in support of the sisters. At the end of the statement, the Methodists added that they had heard from their correspondent (undoubtedly William Chaplin) by letter dated October 16. He urged them to "[l]et the idea of rapid action be impressed upon the minds of all our friends. My only regret now is that your great meeting must be delayed for a week." To extend their appeal even further, the Methodist ministers reached out to ministers of other denominations to join them at the rally. Everything was in place; never before had the New York clergy come together so publicly in the aid of slaves.

But before the evening at the Tabernacle could take place, crisis struck. Mary and Emily's supporters had missed the deadline in getting the money to Bruin, and now that he was putting together a coffle to move overland to the South, the trader was planning to send Mary and Emily with it. He told the sisters to prepare for the overland trek. William Chaplin learned that they were to be part of a contingent of thirty-five slaves who would be moving out of the slave pen, and told his friends in New York that the traders had fitted up two teams of horses with provisions and a camp tent. They would be heading to Alabama or Mississippi, stopping on the way, as was the custom, "to sell, buy, or swap" slaves. "Gay calico was brought" in for the girls to sew into new dresses so that they would present well to any buyers they might encounter on the way. It was common for coffles to stop at plantations and at the Richmond auction houses to buy and sell. Bruin told Chaplin that he didn't want to send Mary and Emily out with the coffle, but he was embarrassed that the deadline had passed and he hadn't received the money as promised. Now his partner, Captain Henry Hill, who hadn't wanted to return the girls from New Orleans, was insisting that they be sent south.

When one of Bruin's daughters realized that Mary and Emily were preparing to leave on the coffle, she begged the two young women not to go. The sisters gently told her that it was not their choice; it was her father who was making them go. The tearful girl told them that she would make her father change his mind.

The night before the coffle was to leave, Mary broke down weeping. Emily attempted to comfort her, but she also knew that if they were sent south this time there was little chance they would ever return home again. At that point, Bruin entered the slave quarters, and Mary and Emily pleaded with him not to put them on the coffle. Mary threw herself on her knees, begging him to let them stay. Knowing that his daughter had returned home to plead their case with her father, Mary pointedly asked him how he would feel if his daughter were being sent away.

The next morning, as Bruin was preparing for the coffle to leave, Mary crouched in agony in a corner of the slave quarters while Emily looked out a small window overlooking the yard in the rear of the

Alexandria slave pen, watching the line form in the yard, the men assembled two by two in the front followed by the women and children stretched out in a similar way behind them. They could hear the sounds of the fiddle and banjo already beginning to play. The music would set the pace for the walk, and the slaves would likely be ordered to sing.

As the gates of the prison complex swung open, the coffle began to move slowly forward. Emily tensely watched as the end of the line passed out from the yard and the gates began to close behind them. She screamed to her sister that they were saved. The coffle had headed out without them.

William Chaplin and other supporters had come up with a new proposal that saved the girls at the last minute. They offered to pay Bruin a $600 deposit, which would be forfeit if they failed to produce the balance of the purchase price by a new deadline. Bruin readily agreed. He could now make a handy bonus in addition to what he would still be able to sell the sisters for in New Orleans if they couldn't raise the money, and it seemed more and more unlikely that they would ever be able to do it.

According to a report later published in the *Salem (OH) Anti-Slavery Bugle,* the major portion of that money was secured by one of Mary and Emily's brothers-in-law, very likely John Brent, using his house as security to borrow money that was added to what they had been able to collect from family and friends in the city. Some years later, Congressman Giddings wrote that he had been approached by one of Mary and Emily's brothers and asked to contribute money for his sisters' freedom. As Giddings recalled it, this encounter happened before the escape attempt. However, there is no evidence that any attempt had been made to raise money to free the sisters before they boarded the *Pearl.* It is far more likely that it occurred at the time the family was attempting to raise the $600 to keep Mary and Emily from being taken south with the coffle.

Chaplin sent a letter to supporters in New York to tell them the girls had been saved again, adding a startlingly new encomium from the slave trader. "Bruin gives the girls the very highest character," and believes that "they are equal to any white girls, let them be who they may." Bruin told him "[I]f there is a *real Christian* upon earth, he believes Mary Edmondson [*sic*] is one."

The Methodists were able to attract a number of clergymen from outside their own church. The Reverand John Dowling, D.D., a highly respected Baptist clergyman and scholar agreed to attend the public meeting at the Broadway Tabernacle. So did Congregationalist preacher Henry Ward Beecher. Beecher had been approached personally by Paul Edmonson, who had taken the Fulton Ferry at the foot of Manhattan to see the still new but increasingly popular preacher at the Plymouth Church in Brooklyn. Beecher found the older man sitting on the steps of his home, brought him inside to listen to his story, and then accepted his invitation. Meanwhile, the organizers from the Anti-Slavery Society were widely distributing the story of the Edmonson sisters throughout the city to encourage attendance at the rally.

On the evening of October 23, the two-thousand-seat Broadway Tabernacle at Thirty-fourth Street was filled to capacity with an excited crowd primed to hear of the lovely young women who were about to be forced into prostitution. Dr. Dowling began with an impressive speech "replete with noble feeling and impressive points." But it was Henry Ward Beecher who shook the people to their very souls and transformed the gathering into an uproarious revival meeting. He also transformed himself that night into a powerful leader in the antislavery cause.

Since his ordination in 1837 and his first posting to Indiana, the son of Lyman Beecher, one of the country's most famous and controversial preachers, had taken caution to an extreme in his reluctance to take a stand on slavery. Even when directed by his synod in Indiana to do so, Beecher had equivocated.

Neither was Beecher's famous father active in the antislavery movement, though he recognized that slavery was wrong. But on his list of wrongs to right, slavery fell well below his war with the Catholic Church and Unitarianism, a belief that had crept into Boston despite Beecher's fierce resistance. When William Lloyd Garrison attempted to enlist him in his fight for immediate emancipation shortly after he was released from jail in Baltimore, the prominent minister told him he already had too many irons in the fire. Now Henry had found a cause that would make him even more famous than his difficult and eccentric father, a man who had enthusiastically applied corporal punishment to his children, banned Christmas celebrations and secular books, and, in a lighter moment, dangled his young daughter out of an attic window by her arms.

A restless Henry Ward Beecher began to look beyond Indiana at a time when rumors were circulating that a number of female congregants were becoming inordinately close to the married preacher. In June 1847 the thirty-four-year-old Beecher traveled to New York to successfully "audition" for the position of minister at the new Congregationalist Plymouth Church forming across the river in Brooklyn.

Once settled there, Beecher soon came under the influence—and charms—of Lewis Tappan's passionately antislavery daughter, who was married to one of the church's financiers. As she and Beecher became closer, he finally began to speak out against slavery. The story of Mary and Emily Edmonson touched him more than any discussion of the three million enslaved people spread across the South had ever done. At the Tabernacle, he looked out over the packed pews and told the rapt audience that "we have not come here to discuss the general question of slavery." He said "whatever we may believe in relation to the general subject of slavery, we shall all be of one mind in relation to the fact which has called us together tonight. It is a plain question of humanity, and will admit of but one answer."

Beecher acknowledged that the amount of money being asked for

Mary and Emily was exorbitantly large and said he wished it were less. And he knew that some of them wondered whether they would now be asked to buy every slave who was put on the market. But this case was so unparalleled that they had to respond. "I should be ashamed if it were written down, that such an assembly was gathered here of more than two thousand souls . . . and the poor pittance of $2,000 could not be raised." He was saving souls now, ones that were endangered by slavery.

That night, Beecher—with hair flowing longer than was fashionable and an outfit that looked more appropriate for the western frontier—found a voice that would propel him to the forefront of the antislavery movement, however erratic his activism would be. With the passion of a convert, Beecher offered up a hue and cry that was as much about salvation from prostitution—a subject to which he had always allotted a good deal of attention—as it was about slavery. "A sale by human flesh dealers of Christian girls!" he exhorted the audience. Beecher looked around him and, pointing to a venerable Methodist, told the excited crowd, "I know no names of Baptist, Methodist or Presbyterian. I know men and Christians; that is all I know." And then he acknowledged Paul Edmonson, saying that he had seen this old man and "he seemed to me just as good at grief as any other, and it struck me that if he was black he seemed, after all, to act very naturally for a distressed father."

Beecher asked them to put themselves in Edmonson's situation and envision their own daughters in bondage. "Suppose them so comely," he continued, "that no price less than $3,000 would purchase them. Suppose this, and act as you would act then!" Again, drawing their attention to Edmonson, Beecher said that "his sons are long ago sold as slaves to labor on Southern plantations. His daughters, unless we can do something to detain them, must go too, to a worse fate. But I trust in God and I trust in you that it shall not be heard from New York that an appeal like this was not [sic] made in vain, and that you will make it heard that these girls, must not, shall not, be slaves—they shall be free."

An observer reported that, after Beecher spoke, the people in the pews were visibly shaken. The collection basket was passed around twice. Beecher had seen to it that the crowd was determined not to leave the Tabernacle that night until all money had been raised to protect the purity of these two young women. So the basket was called for again. This time, men emptied their pockets and women tore off jewelry, while others shouted out pledges of money. A resounding cheer went up when it was announced that they had raised enough money to free Mary and Emily.

Beecher later said that "of all the meetings I have attended in my life, for a panic of sympathy I never saw one that surpassed that." A correspondent for the *Rochester North Star* who was in the Tabernacle paid Beecher the ultimate compliment. She wrote that Beecher "in sentiment and witty sarcasm, reminded me of our own incomparable [Frederick] Douglass." Thanks to Mary and Emily Edmonson, Henry Ward Beecher had become another star on the firmament of the antislavery circuit. And thanks to Beecher, the sisters were nearly home free. The people in the Broadway Tabernacle lingered together that night, delighted that they had been a part of such a rally. It was a badge of honor to have been at the Broadway Tabernacle that night.

When the celebrants had left and the money was counted, the organizers were horrified to discover that they had not collected the full amount needed to free Mary and Emily. There may have been some confusion over what was pledged and what was received. The *New York Evangelist* reported that they were short $825, while the *New York Tribune* set the figure closer to $300. The *Christian Advocate and Journal* gave the most detailed report. It reported that $656.33 in cash had been collected along with pledges of $908.50.

Word of the spectacular evening at the Tabernacle spread and no one wanted to spoil the memory of the night when New Yorkers saved two young virtuous Methodist slaves. The *National Era* reported that they "rejoice to hear of the success of these efforts," adding that "[t]he family of Edmonson are highly esteemed, and their case has greatly interested some of the citizens of this place."

Nearly the entire sum needed to free Mary and Emily was made up by collections taken in Methodist churches across New York City and even in Jersey City, New Jersey. Short just $47.77, the committee accepted a donation in kind from Buell & Blanchard, the Washington printer of the *National Era*. They donated two thousand copies of a pamphlet containing important congressional speeches, which could be sold to make up the shortfall.

Paul Edmonson, William Chaplin, and the rest of the support committee were enormously relieved with the success of their fundraising venture, and the Methodist clergy were pleased that they had gone a long way to redeem some portion of the church's reputation. William Lloyd Garrison was happy that the efforts to free Mary and Emily had succeeded, but felt the need to temper their self-satisfaction. "While we should be sorry to turn aside from them one drop of sympathy, we claim for one and a half million of their sex, who are this day, in this land exposed to all to which they were exposed; we claim for them at least equal sympathy and equal efforts for their deliverance."

On November 2, William Chaplin wrote to Gerrit Smith from New York, noting that he was about to leave for Washington and that he hoped to see Mary and Emily freed from Bruin's pen no later than the following Monday. He told Smith that the "result of this effort has been most happy upon this city community." Chaplin's letter revealed that he was as much involved in the Underground Railroad in Washington as he had ever been. He told Smith of a large number of people who needed help, including forty people in Hagerstown, Maryland, and a young man who had been on the *Pearl* and was now in a Baltimore slave pen.

Paul Edmonson returned by train to Washington with Chaplin, and, with as little delay as possible, the two men made their way to Alexandria. When they arrived at Bruin's slave pen, the sisters were sewing near a window in the trader's home. Emily looked out and caught sight of "that white man we have seen from the North." As she quickly alerted Mary, both girls looked out and realized the white man was not alone. Their father was with him. Mary and Emily ran shouting through the house into Bruin's office and then out to the street with the trader chasing after them. They flew into their father's arms and begged to know if he had the money to free them. He gently asked them to go back in and wait while he and Chaplin met with Bruin.

Before the slave trader prepared the bill of sale that would transfer the girls' ownership to William Chaplin, he had a complaint to register. Bruin had been hurt that Henry Ward Beecher had spoken ill of slave traders without making an exception of him. He said that he had surely shown more care and more humanity than most any other slave trader would have done under the same circumstances. He would have some corroboration from Harriet Beecher Stowe a few years later. She described Bruin as a "man of very different character from many in his trade" and added that he had treated the Edmonson sisters "with as much kindness and consideration as could possibly consist with the design of selling them." When Bruin received his money, he handed over the following bill of sale:

Received of W. L. Chaplin twenty-two hundred and fifty dollars, being payment in full for the purchase of two negroes, named Mary and Emily Edmondson [sic]. The right and title of said negroes we warrant and defend against the claims of all persons whatsoever; and likewise warrant them sound and healthy in body and mind, and slaves for life.

Given under our hand and seal, this seventh day of November, 1848. $2,250 BRUIN & HILL. (Seal.)

While Chaplin and Paul Edmonson were finalizing the sale—for they were in fact purchasing the sisters—the girls were impatiently waiting to find out if they were truly free. According to Paynter's book, the messenger of very good news was one of the young Bruin girls, who ran up to them, clasped a hand of each sister, and cried out, "You're free at last! You're free at last!" Emily literally jumped for joy, and both girls shouted, clapped their hands, and embraced their father in relief.

The sisters said good-bye to the Bruin daughters and even managed a cordial good-bye to Bruin, who, determined to show that he was a kind man, took two $5 gold pieces from the money he had just been paid and pressed one in each girl's hand.

Paul Edmonson splurged on a carriage, and they set off across the Potomac River to John and Elizabeth Brent's home in Washington, where family and friends were waiting for them. That evening, Chaplin sent a telegram to New York City that simply said, "Thank God! Mary and Emily Edmonson are free!"

According to an abolitionist newspaper, the next day Chaplin went to city hall and executed a formal deed of manumission in which, for the consideration of one dollar and the claims of "humanity, justice, and republican freedom, and Christian brotherhood," he freed "the sisters Mary Jane and Emily Catherine Edmonson, daughters of Paul Edmonson, and they are hereby, each of them, declared forever free from any and all restraint or control." The manumission document was witnessed by H. Naylor, a justice of the peace who had also witnessed the freedom of the Bell family that had been overturned in court. Chaplin further acknowledged that the manumission was "his free act and deed, and the negro girls therein named to be henceforth free, manumitted, and discharged from all persons and claims whatsoever."

For the first time in their lives, Mary and Emily belonged to no one but themselves. They could hardly be the same young women who had walked through a darkened city to board a small schooner. Yet, through seven months of uncertainty and dreadful living circumstances, Mary and Emily's faith stood steadfast. The journey on the *Pearl*, in the end, did bring them freedom, though the majority of the fugitives onboard were not so fortunate. The two young women would not forget their brothers and the others from the *Pearl* who were sold south to join a vast sea of slaves that would number nearly four million by the outbreak of the Civil War.

SEVEN

More Legal Maneuvers; the Sisters Head North

The legal maneuvers in Washington were far from over. In late November, hearings began on Daniel Drayton's appeal of his larceny convictions. Arguments were held before judges William Cranch, James Morsell, and James Dunlop, the three men who comprised the District of Columbia Circuit, which heard civil trials in the jurisdiction and also sat as an appellate body for criminal cases. Richard Hildreth of the Boston support committee was ready to open the arguments for the defense. Barton Key, whom Drayton, sounding very much like Hildreth, later described as "better fitted to bawl to a jury than to argue before a court," was representing the District of Columbia with the assistance of Joseph Bradley, Samuel Edmonson's former employer and the attorney for the City of Washington. The man who had represented the Bells in their legal quest for freedom was now arguing to convict the captain who had participated in an illegal plan to free them.

More than a week was taken up with the large number of errors Drayton's lawyers claimed were committed. James Mandeville Carlisle, the local attorney representing Daniel Drayton, presented arguments on behalf of the defense along with Horace Mann and Richard

Hildreth. Mann had become increasingly impressed by Carlisle, describing him to his wife as "a young man, rather small but beautiful, dignified and gentlemanly . . . of Irish descent and full of Irish fire." Hildreth was less impressed; he said Carlisle was a "little too apt to wander from the matter immediately at hand," while arguing the case to the jury, but admitted that he was "partly well satisfied at the position in which the case was left."

Hildreth argued that Judge Crawford's legal definition of larceny was "rotten," unsupported by a single adjudged case in any book, and even contrary to "the whole course of Southern legislation." Apparently, Judge Crawford took the comments personally, because Hildreth later clarified that his words were meant only for the instructions and not for the judge. Horace Mann added that the servitude of the fugitives had not been proved, and therefore they could not be stolen any more than someone could be charged with stealing a fox. While Mann was presenting his case, Barton Key passed him a few lines of doggerel that he had just scribbled, which ended "Pursuing hounds say he's mistaken, at least so far as to the taking." When Mann finished his argument and read Key's verse, he flipped the paper over and responded in kind. His ended with:

> *Foxes do not eat foxes—brute natures have bounds,*
> *But Mr. District Attorney, out-hounding the hounds,*
> *Hunts men, women, and children, his pocket to fill,*
> *On three hundred indictments, at ten dollars a bill.*

The arguments concluded in mid-December, and the circuit court announced that it would need at least a fortnight to deliberate. There was still the possibility of more trials against Drayton—Sayres's cases were settled—and, while they waited for the court's decision, another fund-raising appeal was sent out by the Boston Committee. Lewis Tappan responded that he had not sent money for the men's defense because he felt an obligation "to aid some of the poor colored people who took passage in the *Pearl,* also those who took an interest in helping them to asylum, and likewise the family of Drayton." Tappan, who had earlier advised the committee to take a lesson from how he had raised money to assist the legal fund for the mutineers of the slave ship *La Amistad,* pointed out how "the New Yorkers took up the case of the Edmonson girls," and asked, "why did not the Bostonians act as promptly and efficiently . . . ?"

On February 19, 1849, in a decision that took Judge Cranch nearly four hours to deliver, the court struck down Judge Crawford's broad definition of larceny in a 2–1 vote. The court held that to make a charge of larceny stand, the district attorney would have to prove that Drayton had profited in some way. Judge Dunlop cast the dissenting vote, though he should not have been allowed to serve on the panel, because his wife's sister and her aunt each owned two fugitives on the *Pearl.* It is not surprising that he voted against overturning Drayton's conviction. However, Drayton still had more charges pending against him.

Meanwhile, opposition to Washington's ongoing slave trade continued to build. The *Independent,* a new antislavery newspaper in which Henry Ward Beecher would express an increasingly radical voice, weighed in. "Recent events, especially those connected with the affair of the sale and redemption of . . . the Edmonson family, have greatly aroused the public mind with regard to the atrocities of the trade in human beings, now greatly carried on at Washington City."

In December 1848 Rep. Daniel Gott, of New York, offered a resolution asking the Committee for the District of Columbia to report a bill prohibiting the slave trade in the District. Gott argued for the bill on the grounds that "the traffic now prosecuted in this metropolis of the Republic in *human* beings, as chattels is contrary to natural justice and the fundamental principles of our political system, and is notoriously a reproach to our country." As Horace Mann waited for a decision from the three-judge panel, he worked to support Gott's resolution. A Southern congressman attempted to swat the resolution away with the usual motion that it be laid on the table to end further discussion. But this time it didn't work. By a vote of 85–82, his motion failed; and, to the alarm of the slave power, after lengthy and contentious discussion, the resolution was adopted on a vote of 98 to 87, which meant that the resolution would be sent to the Committee of the District of Columbia instructing them to prepare a bill banning the slave trade.

The coverage of the fugitives of the *Pearl* being paraded through the streets of the District of Columbia to be jailed and then sold to traders, and the widely circulated story of the railroad car of fugitives saying good-bye to their loved ones as they waited to be transported to Hope Slatter's slave pen in Baltimore, appears to have contributed to a change of heart in a number of congressmen. On January 31, 1849, a bill to end the slave trade in the capital was introduced in the House.

Angry Southern legislators immediately called for a separate session of their own—closed to members of the press—to consider ways of preventing Northerners from trampling on the Constitution by banning the slave trade in the nation's capital, which is how they viewed such legislation. Threats of disunion became louder and the opponents of the bill successfully tabled it. On February 23, 1849, as the congressional session was coming to an end, a frustrated Horace Mann rose to speak. He said that a "bill was introduced into the House to abolish the domestic slave trade in the District of Columbia—here in the center and heart of the nation—and seventy-two representatives . . . voted to lay it on the table, where, as we all know it would sleep a dreamless sleep." After describing the horrors of the now-banned African slave trade, Mann claimed that "[b]y authority of Congress, the city of Washington is the Congo of America."

Abraham Lincoln, who had consistently supported the Wilmot Proviso to ban slavery from the new territories, voted against the bill to end the slave trade—most likely because he was at work drafting his own legislation to end slavery in the capital. Lincoln's plan provided for a system of gradual emancipation, which had ended slavery across much of the North, but then added financial compensation for the owners who would lose their slave property. He also added that any such program would first have to receive the consent of the white voters of the District of Columbia. In January 1849, Lincoln's bill was read on the floor of Congress and published in the *Congressional Globe*, but it found such little support that he quietly withdrew it from circulation. It found even less support among the radical abolitionists.

To the surprise of Horace Mann, District Attorney Key exercised his option to prosecute the remaining larceny indictments even though the first two convictions had been overturned. The committee confessed that it had no funds to continue paying James Carlisle for the ongoing trial work. Wendell Phillips, a charismatic and powerful Garrisonian, stepped in to help by combining Samuel Gridley Howe's report on his visit to Daniel Drayton with Richard Hildreth's summary of the trials to produce a pamphlet that could be used to solicit funds for the defense work. Phillips sent the material to George Thompson, one of Britain's leading antislavery advocates, and it was published in England under Dr. Howe's name. That appeal may have helped retain Carlisle's services.

Then Horace Mann, weary from the repeated trials and anxious to turn his full attention to his congressional work, informed the Boston Committee that he wished to withdraw as legal counsel. The Boston Committee urged him to stay on, and Carlisle clearly agreed, writing to Mann that for all his "bitter anti-abolitionist feelings," he would very much regret losing the case. Mann stayed.

At the conclusion of the next larceny case against Drayton, the jury came back with a verdict of not guilty in less than thirty minutes, and Mann expected the prosecutor to drop the remaining indictments, just as he had done with Sayres. But Key would not give up; he scheduled yet another trial on larceny charges. But this time, he turned the prosecution over to General Walter Jones, one of the most respected members of the Washington bar.

Drayton's fourth trial began on May 12, 1849. Jones was a far more formidable opponent than Key. He called Edward Sayres as a witness. Sayres testified that the *Pearl* was taking the fugitives out of Washington but that strong winds had prevented him from sailing up the Chesapeake. But General Jones did no better than Key; Drayton was again acquitted. Key finally saw no point in more trials. He agreed to drop all of the outstanding larceny indictments in return for Drayton's pleading guilty to seventy-four charges of the illegal transportation of slaves.

When Drayton and Sayres returned to Judge Crawford's court to be sentenced, the judge made it clear he believed that others above Drayton and Sayres were "acting under the garb of philanthropy" to orchestrate a massive attempted escape. Nonetheless, he said, the two men before him would have to pay for their crimes. Edward Sayres was fined $100 for each of the seventy-four counts of illegally transporting fugitives, totaling $7,400, plus costs. Drayton, who was considered the more complicit of the two, was fined $140 for each fugitive, totaling $10,060, plus costs. Crawford allowed as how he had reduced Drayton's fine from $150 per fugitive because he had been incarcerated for a year. It was an improbable sum to collect, particularly in light of the fact that the Boston defense committee had barely been able to raise enough money to pay Carlisle's retainer of $500 and cover Mann's and Hildreth's costs. Both men would have to remain in jail until the fines were paid. It seemed hardly to matter that they had been acquitted on the larceny charges. In Philadelphia, Charles Cleveland was continuing to solicit support for the families but with little success. Cleveland sent out one appeal hoping to collect $300.00 but netted only $132.25.

In the midst of Drayton's trials, the property-holding white men of America were preparing to elect a new president. Both parties—Democratic and Whig—were exhibiting deep rifts. In the summer of 1848 antislavery factions arrived at their respective party's conventions determined to craft a platform that would ban slavery from all of the territory recently acquired after the Mexican War. Proslavery forces were determined to extend slavery into those territories as far as possible.

Senator John Calhoun, the powerful Whig from South Carolina, former vice president, and leading defender of the Southern way of life, had followed his party's line and even had spoken out forcibly against the Mexican War. But his reasons were very different from those of the Conscience Whigs. Calhoun feared the South might well lose the all-important battle over the extension of slavery into the newly acquired lands and then end up outvoted. But the war had been waged and won, and the issue of whether that land would be slave or free was becoming more and more heated. Calhoun now argued that slave owners had joint property rights in the newly acquired territory and consequently were entitled to settle it with any property they should choose to take with them, including slaves. If Congress banned slavery in the new lands, Calhoun threatened, the South had only one other card to play: disunion.

The deep rifts among the Democrats became permanent cracks at their respective party conventions. The New York Barnburners, furious that a rival faction of Democrats was seated at the national convention, lived up to their nickname and bolted the party. At the Whig convention in early June, the delegates nominated recent war hero Zachary "Rough and Ready" Taylor, a political neophyte who owned some hundred slaves scattered over several plantations in Louisiana and Mississippi. The party that had opposed the war with Mexico had turned to a slave-owning war hero as a way to appeal to Southern voters. The best that candidate Taylor could offer on the question of whether slavery should be extended to the territories was a promise that he would sign whatever legislation Congress passed. The antislavery Conscience Whigs were now in the same predicament as the antislavery Democrats, and they too were ready to bolt.

Salmon Chase and the Free-Soil Party were waiting for them, and a convention was already scheduled to be held in August in Buffalo, New York. During the same spring that he had been asked to represent Captains Drayton and Sayres, Chase was spearheading a party that would bring together people of all political stripes as long they supported a ban on slavery in the new territories. That would include a large segment of white voters whose prime concern was eliminating slave labor from the territories. Unfortunately, many of them wanted to eliminate free blacks as well.

The Wilmot Proviso had managed to pass the House of Representatives by then, but not the Senate, which still had sufficient votes from Southern senators and sympathetic Northern senators to block it. But it remained a vivid reminder to Calhoun and his followers that their only strength rested in maintaining that balance of power, which meant extending slavery. If slavery was banned from the new territories, the free states that would come out of those territories would outweigh the slave power, which would then be unable to protect Southern interests. On July 24, just days before Drayton's first trial began in Washington, a Free-Soil organizational meeting packed Baltimore's Union Hall. Given the anomaly of a Free-Soil Party in the slave state of Maryland, the organizers crafted their resolution very carefully to make sure the slave owners of Maryland were not directly threatened. It proclaimed that "[w]hatever may be the evils [of slavery]—and they are too palpable to be denied—it is for her own people to say how and when they shall be removed. . . ." Virginia followed with a Free-Soil convention in the largely Quaker-populated town of Waterford on August 20, 1848.

Nearly fifteen thousand excited delegates came together at the national Free Soil convention in Buffalo. In addition to David Wilmot and Salmon Chase, new converts to the party included Joshua Giddings, Charles Sumner, and Charles Francis Adams, the son of former president John Quincy Adams. Giddings had changed in the four years since the last election, when he had enthusiastically supported the candidacy of slave owner Henry Clay, who lost to Democrat James Polk.

No longer would he support a presidential candidate who owned slaves. Four months earlier, he had faced a riotous crowd at the D.C. jail, received death threats at his boardinghouse, and been physically jostled on the floor of the House by a particularly angry Southerner, all because he supported ending slavery in the District of Columbia. At the convention, Giddings exhorted the inflamed crowd that the political conflicts were now "between slavery and freedom."

But not all antislavery Whigs agreed: Abraham Lincoln, a moderate who continued to favor compensated and gradual emancipation; Thaddeus Stevens, a radical who wanted to end slavery immediately; and Horace Mann, whose maiden speech in Congress was an attack on slavery, remained committed to work within the Whig Party. The Free-Soil meeting, held in Newton, Massachusetts, supported Mann even if he remained a Whig because he was "heartily co-operating with us in the pending struggle between the antagonistic forces of Freedom and Slavery."

The Free-Soilers nominated former Democratic president Martin Van Buren to head the ticket and selected Charles Francis Adams to balance it as his running mate. In the end, the new party failed to carry a single state, and General Zachary Taylor, the Whig candidate, won the election. However, the new party made its mark in Congress. Salmon Chase was elected to the U.S. Senate from Ohio, along with thirteen congressmen, a strong swing block that abolitionist Joshua Leavist hailed as standing for "Free soil, Free speech, Free labor, and Free men." The year 1848 saw the end of the era when both the Democrats and the Whigs could appeal to voters across the North/South divide. Slavery had emerged as an issue that could not be ignored at party conventions or in party platforms. The Free-Soil Party may not have made a strong showing in the presidential run of 1848, but its platform would soon become the base of a new party, the Republican Party.

Broadway Tabernacle Revisited

In late November, Mary and Emily Edmonson made preparations to travel to New York with William Chaplin and their father. Chaplin wrote his friend Gerrit Smith in Peterboro, New York, to tell him that he was coming north with the sisters, who were to appear at a second rally at the Broadway Tabernacle. Chaplin urged Smith to come into the city to witness it. Henry Ward Beecher, Chaplin told Smith, "is in exercise at the thought" of participating at a rally that would present the very young women he had helped to redeem from slavery.

In Chaplin's ever-evolving plan to shake the North out of its complacency toward slavery, he touted the redemption of Mary and Emily as the beginning of an important new campaign. "This case has excited extraordinary interest in New York," he told Smith, "and has done and will do more for the antislavery cause" than anything that had come before. The Edmonson sisters will demonstrate to the North "what sort of people are the victims of the slave traders in the Nation's Capital." The more immediate purpose for the rally was to ask the people who had contributed to the sisters' freedom to step forward to fund their education.

Mary and Emily's journey to New York put them on free soil for the first time in their lives—and in the largest city in the United States. New York City's population was just under half a million people, more than ten times the population of Washington and four times that of New Orleans. The sisters saw no slave coffles in the streets of New York and the black people around them answered to no local masters. New York City's black community had deep roots going back to the days of the city's founding by the Dutch. Slavery had been unrestricted until 1799, when New York instituted a system of gradual emancipation in which children born to slaves would be freed after twenty-five years of slavery. In 1827 the state finally declared that all persons, black or white, born at any time in New York were free.

But not all of New York's blacks were technically free. Like the Reverend James Pennington, the Presbyterian minister from western Maryland, many were runaway slaves and kept a careful watch on strange white men looking at them. Most Northern states had devised their own laws to make it more difficult for slave traders to apprehend an owner's missing property, but runaways were still recaptured and taken away. And while the black New York community was free, prejudice was rampant and job opportunities were limited. Like most states in the North, what public education was offered to blacks was inferior and segregated. Black leaders in Boston were suing to integrate the schools in their city, while Frederick Douglass was fighting the shameful treatment of his daughter in the schools of Rochester, New York.

It's unlikely that Paul Edmonson could have prepared Mary and Emily for the noises, smells, and excitement of a New York that had exploded in size within the past twenty years. With the construction of the Erie Canal, which linked New York City to points farther west, and the ongoing arrival of immigrants filling its tenements, New York was a bustling, crowded, and still growing economic center.

Before the public rally, Mary and Emily had been able to see a cross section of the city as Chaplin took them on a triumphant round of visits to meet the New York ministers who had sponsored the first rally at the Tabernacle. These same powerful spiritual leaders had been asked to support the upcoming rally, and Chaplin knew that a meeting with the sisters would only make them more committed to raising additional sums of money.

On December 7, Mary and Emily stood inside the Broadway Tabernacle with Henry Ward Beecher, who was eager to lead a second campaign on their behalf. With the Tabernacle nearly filled by many of the same people who had contributed to Mary and Emily's redemption, Beecher began by congratulating them for their earlier support. Through their generosity, he told them, Mary and Emily Edmonson "are here with us FREE." Beecher revisited the slave trade in Washington, D.C., with new information received from the gentlemen involved in the rescue of the sisters. William Chaplin had clearly passed on more stories related to the escape of the *Pearl*. Touching on the attempted sale of Mary Ellen Stewart, Beecher recounted how ruffians in the nation's capital on occasion attempted to seize young women at public water pumps to spare their owners the sight of a struggle.

MARY AND EMILY EDMONSON

After incarceration in the D.C. jail and slave pens in three different states, the teenaged Mary and Emily Edmonson (previous page) likely had this daguerreotype taken along with their mother Amelia's (left) when they met in New York in 1852 to enlist Harriet Beecher Stowe's help in freeing the two youngest siblings.

Amelia's eldest daughter, Elizabeth, and son-in-law John Brent, who helped raise money to free Mary and Emily, were leaders in Washington's black community and were involved in establishing both Asbury (United) Church and John Wesley A.M.E. Church.

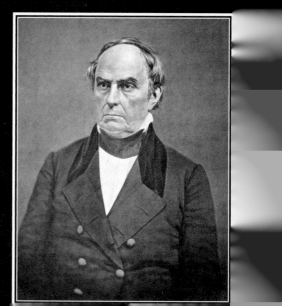

Former first lady Dolley Madison (above right) executed a bill of sale to Pollard Webb (above left) for family slave Paul Jennings, who is said to have helped plan the *Pearl* escape.

Senator Daniel Webster bought Jennings from Pollard, freed him, and then executed a contract whereby Jennings, his new butler, worked off his purchase price.

Two white men of very different backgrounds came together to plan the attempted escape from Washington. Daniel Drayton (top), the sea captain from a hardscrabble family, spent more than four years in prison for his part. The Harvard-educated Underground Railroad operative William Chaplin (below) was captured in a later escape attempt out of Washington and, charged with attempted murder, jumped bail.

The Potomac shoreline around the time of the *Pearl* escape (above) shows a lonely schooner near the high bank and the still-rural nature along much of the river's length inside the District of Columbia. The map (right) shows the journey of the *Pearl* down the river to where it was caught near Point Lookout. They had planned to traverse the Chesapeake Bay and disembark at the Frenchtown landing at the head of the bay.

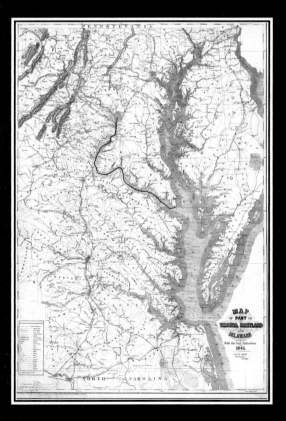

John Plumbe, Jr., the "Daguerre of Washington," took this earliest known photograph (1846) of the U.S. Capitol (top). The Charles Bullfinch dome was still there in 1848. The 1863 Matthew Brady photograph of the Smithsonian Institution (bottom), shows a residential neighborhood to the south where, at the time of the *Pearl* escape, William Williams and Joseph Gannon operated slave pens.

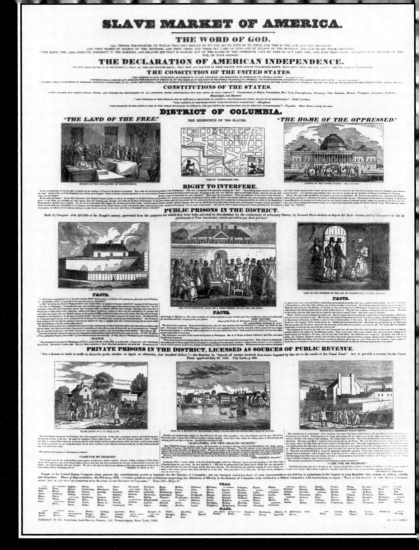

Broadside produced in 1836 by the American Anti-Slavery Society depicting the slave trade in the capital. On the top, a map shows where slaves were held at the D.C. jail, and the private slave pens of William Robey and Joseph Neal. To the right of the map, slaves are led in front of the Capitol. In the middle of the second row, a free man is sold to pay fees at the D.C. jail and an enslaved mother and her children are held inside that same facility. The bottom row shows a coffle leaving Neal's slave pen, the Alexandria waterfront where slaves were loaded for Southern markets, and slaves moving out of the Franklin & Armfield slave pen, which owned three vessels, likely heading for one of those ships.

Both images appeared in Jesse Torrey's *Portraiture of Domestic Slavery in the United States*, published in 1818. The surreal figure jumping from a tavern at 13th & F Streets depicts the woman who tried to commit suicide rather than be sold south without her husband. Badly injured, she lived and was interviewed by Torrey. A coffle (below) leaves a Washington slave pen heading south at the time when the domestic slave trade was rapidly expanding.

A Slave-Coffle passing the Capitol.

TO THE
CITIZENS OF WASHINGTON.

It is well known to you that events have transpired within the last few days, deeply affecting the peace and character of our community. The danger has not yet passed away, but demands increased vigilance from the friends of order.

The cool, deliberate judgment of the People of this community, unexceptionably and unequivocally declared, can, and will, we doubt not, if the Law is found insufficient, redress any grievance, in a manner worthy of themselves; but the fearful acts of lawless and irresponsible violence can only aggravate the evil.

The authorities, Municipal and Police, have thus far restrained actual violence; and they now invoke the citizens of Washington to sustain them in their further efforts to maintain the peace and preserve the honor of the city.

The peace and character of the Capital of the Republic *must* be preserved.

The Mayor of the City (confined to his bed by sickness) fully concurs in the above.

W. LENOX, *Pres. Board of Aldermen*,
J. H. GODDARD, *Capt. Auxiliary Guard.*
April **20, 1848.**

The handbill (top) was hastily prepared by city authorities in an attempt to stem the pro-slavery mob who had promised more riots. Gamaliel Bailey (middle) was the editor of the moderate antislavery newspaper, the *National Era*, which the mob wanted to shut down. The modern photograph of the Smithsonian American Art Museum and National Portrait Gallery, the former U.S. Patent Office, shows the southern facade where the forces wanting to close the newspaper gathered.

In Congress, Rep. Joshua Giddings (top) lauded the slave escape as being in the tradition and spirit of the American Revolution; Rep. Horace Mann (middle) accepted the job of lead defense attorney for Capts. Drayton and Sayres; and Charles Sumner (bottom) masterminded the presidential pardon that released the two men from prison.

President James Polk (top left) urged federal employees to calm the mob but sympathized with the slave owners; four years later, President Millard Fillmore (top right) signed the presidential pardons for Capts. Drayton and Sayres; and the partly fanciful rendition of City Hall (bottom), where the free blacks were required to register their freedom, the trials of Drayton and Sayres were held, and the slaves of the District of Columbia were brought in April 1862 to assess their worth.

SOUTH FRONT OF THE CITY HALL,
Washington City.

Joseph Birch, a prominent Washington slave trader, moved his business to the former Franklin & Armfield slave pen, now the headquarters of the Northern Virginia Urban League in Alexandria, in 1850 (top) when the slave trade was banned in the District of Columbia. A watercolor shows a slave auction in Richmond (middle), the city where *Pearl* fugitive Grace Russell was taken to be sold.

A watercolor of a slave pen in New Orleans was done just after the Civil War. It had been owned at various times by Joseph Bruin, the trader who purchased the Edmonsons, and his partner Jonathan Wilson. Hope Slatter also traded here.

The Great Cazenovia Fugitive Slave Law Convention of 1850. Mary and Emily flank Gerrit Smith, the radical antislavery philanthropist, just behind the seated Frederick Douglass. The sisters sang abolitionist songs and one publicly pled for help for William Chaplin, who had been arrested two weeks before with two fugitive slaves in a carriage heading north just over the District line in front of Francis Blair's Silver Spring estate. The daguerreotype is a rare image of an antislavery rally.

Harriet Beecher Stowe (above left) found the funds to support Mary and Emily's studies at Oberlin College, after her brother (above right), on the cusp of becoming a celebrity preacher, led the meeting at the Broadway Tabernacle in New York that raised the money to purchase the sisters' freedom.

After Mary died in Ohio, Stowe arranged for Emily to work for Myrtilla Miner, who had established a school for colored girls in the capital.

CELEBRATION OF THE ABOLITION OF SLAVERY IN THE DISTRICT OF COLUMBIA BY THE COLORED PEOPLE, IN WASHINGTON, April 19, 1866.—[Sketched by F. Dielman.]

For many years, the African-American community in the District of Columbia celebrated the April 1862 emancipation that brought freedom nine months before the Emancipation Proclamation was issued. A jubilant crowd (above) gathered outdoors to celebrate a few years after it was issued. Lincoln's Emancipation Proclamation, issued January 1, 1863, freed slaves who were in areas still in rebellion on that date. Lincoln also formally authorized the formation of black troops, such as these from the District of Columbia (below).

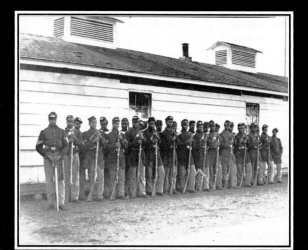

Thought to be taken in 1885 or 1886, this photograph (top left) shows Emily with her four grown children, Emma, Ida, Fannie, and Robert. The inscription on the photo states that Ida is proudly displaying her engagement ring. Emily's brother Samuel (top right), shown here later in life, lived in England and Australia for a while after escaping from New Orleans, and then became a property owner in Anacostia. Edmonson descendants Paul Johnson, his wife, Amy, and Diane Young and her daughter Dawne (below) celebrate their family's rich history near Cornfield Harbor in 2002.

Beecher also had news to report from his "friend" Joseph Bruin that night. The Alexandria slave trader had written to the preacher to say that he had been offended by what had been said about him at the first rally in New York. Bruin complained that even if he might be a "magnanimous, noble, most Christian slave trader," Beecher and his like would not touch him with a "ten-foot-pole." To roars of laughter, Beecher answered, "I think we would."

Beecher triumphantly held Mary and Emily's bill of sale over his head and castigated the legalities of selling slaves that likened them to animals or objects that needed to be warranted from defect. A radicalized Beecher then proclaimed that "slavery is a state of suppressed war—[and] the slave is justified in regarding his master as a belligerent enemy."

The Reverend John Dowling, D.D., the Baptist minister who had participated in the first rally for Mary and Emily, could not attend that night but sent a letter that was read at the Tabernacle. He told the crowd that the sisters had come to visit him the previous Sunday morning at his church on Bedford Street and that he had seen their faces and "marked their grateful happy countenances and their pious devotional behavior as they united in offering up thanks to God for their deliverance."

The Reverend Samuel H. Cox, D.D., from the First Presbyterian Church on Henry Street in Brooklyn, stepped up to the platform to address the crowd. Cox reported that Mary and Emily's gratitude for being freed was profound and from the "deepest debts [*sic*] of their hearts" and that he could not have expected "more propriety" from the daughters of Queen Victoria. He reported that Mary and Emily had told him that neither of them knew their letters before the escape but, in the few weeks since they gained their freedom, Mary had learned the alphabet, and Emily was just behind her. Dr. Cox added that the sisters had confided in him that they feared their youngest sister, Louisa, still a slave in Maryland, was in danger of being sold. Louisa was currently valued at $400 but that figure would sharply escalate in just a few years. However, when the call was made for contributions to Mary and Emily's education fund, the spirit of giving moved few New Yorkers that night. Even Beecher couldn't make an appeal for the sisters' education fund as exciting as the appeal to save them from the evils of sexual exploitation. A second meeting at the Tabernacle a week later did little better.

It is likely that the often ill Gerrit Smith was unable to take up Chaplin's invitation to meet him at the Tabernacle. But there is evidence that Mary and Emily made the 250-mile journey from Manhattan to Gerrit Smith's small hamlet of Peterboro, in Madison County, New York, to begin their education. The *Herkimer Freeman,* published in Little Falls, New York, reported that the colored Methodist sisters, from a family of fifteen slave children, who had recently escaped the "horrors of the Southern prison-house," were now attending "a school in the quiet neighborhood of the great philanthropist." The unnamed sisters appear to be Mary and Emily Edmonson.

The newspaper also reported that the sisters had appeared at an antislavery event with the Reverend Henry Highland Garnet, an abolitionist and Presbyterian minister who was a fellow Marylander. Born into slavery in Kent County on the Eastern Shore, Garnet and his entire family escaped when he was a child. The minister and black leader introduced Mary and Emily to the audience, assuring the crowd that the girls were now safe because "there are yet two places where slaveholders cannot come—Heaven and Peterboro."

Garnet had become one of the antislavery movement's most militant theorists. At the Negro National Convention of 1843 in Buffalo, New York, before Frederick Douglass and John Brown had developed a more militant and less-than-nonviolent stand on slavery, Garnet delivered an address to the slaves of America that openly called for revolt. He told them that "you had far better all die—*die immediately,* than live slaves, and entail your wretchedness upon your posterity. . . ." He also warned "there is not much hope of redemption without the shedding of blood."

Gerrit Smith had hired Garnet to assist him in a project to distribute parcels of his hardscrabble upstate New York land to landless black families, though one parcel of that land was deeded to a white abolitionist named John Brown, who moved there with his large family. After the Supreme Court issued its 1857 *Dred Scott* decision, which denied all blacks the right of citizenship, a discouraged Garnet became a leader in the African Civilization Society, which hoped to set up their own independent colony in Africa.

It's not known how long Mary and Emily stayed in Peterboro; in fact, much of their activity during the next few years is unknown. On December 15, 1848, Frederick Douglass reported in his paper that Garnet had moved some eighty miles west to Geneva, New York, where he was operating a school during the week and preaching on Sundays. It is possible that Mary and Emily accompanied him. A year later, the sisters were living in Macedon, New York, where they were continuing their studies in the home school of William R. Smith, a close friend and ally of William Chaplin. Smith worked as an operative in the Underground Railroad, and Mary and Emily were no doubt pleased to be a part of a home where people were helping runaways make their way farther north. Smith did not make his living from the school. The *National Era* in Washington noted that "our friend" William R. Smith was the proprietor of a nursery for fruit and ornamental trees and plants in Macedon.

At the Smith school, Mary and Emily learned the fundamentals of reading and writing and clearly made a strong impression in the home because plans were made to raise money for them to pursue teacher training. In October 1849, five New York women, including Hannah C. Smith, established a committee to finance the next phase of Mary and Emily's education. The committee issued a public statement that described the Edmonson sisters as young women from a good family with "most exemplary industry and a rare deportment for propriety." The statement added that the sisters were "anxious to acquire information that will, in every way, render them competent and effective as teachers and examples among their people in the District of Columbia." They planned to extend the program to more young women of color who would go back into the black communities of the Upper South to teach. There is no indication that the organization ever progressed much beyond that appeal.

Mary and Emily would go on to college, but it would not be for another two years. In the meantime, they spent considerable time in the Syracuse home of Jermain Loguen, one of the Underground Railroad's most prolific and bold conductors. When the sisters later enrolled in New York Central College in McGrawville, New York, their admission records described them as coming from two home cities: Syracuse and Washington, D.C. A few years later, when Emily returned to Washington, she expressed an interest in returning to the Syracuse home of Jermain Loguen, whom she described as a "brother" to her.

When Emily and Mary lived in the Loguen home they undoubtedly administered to the needs of runaway slaves arriving at any time of night or day, helping to feed and clothe them and then prepare them for the next leg of the journey. The sisters became even more steeped in the politics of radical abolitionism. Loguen worked closely with Gerrit Smith, even naming a son after the Peterboro philanthropist. He operated his cell so blatantly that he sometimes placed advertisements in the newspaper offering shelter to runaway slaves. Smith and Loguen would soon put their beliefs on the line when Congress passed a new Fugitive Slave Act with extraordinary enforcement provisions.

EIGHT

The Fugitive Slave Act and the Great Protest Meeting

Tensions over the extension of slavery worsened when California petitioned to be admitted to the Union as a free state in 1850. California was thought by many Southerners to be an ideal land for slavery, but gold fever had transformed it almost overnight into a largely Northerner-populated territory that preferred free labor for white settlers.

Threats and angry harangues were traded—Senator Henry Foote even pulled a pistol on the Senate floor. Senator Calhoun established a new social policy in which he refused to speak to any legislator he deemed hostile to the South. But, as a gentleman, he would reply if spoken to first. Other Southerners followed suit in a strained dance of manners.

Senator Henry Clay of Kentucky, a founder of the Whig Party and a hero to many of its younger politicians, stepped forward yet again to craft a compromise to dampen hostilities. In 1820 Clay had designed the compromise that admitted Missouri to the Union as a slave state, cut off a part of northern Massachusetts to form the free state of Maine, and restricted slavery to Louisiana Purchase land that fell below 36 degrees, 30 minutes north latitude.

Thirty years later, Clay pulled together an omnibus package of pending legislation, known as the Compromise of 1850, in an attempt to quell the conflict over slavery once and for all. He proposed that California be admitted to the Union as a free state, while the residents of the remaining land gained by the Mexican War—the huge Utah and New Mexico territories—would decide whether to be slave or free under the doctrine of popular sovereignty. To make the deal more appealing to the South, the Compromise supported the passage of a stronger federal Fugitive Slave Act. Southern politicians and newspapers had long railed against their loss of "property" to the North and their inability to easily retrieve runaways, because many Northern states had passed laws to nullify the provisions of the Fugitive Slave Act of 1793.

The proposed new Fugitive Slave Act would not be so easily thwarted. Rep. John Mason of Virginia had drafted an act that provided a federally enforced system that would give wide evidentiary latitude to slave owners or their agents to reclaim runaways. Federally appointed commissioners would receive a fee of ten dollars if they determined that the runaway should be returned to his or her owner and only five dollars if the alleged fugitive was determined to be free. It was argued that more work was involved in returning a runaway than setting one free but the effect tipped the scale even further in favor of the slave owner, in more than just appearance.

Unlike the 1793 Act, U.S. marshals would be authorized to forcibly deputize citizens to assist in returning runaways to their owners, and those who interfered with the provisions of the act were subject to criminal charges. The alleged fugitives would have no right to a trial. If passed, the new Fugitive Slave Act would have an immediate and devastating effect on runaway slaves who had fled to the North and lived there for years.

Then, to provide something for the increasing number of antislavery voices being raised in the North, Clay's package included the bill to abolish the slave trade in the District of Columbia. Free-Soil and sympathetic Whig congressmen had continued to push that bill, and many residents of Washington were not strongly opposed to the idea. The recent *Pearl*-related events had left many in the capital willing to be rid of the trade. The city council announced that it was happy to see the elimination of the slave trade because it had become "prejudicial to the interest of our city and offensive to public sentiment." But the abolition of slavery in the nation's capital would be going too far. When Rep. William Seward attempted to attach a clause to the bill to include a program of compensated emancipation—much like the one proposed by the Abraham Lincoln the year before—it was rejected.

Such a far-reaching and politically precarious compromise could only succeed if strong voices from both the North and the South gave it substantial support. The powerful Senator Daniel Webster, Paul Jennings's employer and a presidential aspirant, became the leading advocate for the Compromise for the North and assured the South that he would wholeheartedly support the new Fugitive Slave Act. Webster believed that if he spared the Union from conflict over slavery, his presidential bid would succeed. If he'd been right and lived long enough, Paul Jennings would have served two presidents in the White House.

Webster threw himself behind the Compromise bills and attacked the abolitionists, who had immediately condemned the proposed Fugitive Slave Act, for their inflexibility. On the floor of Congress, he proclaimed that in the past twenty years they had "produced nothing good or valuable," adding that the money abolitionists spent attacking slavery could have been put to better use by purchasing slaves and sending them to Liberia. The ambitious senator from Massachusetts became the pariah of antislavery activists.

The leading voices of the abolitionist movement focused their energies on defeating the Fugitive Slave Act. Had Frederick Douglass not allowed supporters to raise funds to purchase his freedom, the new act would have given his owner unrestrained power to drag him back to Maryland. Mary and Emily's friend Jermain Loguen, still wanted by his owner in Tennessee, would also be in serious jeopardy. And James Pennington, the New York minister whose church had contributed fifty dollars to Paul Edmonson for his daughters, felt he was in such jeopardy that he soon left for Europe, where he toured as a very successful antislavery activist, sometimes accompanied by a series of panoramic views of slavery designed by William Wells Brown, another black abolitionist traveling in England. The fifth view included an ocean view with the schooner *Pearl* and the slave ship *Franklin,* which once transported thousands of slaves from Alexandria to the Lower South.

The Great Cazenovia Fugitive Slave Act Convention

In the summer of 1850, Emily and Mary were invited to attend a convention in Cazenovia, New York, organized to protest the pending Fugitive Slave Act. Cazenovia, in Madison County, New York, was just nine miles from Gerrit Smith's Peterboro but offered more plentiful accommodations and better transportation facilities. Smith, whose long shadow extended over Madison County and Cazenovia in particular, was the prime mover behind the convention.

The published notices for the convention assured all that they would be "bid a most cordial welcome by the good people of Cazenovia." However, not all of the town's leaders agreed with that assessment. On August 14 the *Madison County Whig* claimed that most of the residents had little sympathy for abolitionists whose meetings drew only a "few idle women and children" and largely attracted "strangers from abroad." The paper concluded that "[t]he tender of our hospitalities is therefore unauthorized."

But the town had a strong history of antislavery sympathy. A survey of documents conducted by Russ Grills, Cazenovia's town historian, shows that more than three hundred residents of Cazenovia and nearby towns had joined antislavery organizations, contributed to their activities, or signed antislavery petitions at some time. Ironically, H. A. Coolidge, the editor of the *Madison County Whig* who had questioned the town's welcoming of such a convention, is on that list. But signing petitions and contributing to antislavery societies did not necessarily make one a radical abolitionist or an opponent of the Fugitive Slave Act.

On May 1, 1850, the *Madison County Whig* listed two hundred signatories—including Coolidge—who supported Clay's compromise bundle for "the settlement of the slavery question."

One of those "strangers from abroad" was the charismatic Frederick Douglass, already famous for his 1845 autobiography, the *Narrative of the Life of Frederick Douglass, an American Slave*. He had become a powerful antislavery orator who often told his own incredible story under the yoke of slavery. A close political ally of Gerrit Smith's, Douglass made his way to Cazenovia from Rochester, New York, where he had moved in 1847 to begin publishing his own abolitionist paper, the *North Star*.

Gerrit Smith and the other organizers reached out to leading abolitionists to join the rally. One who answered the call was the Reverend Samuel May, Louisa May Alcott's uncle, who was a member of the Drayton and Sayres defense committee in Boston. He had since moved his Unitarian ministry to Syracuse and joined Jermain Loguen's Underground Railroad network. James Caleb Jackson, a member of the Liberty Party and the publisher of the *Albany Patriot*, agreed to participate, as did George W. Clark, a leading composer and singer of antislavery songs. Loguen, a runaway slave of many years who had reached freedom by stealing his owner's horse in Tennessee to make his way north—and then set the horse free to make its way back to its owner—would play a prominent role at the convention.*

When the Edmonson sisters arrived in Cazenovia, Mary was about seventeen years old, and Emily, about fifteen. In the two years since they boarded the *Pearl*, the sisters had moved from slavery to freedom and from illiteracy to a growing confidence in their learning. They had traveled far more widely than imaginable for most Americans, moving by schooner, carriage, steamboat, an ocean-sailing brig, and railroad. They had walked through the streets of New Orleans and New York

---

* Ten years after the Cazenovia convention, the widow of his owner would write to Loguen to demand the $1,000 she believed he was worth. She also grumbled that the horse was never the same again.

City, and no matter where they went, the sisters made fast friends and gained support. They had become celebrities in abolitionist circles for their moral courage, bravery, lovely singing voices, manners, and beauty.

The sisters were looking forward to seeing many of their friends and supporters in Cazenovia, particularly William Chaplin. In 1849 the man who helped design the escape on the *Pearl* had attempted to begin his own newspaper in Albany, New York, called *Chaplin's Portfolio*, but little was ever heard about it beyond its announcement in the *National Era*. It was billed to serve "its readers with a large amount of miscellaneous matter, selected from a great variety of sources, with taste and judgment. . . ."

Chaplin had returned to Washington and was back at work in the Washington Underground Railroad cell. A few weeks before the convention was to open, he left Washington on the Seventh Street road to make his way north in a hired private carriage with two fugitive slaves, named Allen and Garland, secreted in the back. He had been planning to arrive triumphantly in Cazenovia with the runaways to underscore the campaign against the looming Fugitive Slave Act. To make his entrance all the more provocative, the fugitives belonged, respectively, to Georgia congressmen Robert Toombs and Alexander Stephens, the latter of whom was described by Lincoln as "a little slim, pale-faced, consumptive man."

John Goddard of Washington's auxiliary guard—the same man who had interrupted the 1843 escape organized by Charles Torrey at the home of John Bush and had stood in the doorway to block the attack on the *National Era* office in 1848—had been alerted to the escape. As Chaplin crossed the line taking him into Maryland near Francis Blair's "Silver Spring" estate in Montgomery County, Goddard leapt out from the shadows and thrust a rail into one of the carriage's wheels to lock it. Goddard's aides reached up to pull Chaplin off the driver's seat and, as they began to rain blows on him, twenty-seven pistol shots rang out from inside and around the carriage. The account in the *Daily National*

Intelligencer claimed that Chaplin fired a pistol at one of Goddard's men, and the bullet went through his hat. Garland was shot in the shoulder but still managed to flee. The other fugitive was captured alive only because his large pocket watch had deflected a bullet.

Chaplin, who had again designed a dramatic escape that failed, landed in the Blue Jug, where the captains of the *Pearl* still languished. It was a rueful reunion for Chaplin and Drayton, though it is unlikely they were allowed to spend any time together. In a replay of the events surrounding the *Pearl* escape two years earlier, a mob began to collect around the *National Era* as word spread through the city. Walter Lenox, the proslavery mayor of Washington, D.C., who had been involved in attempting to quell the mob who wanted to destroy Gamaliel Bailey's printing press two years earlier, went directly to the Blue Jug to obtain a disclaimer from Chaplin exonerating Bailey. Washington mayors frowned on mob actions, whatever the cause, because of the negative attention to the city they invariably drew. This time, the mob dissipated.

When Gerrit Smith learned of Chaplin's arrest a few weeks before the convention, he sent Theodosia Gilbert, Chaplin's thirty-one-year-old fiancée and part owner of the Glen Haven water cure facility, to the District of Columbia along with Quaker abolitionist Joseph Hathaway. With the help of Free-Soil senator Salmon Chase, they were admitted to the jail, where they found Chaplin in manacles, sleeping on a bed of straw with a swollen and injured head.

At some point, likely during that visit, Seth Concklin, a risk-taking antislavery operative, arrived in Washington with a plan to break Chaplin out of prison. It never was executed. Not long afterward, Concklin was murdered by slave catchers after making a dangerous trip into Alabama to try and free Peter Still, the brother of Philadelphia Underground Railroad operative William Still. Chaplin's fiancée wrote to Still to say that she would never "forget that night of our extremest peril (as we supposed), when [Concklin] . . . proffered his services at the hazard of his liberty . . . in behalf of William L. Chaplin."

Gilbert and Hathaway returned to New York in time for the Cazenovia convention, which now took on a far more militant tone than had
been originally planned. After Chaplin's arrest, a second call was issued incorporating more radical language. It invited opponents of the
proposed Fugitive Slave Act to come to the convention "determined
that the two hundred thousand pirates who hold three millions of our
countrymen in slavery, and rule the whole nation besides, shall, no longer, be permitted to do either."

At 10:00 A.M. on August 21, 1850, the Great Cazenovia Fugitive
Slave Law Convention opened in the packed Free Congregational Church
on Lincklaen Street in the center of town. The "free" church, one of a
number established around the North on antislavery principles—when
most churches refused to condemn slavery outright—was designed to
hold four hundred people, but so many people arrived, including at least
fifty fugitive slaves, that hundreds of people were left outside. Frederick
Douglass, a veteran runaway slave, was elected president of the convention, and his first piece of business was to devise a plan to support Chaplin. Joseph Hathaway recounted the details of his visit to Washington,
and committees were quickly formed to raise the considerable amount
of money needed for his bail.

Mary and Emily were devastated that their friend was now in the
Blue Jug where they had spent several days and nights after their capture.
In a letter published in the *Rochester North Star*, Douglass's trusted assistant Julia Griffiths, who was at the convention, wrote that the Edmonson
sisters "were closely attached to Mr. Chaplin" and "one of them was resolved to say a few words at the Convention on the subject of his arrest
and imprisonment." The sister who stepped forward was very likely
Mary Edmonson. The older of the two young women carried herself
with a stature and maturity that went far beyond her seventeen or eighteen years. This was a young woman who had even elicited superlatives
from Joseph Bruin, the slave trader in Alexandria. In a time when the
inclusion of women in prominent roles had split abolitionists in America,
a young woman of color, a former slave and fugitive on the run, stood

before that overflowing gathering to speak in public. Griffiths told her friend that "[y]our eyes and heart . . . would have overflowed, could you have heard and seen that young and noble-hearted girl, appeal, in words of simple and touching eloquence" on behalf of their friend. Griffiths also noted that when Douglass rose to speak, it was "over the heads of the Edmonson girls."

The sisters were also asked to sing on several occasions during the convention. The *Cazenovia Republican* reported "the marvelous way . . . the colored Edmonson sisters" sang "I hear the voice of Lovejoy on Alton's Bloody Plains." Newspaper editor Elijah Lovejoy had been one of the movement's earliest martyrs, and the sisters no doubt sang with Chaplin very much in mind.

Jermain Loguen was appointed head of a committee formed to report on a proposed letter that was to be addressed to American slaves from the fugitives who had fled slavery. But it was Gerrit Smith who read the forty-two-page draft—a document that everyone acknowledged he had written. After some debate on the subject, Douglass insisted that the fugitives themselves should review the letter before it was issued. When discussion ended, the Cazenovia Fugitive Slave Act Convention adopted one of the most radical attacks on slavery that had ever come out of an antislavery meeting. The letter read:

> When the insurrection of the Southern slaves shall take place, as take place it will unless speedily prevented by voluntary emancipation, the great majority of the colored men of the North, however much to the grief of any of us, will be found by your side, with deep-stored and long-accumulated revenge in their hearts, and with death-dealing weapons in their hands.

The letter exhorted Southern slaves not to hesitate in violating their own sense of propriety to bring about their escape, advising them, in obvious tribute to Jermain Loguen, to take the "fleetest" of "your masters' horses" and "break your masters' locks" because their right to slave property is "but a robber-right." The letter concluded "by all the rules of war, you have the fullest liberty to plunder, burn, and kill, as you may have occasion to do so to promote your escape." Hugh Humphreys's detailed monograph on the convention, published by the Madison County Historical Society, noted that "many abolitionists in the throng must have squirmed at the idea of putting their stamp of approval on the resort to violence to free the slave."

Punctuated by songs from Mary and Emily and others, the first day of the convention finally came to a late end. By then, the crowd had grown to some two thousand people, and larger accommodations were needed. They gratefully accepted the offer of Grace Wilson, a teacher and antislavery activist, to use her orchard located on Sullivan Street, just one block west of the Free Church.

The next day a platform was set up under one of Wilson's fig trees, and fugitives from slavery described their escape experiences for the crowd. At one point, it was announced that a telegram had been received claiming that Captain Goddard of Washington would be in Cazenovia that very day. Frederick Douglass called out for Goddard to step forward, assuring him that he would be treated kindly. There was no response. It was unlikely that Goddard had made his way to Cazenovia, and it is unclear what business would take him there, since he had William Chaplin safely locked up in the Blue Jug.

There were more resolutions to finalize before the final day of the convention could adjourn. It was resolved that any civil servant who made a person's complexion a bar to either social or political equality could not be supported in an election. Another resolution proclaimed that any goods that were the product of slave labor should not be purchased or consumed, the position of the American Free Produce Association. The last resolution returned to William Chaplin. It stated that:

> We call on every man in the Free States, who shall go
> to the polls at the approaching elections, go with this

motto burning in his heart and bursting from his lips: "CHAPLIN'S RELEASE, OR CIVIL REVOLU- TION."

Gerrit Smith hastily explained that civil revolution "implied no bloodshed." It would be a "revolution in civil things" that "did not ask for blood and did not forbid bloodshed." With that last slightly modi- fied radical cry in support of Chaplin, the convention came to an end.

The Southern press devoted extensive coverage of the Fugitive Slave Act debate in Congress and was particularly outraged by the convention in Cazenovia. Attacking it as a "witches cauldron," one claimed that a meeting "more diabolical in its character and tendencies . . . was never held out of Pandemonium." The rhetoric of the convention was even too radical for most abolitionists. The *Pennsylvania Freeman* dissented from the sentiments voiced at the convention and—even more of a blow—the *Liberator,* after printing extensive coverage of the convention, retracted its support and published a report that referred to its organizers as violent men. In the end, perhaps the only newspaper that enthusiastically sup- ported the convention was Frederick Douglass's *Rochester North Star.*

Daguerreotype

The Great Cazenovia Fugitive Slave Act Convention produced a price- less and extremely rare artifact: a daguerreotype taken in Grace Wil- son's orchard by Cazenovia resident Ezra Greenleaf Weld, the brother of leading abolitionist Theodore Weld.

Weld's daguerreotype shows Mary and Emily Edmonson standing on either side of Gerrit Smith, who is wearing his trademark and much- outdated Lord Byron collar. Mary, wearing a white dress and a demure matching bonnet tied with wide ribbons under her chin, looks calmly and directly out at the crowd. She is taller than every man standing on the platform save Smith. A wide plaid shawl covers her shoulders and arms and hangs down the front of her dress past her knees. Emily is similarly dressed, but it is unclear if she is wearing a plaid dress or if one end of her plaid shawl is crossed over the front of her dress and thrown over her shoulder—a fashionable trend of the day. Emily, as verified by the slave manifest of the *Union* brig in Baltimore, is much the shorter of the two sisters. Her face is also a little rounder; but the girls share a strong family resemblance. The camera catches Emily looking sideways out at the convention. A man who looks very like the abolitionist Theodore Weld is sitting on the platform in front of Douglass.

The daguerreotype was specifically commissioned to send to Chaplin in prison, and, for that reason, Chaplin's fiancée, Theodosia Gilbert, is the central figure of the image. She is placed at a table on the platform next to a seated Frederick Douglass. The fact that Douglass, the president of the convention, is seated just to the side of the table where Gilbert is indicates that he had temporarily shifted over to give her his place. The daguerreotype shows a noticeably large number of women on the platform, and a sea of bonnets in front of them, evidence of how women had become a significant part of the abolitionist movement. According to an eyewitness at the rally, Gilbert was wearing bloomers, a costume that had just been designed by Elizabeth Smith Miller, Gerrit Smith's daughter, and then taken up by Amelia Bloomer.

At the end of September, President Fillmore signed both the Fugitive Slave Act and the act banning the slave trade in the District of Columbia as part of the Compromise bundle of acts. Many Northerners, weary of the debate, initially welcomed the Compromise as a magic bullet that would settle these issues once and for all. It made little difference to the enslaved who lived in the capital. Slave owners still retained the right to sell their slaves. The only change was that traders could not operate their holding pens in the capital. James Birch, the Washington slave trader who had purchased the kidnapped Solomon Northup, simply crossed the river to Alexandria and purchased an interest in the old Franklin & Armfield slave pen.

Many across the North were shocked to find that a summary kind of justice in support of slavery would now play out in their states because of the Fugitive Slave Act. Notwithstanding the risk of a six-month jail term and a $1,000 fine, a number of citizens in several cities joined a movement that resulted in just what Gerrit Smith had proposed at Cazenovia: civil resistance. In Boston, when agents came to claim William and Ellen Craft, two high-profile runaway slaves who traveled widely through the North to speak on the antislavery circuit, black and white antislavery activists came together to stop them. The Crafts had escaped from Georgia by train with the fair-skinned Ellen disguised as a young white gentleman and her darker-skinned husband as "his" servant-slave. Ellen had hung her hand in a sling to explain her inability to sign her name.

When word of danger reached them, the Crafts hid in the home of Lewis Hayden, a long-standing fugitive from Kentucky and staunch antislavery activist. An armed Hayden placed barrels of explosives on the front porch of his house and threatened to blow up anyone who tried to enter. At the same time, white members of the vigilance committee surrounded the slave owner's agents to hinder their every movement. Before a warrant could be successfully served on the Crafts, the couple was clandestinely spirited out of Boston and on to safety in Great Britain, where they became prominent speakers for the cause.

Boston abolitionists acted quickly when runaway Frederick Jenkins—previously known as "Shadrach" on the Virginia plantation he had escaped from—was snatched from the Boston coffeehouse where he worked and taken into court. When the U.S. marshal guarding Jenkins became distracted, Lewis Hayden led a group of black men to surround the prisoner and, before the authorities realized what had happened, they had marched him out the courtroom door to freedom. Senator Clay, the author of the Compromise, may never have known it, but he shared a history with the man who helped flout the law he had pushed through Congress: Hayden was the son-in-law of one of Clay's Kentucky slaves.

But the federal authorities in Boston would not be so lax next time.

In April 1851 a bricklayer named Thomas Sims was taken into custody as a runaway from Georgia. To prevent a similar incident, the doors of the courthouse were chained, and the building was surrounded by city police and newly deputized assistants. All legal maneuvers failed to stop the return of the runaway. Sims was surrounded by hundreds of police officers during his march to the wharf to board a ship headed to Savannah. On his arrival in Georgia, the twenty-three-year-old runaway was given thirty-nine lashes in the public square of the city.

Opposition to the Act in Syracuse, New York, was fierce. On October 1, 1851, when U.S. marshals arrested barrel maker Jerry McHenry as a fugitive from slavery, the city happened to be hosting Gerrit Smith's Liberty Party—and so was swollen with more than its usual share of abolitionists. When church bells rang out the signal that a fugitive slave had been seized, a crowd of would-be rescuers quickly assembled at the jail. Jermain Loguen, Samuel May, Gerrit Smith, and others battered down the door to remove McHenry in what would become known as the "Jerry Rescue." McHenry successfully escaped to safety in Canada along with a number of the men who had aided him.

Some attempts to reclaim slaves turned violent. In the small town of Christiana, Pennsylvania, free blacks rallied to resist the efforts of U.S. marshals, who had arrived in the company of a Maryland slave owner to collect his runaways. White Quakers arrived at the scene of the struggle to bear witness. Guns were pulled, and in the course of the confrontation, the owner was shot dead. The two fugitives managed to escape and make their way safely to Rochester, New York, where Frederick Douglass quickly put them on the last evening boat to cross Lake Ontario to safety in Canada. The Quakers were unsuccessfully prosecuted for failing to come to the aid of federal marshals.

In the end, about three hundred fugitives were returned to their owners in the South, and federal commissioners released only eleven of the captured fugitives because they were, in fact, free. At least twenty-two escaped with the aid of black and white antislavery activists. But far more lives were disrupted by the threat of capture. The Fugitive Slave

Act resulted in a pre–Civil War migration of fugitive slaves of significant proportions. Thousands of fugitives, fearing they would be returned to slavery, fled the United States for Canada. They didn't flee from slavery in Maryland, Virginia, or North Carolina. They left Boston, Cincinnati, Pittsburgh, and small towns spread across the North. Instead of being chased by slave hunters with dogs, they were hounded by federal agents. In his monograph on the Great Fugitive Slave Act Convention, law professor Hugh Humphreys states that "[t]he magnitude of the tragedy is apparent from a casual scan of the Northern papers: black city parishes almost totally abandoned; blacks moving by rail, and by foot along the tracks; hundreds of blacks leaving Northern cities en masse; blacks arming themselves in preparation for the move."

When the enormity of the Act was realized, there was a decided change in public opinion in the North, and it may have done more to expand the antislavery movement than anything else had done up to that time. The *Madison County Whig*, which had published signatures from townspeople heartily supporting the Compromise of 1850, now ran a statement demanding the repeal of the Fugitive Slave Act.

Mary and Emily threw themselves into the fund-raising events to meet William Chaplin's bail. They spent much of September 1850 making appearances in small towns that stretched across 175 miles of upstate New York. They kept to a grueling schedule, appearing before the public almost daily—even on Sundays, because they were doing the Lord's work.

On September 18, 1850, the same day that President Fillmore signed the Fugitive Slave Act into law, Judge William Cranch set Chaplin's bail at $6,000. His supporters were able to meet that bail, but he was released only to be immediately turned over to the waiting arms of Maryland authorities, who took him directly to the Rockville jail. The ramifications of the charges against him were far more serious in Maryland than they were in the District of Columbia. In addition to two counts of larceny for attempting to steal the slaves belonging to Congressmen Toombs and Stephens, and two counts of assisting runaways to escape, he was charged with three counts of assault and battery with intent to kill Captain Goddard and two of his men. At his bail hearing before the judge, with his fiancée and close friend William R. Smith by his side, Chaplin's bail was set at a staggering $19,000.

The sisters continued to make the rounds of New York towns, raising their voices in song in sixteen venues in as many days. Their last appearance was on September 25 in Vienna, New York, just thirty miles from Cazenovia, where they seemed to close the circle from the beginning of the campaign at the Great Fugitive Slave Convention in August. They likely retired to the Loguen home to recover from the strenuous tour.

With Gerrit Smith putting forward the bulk of the bail money to get Chaplin out of the Rockville jail, his supporters were still required to find a propertied Maryland resident to stand surety for his release. Wealthy Baltimore Quakers demurred, informing Chaplin's supporters that they found it safest not to get involved in such activities, particularly when guns had been involved. In desperation, one of Chaplin's supporters approached one of the Campbell brothers, described as the "successor of the notorious Hope H. Slatter," to ask if he would go surety for Chaplin's bail. Enjoying the irony of standing as a benefactor to an abolitionist charging with stealing slaves, Campbell agreed. However, a wealthy Maryland slave owner stepped forward who was considered more palatable than a slave trader.

In January, 1851, Chaplin was released from the Montgomery County, Maryland, jail and immediately fled, forfeiting $25,000 in bail money owed both to the District of Columbia and Montgomery County, Maryland. Back in the Blue Jug, Daniel Drayton learned that money had been found to gain Chaplin's freedom while he and Sayres remained incarcerated, unable to pay their fines. A short time later, Drayton made it clear to William R. Smith that Chaplin's supporters should not blame him if he revealed Chaplin's involvement in the *Pearl* escape. He told Smith that his "chains" weighed "so heavily upon his limbs he should lose his power of endurance and seek that relief which his fellow citizens have not afforded him." A short time later, William Smith informed Gerrit Smith that Drayton had contacted him through a friend to urge that a "confidential agent" be sent to Washington to participate in a plot to free Drayton for only a "moderate sum of money." William Smith told his wealthy friend in Peterboro that he wrote back that he could do nothing unless Jacob Bigelow would produce a "certificate of good character" for this "friend." Nothing more came of it and, somehow, Drayton was again mollified and continued to maintain his silence. But the fact that Gerrit Smith was informed of Drayton's proposal indicates just how closely he was concerned with the goings-on in Washington.

Chaplin was freed in time to attend a convention in Syracuse to plot strategy to overturn the Fugitive Slave Act, which was attended by Gerrit Smith, Jermain Loguen, and other stalwarts of the New York abolitionists. While they joyously welcomed Chaplin, they did not forget Drayton and Sayres. The convention resolved that "[i]nasmuch as the imprisonment of Drayton and Sayres for aiding their fellow men to escape from the horrors of Slavery, is an imprisonment for what not only humanity and religion pronounce a virtue . . . it would be . . . a lawful as well as a humane and religious act, to demolish the prison." Loguen said lovingly of Chaplin, to great cheers, that "[t]here are many happy families in New York and Canada, who owe the privilege of breathing free air to your labors."

But some of that love for Chaplin soured when the repayment of the money donated for his bail became a sore subject. Chaplin was expected to mount an intensive campaign to raise funds to reimburse those donors. To add to the problem, David Hall—the Washington lawyer who had initially aided Horace Mann in the defense of Drayton and Sayres—and two others had put up their property as surety that Chaplin would appear for trial in the capital, and they were now in danger of having that property seized.

In June 1851 Chaplin set out on a speaking tour to appeal for funds in small towns across New York. Frederick Douglass was so thoroughly impressed with Chaplin's speeches that he suggested either that he be conferred with a doctor of divinity degree or nominated for the presidency—though only if Gerrit Smith were not available. On August 12, 1851, William Chaplin married Theodosia Gilbert at the water cure facility in Glen Haven, New York. At the wedding, Gerrit Smith's daughter presented Chaplin with a commemorative silver pitcher that had been purchased with dimes collected for that purpose at the Cazenovia Convention. The pitcher was engraved "TO WILLIAM L. CHAPLIN IN PRISON from one thousand of his friends: A TESTIMONIAL of their high regard for his character. August 8th, 1850." It had originally been planned to send the pitcher to the Washington jail, but it was later thought more prudent to hold it for him until a more suitable setting could be found.

But the enormous amount of money that he needed to coax out of antislavery supporters simply did not materialize, and a weary Chaplin began to distance himself from the entire matter. After one more round of fund-raising, Chaplin retired to Glen Haven, abandoning all further antislavery work. To the disgust of many and the embarrassment of Gerrit Smith, Chaplin simply gave up any further attempt to repay the people who had put up the money for his bail. There is some evidence that Chaplin left the Maryland jail with his mind permanently altered and his health ruined. An old colleague who saw him after his retirement reported that no slave owner need ever fear William Chaplin again.

New York Central College and Mrs. Stowe

Mary and Emily left the fund-raising circuit to enroll in the primary department of New York Central College in the fall of 1851. A notice of their enrollment was sent to the *New York Tribune, Frederick Douglass' Paper* (the former *Rochester North Star*), and other sympathetic papers. The Reverand Wilbur Tillinghast, one of the founders of the college and a professor of mathematics, explained in the notice that William Chaplin was no longer able to bear the burden of their education. Tillinghast, a Baptist minister who had met Mary and Emily three years earlier when he offered a prayer at an antislavery meeting in upstate New York, stated that he was paying the forty dollars needed for the sisters' expenses. He added that he hoped others would "share the privilege" of funding the sisters' education. Apparently, the committee formed by the women in upstate New York to send Mary, Emily, and other young black women to college had disbanded.

Central College began construction in 1848, the same year that Mary and Emily boarded the *Pearl*, and soon opened its doors to 150 young men and women, a small minority of whom were African-American. Manual labor, an important tenet of the school, paid male students $.06 an hour for agricultural work on the campus farm, and female students were paid $.03 an hour for domestic work in the kitchen and dormitories. The school showed a strong commitment to its principles by hiring African-American professors. Charles L. Reason, the first black college professor in the country, taught French and mathematics. Professor William G. Allen taught Greek language and the classics, and wrote letters about the school and other topics that appeared in Frederick Douglass's newspaper. George B. Vashon, the first black to graduate from Oberlin College, was versed in Hebrew, Sanskrit, and Persian. He joined the faculty the same year that Mary and Emily enrolled.

Only fragments of records from the college remain, but what there is provides some insight into Mary and Emily's lives. Their names are included in the labor list, indicating that they performed manual labor at the school. Their classmates came largely from the state of New York, but many of the black students traveled from much farther afield, coming from Elgin, Illinois; Philadelphia, Pennsylvania; and even Wilmington, North Carolina. The college records, corroborated by an undated history of the college, indicate that Mary and Emily were not the only fugitives from the *Pearl* enrolled at Central College. Grace Russell, of New York City, also attended the college between 1851 and 1853. The history of the college, located in the files of the Cortland County Historical Society, states that three Central College students—a Miss Russell and the "Edmund" sisters—had been mentioned by Harriet Beecher Stowe in *Uncle Tom's Cabin*. In March 1852, while all three young women were at Central College, the wildly popular story, which had already been serialized in Gamaliel Bailey's *National Era*, was published in book form. Stowe's book delivered slavery into the sitting rooms of the world and quickly became the most influential American novel ever written.

Grace Russell was the attractive young woman William Chaplin had described in the *Albany Patriot*. She had been rescued from a Richmond auction house by her family and their supporters and had also made her way to Central College. In Stowe's concluding remarks, she cited these three young women when she wrote that "the public and shameless sale of beautiful mulatto and quadroon girls has acquired notoriety from the incidents following the capture of the *Pearl*." But when Stowe attempted to detail Grace Russell's story, instead she told the tragic story of her sister, Emily. Two years after the *Pearl* escape, the same man who had owned Grace sold Emily to Joseph Bruin. Abolitionists tried to bargain for the young woman's freedom, but Bruin was demanding the impossibly high sum of $1,800 for her freedom. Reluctantly, they broke off negotiations. Emily Russell, described by Bruin as the most beautiful woman in America, died on a slave coffle walking south. When her mother in New York was told, she thanked God that her daughter had escaped the terrible fate that someone of her beauty was sure to experience.

It seems remarkable that Mary and Emily Edmonson and Grace Russell were at the same college at the same time but in fact, there were few schools of higher learning that they could attend. Unfortunately, it is unknown if the three *Pearl* veterans became close during their studies there. They took very separate paths when they left Central College. Russell spent some time in London under the patronage of the Earl of Shaftesbury. After she returned to America she was invited by an Englishwoman to sit with her at church in

Newport, Rhode Island, after which the attractive young woman was "persecuted" for not sitting in the Negro gallery. Abolitionist Sallie Holley explained that the "summer-visiting slaveholders are rarely disturbed in their pews . . . as a terribly conservative, proslavery atmosphere abounds here still."

Worries on the Edmonson Farm

While Mary and Emily were studying at Central College, their parents were 375 miles away from their daughters, taking care of the farm in Norbeck, Maryland. Quaker William H. Farquhar, a leading educator, farmer, historian, and influential resident of Sandy Spring, Maryland, visited the Edmonson Farm to obtain information for the population and agricultural schedules of the 1850 U.S. Census. He recorded that the farm was valued at $500, and thirty-five of Edmonson's forty acres were under cultivation. Farm implements were valued at $35, and three horses, three milk cows, and five swine together were worth $120. The farm produced 20 bushels of wheat, 250 bushels of Indian corn, 30 bushels of oats, and 20 bushels of Irish potatoes. Profits from the orchards amounted to $5 and the cows produced 150 pounds of butter.

For the population census, Farquhar listed sixty-five-year-old Paul and fifty-eight-year-old "Milly," as Amelia was known, and Louisa Edmonson, even though both Amelia and her daughter were still enslaved and should not have been included in the same category as free people or even listed by name. Perhaps Farquhar, whose long-standing Quaker family was clear about where they stood on slavery, decided to waive such distinctions, at least for the Edmonson family.*

---

* Two men named Farquhar signed the famous 1783 petition from the "People Called Quakers" addressed "To the United States in Congress Assembled," which said, in part, "[w]e have long beheld with sorrow the complicated evils produced by an unrighteous commerce which subjects many thousands of the human species to the deplorable State of Slavery."

Josiah was not named as a member of their household, indicating that he had been hired out to work elsewhere. Later evidence establishes that he was working directly for Francis Valdenar, Rebecca Culver's trustee, who perhaps feared that sending any more Edmonsons into the District of Columbia was too risky a prospect.

Paul and Amelia were increasingly worried about the safety of Louisa and Josiah. The family in Maryland had heard—as the enslaved community seemed to always hear—that the ailing Rebecca Culver's heirs were in discussions with Bruin & Hill slave traders. Francis Valdenar informed Paul Edmonson that he could purchase his wife and two children for the total sum of $1,200, indicating that if he didn't come up with that amount, they would be sold. It was unlikely that he would attempt to sell Amelia; she was virtually worthless on the slave market at her age.

The family again looked to Paul to go north to try to find the money to free his two children, but he could only raise $100. When Paul became too ill to try again, Emily, Mary, and Amelia took over the task of raising the money for the last two enslaved Edmonson siblings in Maryland. Mary and Emily had already journeyed to Brooklyn from Central College to meet Harriet Beecher Stowe, who was staying at the home of Henry Beecher Ward. While Stowe was visiting with her favorite brother, her publisher's printing presses were operating twenty-four hours a day to meet the demand that was sweeping the country and the world for *Uncle Tom's Cabin*. The unexpectedly lucrative success of her novel had given the novelist the means to extend a helping hand to many slavery-related causes. At some point, perhaps after that visit, Stowe began to contribute to Mary and Emily's expenses at Central College.

It may have been Mary and Emily's idea to bring their mother to Brooklyn. With the help of one of her free grandchildren who had been taught to read and write, Amelia wrote to her daughters agreeing to meet them at the Beecher home. The prospect of a slave trader—likely Joseph Bruin, with whom Valdenar had already done business—getting two more of her children had propelled her to action. There is no record of whether Valdenar knew of her trip and approved it, or whether she left without his knowledge. But her husband, children, and home were in Montgomery County; there was little doubt that she would return.

Amelia Edmonson went "directly to the Rev. Henry W. Beecher's house," to meet Mrs. Stowe. Neither woman would be disappointed. Mary and Emily, whom Stowe described as "fine-looking mulatto girls, with very interesting faces, pleasing manners, and sweet voices," introduced their mother to Stowe "with the air of pride and filial affection." Amelia made an immediate strong impression. Stowe saw before her an older woman, wearing a plain black Methodist bonnet with a modest white cap beneath it, who carried herself with great dignity.

According to Stowe, Mary and Emily had not seen their mother in four years, indicating that they hadn't been home since they were freed from Bruin's pen in Alexandria. Amelia found her daughters changed after four years of living in the North. Not only had they grown into confident and poised young women, they spoke with the passion of radical abolitionists. They had leapt from a life of servitude to one of antislavery activism, living, working, and traveling with some of the most important abolitionists of their day.

Amelia told Stowe of the horror of seeing her six children on the *Pearl* sold to slave traders, to which Mary and Emily responded with "bitter language against all slaveholders." Their response shocked the deeply religious Amelia. "Bitter" did not hold with her view of true Christian piety. When she admonished her daughters to "hate the sin but love the sinner," they demurred. Slave traders are wicked, they told their mother; one of her daughters said that if she were ever taken as a slave again she would kill herself. The Edmonson family had encountered a generational divide in dealing with the sorrows that slavery had wrought.

Amelia touched Stowe deeply. The now famous author described her as "a woman of very strong character, and though wholly uneducated, of uncommon intellect and of the most remarkable piety." She told her husband, Calvin Stowe, that until she met Amelia, she had not met a "living example in which Christianity had reached its fullest development under the crushing wrongs of slavery." In Amelia, Stowe had found a woman as Christlike as Uncle Tom. The central character in her book was partly based on Josiah Henson, another fugitive slave who had lived in Montgomery County, Maryland; he had gone on to reach prominence in Great Britain and in the black community in Canada. "I never knew before what I could feel till, with her sorrowful, patient eyes upon me, she told me her history and begged my aid," Stowe wrote to her husband.

That day, the writer made a commitment to free Josiah and Louisa, Amelia's last children on the farm, and their mother, too, telling Amelia that if she couldn't raise sufficient money to free them, she would pay it herself. But an appeal coming from Harriet Beecher Stowe would not be taken lightly. A number of Brooklyn women quickly offered to host fund-raising meetings in their homes where Amelia would patiently repeat her story. The women were so taken with Mary and Emily's mother that they requested she sit for a daguerreotype so they could remember her visit. That image is preserved in the 1930 book written by John Paynter, Amelia Edmonson's great-grandson. She is wearing a white cap tied under her chin and a pale-colored shawl over a dark dress; she looks much older than her years. Her face is gentle, her demeanor calm, and her gaze is steadfast. She has, after all, just succeeded in saving two children from the slave traders.

Paynter's book also includes a daguerreotype of Mary and Emily, an image likely taken in New York City at that same time. The sisters are wearing matching print dresses buttoned up the front, with long sleeves ending in soft lace cuffs. Their modest dresses are topped with lace collars that circle their necks. With their hair parted identically in the middle, then draped gently down over the ears and finally pulled up into a bun high on the back of their heads, they nearly looked like twins. A small black knit or crocheted cap appears to cover each bun.

Mary is standing—each girl is identified with a handwritten name just over her head—with her arm resting gently on the seated Emily's shoulder. They look like serious, attractive young women with the rest of their lives before them. After the visit, Stowe wrote that the sisters "had acquired the rudiments of a primary education, they can write a legible hand, and have some knowledge of grammar, geography, and arithmetic." The home school in Macedon, New York, and the year at Central College had moved them forward significantly. She added that Mary and Emily were anxious to give back for all that had been done for them by teaching school in a fugitive community in Canada.

Stowe quickly assembled the money needed to free the remaining enslaved Edmonsons, but for once the money turned out to be the least of the problem, and negotiations with Valdenar turned out to be far more complicated than Stowe had imagined. He informed her that he couldn't free the Edmonsons right away because he needed Josiah to work his fields. Then, to Stowe's increasing frustration, he demanded an additional $300. But the writer had committed herself to free Amelia and her children, and she would pay the extra money even if it seemed like extortion. Valdenar knew he was dealing with a wealthy woman who had committed herself to free this family.

At the same time Stowe was negotiating with the difficult Valdenar, she was also making plans for Mary and Emily. She decided to continue their education by sponsoring Mary and Emily's enrollment in the preparatory division of Oberlin College in order to "perfect their education . . . [and] place in the Canadian field two well educated and efficient missionaries, from whose energy and zeal much may be hoped."

To raise the money for their tuition and board at Oberlin, Stowe wrote an eight-page *History of the Edmonson Family* to send out with appeals. She concentrated on schools for young women, including one operated by her sister Isabella Beecher Hooker. That appeal circulated with a list of sponsors vouching for the importance of the cause. Harriet Beecher Stowe's newfound fame had led to an acquaintance with Jenny Lind, the most famous and sought-after singer in the world, who was finishing an enormously successful American tour with concerts in New York. A letter from Stowe garnered a $100 donation for Mary and Emily from the "Swedish Nightingale." Lind even gave permission for her name to be put at the top of the list of subscribers, even though such donations had caused problems in the past for her with P. T. Barnum, her American agent, who was concerned about her Southern engagements. A few years earlier, Thomas Ritchie, the editor of Washington's *Daily Union* newspaper, wrote to Barnum at his hotel in Baltimore to ask if there was any truth to "the insidious report . . . [that] she has presented an association of abolitionists in the North with one thousand dollars, for the purpose of promoting their alarming and detestable projects." Barnum promptly answered, as was clearly the point of the public exchange, that Lind had never "given a farthing for any such purpose."

NINE

The Struggle to Free Drayton and Sayres; Mary and Emily Go to Oberlin

While Mary and Emily were preparing to leave for Oberlin to begin their studies, Daniel Drayton and Edward Sayres remained incarcerated in the Blue Jug, unable to pay fines of more than seventeen thousand dollars. It must have been particularly disheartening for Drayton and Sayres when the 1850 U.S. Census was conducted at the Blue Jug. The U.S. marshal recorded each inmate's offense next to his name, and Drayton and Sayres were the first and second of the fifty-one inmates to be listed, with the crime of "theft" written next to each man's name. Even though the only crime for which they were convicted was the illegal transportation of slaves—not theft—they were still, at least in the eyes of the U.S. marshal, slave stealers.

Drayton managed to be listed twice in that census. In addition to his listing at the District of Columbia jail, he was included for Philadelphia's Ward 5, in the Northern Liberties, as a forty-eight-year-old sea captain. He was listed with his forty-nine-year-old wife, Elizabeth, and the couple's six children, ranging from six-year-old Sarah to twenty-five-year-old Eliza. His wife may have simply told the census taker that her husband was not at home.

Horace Mann kept in touch with the men to assure them they had not been forgotten, while the Boston Committee unsuccessfully wrestled with strategies that would release them from jail. The Maryland statute under which the captains were convicted complicated efforts to free them. It required the two captains to pay one-half of the fines they owed to the owners of the fugitives. The remaining half would go to the County of the District of Columbia. Whatever solution they came up with would somehow have to involve the slave owners.

According to the *National Era*, a "gentleman visited the men once a week" and other visitors occasionally were admitted to the jail to see the two men. On May 17, 1850, a man from Pennsylvania named H. M. Darlington visited Horace Mann and then carried a message from the congressman to Captain Sayres. He later told Mann that he "had read of such places—but seeing and feeling are more vivid interpretations of misery than words."

Drayton was often discouraged, as his July 30, 1850, letter to Horace Mann revealed. "I am very anxious to see you . . . [and] wish to confer with you *Solus*. I hope that you have written to friends—for some pecuniary aid." He had, clearly, greatly increased his writing skills while in prison.

Professor Cleveland was still the primary support for Elizabeth Drayton, but theirs had become an increasingly contentious relationship. Letters to Mann indicate that Cleveland was becoming increasingly annoyed with Mrs. Drayton. The professor described her as "one of the most unreasonable, ignorant of women I have ever met with," and "most heartlessly ungrateful" in the face of all he had done for her. He reported that eight months earlier, Mrs. Drayton had received "a very handsome offer" from some people in Massachusetts to take two of her children and raise them in their home. Cleveland said that even her husband supported the plan. But she absolutely refused to send her children away to be raised by someone else. Cleveland told Mann that he was "completely disgusted with her" and "were it not for her poor husband I would do no more for her."

Someone in the antislavery community must have raised concerns about whether Cleveland had provided sufficient care for the Draytons, because he wrote to Mann to ask him to confirm that he had done everything he could to help the family. He reminded Mann that he had given Drayton "full liberty to state publickly [*sic*] all the knowledge that I had of the expedition of the *Pearl* and how much I had aided him." But Cleveland mysteriously added that if he talked publicly, it "must be the truth, and the whole truth." There is no record of Mann's response.

Cleveland wrote to Mann to discuss a plan proposed by Daniel Radcliffe, the Washington attorney who had led the committee that tried to convince Gamaliel Bailey to shut down his printing press. Radcliffe was now suggesting that for $1,000, he would mount a campaign to persuade the slave owners to waive the fines owed to them by Drayton and Sayres, which should clear the way to a pardon. Cleveland suggested paying Radcliffe $400 up front and the remainder if he could complete the task by the winter of 1851–52. Radcliffe seemed a practical choice, because he was well known in the city and acquainted with many of the slave owners. Cleveland reported that $200 of the initial payment had been donated by Gerrit Smith, and he was well on the way to raising the remaining $200. As part of this campaign, Mrs. Drayton would go to Washington to personally appeal to the slave owners to help her husband.

Mann gave his blessing to the plan. On March 21, 1851, Cleveland sent a check for $400 to *National Era* editor Gamaliel Bailey to pay Radcliffe directly, because he thought it safer not to alert bank officials in Washington that money was coming in from the North on behalf of Drayton and Sayres. But the scheme stalled. Eight months later, the men were still incarcerated and completely out of funds to help them pass the time more comfortably in the uncomfortable jail. In October 1851 Bailey announced in his newspaper that they had received and spent $120 in donations to aid Drayton and Sayres over the past year, but that it was gone, and they needed more money to keep them "comfortable during the next winter." A month later a letter in the *Era* suggested that "the season of our annual Thanksgiving is at hand," and would prove the ideal time for friends to "pass around the plate for Drayton and Sayres" at their table.*

In January 1852 Cleveland wrote to Mann to say that he had not heard from Radcliffe but twice since he had been paid ten months earlier. In his memoirs, Drayton revealed considerable unhappiness about the petition plan. He wrote that Radcliffe had been paid handsomely but had done little. Drayton said that he repeatedly begged for Radcliffe to bring his wife to Washington to meet with the slave owners, but he never heard anything. As Drayton became increasingly frustrated, he lashed out at Cleveland. On January 19, 1852, Cleveland wrote to Horace Mann, enclosing a letter from "poor Drayton." He told Mann that he could hardly make out Drayton's letter but "it seems someone told him I have $1,000."

Gamaliel Bailey attempted to jump-start the campaign to persuade owners to sign the waiver. He assured his readers, and the slave owners, that he and his newspaper "disapproved of the act" that landed the men in jail. But, Bailey asked, "how can they ask God to forgive their trespasses as they forgive those who trespass against them, while they are inexorable against the prayers of these incarcerated men?"

In February 1852 Radcliffe wrote to Cleveland to say that he and Dr. Bailey thought it was time to send Mrs. Drayton on to Washington to lobby the slave owners. But, much to Cleveland's annoyance, Radcliffe suggested that the professor provide her with money for a stay of three or four weeks. The professor grumbled to Mann that Radcliffe should be paying for these expenses out of the advance already sent to him but added that he would pay if he had to. When Cleveland went to Mrs. Drayton's home to tell her the news, he found her destitute and promised her money to get proper clothing for the trip. He also said he

---

* Most states sponsored a Thanksgiving Day at that time, though it would not become a national holiday, i.e., celebrated on the same day, until Lincoln's presidency.

would provide money for her travel expenses and a week's board for her and one child.

To Cleveland's annoyance, Mrs. Drayton insisted on making her way to Washington by way of the Chesapeake and Delaware Canal, where her husband had sailed the *Pearl* on his way to Washington. Apparently, there were cheaper ways to travel, but one of her sons worked on the canal, and she was adamant. In Washington, it took two months for Radcliffe and Mrs. Drayton to make the rounds of the slave owners. Daniel Drayton reported that some signed the waiver with alacrity, others with some urging, and that a few still maintained that the captains should be hanged or, alternatively, tarred and feathered. Francis Dodge Jr. of Georgetown, whose family owned the steamboat that captured the *Pearl*, refused to sign. Drayton also reported a sad encounter when his wife visited one of the owners in Alexandria. This woman had sold the young man who had attempted to escape on the *Pearl* but still owned his mother. When Mrs. Drayton visited her home, the woman brought out the former fugitive's mother, who had been convinced that the loss of her son was the fault of the abolitionists. The distraught mother told Mrs. Drayton that she would have to do without her husband just as she had had to do without her son.

By the time they finished, Radcliffe and Mrs. Drayton had persuaded a bare majority of slave owners to release their claims against the captains. It was possible that this could lead to a presidential pardon, which seemed to be the only hope of getting the two men out of jail. Charles Sumner of Massachusetts, recently elected to the Senate, had already begun to work quietly to solicit President Fillmore to release the men. But while Fillmore still had a chance to be renominated for president by his party, a pardon was unlikely.

In the early spring of 1852 Sumner submitted a written argument to the White House concerning the president's authority to grant a pardon in this case. He also suggested that Fillmore could, alternatively, release the men from any further jail time but leave them still financially liable to the slave owners who had not waived the fine. When Fillmore lost the Whig nomination for reelection, their chances of success vastly improved. He now had far less to lose by signing a pardon.

Sumner next turned his persuasive powers on Attorney General John J. Crittenden of Kentucky and finally convinced him that the president had authority to issue such a pardon. The attorney general notified President Fillmore that he no longer saw any impediments to the pardons, and on August 11, Fillmore wrote to Sumner that he had executed the pardons. However, they weren't officially signed until August 12. The musty ledger-sized docket book for the District of Columbia courts has this simple sentence scrawled across the pages recording Drayton and Sayres's convictions for the illegal transportation of slaves: "Pardoned by the President on August 12, 1852."

Sumner arrived at the jail as soon as the pardons had been delivered and demanded the immediate release of Drayton and Sayres, but the U. S. marshal refused. He had received word from Fillmore's secretary of the interior to hold the men until the next morning. Drayton later said that the Virginia authorities wanted an opportunity to prosecute the two for theft and the illegal transportation of two *Pearl* fugitives who had been owned by Virginians.

The alarmed senator hurried to the office of the *National Era* to consult with Lewis Clephane, the *National Era*'s twenty-three-year-old business manager, who was apparently in charge of removing the two men from the District of Columbia. Both men were particularly concerned that, like Chaplin, the men would be released from a District of Columbia jail only to be immediately incarcerated in another jurisdiction. Sumner and Clephane returned to the jail to argue for the men's release, and it may have helped their cause that there were signs that the usual mob was beginning to form. The marshal relented. As the door of the Blue Jug opened and Drayton and Sayres walked out, the black prisoners left behind—some free, some captured runaways, and some put there to prevent their running away—gave three loud cheers for the two captains. After four years, four months, and a few more days of incarceration, Drayton and Sayres were free.

But that didn't necessarily mean they were safe. Clephane, a native Washingtonian, first hurried them to his home near Twelfth and G Streets, which was just one block from the home that Mary Edmonson had quietly slipped away from to join Samuel and Emily for the walk to the schooner. The men were given their evening meal in the home built by Clephane's Scottish grandfather, an artist who had arrived in the city in its very early days. He had once sold picture frames to Mrs. William Thornton, the wife of the architect of the Capitol and the subject of the attempted axe murder that caused so much trouble in 1835. While the men ate, Clephane made plans to get them out of the city as soon as possible.

Clephane thought it best to transport the men by carriage to Baltimore after nightfall. But days of rain had left bridges down and roads treacherously difficult to navigate. Clephane scoured the city to find a carriage and a driver who would be willing to make the dangerous trip in the worst of conditions for a substantially higher fee than normal.

By 10:00 P.M., Clephane and the two men were in a carriage heading to the railroad station in Baltimore, where they hoped there would be no one looking out for them. But when they tried to ford a river near Bladensburg, the horses nearly lost their footing, and the driver insisted they would have to turn back. Clephane, determined that they would go forward, pulled the large iron key that opened the door to the *National Era* offices from his pocket, pushed the hard metal into the back of the driver's head, and ordered him to keep going. Feeling what seemed to be a gun, the driver obeyed him. By the light of dawn, they reached Baltimore, where Drayton and Sayres were put on different trains. Sayres went directly to Philadelphia, but it was thought safer for Drayton to go first to Harrisburg and then make his way east to Philadelphia, where his family was waiting for him. So was Professor Cleveland. He gave Drayton $100—Sayres received the same—to get them back on their feet. He also promised that he would try to find another $200.

The reactions to the men's release varied greatly in the Washington newspapers. The *National Era* was exultant, describing Charles Sumner as "indefatigable in his exertions to secure the pardon of these men." The *National Intelligencer* matter-of-factly set forth the bare facts and noted that the "power of the President to remit the imprisonment, under the circumstances, was affirmed by the Attorney General." The *Union*, Washington's proslavery Democratic newspaper, was apoplectic. A United States president had released two men who fit the template of a "negro-stealer," it cried. It's not the "abduction" of the property that is so very upsetting to the Southern people, the paper explained. It's the fact that the Northern slave-stealers infect the minds of the slave and "make them dissatisfied with their lot."

A few weeks later, Gamaliel Bailey described the efforts that led to the pardon in the *National Era*. He applauded Professor Cleveland, with whom he had worked in the attempt to gain the waivers of the slave owners, and reported that it was Cleveland who had raised the money to pay the Washington attorney to solicit the releases from the owners and had supported Mrs. Drayton for a two-month stay in the capital. And, he added, it was Cleveland who had looked after Mrs. Drayton, paid her rent and fuel expenses in Philadelphia, and even assisted her in opening up a small shop. "We know of no man more humane and liberal, albeit his alms are done in secret," the paper concluded. He did not discuss why Cleveland found Mrs. Drayton destitute when he went to talk to her about the petition campaign.

But Drayton credited only Charles Sumner for gaining his release. The professor later complained to Horace Mann that "Capt. Drayton has behaved with great ingratitude towards me after all I did for him— the money raised—the time spent—the exertions made—the solicitations felt in his behalf." Cleveland remarked with some bitterness that Sayres had been far more grateful for his help than Drayton had been. Sayres took his $100 and disappeared to regain what he could of his life. Census records show little trace of him.

Cleveland was clearly disturbed that Drayton had been telling antislavery activists in Boston and other cities that he had "done very little" for him when he was in the Washington jail. A defensive Cleveland wrote to Mann to say that if he could see his journal, Mann would be astonished at all he had done. Unfortunately, his journal has not been found. But Cleveland said that he would let his bad feelings go, as Drayton was "in feeble health and I pity him." He mentioned that he would be sending another $10 to Drayton within the month.

After spending a few weeks with his family in their Philadelphia home, Drayton left to speak at an antislavery meeting in Dartmouth, New Hampshire. The crowd resolved that truth and righteousness would crown a rejoicing Drayton's "labors with abundant success." They also promised to give "our quota of material aid." On September 30, 1852, he appeared at the Liberty Party National Convention in Syracuse, on a dais with Gerrit Smith, Jermain Loguen, and Frederick Douglass. Drayton told the crowd that he had been offered $1,000 to reveal the names of the other people involved in the *Pearl* escape, but he had kept his silence.

The next day, Drayton joined a celebration to mark the first anniversary of the Jerry Rescue in Syracuse that had sent many of New York's leading antislavery activists scuttling over to Canada to lay low. Even William Lloyd Garrison joined this gathering. While the famous editor of the *Liberator* still had little use for political parties, he had become increasingly supportive of open resistance to the Fugitive Slave Act and had taken part in actions in Boston to resist returning runaways to slavery.

Drayton spoke briefly of his involvement in the *Pearl* escape in front of a crowd that the *New York Tribune* estimated at two thousand people but which Douglass's paper put at five thousand. It is unclear whether Drayton had the personality to develop into a regular antislavery speaker, but there was no doubt that even if he did, his poor health would prove an obstacle. Gerrit Smith made a plea for charitable contributions to help Drayton and his family.

When Drayton visited Boston, he went to Horace Mann's home. After he introduced himself to Mary Mann, he thanked her for the sacrifice she made when her husband had to remain away from home to attend to his trials and reported that Mann had come to see him in prison to lift his spirits. He told her that the two men spoke about how they longed to see their families. He also visited members of the Boston Committee, who realized how badly prison had broken him. They quickly disseminated a notice addressed "To the Friends of Humanity" announcing that Captain Drayton's health was "seriously compromised" and that he would need support to take care of his large family. But Drayton never got back on his feet financially. A plan developed to publish his memoirs, with Richard Hildreth, who had taken extensive notes of all the trial proceedings, taking a substantial hand in writing the book.

Oberlin College

In the summer of 1852 Mary and Emily prepared for their journey to Oberlin, Ohio, to attend the Young Ladies' Preparatory School at Oberlin College. Harriet Beecher Stowe covered Mary and Emily's traveling expenses and bought each of the young women a new outfit of clothing. She also made arrangements for them to live in the home of Henry Cowles, Oberlin's Congregationalist minister, editor of the *Evangelist* newspaper in Oberlin, and a member of the college's board of trustees. His wife, Minerva, was on the board of managers for the Female Department of the school, and the Cowles children attended various programs within the school. The Cowles family regularly took in students who attended the college.

Progressive Presbyterians founded Oberlin College in 1833. The highly respected Charles Finney, a leading revivalist and the first minister of the Broadway Tabernacle in Manhattan, agreed to join the faculty of Oberlin as a professor of theology—but only if the board of trustees allowed the faculty to admit students irrespective of color. Students of color were encouraged to apply and soon made up five percent of the population. Oberlin became one of the earliest interracial colleges in America.

Shortly after Finney arrived at the school, Cowles was hired to teach language and Old Testament literature. A pleasant man, if not the most noteworthy of teachers, Cowles had been put to work as the editor of the rather cheerless *Evangelist* newspaper before Mary and Emily arrived.

The town of Oberlin was very different from the rest of Ohio. While black children in Cincinnati and Cleveland were generally relegated to a poorly financed segregated school system, Oberlin's schools were integrated and well supported by the community. There were strict black laws on the state books dating back to 1804, but they were seldom enforced in Oberlin. Not long after Mary and Emily began their studies, a state senator proposed a law that would prohibit any black or mulatto person not then a resident from settling in the state. Blacks already living in Ohio would be required to post a good behavior bond to remain. The law didn't pass, but it both reflected and generated extensive hostility toward free blacks outside the oasis of Oberlin.

The Underground Railroad frequently ran through Oberlin, and a number of the town's black residents became intertwined with both the antislavery movement and the campaign for social justice for black Americans. Lewis Sheridan Leary, a black harness maker in the town, would later die in John Brown's raid on the federal arsenal in Virginia. Attorney John Mercer Langston, a graduate of Oberlin and the son of a white plantation slave owner who had left him a sizable fortune, attended the theology school at Oberlin when Mary and Emily were there. He would practice law in Oberlin and, after the Civil War, would serve as the founding dean of Howard University's law school, a diplomat, and a U.S. representative from his home state of Virginia. Both Leary and Langston are linked to one of America's leading poets of the twentieth century, Langston Hughes. Leary's widow married abolitionist Charles Langston, John Mercer Langston's brother; the poet was her grandson.

The children of black leaders well known to the Edmonsons were drawn to Oberlin. Frederick Douglass's daughter Rosetta would arrive two years after Mary and Emily and stay for a year. John Cook, the son of the prominent minister and the teacher who had written a letter of support for Mary and Emily, attended Oberlin and went on to be a faculty member of Howard University's law school and the first superintendent of Washington's school district for colored students.

Not all of the black students at Oberlin relied on the largesse of sympathetic white people. George Vashon, the lawyer who taught at New York Central College, was the well-dressed son of a man of means. His father, John B. Vashon, owned a barbershop in Pittsburgh and nearly twenty years earlier had contributed the sizable sum of $50 to William Lloyd Garrison to help set up the *Liberator* newspaper. But a good number of Oberlin's black students were the children of struggling skilled workers, some of whom lived in slave states, where it was against the law for free blacks to be educated.

A handful of students at Oberlin traveled from other countries—with a good sprinkling coming from Great Britain, and a few from as far away as Africa. Sarah Margru Kinson, a native of Bendembu in the Mandingo country of Africa, first arrived in America at the age of six, as a young slave aboard *La Amistad*. After she and her shipmates were freed and then returned to Africa, Kinson returned to America to study under the sponsorship of Lewis Tappan, the New York abolitionist. A convert to Christianity through her exposure to evangelical abolitionists, Kinson went back to Africa to teach school.

Octave F. Chevalier, from Nachitoches, Louisiana, came from a background nearly as exotic as the young woman from the *Amistad*. The 1860 U.S. Census listed a Chevalier family in Nachitoches with real estate property valued at $80,000 and personal property at just over $5,000. A forty-five-year-old mulatto woman named "F. Chevalier" was listed as the head of family, which included a son named Octave Chevalier. Madame Chevalier also appears as the owner of six slaves on the slave schedule for the 1860 Census. Ten years earlier, the 1850 U.S. Census reveals that a mulatto woman named Francine lived with a white man named Chevalier and their children, and that she used the surname Chevalier. That man's name did not appear on the 1860 U.S. Census, most likely indicating that he had died, and that Francine Chevalier became the owner of a significant estate. It's doubtful that Oberlin students knew they were sharing classes with the son of a black slave owner.

Before Mary and Emily left for Oberlin, Mrs. Stowe wrote to Mrs. Cowles to prepare for their arrival. She told her that Mary and Emily "are of a *noble* family," and that she wanted them to have an education that strengthened and developed "their reasoning powers & judgment rather than their taste & imagination, which are generally active enough in girls of their class." Mary and Emily may have been from a "noble" family, but they were still burdened by the drawbacks of class. According to Stowe, Mary and Emily had naturally fine musical abilities; one of the most essential elements of their teacher training was a "thorough knowledge" of vocal music. She also thought it important that they learn the nicer parts of housekeeping, and suggested that they be taught how to cut and fit fabric and master fine sewing. These were skills, she believed, that would be useful for them when they began teaching in a settlement in Canada.

Stowe worried that the years Emily and Mary spent in New York, under the influence of questionable "advisors," may have led them to suffer spiritually. In her letter to Cowles, she said, "I should like them to imbibe that style of piety of which I have seen many examples from Oberlin—a kind which is pure, peaceful, humble, self denying and willing to spend and be spent anywhere for Christ." Stowe remarked that she wanted the sisters to be taught to follow their mother's example and learn to love and pray for the "bitterest enemies of their unhappy race," undoubtedly thinking of Bruin.

Clearly unhappy with how William Chaplin had taken care of the sisters, Stowe reported that Mary and Emily had been under the control of "an unprincipled man who on pretense of raising money for their education made a show of them in public exhibitions." Stowe may have exaggerated the charges against Chaplin, but it was clear that she strongly disapproved of displaying young women on rounds of fund-raising appeals before strangers.

Through letters to the Cowleses, Stowe sent news about the efforts to free the three Edmonsons in Montgomery County who "yet abide in bonds." While Stowe corresponded with Francis Valdenar in Maryland, unable to finalize a deal with him that would let them go, Mary and Emily became immersed in *Adam and Colburn's Arithmetic, Bullion's English Grammar, Modern Geography*, and *Andrews and Stoddard's Latin Grammar and Reader.*

The sisters may have had some trouble adjusting to being so far away from their family and the many friends they had made in the New York area. Twelve- or thirteen-year-old Mary L. Cowles, the youngest of the five Cowles children still at home, wrote a newsy letter to an aunt that mentioned the new boarders from Washington. She told her aunt how much her family was enjoying having Mary and Emily living with them and said "for a few days they have been happier than before" because of visits from "old acquaintances" Gerrit Smith and Frederick Douglass.

Stowe also corresponded directly with the sisters; unfortunately, the letters from Mary and Emily were not preserved. But Stowe's letters open a window into Mary and Emily's progress at Oberlin. In October Mrs. Stowe was delighted to get her first letter from Mary because, she told her, all the earlier letters had come from Emily. She told her that her handwriting was already much better than she had expected it to be at that point. With a little care, she predicted, she and Emily would both write a handsome hand. Stowe had frustrating news from Montgomery County: Amelia and her two children still had not been freed, because "Mr. Valdenar says that sickness & other causes have so put back his work that he cannot spare your brother yet."

Stowe continued to raise money to cover Mary and Emily's expenses at Oberlin. Two benevolent sewing societies in the church of one of the many Beecher brothers sent donations, and the young ladies at Miss Porter's School in Farmington, Connecticut, held a fair that

brought in the considerable sum of $110. Stowe gave very specific in-
structions to Mrs. Cowles in regard to the notes she wanted Mary and
Emily to send to the students at Miss Porter's. Please see that "the girls
could write a pretty, simple note, first acknowledging the kindness of
all the ladies together, and then expressing the pleasure that they feel in
being remembered by those of their own age."

While the Cowleses opened their hearts to Mary and Emily, everyday life at Oberlin was certainly less exciting than the round of antislavery conventions, songs, and speeches, or the sudden knock on the
Loguen door by fugitives on their way to Canada. College students
were not allowed to play chess or any game of chance or skill, and theater was also forbidden, although an exception would be made for *Uncle
Tom's Cabin*.

Mary and Emily spent a quiet Christmas in the Cowles home—all
Congregational Christmases were quiet and differed little from the
Sabbath. Young Mary Cowles, who had formed a strong attachment to
both sisters, described a typical Sabbath at the Cowles home. It began
with morning services at the church, followed by a return visit in the
afternoon for communion. The Congregational Church sat three thousand people and was nearly full every Sunday with students and townspeople coming to hear the well-known Rev. Finney preach. The rest of
the Sabbath was a day of quiet reflection and more prayer.

A visitor to the Cowles home on another Sabbath described a weary
day of two long sermons and then a family religious service in the home
before another evening lecture in the church. Dr. Harriot K. Hunt, one
of the first women doctors in the country, reported to a friend that she
"thought she would be suffocated with the awful solemnity."

Mary's health became an ongoing concern almost as soon as the sisters
arrived at Oberlin. In a letter dated August 4, 1852, Stowe, informed
that Mary was having "spinal difficulty," advised that she should wear
a wet bandage over the affected area as was typically done as part of the

increasingly popular water cures. By March 1853 Mary's health began to deteriorate alarmingly, and Stowe was immediately informed. "I am pained to hear of the alarming symptom of Mary's complaint," Stowe wrote Minerva Cowles, adding that she had her consent to use any measure that would help Mary. While Stowe exercised extensive and sometimes patronizing control over the sisters, she had a very real affection for them, urging Cowles to give Mary the same care she would have given to Stowe's own daughter. She suggested that it might help if a gentle horse could be found for Mary to ride and that she should be exposed to as much open air as possible.

As Mary continued to deteriorate, the sisters decided they wanted to go home to be with their family in Washington. But Stowe rejected the plan for several reasons. First, she believed that "a journey to Washington at this time would develop consumption at once." Second, she was concerned for their safety. In response to charges that *Uncle Tom's Cabin* was an unfair representation of slavery, Stowe had compiled a nonfiction account of slavery from eyewitness accounts, runaway slave advertisements, and other sources, and included a full chapter on the story of the Edmonsons. The new book was to be soon published as the *Key to Uncle Tom's Cabin*. Stowe was worried that with its publication "the state of popular feeling in Washington might subject the girls to some annoyances." The sisters remained in Oberlin.

The cold baths and other remedies administered in an attempt to restore Mary's health all failed. By the end of April, Frederick Douglass announced in his newspaper that Mary Edmondson "now lies dangerously ill, and is not expected to live." Paul Edmonson traveled to Oberlin to be with his dying daughter, as Emily struggled with the impending loss of her beloved sister. The two young women—Mary had turned twenty the previous November and Emily was now eighteen—had been together as sisters, friends, and confidantes in slavery and in freedom. Now Mary was slipping away. Emily's adored sister was dying of tuberculosis.

When he reached Oberlin, Paul Edmonson joined the twenty-four-hour vigil at Mary's bedside. Even thirteen-year-old Mary Cowles took her turn. Five years later, she recalled "the watchings here, day-watchings and night-watchings by the sick one." She wrote, "then, after many nights death came, and he took our place at watching and would not let us care any more for Mary." Paul and Emily were at her side when she died. A deeply affected Mary Cowles wrote:

> The aged, sorrow-burdened father might bow his
> head silently into his bereavement, Emily might weep
> and wail and wring her hands, but Mary would never
> speak to them again with her beautiful voice, its last
> tone died out here. . . . Mary who had been the earnest
> Christian—she was now all that she had been to us only
> in heaven, and the Christian had taken the better name
> of angel.

Henry Cowles's *Evangelist* published an obituary that reported Mary Jane Edmonson died of pulmonary consumption at the age of twenty years and six months on May 18, 1853. It referred readers to the *Key to Uncle Tom's Cabin* for a brief sketch of Mary's early history. She died, the obituary read, "in the hope, as she expressed herself, that 'she should be happy in the kingdom.'"

President Finney officiated at Mary's funeral at the Congregational Church. Her fellow students and other members of the community gathered together with her father and sister and the Cowles family to honor Mary Edmonson's last journey. An unsigned eyewitness account of the funeral appeared in the *Cleveland True Democrat*, the newspaper that gave extensive coverage to the *Pearl* escape. The correspondent, very likely former Rep. Edwin Hamlin, wrote that Paul Edmonson had seen his daughter in the hands of slave traders and now, in the words of President Finney, he had come "to see her off to heaven."

The reporter continued that he had seldom been more deeply moved or had his "indignation more thoroughly aroused against the awful sin of slavery . . . the sorrowful spectacle, and painful story of the aged father and sorrowing sister, then about to follow the long afflicted and sorely tired one to the grave." He closed his report by asking how long will "men who profess to be Christians, aid in upholding by their votes the great and damnable iniquity of American slavery." Mary was buried in Oberlin's Westwood cemetery.*

Emily could not stay at Oberlin without Mary, and she returned to Washington with her father. In a letter dated June 3, 1853, in a handwriting that would make Harriet Beecher Stowe proud, Emily Edmonson told the Cowleses that her "heart still lingers around Oberlin, for I have left there beneath the green turf, one that I loved as I did myself." She told her "dear friends" at Oberlin that her mother was in the city when they arrived in Washington and that she had read her mother the letter that Mrs. Cowles had sent expressing their deep sympathy. She told them that it helped cheer her mother's "sad heart very much."

Emily graciously thanked the Cowles family for their "kindness to us," which she said she would never forget. But she did add that the only regret she and all their friends in Washington had was that the sisters did not come home "when Mary wanted to come, early in the Spring." Emily wrote a good letter; it was honest and straight from the heart.

Emily's mother dictated a letter for Mrs. Cowles. An enslaved woman addressed the wife of a college professor and administrator of the girls' preparatory school as "sister," and thanked her for the kindnesses shown her daughter. Amelia said that she was sorry she couldn't be with her "dear child in her last moments but I feel very glad to hear that she suffered for the want of no assistance."

In a letter dated December 12, 1853, Harriet Beecher Stowe wrote to Mrs. Cowles after she returned from a hectic and well-received

---

* It is possible that Mary was buried in the circle reserved for the college's students. Westwood cemetery was later moved to another location. There are no records that establish whether her remains were removed or, if they were, where they are now buried.

European trip. She thanked her for all she had done for Mary and then responded to comments that Mrs. Cowles had made about Emily. "That you should have met with some things to try you in Emily, I am not surprised; she has been through enough to ruin five ordinary girls." As close as the sisters were, there was no doubt that they were different. Emily was very much a part of this world, while Mary seemed to always be closer to the spiritual world. Emily, in particular, might have found those Sundays difficult, and she may well have retained some resentment that they had not been allowed to go home so that Mary could be with all her family at the end. Stowe also told Mrs. Cowles that Emily would be "going into a family of a lady in Washington, where she will assist in the care of young children and in return, receive some facilities for education."

Emily had come full circle. She had now returned to Washington as a literate free woman and would begin to make her new life there.

TEN

Emily Comes Home;
Samuel Edmonson Escapes Again

Harriet Beecher Stowe never gave up on her attempt to convince Francis Valdenar to let her purchase the last three Edmonsons still enslaved in Maryland. She finally succeeded. All of Emily's immediate family in the Washington area were free. Only Samuel, Ephraim, and John remained enslaved.

Emily settled back into Washington surrounded by the growing families of her married sisters Elizabeth, Martha, Eliza, and Eveline, and her brother Richard, who had returned from New Orleans as a free man. Her parents weren't far away, and they frequently came into the city to see their family. Emily had returned to a city where, as Stowe predicted, her books on slavery had produced a negative reaction. During Stowe's triumphant spring tour of Europe, while Mary Edmonson was dying with consumption in Oberlin, Washington's *Evening Star* newspaper weighed in on the now famous author in particular and on the abolitionist movement in general. The paper claimed that the abolitionists had shrunk from a faction into a shadow and that they are "now the disgust and disgrace and execration of the wise and decent of every community." The paper urged that people see these deluded persons as they are, including "such traitors as Mrs. Stowe."

Washington had changed while Emily was away, and the white population of the District of Columbia was increasing dramatically. Between 1850 and 1860, it would jump from almost thirty thousand to more than fifty thousand, with the foreign-born portion of the number increasing at a much higher rate than the native-born. Although white Washington continually braced itself for an onslaught of blacks from Virginia and Maryland, the free black population of the District rose only modestly, from 10,059 to 11,131 during that same period. However, population figures concerning African-Americans were always somewhat artificial. Runaway slaves from Virginia and Maryland disappeared into the black community with no interest in making their presence known.

Free blacks also had good reason to lay low. Until reduced to $50 in the early 1850s, free blacks were required to register their presence in the city and pay up to $1,000 for a good behavior bond to reside in Washington. In 1843 Daniel Payne, the newly appointed itinerant preacher for the African Episcopal Methodist independent black church, arrived at the Israel A.M.E. church on the "Island," the neighborhood south of the Mall leading down to the river. Later one of the leading bishops of his church, Rev. Payne wrote in his autobiography that he was forced to "comply with a barbarous law of the District of Columbia, and give a bond of one thousand dollars to secure my *'good behavior.'*" For many newly arriving free blacks, $50 was not much different from $1,000, because they didn't have it. Blacks were still required to obtain permission to gather in groups larger than seven, and the curfew still applied, though sometimes it was enforced and at other times ignored. In 1854 "only 8 of the 603 persons sent to the workhouse were committed for being 'out after set hours' and only two of being 'resident without bonds.'" Of course, those were the only ones caught.

In 1850 the number of enslaved in the city stood at 3,687, a considerable reduction from 1820, when the enslaved population peaked at 6,277. It is impossible to know exactly how many of the city's slaves were sold south, had run away, or were freed. Although slave trading had been outlawed in the District of Columbia, slave owners who lived there were entitled to sell their slaves in any way they chose.

One former inmate of a slave pen returned to Washington in an attempt to redress the egregious wrong he had experienced. In January 1853 the now free Solomon Northup instituted a criminal prosecution against James Birch, the slave trader who had put him in the Williams slave pen and then sold him south. Senator Salmon Chase and Northup acted as counsel for the prosecution, but the slave trader also retained an excellent attorney—Joseph Bradley, the highly respected lawyer who had once represented the Bell family and employed Samuel Edmonson as a hired slave. Birch was exonerated.

Emily had returned to a Washington that was showing a number of physical improvements. The public gardener was planting three hundred trees on Pennsylvania Avenue west of the White House in an effort to beautify the city. Railroad transportation had progressed. When the slave trader Hope Slatter was taking fugitives from the *Pearl* to his slave pen in Baltimore, the railroad cars at Second Street and Pennsylvania Avenue were pulled by horses to engines that were waiting on the tracks just outside the city; the journey took two and a quarter hours. Now steam engines could pull the cars right into the new terminal at New Jersey Avenue, just a few blocks north of the Capitol, which cut the travel time considerably.

One of the most heralded events in the city was Clark Mills's completion of his statue of Andrew Jackson for Lafayette Square. On January 8, 1853, the anniversary of the battle of New Orleans, twenty thousand people joined President Millard Fillmore, members of both houses of Congress, and enthusiastic residents in the square to listen to a speech from Senator Stephen Douglas, the feisty and ambitious Democratic senator from Illinois. A much relieved Mills, who once threatened to throw himself into the Potomac over problems with government allocations, could finally celebrate the completion of his work.

Francis Dodge, whose three slaves were captured on the *Pearl*, was prosperous and living in a lovely new villa designed by Andrew Jackson Downing and Calvert Vaux, two of the premier designers and architects of their day, on the southwest corner of today's Thirtieth and Q Streets, in Georgetown. He had become the secretary of the budding Metropolitan Railroad Company, which some years later would cut through Montgomery County, creating new suburbs and propelling an early movement out of the city for newer housing stock with access to the city. In the 1850 slave schedule for the District of Columbia, Dodge claimed ownership of three slaves: a man aged about forty years, and two girls, aged nine and eleven years old.

Former mayor W. W. Seaton, still the editor of the *National Daily Intelligencer,* was the proposed president for the railroad and also served on the executive committee of the American Colonization Society along with attorney Joseph Bradley and Harvey Lindsly, the physician who had written letters of support for Mary and Emily which their father took to New York. Even though Liberia had declared its independence at the urging of the Colonization Society, which could get little federal support for the colony, the society was still engaged in encouraging free blacks to emigrate. Captured slave ships continued to provide new residents for both Liberia and Sierra Leone. Other illegal shipments made it safely to Cuba and even into Alabama through the Gulf of Mexico.

The same month that Emily returned, a fifteen-foot shark made its way up the Potomac as far as Fort Washington, and the city announced that the ten o'clock curfew for blacks would be strictly enforced. In southeast Washington, workers had begun construction on a lunatic asylum that would be the first of its kind in the country, after the indefatigable reformer Dorothea Dix had come to Washington to lobby the government to support her progressive ideas for treating the mentally ill. She succeeded in convincing the federal government to purchase St. Elizabeth's, the 320-acre tract of land owned by Thomas Blagden, the wealthy Washingtonian who had loaned money to the Bell family to save several of them from being sold south.

New gangs called the "Gumballs, Peelers, Lemons, Killers, Screwbolts, and Reubenites" were formed in Washington, which the *Evening Star* claimed were heavily influenced by Baltimore cutthroats. Gangs of black Killers and Peelers also formed, and the paper noted that if "called upon to judge of the decency and intelligence of the different gangs . . . the negro rowdies were superior in both respects to the whites."

Death certificates would not be instituted for twenty more years, but the Board of Health reported mortality summaries, which were published in the city directories. For the eighty Washingtonians who were interred in May 1853, the Board listed forty-three distinct causes of death. Consumption, with eleven deaths, was the largest single factor. Five persons died of unknown cause. Typhoid fever, convulsions, and scarlet fever each accounted for four deaths. Insanity caused by alcohol and marasmus, another name for starvation, were each the cause of one death. At the end of the summary, the writer remarked that the "colored population died in greater numbers during the winter months . . . proving that they cannot endure cold as well as heat." Little consideration seems to be given to the fact that a far greater degree of poverty in the black population would have contributed to their higher death rate in the winter months.

Shortly after Emily returned from Ohio, Captain John Goddard, who had defended the *National Era* from attack and saw to the incarceration of the *Pearl* fugitives and their orderly sale to slave traders, was dismissed from the auxiliary guard after nearly eleven years of service. The new captain led the guard in the usual round of corralling public drunks, disorderly residents, and surprisingly frequent incendiaries. Officers were kept unusually busy on Sundays catching Sabbath law offenders. Drinking and gambling were clearly forbidden, and so were activities that, more recently, have become Sunday staples. One Sabbath, fifty people were engaging in outdoor "demoralizing games" in the northern part of the city. Thirteen officers broke up the affair and then chased the players through the marshes in a "hard race" that netted eight arrests. They may have broken up a pickup game of baseball.

Even though the slave trade had been banned, Washington was not finished with slave auctions. The U.S. marshal continued to auction slaves in front of the jail to satisfy legal liens on slave owners' property. It was also legal for private auction houses in the city to advertise estate sales that included slaves. Two black children, a sister and a brother, were part of the estate sale for Jesse Brown, the late proprietor of Brown's hotel, held at the premises of the auctioneer at the corner of Tenth Street and Pennsylvania Avenue. The deceased had restricted the sale of the boy to the local area. The former owner's brother, Marshall Brown, bid for the boy and thought he had won the auction for the sum of $325. But a slave trader who had also been bidding claimed that he had won the auction. In the end, the auctioneer offered the trader $25 to abandon his claim on the boy, and the man accepted it. The sister was less fortunate. She was sold to a Judge Sturgis, a Georgian, and was likely removed from the city.

Two years later, Washington authorities announced they would be strictly enforcing the 10:00 P.M. curfew for all persons of color, a move applauded by the *Evening Star.* A particularly noxious enforcement clause of the law provided that a police guard would be charged $50 for failure to enforce it. A disheartening incident occurred when the guard broke up a private meeting of twenty-four "genteel colored men," as they were described by a local newspaper, who had gathered to raise money to free an enslaved woman. The guard confiscated a list of pledges made toward the woman's $650 purchase price. Rep. Joshua Giddings had promised $1, Senator William Seward $5, and Rep. Gerrit Smith $30. (Smith was elected to Congress in 1853 on a swell of antislavery sentiment resulting from the Fugitive Slave Act. But he had never much enjoyed the political swirl and, in bad health, would soon resign his seat and returned to Peterboro.) The guard also confiscated several books from the meeting, including "the Holy Bible, Seneca's *Morals,* and *Life in Earnest.*" Four of the free men were ordered to serve a term at the city workhouse. One of the enslaved men received six lashes.

The Miner School

Through the intercession of Harriet Beecher Stowe, Emily began to work in a two-year-old Washington school established by Myrtilla Miner, a determined and somewhat imperious thirty-six-year-old white woman from Madison County, New York. Miner arrived in the slave territory of Washington in the fall of 1851 to open a school to prepare black girls to become teachers and missionaries. She had also spent time at the William R. Smith family school in New York, where Mary and Emily once studied, though it does not appear that their paths ever crossed. While Miner was at the New York school, Asa Smith, William R. Smith's father, suggested that she open a school in the District of Columbia for young women of color, an idea that closely follows the plan the local committee of women had formulated with the Edmonson sisters in mind.

Miner grew up on a farm in North Brookfield, New York, not far from Cazenovia. After a stint of home schooling, she attended a publicly supported school and, like other young people in that area, picked hops, the area's staple crop, at harvest time. She gravitated toward teaching and was able to continue her studies at the Young Ladies Domestic Seminary in nearby Clinton, New York, by deferring her fees.

Miner taught in Rochester, New York, and Providence, Rhode Island, but became restless. In July 1846 she was on her way to teach at the Newton Female Institute in Whitesville, Mississippi. Three years later, a seriously ill Miner returned to New York a substantially changed woman. She had not become a radical abolitionist in support of immediate emancipation, and she remained convinced that the only practical way to end slavery was to do so gradually. Nonetheless, her firsthand view of slavery in Mississippi, where she had been forbidden to teach black children, free or enslaved, incensed her, and she decided to accept the challenge to open a school for young black women in Washington. She began by soliciting support from Frederick Douglass, but he discouraged the idea, considering it so ill-advised that it bordered on madness. Gerrit Smith declined to aid the venture. But Henry Ward Beecher thought it an excellent idea and promised to send money for furniture.

In preparation, Miner wrote to a number of people in Washington for support. Gamaliel Bailey did not respond, but Jacob Bigelow, the attorney who had been involved in aiding the Edmonsons and other passengers on the Underground Railroad, offered to make contacts in the black community for her. On October 21, 1851, Bigelow wrote Miner to say that he had seen "Mr. Brent and the other parties" on her account. He reported that they were interested in sending students to her and might also be able to provide rooms for the school. Bigelow also advised Miner that he thought it best that she should make a decision about where to commence her school in person. He may have been giving her a warning to come and see what she was getting into for herself. Miner said that Bigelow was the only person she had written who responded with encouragement. However, she added, after her arrival, "he became alarmed by my exampled boldness and seemed studiously to avoid me."

Miner also wrote to the Reverend John F. Cook, who had long been educating free black children in Washington, and he wrote back to her in Macedon, New York, to wish her well. However, a man who had nearly lost his life in the Snow Riot and had worked for years under the constant strain of operating a school for black children in slave territory made it clear that it would do neither of them any good to work together publicly. He assured her that their schools would not be in conflict. Cook's school struggled to teach about 150 boys and girls basic literacy with limited funds. Miner's school would be offering a curriculum that extended to teacher training. A few years later, Cook would write to Miner to say that he wanted to entrust her with his daughter Mary Victoria and asked her to advance her quickly in the "seminary."

Miner arrived with all of a hundred dollars in hand, a promise of future aid from Beecher, and teaching support from Quaker Anna Inman from Rhode Island. Her first classes for six students began in December

1851 in a low-ceilinged fourteen-by-fourteen-foot room rented to her for seven dollars per month by a black man named Edward Younger. One of Emily Edmonson's sisters, Martha, was married to a man named Edward Young; it is very possible that he was Miner's first landlord and that his name was distorted. John and Elizabeth Brent would soon enroll their daughters in Miner's school. So would Ellis Brent, John Brent's brother and longtime member of the Mt. Zion Church in Georgetown.

In a recruitment effort, Miner approached the Rev. John W. Bull, the white associate minister assigned to Asbury Church. But Bull was hostile toward the school, Miner reported to Frederick Douglass's assistant, Julia Griffiths. Miner told her that the minister was not at Asbury by choice and would "do nothing to aid me." Bull would actually attempt to block her efforts. He approached Mayor Walter Lenox and suggested that Miner be barred from operating a colored school in Washington. The implacable Miner followed up Bull's visit to the mayor with one of her own and was pleased when Lenox assured her that there was no law against her operating the school. The mayor added that he believed she would be able to run the school without the slightest molestation.

Some six months after Miner's school opened, the number of students rose to forty-one, and her little classroom was stocked with carpet, desks, textbooks, and a small, select library. She told Griffiths that she would very much like to receive *Frederick Douglass' Paper* as her students had heard of him but knew little of his work. She let it be known that a number of editors regularly sent her their newspapers, including Horace Greeley of the *New York Tribune* and Gamaliel Bailey of the *National Era*. Her school was on its way.

Miner's assertiveness also extended into the political sphere. Miner went to the White House to speak directly to President Fillmore about the imprisonment of Daniel Drayton and Edward Sayres. But Fillmore always managed to elude her. Miner was forced to write the president to complain that she had been allowed to sit in a waiting room in the President's House that made her wonder if she had, "by some magic, been transported to the palace of the sham President Louis Napoleon or to the mansion of some aristocratic boor of the South." Turning to the purpose of her visit, Miner urged Fillmore to release the *Pearl* captains, adding that with more than half the claimants signing a waiver for the fines they were owed, "justice is satisfied." Miner had one more request of the president. She asked for a donation for the "normal [teacher's] school for colored girls which has been in successful operation the past six months in this city."

After Miner's first meeting with Emily, the older woman wrote to Harriet Beecher Stowe to say that she was pleased with the young woman and thought she had "much native power" that would allow her to become fully qualified to take charge of a primary school and even "control a larger advanced class with an assistant qualified to teach the higher branches."

But Emily wasn't so sure the plan suited her. She told Miner that she might return to Syracuse to stay with the family of Jermain Loguen. Miner thought this was a bad idea. "I fear," Miner dramatically told Stowe, "she will be petted & spoiled, rather than ennobled . . . by great quiet thoughts." She also reported that she had visited Oberlin the summer before and had spoken with the Cowles family about Emily. The religiously conservative Cowles had told her that the young woman who had stayed with them "was too fond of admiration." Miner feared that if Emily were to return to Syracuse, she would marry too soon. She doubted Emily would be able to keep her health under the excitement that might bring.*

The combined forces of Harriet Beecher Stowe and Myrtilla Miner proved too much for a young woman of eighteen to withstand; Emily remained in Washington. She became Miner's assistant, replacing Anna Inman, the young Quaker woman, who had had quite enough of working for the demanding Miner.

---

* Marriage was a real concern for Miner. When female teachers married, it was customary for them to retire immediately from the classroom. It would take some fifty years for the public schools of the city to accept married women as teachers.

Mrs. Stowe was a strong supporter of Miner's school and had recently given a generous gift of $1,000 from what she and her husband called her "Uncle Tom" money. Miner put that money toward the $4,000 needed to purchase an old fruit-and-vegetable farm for their school.

Miner and Emily moved onto the new three-acre campus, which occupied the whole of Lot 115, bordering the southern edge of Pacific Circle—today's Dupont Circle. Surrounded by fruit and shade trees and remnants of the raspberry, asparagus, and strawberry patches from the truck garden, they prepared the buildings for the school and set up their living quarters. Miner wrote a friend "Emily and I live here alone, unprotected, except by God. The rowdies occasionally stone our house in the evening." After classes resumed, they received a written threat that if Miner and the "young niggers" were not out of the house by April 10, it would be set on fire. Stones sometimes flew over the fence. Miner and Emily were once surprised to find that the city's auxiliary guard on night watch in the area had arrived to help them by chasing ruffians away with large clubs.

It took a few weeks to have a picket fence erected around the premises and the house fixed with proper locks. The two women had a message of their own to pass to rancorous neighbors. When a menacing group approached the school, Miner stood at the window holding the revolver in plain view and shouted out that she would use it.

On the advice of Samuel Rhoads, a Quaker abolitionist in Philadelphia who was her most supportive board member, Miner invited Paul and Amelia Edmonson to move into one of the cottages on the new campus, where Paul could cultivate a large garden and the family's dog could bolster their security. She thought the couple would be a good influence on Emily. Paul and Amelia's youngest son and daughter came as well and likely began working in domestic service in the city. But now the wages they received were theirs to keep and they could make their own decisions about where they would work. A few years later, the 1860 U.S. Census recorded that Emily's brother and sister were working as live-in house servants in the household of the commander of the United States Navy.

Forty-five students were soon enrolled in the school; three girls boarded. In spite of Miner's testy ways, the school was prospering, and they would be left in relative peace—for a while.

The Far-flung Journey of Samuel Edmonson

Five months after Mary died, a death in New Orleans propelled Samuel Edmonson into a new life. For nearly three years, Samuel had worked in the stately stone and stucco home of Horace Cammack at 79 St. Louis Street, in the heart of the French Quarter. Huge iron gates opened to a driveway that rimmed a manicured lawn graced with trees and beautifully landscaped flowers. The English-born Cammack sold American cotton to the mills of England and moved in the highest circles of New Orleans society with his attractive French Creole wife. He had also become involved in railroad companies that were mushrooming across the country and, in 1835, he was the New Orleans commissioner to the Nashville Railroad Company.

In the 1850 slave schedule of the U.S. Census, Cammack listed six slaves; all were described as mulatto and, as was the practice, none were listed by name. Two of the three males claimed by Horace Cammack were twenty-six years old; one of them was undoubtedly Samuel. The third was a nine-year-old. Two of the three women were thirty-five years old, and the third was twenty-two.

Samuel was responsible for keeping Cammack's table as elegant as he had once kept Joseph Bradley's in Washington. He planned the meals, purchased the food, and kept the key for the wine cellar. Arguably, he was as well situated as a slave could possibly be. But circumstances could change suddenly in a slave's life, and he was still subject to sale at any time.

Samuel's circumstances began to change for the worse when Cammack's son, Thomas, returned home from college and took a thorough dislike to the new servant from Washington, D.C. Verbal abuse, followed by strong threats of physical abuse, led to a struggle in which Samuel struck the first blow. Thomas Cammack immediately called for the police to come and take Samuel to jail. Slave owners typically used the "calaboose" to punish recalcitrant slaves, paying the jailers extra when they needed a slave to be whipped. Although physical violence was a line that masters seldom allowed their slaves to cross, the older Cammack, perhaps aware of deficiencies in his own son, removed Samuel from the jail and returned him home. The matter, the senior Cammack told Samuel, was to be forgotten.

The son's animosity may have been caused by the fact that Delia Taylor, "a lady of much beauty and refinement," who was the personal maid to Mrs. Cammack, had fallen in love with Samuel. Whatever protection Samuel had received from his owner evaporated when Horace Cammack died in a severe storm off the coast of Norway in October 1853. The inventory of the assets Cammack left behind was duly filed and included a slave named Samuel, valued at $1,000. Samuel was now completely vulnerable to Thomas Cammack's abuse. Even Mrs. Cammack realized that Samuel could not stay in the home any longer, and she sent him to work for her close friend Mrs. Slidell, who lived at 81 Bourbon Street.

In his account of that time, John Paynter offers no details about the Slidell family. In all likelihood, Samuel was instructed to make his way to the New Orleans home of John Slidell, a transplanted New Yorker who had married into a prominent family just as Cammack had done. Slidell had served as a U.S. congressman and would later go on to the Senate before serving a prominent role as an envoy to France for the Confederacy.

But Samuel chose a different option. With the help of his brother Hamilton, he purchased forged free passes and planned to lead his wife and young child north following the river. But he quickly abandoned that plan: a journey in unknown territory was too fraught with danger.

He decided to make his way out of New Orleans alone and then see to his family.*

Samuel found a merchant ship with a British captain that was scheduled to leave immediately for Jamaica. Sufficiently light-skinned and well versed in the dress, manners, and accents of a gentleman, he could easily pass as a white man inside a dimly lit ship's cabin. Samuel presented himself as a West Indian merchant who needed to return home after a trip to New Orleans to look for lost goods. The agreeable captain offered him a berth in the cabin, and Samuel returned to the Cammack home to tell his wife that he was leaving. But word had already reached the household that he had never reached the Slidell home. Delia tearfully told him that Thomas Cammack had already sent officers out to look for him; he had to leave immediately.

Samuel made it safely back to the ship with only one last obstacle to face: inspection. An official from the Custom House boarded the vessel for the customary review that included keeping an eye out for runaways attempting to stow away on ships leaving New Orleans. When the captain told him there was a Jamaican merchant on board, the inspector asked to see him. Face-to-face with Samuel in the dim light, the official accepted Samuel as the merchant he claimed to be and continued on with his inspection.

Samuel reached Jamaica safely. Then, according to Paynter's story, he left for Liverpool, England, most likely working his passage across the ocean as a waiter on a ship. In England he found work in the home of a wealthy merchant he had once served in his deceased owner's home in New Orleans. Later, Samuel left England for Australia, again likely working as a waiter, or as private servant to the captain of the vessel.

Most important, Samuel made good on his pledge to free his family,

---

* Paynter states that Samuel and Delia had a son in New Orleans. Later census data fails to show any children until a few years later. However, a child born during Samuel's stay in New Orleans may have died.

though there are no details as to how he did it. When Samuel later returned to Washington from overseas, his wife and children were with
him. The U.S. Census of 1870 states that his eldest child, eleven-year-
old David, was born in England. Two younger ones, eight-year-old
Robert and six-year-old Amelia, were born in Australia. His wife,
Delia, was described in that same census as a "native of New Orleans."

Daniel Drayton and Others Confront Cleveland

Daniel Drayton never regained his health or shed his dislike of Charles
Cleveland, the Philadelphia professor who had been charged with looking after his family. The captain's resentments spilled out in a hostile
letter that was hand-delivered to Cleveland by Mrs. Drayton in the fall
of 1853. The contents of that letter are unknown, but Cleveland's response is preserved among the letters of Lysander Spooner, the constitutional scholar and abolitionist who visited Drayton twice daily when
he was ill in Boston.

A seemingly puzzled Cleveland replied to Drayton that he was "either labouring under some delusion, or else set upon by some wicked
person." Cleveland then detailed all that he had done for Drayton and
his family while he was imprisoned, finished by enclosing five dollars
with the letter, and signed it his "well wisher."

Drayton had moved to Boston for a while, likely to work on his
memoirs with Richard Hildreth. He stayed with Francis Jackson, a
leading member of the Boston Vigilance Committee, and became well
acquainted with other prominent abolitionists in the city. These new
supporters could readily see that the captain's health would never return and that he would need financial support indefinitely. They published notice of their campaign to raise money for his support in the
Boston Commonwealth, a newspaper owned by Samuel Sewell of the
original Boston committee for Drayton and Sayres's legal support.

When Professor Cleveland saw the appeal in the *Commonwealth*, he
read it as an implicit criticism of his own efforts and was not pleased. In
his own defense, Cleveland wrote to the *Commonwealth* detailing how

he had raised more than seven hundred dollars to support Drayton and his family over the years and asked that his account be printed in the *Commonwealth*.

But the three men who were mounting the campaign to aid Drayton saw to it that Cleveland's letter never ran in the newspaper. On February 11, 1854, Wendell Phillips, Francis Jackson, and Lysander Spooner jointly signed a letter to Cleveland that said they believed the purpose of his letter was to discourage contributions and asked why he would do such a thing, particularly because it was generally believed that Cleveland had persuaded Drayton to undertake the escape attempt. They suggested to him that his duty to aid Drayton "will not be ended so long as he has life, is in ill health, and in want of the comforts of life." The Boston men added that in their view the total amount Cleveland had raised over the years was not very significant.

Richard Hildreth, who had sat in the courtroom with Drayton for more than twenty days of trial and was working with him on his memoir, probably knew Drayton better than anyone. He was made privy to the joint letter addressed to Cleveland and added an important postscript. He pointed out that Drayton's "steady firmness saved Mr. Cleveland from a danger which he was very anxious and earnest to avert."

Their letter elicited an agitated reply from Cleveland in which he first said that even though the three men did not know him personally, he had flattered himself that they "knew enough about my character to know that I could do nothing 'designed' to lessen" contributions for Drayton. He then laid out a detailed account of his dealings with Drayton in order to "qualify or dispel" the supposition that he had induced Drayton to undertake the escape attempt. Cleveland described his first meeting with Drayton in 1847, when the captain came to his house asking for the rest of the money he was owed for helping the Stevenson family escape from Washington. Cleveland argued that he had given Drayton a careful warning that if he should take on the job of carrying fugitives out of Washington again, it would be *"at his own cost and entirely at his own risk."*

In reply to Cleveland's defense, the Boston men were polite but unconvinced. They reaffirmed their belief that any person or persons who benefited from Drayton's silence were now "bound in honor and conscience to look after his wants during life." That letter seems to have ended their correspondence. Cleveland remained involved in the Philadelphia Vigilance Committee with William Still, who spoke highly of him in his book *The Underground Railroad*.

Drayton's supporters in Boston hoped that he could raise sufficient money to live on from his memoirs. *The Personal Memoir of Daniel Drayton*, written with substantial help from Richard Hildreth, was published in 1854 and cost thirty-eight cents for the bound copy and twenty-five cents for the paper.* But Drayton's book sold only modestly. In August 1855 a restless and far-from-realistic Drayton proposed to Francis Jackson that he mount another escape attempt, but the Boston abolitionist advised time and caution, adding "[d]o not despond Captain . . . abolitionists must never despair." Of course, nothing more came of it. But Drayton remained a hero in the black community; many copies of his book were sold in black churches, where he was always welcomed.

Bleeding Kansas; Emily Returns North; Closer to War

Fallout from the Fugitive Slave Act and the ongoing fight to prevent the extension of slavery consumed the antislavery forces. The always optimistic Joshua Giddings was convinced that the growing Northern revulsion for the forced return of runaways would help their cause. The Ohio congressman pointed out on the floor of Congress that few members from the free states who had supported the Compromise of 1850 "have survived the storm of public indignation." Daniel Webster, now dead, had had his presidential hopes "blasted and withered" by the

---

* Drayton's book is often cited with an 1855 publication date. However, the University of Michigan has a copy published in 1854 and Drayton's correspondence clearly indicates that it was in print as early as January 1854. It was likely reprinted in 1855.

whole affair. Giddings warned that recent elections in Massachusetts, New Hampshire, and Ohio had all turned on the question of slavery. From the sound of it, the antislavery forces were on a groundswell.

But Giddings was wrong. While both the Fugitive Slave Act and the enormously successful *Uncle Tom's Cabin* had greatly increased Northern antipathy toward slavery, the vast majority of people in the North were apathetic about slavery, and hostility toward free blacks was growing in some states. Although efforts to resuscitate a law that would preclude free blacks from moving to Ohio failed, Illinois succeeded in passing just such a law in 1853. Indiana revised its constitution to accomplish that same end. Many free blacks had good cause to fear for their well-being, and some began to see some value in emigration. The *Washington Evening Star* reported that "colored residents of Circleville, Ohio, are about sending an agent to Liberia, to seek out a home for them, as are the colored people of Cleveland."

Serious conflict soon broke out over Kansas. Both Kansas and Nebraska were part of the land that had come into the control of the United States as part of the Louisiana Purchase nearly fifty years earlier. That land was still subject to the provisions of the Missouri Compromise of 1820, which prohibited slavery there because it was north of the 36°, 30' latitude. But angry Southerners had watched California enter the country as a free state and felt strongly that something had to be done. They decided that they would make their stand in Kansas. Democratic Senator Stephen Douglas of Illinois, who wanted Southern support to develop railroad and other interests in the territories of Kansas and Nebraska, sponsored the Kansas-Nebraska Act of 1854, which would allow the territorial legislatures to determine whether they would be free or slave by popular sovereignty.

The Kansas-Nebraska Act passed, and Henry Clay's Missouri Compromise of 1820 was nullified. It was a devastating setback for antislavery forces and led to an intense and violent struggle over slavery that became the preamble to the Civil War. This new tension played out in a territory that would soon be known as "Bleeding Kansas." Supporters of slavery urged their followers to flood into Kansas to set up homesteads. Emigrant aid societies, formed in the North, sponsored settlers who opposed slavery. Henry Ward Beecher provided funds to purchase guns for the antislavery forces that became known as "Beecher's Bibles," while votes were manipulated by the Southern forces, primarily by sending Missouri residents in to claim resident rights. Political conflict turned vicious, and the country moved irrevocably toward war.

In November 1854, six months after the Kansas-Nebraska Act passed, Myrtilla Miner returned from a fund-raising trip in the North to find her assistant packing a bag to head to New York. The Edmonson family had learned, likely through Emily's brother Hamilton in New Orleans, that the owner of one of the Edmonson brothers was willing to sell him for $800. With help from friends and supporters, quite likely through Harriet Beecher Stowe, the family had managed to pull $600 together. Emily would now go to New York to plead for help to collect the balance.

The fund-raising circuit in New York was surprisingly crowded with desperate family members trying to raise a loved one's ransom jostling with one another to plead for help from the same people over and over again. Emily knew there was a limit to the number of times people could be moved to give, but she was experienced and had some powerful contacts in New York.

In December Jermain Loguen, the always active Underground Railroad leader and Emily's very good friend, introduced her to members of the Rochester Ladies' Anti-Slavery Society, who were hosting their annual fund-raising fair. This was not a modest affair. It was held at the Corinthian Hall, an imposing structure built in 1849. Donations for the fair had arrived from Leeds, Glasgow, Liverpool, and countless other cities and towns across Great Britain. Mexican supporters sent a box of toys and a large piece of beautiful coral, which unfortunately had broken into small pieces in transit. The purpose of the fair was to raise money to assist fugitive slaves on their journey to Canada. The previous year, the Rochester women funded fifty-eight fugitives.

Emily spoke on the last day of the fair, and her story was so deeply affecting that the organization immediately planned for a second appeal. The Corinthian Hall was offered at no charge for the night of December 31, and Frederick Douglass came to the hall in support of Emily. Four and a half years after the Cazenovia Convention and the excitement surrounding the arrest of William Chaplin, Douglass and Emily were again together, addressing an antislavery gathering. Though many of those present were familiar with the story of the Edmonson family from *Key to Uncle Tom's Cabin*, it turned out to be "a new and more thrilling" account when given by the surviving Edmonson sister, which, unfortunately, was not transcribed. Frederick Douglass then lifted his impressive and always persuasive voice to ask the audience to help Emily. She finished up her visit to Rochester with the substantial sum of $160 to put with the $600 they had already pulled together. It was an enormously successful trip.

When they were so close to their goal of $800, Emily and her family suffered a heartbreaking setback. They entrusted $300 to a man claiming to be the son of a distinguished New York clergyman. He turned out to be a swindler and absconded with the money. Emily had no choice but to return north to plead for help to make up their loss. Finally, on July 27, 1855, Frederick Douglass's newspaper announced that Emily's brother was now back at home with his parents.

None of the reports revealed which of Emily's two still enslaved brothers was freed by this effort, but it had to be Ephraim, the oldest of the six siblings who had set out on the *Pearl* to find freedom. His name soon appeared in the City Directory of Washington, D.C., and also on a land deed for property purchased with his father and other siblings. John Edmonson's name never resurfaced in Washington.

Meanwhile, Myrtilla Miner managed to embroil her school in controversy. Black abolitionist George T. Downing accused Miner of supporting the American Colonization Society, favoring light-skinned blacks over those with darker skin, and disparaging the black educator John Cook. There was some truth in all three accusations, though some black radicals had already begun to support emigration—though outside of the mandate of the American Colonization Society.

The significance of skin color was an issue that had always bedeviled white abolitionists. Many thought it effective in their attacks on slavery to point out that some slaves could pass as white or had just a tint of the "sable brush." Miner once described one of her students to her brother as "beautiful—tho' dark—and she speaks French with great ease." Unfortunately, that emphasis seemed to imply that light-skinned blacks were more worthy of help than darker-skinned ones. Undoubtedly, a good number believed that.

George Downing's allegations against Miner may have stemmed from an article that had appeared in *Frederick Douglass' Paper*. Miner had gone north for a fund-raising trip, accompanied by two light-skinned children from her school, and paid a visit to Rochester. In an article likely written by Douglass's white assistant, Julia Griffiths, who had been in correspondence with Miner over the school, the paper reported, "We have just had a call from Miss Miner, accompanied by two of her darling little scholars, the latter so nearly white as to make it almost impossible for the unpracticed eye to identify them with the African race."

Supporters who had seen the positive side of Miner's work, including Samuel Rhoads, a Philadelphia Quaker on the school's board of trustees, and Gamaliel Bailey of the *National Era*, attempted to defuse the controversy, praising the good work that she had done. The school continued to attract more and more young women, including Rev. Cook's own daughter.

In addition to the attack from Downing and the ongoing hostility from many residents in Washington, Miner's increasing physical ailments may have further compromised her judgment, which often taxed the patience and good will of trustees, teachers, pupils, and parents. Her intemperance worsened during a dispute with parents Elton Brent—John

Brent's brother—and his wife, Jane. Miner had disciplined their sixteen-year-old daughter Caroline for an unspecified dietary violation, and her parents had apparently inquired as to how they could appeal Miner's actions. Miner bluntly informed the Brents that "there was no 'appeal' to any higher power but God—& of him I am not afraid. . . ." She added that she hoped their "eyes [would] be opened to comprehend what dreadful endurance is involved in this mission to raise a people who constantly turn back to their idols, & sigh for the 'flesh pots of Egypt.'" In case the Brents might have misunderstood just how aggrieved she felt, Miner signed her letter "Farewell (I only pray God to let me die)." Miner's views were insulting and alarming, even if voiced by a woman who was risking her safety and health to operate a school for young black women in slave territory. She was fortunate that her letter did not fall into the hands of George Downing.

At the same time, the school was succeeding in its mission. By 1855 Emily Brent, Emily Edmonson's niece and Caroline's cousin, had completed her course of study and was successfully teaching black children in Wilmington, Delaware. Amelia Brent would also complete her course of study.

There are few details of Emily's life after her fund-raising trips north except for the intriguing fact that about the time she returned, she had become Emily Fisher. A deed of trust for part of Lot 4 in Square 313, located a few blocks north of Asbury Methodist Church and recorded on February 25, 1860, states that Paul Edmonson purchased the land with four of his children: Ephraim, Josiah, Louisa, and Emily C. E. [Catherine Edmonson] Fisher. Although the name change presumes that Emily likely married, there is no record of a marriage to a man named Fisher in the District of Columbia. It is conceivable that she married while she was in New York raising money to free Ephraim, but if she did, that marriage had ended by April 5, 1860. The union records of the District of Columbia show that, on that date, Emily Fisher married a man from Montgomery County named Larkin Johnson.

There is one other explanation for Emily Edmonson becoming

Emily Fisher: her own safety. The story of the strong-minded young woman—whose views on slave owners were radical enough to shock her own mother and Harriet Beecher Stowe—had been published for all to read in the *Key to Uncle Tom's Cabin*. Her recent trip north took her to public platforms where she had again joined forces with Frederick Douglass and other "ultras." If this were to come to light in Washington, it would draw dangerous attention to both Emily and the school.

Emily may have found it prudent to borrow the surname of David Fisher, another leading member of Washington's black community. The City Directory for 1858 shows David Fisher living near Fourteenth and N Streets; Paul Edmonson and his family lived very close to him. Later directories show the Edmonsons back on Twentieth Street, and the U.S. Census of 1860 shows Fisher living near the Brents in the household of Edmonson family friend Paul Jennings. Although Fisher was a prosperous widower working as a furniture dealer, there is no evidence that he married Emily. He was very much alive when she married Larkin Johnson, and there is little likelihood that they had married and divorced. Provisions for divorce in the District of Columbia only began in 1860; prior to that, residents were expected to have links to other states in which they could file or, if sufficiently prominent, they could petition Congress for a private bill of divorce. Those case files do not include an Emily Fisher.

In spite of all of Miner's difficult ways, Emily remained strongly loyal to her mercurial employer. In 1855, when Miner traveled north for a water treatment at the largesse of Harriet Beecher Stowe (who had also paid Lucy Mann, Horace Mann's sister, to operate the school while she was away), Emily wrote to her from Washington using the surname Fisher. She told Miner that she was opposed to a proposal to rename Miner's school the "Stowe Institute." After acknowledging all that Harriet Beecher Stowe had done for them, Emily told Miner "I want your name associated with the house as closely as you are bound to our hearts." She reminded Miner that she was the one who left home and friends to risk coming into a city where she did not know what could befall her, a risk that Stowe had never taken. It is quite possible that Emily bore some ill feeling toward the famous author for blocking her and her sister's desire to return home so that Mary could see her family one last time. In any case, when it came to choosing between Miner and Stowe, Emily clearly favored Miner. Others must have agreed, because the school name remained unchanged.

That same letter showed that Emily was closely following the activities of Washington's Underground Railroad. In it, she refers to a well-publicized incident in Philadelphia in which Passmore Williamson, the son of a Miner school trustee, was jailed. He had assisted William Still, the black abolitionist who recorded the names and circumstances of the runaways who came through his Philadelphia station, in the rescue of Jane Johnson, an enslaved woman, and her two children from Washington, D.C. John Hill Wheeler, the recently appointed U.S. minister to Nicaragua, was traveling with the Johnsons to New York, where they planned to board a ship for Central America. Knowing they would be stopping in the free state of Pennsylvania, Johnson traveled with a note prepared by Jacob Bigelow to send to antislavery activists in Philadelphia to ask for help. When the note was successfully delivered, Passmore, Still, and several other black men rushed to their vessel and successfully removed Johnson and her children.

Wheeler went to court to demand the return of his property. After Williamson refused to heed federal Judge Kane's order to turn over the fugitives, he was jailed. In her letter, Emily tartly wondered if Judge Kane thought that when the Declaration of Independence stated that "all men are born free and equal . . . it did not include colored men & women." Emily's words echoed the sentiments of many antislavery people, who were increasingly looking to the founding documents, especially the Declaration of Independence, to support the rights of free black people.

The Edmonson Farm and Further Activity
on Washington's Underground Railroad

In 1855 Emily's parents decided to put their farm on the market and move permanently to Washington, where nearly all their children lived. On December 8, 1855, the *Montgomery County Sentinel* newspaper advertised the sale of:

> a small farm of about forty acres . . . about 15 miles from
> Washington City; a half mile east of the turnpike leading from
> that city to Brookeville, and about six miles east of Rockville. . . .
> There is also a well of excellent water, and a small stream
> running through the lower part of the farm. The soil is good,
> and easily improved. . . . There is a small LOG DWELLING
> and a stable upon it; the former surrounded by a garden
> enclosed by a paling fence.

The advertisement suggested that interested buyers could apply to a lawyer in Washington, or contact Roger Brooke Jr., Esq., a prominent and prosperous Quaker who lived near him. While Paul Edmonson had obviously developed a relationship of trust with a prominent neighbor that crossed racial lines, other advertisements in the paper were a stark reminder of the realities of the day. Directly above the notice of sale for the Edmonson farm, an advertisement announced an estate sale for "a very likely young Negro man, named Henry—slave for life," who would be auctioned in Barnsville, about 20 miles north of Norbeck, under the auspices of the Orphans' Court of Montgomery County.

The Edmonsons' notice for the sale of the farm ran for about two months in the newspaper and shared space with ads from a number of slave traders, including Charles Price and B. O. Shekell, the latter of whom had been a partner of the man who attacked Daniel Drayton with a knife. On January 5, 1856, Price advertised that he was offering very high prices for Negroes and could be found at "his residence below the Catholic Church."

Two weeks later, Price placed a different kind of advertisement. He was now offering a reward of $500 for the capture of "my NEGRO GIRL 'Ann Maria Weems,' about 15 years of age, a bright mulatto, [with] some small freckles on her face." Price added that Weems's parents were free and resided in Washington, D.C., a clear signal to those who sought the award where to start looking. He added that he believed that she had been taken away by someone in a carriage who was probably a white man.

Ann Maria had escaped from Price's home next door to St. Mary's Roman Catholic Church in Rockville, Maryland, where blacks, enslaved and free, including the Weems family, worshipped in the balcony. The unusually large reward indicates that Price was angry, likely because he knew, as his advertisement indicated, that white antislavery activists had played a part in the escape. He was right, of course. The escape of Ann Maria from Rockville, Maryland, had taken nearly two years of extensive planning, experienced several false starts, and involved correspondence between Underground Railroad activists in multiple states and the District of Columbia. It may have been the first escape on the Underground Railroad that Jacob Bigelow directly coordinated with William Still in Philadelphia. Bigelow had contacted Still to say that he wished to transport *"only one SMALL* package to your city." The letter has an introductory tone to it, with the Washington lawyer offering several references to vouch for him, one of whom was Professor Charles Cleveland.

Bigelow's relentless efforts to free Ann Maria reveal the strong bonds of loyalty that usually formed among members of an Underground Railroad cell. In spring 1852 Ann Maria's father, John Weems, a free man of color, had been attempting to raise money to buy his enslaved family when they were sold to a slave trader. With the help of two other prominent black men, Charles Ray, who had attended the Cazenovia Fugitive

Slave Act Convention, and Henry Highland Garnet, who appeared with Mary and Emily in Peterboro, New York, they raised a good deal of money to free some of the family. Much of it was raised by Garnet, who was in England with his family. Stella Weems, another of John and Arrah's daughters, had managed to escape, likely with the help of Bigelow and her father, and traveled with the Garnets.

With Bigelow acting as their agent, they paid $1,000 to free Ann's mother, Arrah, $1,600 for her daughter Catherine, and may have freed two of the brothers. Three brothers were sold south. Arrah became a conductor on the Underground Railroad, working closely with Bigelow and Ezra Stevens. She may have been paid a small stipend for her work, which she saved toward purchasing the freedom of the three sons who had been sold south. On one occasion, she traveled north with a young child to reunite her with her fugitive mother.

The slave trader continued to refuse to sell Ann Maria, so Bigelow paid someone to snatch her from the Price home and bring her into the city, where she was hidden in the home of a black family. As they waited for help to come from Philadelphia, a worried Bigelow wrote to Still to say that they had to move Ann Maria north quickly because "any colored citizen is liable at any hour of day or night without any show of authority to have his house ransacked by constables." He cautioned that there were substantial rewards for information about runaways, which increased the danger daily.

Their plan to take Ann Maria to safety in Canada finally came together. A physician who taught at a medical school in Philadelphia pulled a carriage up in front of the White House and took a seat in the rear. Ann Maria, who had been transformed into "Joe Wright," a coach driver, quickly climbed up onto the driver's seat, took hold of the reins, and began to drive herself to freedom. Four years later, slave trader Price moved his business across the river to Alexandria. He announced in the *Sentinel* that he had purchased Kephart's establishment there; but his agent, William Hickman, would be in the Rockville area.

In addition to Ann Maria Weems's story, Still reported several escapes around that same time that were linked to Gilman's apothecary on Pennsylvania Avenue near Seventh Street. In September 1856 an operative in Canada wrote to Still on behalf of a Washington fugitive named Daniel Neale who had safely crossed the border. Neale wanted to get a message to his friend, John Dade, who lived above Gilman's Drug Store, to ask him to send his trunk of possessions on to him. Before long, Dade put himself on the same Underground Railroad to Canada.

Tensions over slavery in Congress were worsening. Six months before the November elections of 1856, Senator Charles Sumner of Massachusetts delivered a stunningly provocative two-day address on the bloody outrages in Kansas, pointing his finger directly at the Southern politicians around him. He singled out Senator Andrew P. Butler of South Carolina, who was not in his seat, as being particularly culpable. Two days later, Rep. Preston Brooks, a relative of Butler's, entered the floor of the Senate and approached Sumner, who was seated at his desk with his legs tucked underneath the desktop. Injured in the hip in a duel with Louis Wigfall, a fellow South Carolinian who had struck out for Texas, Brooks walked with the aid of a cane topped by a heavy gold medallion in the shape of a lion's head. Butler used that cane to repeatedly strike a seemingly trapped Sumner, hitting him across his head, shoulders, and back. By the time Butler was finally pulled off Sumner, the senator from Massachusetts was severely injured and would not return to his Senate seat for four years. Brooks was fined $300 and resigned from the House, becoming an instant hero in the South; replicas of his cane were sold widely to commemorate the attack. Brooks was quickly reelected and sent back to Washington.

The 1856 elections marked the first presidential campaign of the two-year-old Republican Party. Spurred by the Kansas-Nebraska Act, supporters for a new party met at the Silver Spring estate of Francis Blair near the spot where William Chaplin was arrested. Although Francis Blair was a slave owner and a former Democrat, he strongly opposed the extension of slavery into any of the territories. Some members of the Montgomery County Agricultural Society found this slave owner's new affiliations and beliefs so radical that they attempted to strike him from its rolls until cooler heads prevailed. Gamaliel Bailey had a strong hand in the new party and has been credited with drafting the call for the party's first national convention, held in 1856.

Passage of the Kansas-Nebraska Act galvanized a politically somnolent Abraham Lincoln, whose one term in Congress had barely left an imprint. He joined the Republican Party at the state convention in Bloomington, Illinois, held a week after Charles Sumner was attacked in Congress. An impassioned Lincoln rose to condemn the extension of slavery in any of the territories. William H. Herndon, his law partner, wrote that Lincoln was "newly baptised and freshly born" and "his eyes were aglow with an inspiration." Until his death, Lincoln would never waiver from opposing the extension of slavery westward.

John C. Fremont was the Republican Party's presidential candidate in 1856. He carried all Northern states but five: New Jersey, Pennsylvania, Illinois, Indiana, and, oddly, California, where Fremont had served as governor and then U.S. senator. Lincoln's own strongly Democratic state supported the winning Democratic nominee, James Buchanan of Pennsylvania, who had served long enough in government service to easily qualify as a professional hack, albeit one sympathetic to the Southern cause. The Democrats helped Buchanan enormously by branding the Republicans with the mark of racial amalgamation. Elect Fremont, they threatened, and free blacks would be elevated to social equals in your schools, churches, and even your bedrooms.

The Republicans learned much from their first unsuccessful foray into national politics and regrouped to prepare for the next election. But the country had another crisis to face. A financial panic hit in 1857 and spread across the entire country before expanding to Europe. Washington, then as now, suffered less than the rest of the country when financial troubles hit, but some local merchants were badly affected. The

Dodge shipping business collapsed, and Francis Dodge Jr. was forced to sell his beautiful home in Georgetown.

Fortunately, Paul Edmonson had sold his farm on October 13 of that same year for $800. The family weathered the good times and the bad with the help of a large, loving family and a deep faith that God would see them through. A large number of Edmonson families and friends were living near John and Elizabeth Brent at Eighteenth and L Streets. In May 1856, before the depression took hold, their good friend Paul Jennings had purchased a nearby lot on Square 107 for $1,000.

The John Wesley A.M.E. congregation, formed in the Brent home around the time of the *Pearl* escape, now had a brick church on Connecticut Avenue between L and M Streets, near many of the Edmonsons. Martha Edmonson Young, a founding member of the church, had established the Woman's Aid Society, which raised most of the money needed for the building. After his many years of leadership at Mt. Zion in Georgetown, John Brent's name disappeared from that church's records as he redirected his efforts to John Wesley. It's not clear whether all or only some of the Edmonson family transferred their membership to John Wesley from Asbury, because detailed church records for those early years no longer exist for either church. Emily and other members of her family may have stayed at Asbury or even participated in both congregations at the same time.

In the late spring of 1857 Daniel Drayton's health had reached a critical point. In the five years since he was released from prison, he had moved restlessly from Cape May to Philadelphia, Boston, Staten Island, and, most recently, the old seafaring city of New Bedford, Massachusetts. New Bedford was a city with deep roots in the Underground Railroad and a large black community. It was the town where Frederick and Anna Douglass first settled after the Rev. James Pennington had married them in New York. It was also the town where Washington Underground Railroad operatives William and Lucinda Bush had moved when they left Washington shortly after the *Pearl* escape.

On a June evening in 1857, a despondent Drayton, now a widower and seemingly estranged from his family, spent an evening with Bush, who had become his friend and may well have been the man who approached him to carry a family north to freedom. Drayton told Bush that he had come back to New Bedford to die "and wished to be properly interred." But Bush laughed. He had probably heard that threat before.

A week later Drayton checked into the Mansion House hotel for one night. That evening, he barricaded the door of his room and then swallowed one and a half ounces of laudanum, a commonly used liquid form of morphine. Drayton then rolled up his pants legs, placed his feet in a pan of water, and opened the arteries in his ankles. When he made no appearance the next day, the landlord broke through the barricade and found him dead. He had twelve dollars in his pocket. The *National Era* reported that Captain Drayton died on June 24, 1857. It also carried the report of the *New Bedford Standard* that stated "Capt. Drayton's health was completely shattered by the hardships he had undergone at the hands of the kidnappers."

New Bedford claimed Drayton as one of its own. Led by the mayor and the board of aldermen, the town gave the *Pearl* veteran a hero's funeral at city hall. There is no indication that his family attended, but he would have been honored to know that more than half of the mourners were from the town's black community. The Rev. William Jackson of New Bedford and the Rev. James Pennington of New York, who had supported Paul Edmonson in his attempt to redeem his daughters from slavery, joined white Unitarian minister Rev. Weiss to lead the service.

They buried Drayton in the Rural Cemetery in New Bedford in lot 36 of the Spruce Section. A monument was erected to mark the grave of "Captain Drayton, Commander of the Schooner *Pearl*," but it incorrectly credits him with "saving seventy-six persons." None was saved and most were sold to traders. The conclusion of the inscription, which said "broken by cruel suffering during confinement he died a martyr to his benevolent effort" was more accurate. Drayton's involvement with the *Pearl* escape did not start as a wholly benevolent effort to free enslaved residents of Washington. He was in desperate need of money, and the escape had surfaced as a means of making money, dangerous as it was. But the captain who had shifted from job to job and disaster to disaster ended up suffering hardships and indignities that he could have avoided, or at least shortened, if he had given up the names of William Chaplin and Charles Cleveland. He never did. In a dreary jail in Washington called the Blue Jug, Drayton became something he may not have been at the time his passengers were boarding the *Pearl* near the Seventh Street wharf: a hero.

In 1857 Myrtilla Miner faced far more serious problems than one of her student's violation of the school's dietary rules. Walter Lenox, the former mayor who had assured Miner that there were no rules to prevent her from teaching young black women in the District of Columbia, now launched a public attack on Miner and her school. It was instigated by a fund-raising circular published in the *Boston Journal* by William Beecher, Harriet Stowe's brother, who had joined the school's supporters. Unfortunately, the language of the circular played into the strong fears held by most white Washingtonians that free blacks from neighboring districts would soon invade their territory. Beecher's circular pointed out that there were 500,000 free people of color in the country and they were in great need of teachers and schools. He added that Maryland and Virginia together had 130,000 "equally destitute" people who could benefit from teacher training.

Lenox claimed that the Miner school was manufactured to make mischief by inviting blacks "from every section of the union" into the District of Columbia. He also claimed that their newly educated status would only lead to trouble and "create a restless population, less disposed than ever to fill that position in society which is allotted to them."

Miner could take some small comfort in the fact that at least this time she was not in trouble with abolitionists. Lenox, propelled both by the growing tensions in the country over slavery and an impolitic fund-raising letter for the school that appeared in Northern papers, charged that abolitionists had gained control. He predicted that "our District will be converted into the headquarters of slavery agitation" and reminded readers that "[t]here has been a persistent agitation of the question of the abolition of slavery in this District [and that] is one of the leading purposes of a powerful if not controlling section of the Republican party."

Over the course of his attack, Lenox made a candid observation on the difficulties faced by the black community even as he advocated for the school to be closed. He acknowledged that white immigrants were being favored for work that previously had been held by blacks and recognized that this had put the black community at a disadvantage. The *National Era* again mounted a strong defense of Miner, and her school struggled on. In that issue, Dr. Bailey announced that the office of the *National Era* had moved to the newly erected "Republican Building," at the corner of Indiana Avenue and Second Street.

According to William Still, the Underground Railroad in Washington was doing a "marvellously [*sic*] large business" in the late 1850s. His records show that "William Penn," the pseudonymous Jacob Bigelow, working with Arrah Weems, Ezra Stevens, and other unnamed black and white operatives in the city, sent a steady stream of runaways from the Washington area to Philadelphia. Townsend Derrix escaped from his German owner in Alexandria. William Triplett fled from a woman named Fairfax, likely with some family connection to the Lord Fairfax who had originally settled most of northern Virginia. Mary Jones escaped from Henry Harding, a prominent farmer in Montgomery County whose son was married to Francis Valdenar's daughter. To the delight of Underground Railroad operatives, one fugitive escaped from Rep. John Mason, the author of the hated Fugitive Slave Act.

George Johnson abandoned a large Kalorama estate in northwest Washington, and fugitive Harrison Cary reported to Still that he had been ranked as one of the city's best bricklayers. Some runaways who had been hired out by their owners ran away from the home, hotel, boardinghouse, or farm where they had been sent. Oscar Payne left the Episcopal High School in Fairfax County, where he had been hired out to the Rev. J. P. McGuire. Rebecca Jackson escaped from Georgetown with her daughter and safely reached Philadelphia accompanied by her free husband, Robert Shorter, who carried the surname of a large and well-known black family, many of whom had been born free. A slave owner had once complained in an advertisement that his missing property might well claim to belong to the free tribe of Shorter.

ELEVEN

Dred Scott and the Rise of Lincoln

The very issue of whether the rights set forth in the Declaration of Independence, the Constitution, and the laws of the land applied to "colored people" came before the Supreme Court in *Scott v. Sanford*. Dred Scott claimed that he and his family were entitled to their freedom because his owner had taken them into free territory as well as into the free state of Illinois. Montgomery Blair, the son of Francis Blair and the future postmaster general under Abraham Lincoln, argued Scott's case before the Supreme Court. The antislavery forces were particularly concerned because the proslavery forces were arguing that no state or territory could outlaw slavery. Under the Fifth Amendment to the Constitution, it would unlawfully deprive citizens of property: their slaves.

In 1857 the Supreme Court issued a decision that grievously set back any hope of progress for the black community. It ruled that black people, even if free, were not citizens of the United States and therefore could not bring suit in federal courts. Maryland native Chief Judge Roger Taney wrote the majority opinion, ruling that the rights outlined in the Declaration of Independence did not apply to blacks and they therefore could not bring suit in federal court. Taney also wrote that the federal government lacked the authority to ban slavery in the territories and, as many interpreted the decision, from anywhere in the country. On the face of it, the decision appeared to overrule every emancipation act passed in the Northern states.

Speeches and meetings were organized in major cities in the North to condemn the decision. Under the leadership of Underground Railroad operative William Still, wealthy black abolitionist Robert Purvis, and fiery Quaker Lucretia Mott, a meeting was held in Philadelphia to register their strong opposition to the newest attack on black Americans. The speeches were rousing and strong resolutions spelled out their outrage. But the sharp words of Mary Ann Shadd Cary in the *Provincial Freeman*, the newspaper she founded in Chatham, Canada, after fleeing in the wake of the Fugitive Slave Act of 1850, reflected the despair of many. Those "resolutions amount to nothing," she wrote about the meeting in Philadelphia. "Your national ship is rotten" and you should "leave that slavery-cursed republic." A few months later, the Canadian newspaper reported that the Port of New York began to substitute "native" for "citizen" on black seaman papers. If left to stand, *Dred Scott* would permanently marginalize black Americans to the outer periphery of society.

In 1858 the sharply growing tensions over slavery played out during a contentious senatorial campaign in Illinois. Abraham Lincoln challenged Stephen Douglas to a series of debates throughout the state for an Illinois Senate seat. The debates were covered widely by the press and focused increasing attention on Lincoln. Douglas charged Lincoln and the Republican Party with putting the rights of black people above those of whites and sponsoring miscegenation. In response to Douglas's race-baiting, Lincoln calmly answered that he could approve of freeing an enslaved woman without being required to marry her, and he continued to condemn any extension of slavery westward.

Just as Emily Edmonson had claimed that the rights set forth in the Declaration of Independence applied to "colored people" in her letter to Myrtilla Miner, so did Lincoln. But under hostile questioning from

Stephen Douglas, Lincoln admitted that, like the vast majority of white people in the North, where blacks were proscribed from voting, barred from juries, and relegated to segregated schools, he did not advocate full equality. But Lincoln adamantly argued that blacks had the same right to earn a living and feed their families as white people. The dual blows of the Kansas-Nebraska Act and the *Dred Scott* decision created more Republicans across the North. Kansas continued to be the hot spot of contention over slavery. When a clearly fraudulent referendum supported a state constitution that made slavery legal and proscribed death for abolitionists, even Stephen Douglas, the proponent of popular sovereignty, was appalled. In a move that doomed his presidential ambitions, Douglas publicly condemned the proposed constitution, which passed the U.S. Senate but was defeated by five votes in the House of Representatives.

Lincoln lost to Douglas in a conservative state where the senatorial elections were conducted in the state legislature, but he had made his mark as a national figure.

<hr />

In Washington, crime had precipitously increased in the late 1850s. The Senate began an investigation that reported that "[r]iot and bloodshed are of daily occurrence. Innocent and unoffending persons are shot, stabbed, and otherwise shamefully maltreated, and not infrequently the offender is not even arrested." Senator Andrew Johnson of Tennessee, the future Republican vice president, pooh-poohed the report. He reminded his colleagues that "[p]ockets are picked [and] men are also garroted or robbed" in New York, New Orleans, and Baltimore.

But the most shocking crime of that era did not take place in one of the poorer neighborhoods like Swampoodle, just northwest of the Capitol, near where the Union Station would later be built, or the increasingly dangerous section of the city known as "the Island," cut off by the Washington Canal, south of the Smithsonian. In February 1859, on a well-groomed sidewalk in Lafayette Square, Rep. Daniel Sickles of

New York shot dead Barton Key, the prosecutor who convicted Drayton and Sayres. Key, by then a widower, had been conducting a dangerously indiscreet liaison with the congressman's wife and had rented a house on Fifteenth Street from a black man where the lovers could meet. He would signal Theresa Sickles to meet him at the house by waving a white handkerchief near her Lafayette Square home.

When evidence of the affair eventually reached Sickles, a rising presence in the Democratic Party, he grabbed two seven-inch derringer pistols from his bedroom and shot and killed the unarmed Barton Key, nattily dressed in striped gray pantaloons with matching vest, a white shirt, and a brown tweed jacket. In what became the nineteenth-century equivalent of the O. J. Simpson murder trial, played out in a "dingy little room in the City Hall" still presided over by Judge Thomas Hartley Crawford, Sickles successfully raised one of the first temporary insanity defenses. The murder trial broke "the vulgar monotony of partisan passions and political squabble" but only briefly.

Gamaliel Bailey did not live long enough to see the Republicans put a president in the White House. On June 5, 1859, he died at sea. He had played his role well in the antislavery movement that led up to the Civil War. After the capture of the *Pearl*, the once sprightly editor made a memorable stand in defense of his First Amendment rights to print antislavery articles even while bricks were hurled through the windows of his newspaper, and he encouraged Harriet Beecher Stowe to write the serial for his newspaper that would become *Uncle Tom's Cabin*, an invaluable force in the antislavery crusade. No other antislavery newspaper publishing in slave territory lasted as long as his did.

The next crisis to push the country closer to war took place in a small mountain town in western Virginia. On October 16, 1859, seven months before the national Republican convention was scheduled to take place in Chicago, Captain John Brown, an abolitionist visionary with few scruples about bloodshed, led a failed raid against the federal arsenal in Harper's Ferry, Virginia, with the primary purpose of triggering a slave uprising.

The messianic Brown believed that he was on a mission from God that could not be stopped, and was disappointed when Frederick Douglass refused to join him. Gerrit Smith and Samuel Gridley Howe, radicalized by the Fugitive Slave Act, "Bleeding Kansas," and the *Dred Scott* decision, were among the handful of Northern men who had secretly financed the scheme. After a debacle that left most of Brown's men dead, and those who survived sentenced to death—with not one slave freed—Gerrit Smith suffered a nervous collapse and was institutionalized in New York, while Douglass and Howe fled the country until things calmed down. It didn't take long for accusatory fingers to point at Joshua Giddings. The well-known radical antislavery congressman was compelled to publish a statement that Brown "had never consulted me in regard to the Harper's Ferry expedition or any other expedition or matter."

Senator William Seward of New York, the leading contender for the Republican nomination to run for president that same year, issued a statement condemning Brown and upholding the death sentence. So did Abraham Lincoln. The Rev. Samuel Cox, one of the speakers at the rally in the Broadway Tabernacle to raise money for Mary and Emily, reported to a meeting of missionary workers in New York that he had been asked to send a letter to Gov. Henry Wise of Virginia asking that John Brown be pardoned. Cox explained that he pitied both Brown and Gerrit Smith, but he firmly believed Brown should be hanged. He also suggested that slavery may serve God's purpose and urged his audience to consider the possibility that slavery was God's way of rebuking them for their failure to bring Christianity to Africa. At least slavery had brought the "benighted" Africans to America where they could be taught the gospel.

Ripples from the John Brown raid carried into slave territory everywhere, including Montgomery County, Maryland, where Emily and her siblings had grown up. A grand jury ordered the county sheriff to search all black homes and confiscate guns and other weapons. The day after Brown was hanged, as he was increasingly being viewed in the

North as a martyr rather than a fool, county members formed a militia "for the protection of their homes and firesides, in these times of excitement." Charles M. Price, the slave trader who lived next to St. Mary's Catholic Church and lost Ann Maria Weems to the Underground Railroad, served as an officer in the militia. The county sheriff was instructed to make sure that no blacks were in possession of guns or any other dangerous weapons.

As the debate in Washington focused on the conflict over the extension of slavery into the territories, the movement to end slavery in the District of Columbia remained stalled. Antislavery activists had shifted their attention to the territories, knowing that it was far harder to excise slavery once it had taken hold. Some said that slavery in Washington would soon disappear, but no one seemed to know just when that would be.

The U.S. Census of 1860 showed a decrease of some five hundred slaves over ten years, bringing the total number of enslaved in the District of Columbia to 3,185, while the free black community rose by just over 1,000 to 11,131—although the real numbers of free blacks in the city was likely higher. Washington's blacks were still technically prohibited from operating restaurants, boardinghouses, and other establishments, but they knew how to circumvent those laws. Beverly Snow's restaurant had reopened in the hands of a free black man not long after the riot, and several black caterers were increasingly successful. James Wormley, a caterer and the brother of one of the men who was arrested for acting as an agent for the *Liberator*, had opened a boardinghouse at the family's substantial home at Fifteenth and I Streets. For the U.S. Census for 1850, he exercised some caution by declaring that he had no occupation. In 1860 he allowed that he owned a restaurant, and five servants were included in his household. After the Civil War, he would be the proprietor of one of the city's most elegant hotels, much preferred by European diplomats.

Wormley's boarders before the outbreak of the Civil War included

General Winfield Scott as well as the volatile senator Louis Trezevant Wigfall of Texas, who arrived in Washington with his family in 1859. The senator's daughter later described Wormley's as "even in those days the acme of comfort." Wigfall is said to have killed one man in a duel in 1840 and also maimed the future congressman Preston Brooks, leaving him in constant need of the cane that he used to bludgeon Charles Sumner. Wormley's may have been the site for plotting one of the city's more bizarre schemes. Wigfall led a cabal that planned to kidnap President James Buchanan so that a true Southerner, Vice President John Breckinridge, could become president. Saner minds vetoed the idea, but it's intriguing to wonder what they would have done with poor Buchanan.

Wormley's success was the exception for the black community. Life was a struggle to stay housed, clothed, fed, and employed and the authorities were far more likely to accuse black residents of crimes and enforce penalties they had little chance of fighting. Insidious racism was the accepted norm in Washington, where the large majority of free blacks lived in poverty and oppression with no access to the free education offered to the children of the white population. Emily's siblings paid to send their children to school—the boys likely to the Cook school, and the girls to the Miner school until it suspended operations in 1861. A few years later, after an increasingly unstable Miner set out for California, Senator Henry Wilson would resuscitate the school when he marshaled a bill through Congress that incorporated the Miner school into the public school system.

The Edmonsons took great comfort in the warmth and love of family and good friends and rejoiced in the birth of children and mourned the loss of loved ones. Paul and Amelia were near most of their children and may have stayed in the cottage on the grounds of the Miner school north of N Street near Twentieth Street. There are references to "tenants" in some of the Miner papers, but no names are mentioned after the initial days when the Edmonsons moved onto the school property from Montgomery County. In 1858, the City Directory of Washington listed the Edmonsons' residence as N Street "near Fourteenth Street." In the 1860 directory, Paul Edmonson was again listed on Twentieth Street. In the U.S. Census of that same year, Amelia "Edmuns," described as sixty years old, was listed as the head of the family household, possibly because Paul, listed as seventy-three years old, was ill. It is also possible that Amelia was listed that way for no reason other than the census taker's whim, as reflected in the garbled surname.

On April 5, 1860, the Edmonsons celebrated the wedding of twenty-five-year-old Emily Edmonson Fisher to forty-five-year-old Larkin Johnson in the District of Columbia. After the wedding, the grown woman who had made a remarkable journey to freedom left Washington to return to the rolling hills of Montgomery County, Maryland, to live on a farm just a few miles from where she had grown up. Emily now had a husband who was a near replica of the most important man in her life: her father.

Larkin Johnson had likely lived in Maryland all of his life and doubtless knew the Edmonsons. In a will dated December 10, 1846, Thomas Waters of Montgomery County stated that he did "hereby release from slavery, liberate, manumit, and set free my negro man Larkin Johnson." He also filed an executed document to free Johnson dated December 21, 1848, which was recorded in the Maryland Colonization Society Manumission Book, as required by law. However, the enforcement provisions of that law requiring all slaves freed to leave the state had been long ignored.

At the time Larkin was freed, he had a wife, named Lucy, and a year-old son, named Benjamin. The U.S. Census of 1850 reveals that Larkin and Lucy Johnson were living with four children under the age of six, in Howard County, just north of Montgomery. Five years later, Larkin Johnson purchased ten acres of land for $265 from William S. Bond, a prominent manufacturer of bone dust. His land was located in Montgomery County, just south of a small collection of shops that served Sandy Spring's strong Quaker community, and only a few miles northeast of where Emily had grown up.

Sometime between 1850 and 1860, Lucy Johnson died. When Emily married Larkin, she became stepmother to seventeen-year-old Benjamin, sixteen-year-old Mary, thirteen-year-old Martha, and nine-year-old Charles. In 1860, they were among fifty-one black landholders in Montgomery County, Maryland, who together owned a total of 17,142 acres. The Johnsons would spend the next twelve years in Sandy Spring raising their children and working the farm. The war years were a time of much entitled peace for Emily. Sandy Spring, with its strong enclave of Quakers who had freed their slaves in the late eighteenth century, was one of the least hostile places where a free black family could live in a slave state.

The Sandy Spring Quakers, surrounded by their slaveholding neighbors, were generally not outspoken about slavery, but they lived their beliefs, aiding the black community where possible, and casting votes against measures that would support slavery in any way. In 1842 Lucretia Mott, one of the leading antislavery Quaker activists of the time, visited both the Sandy Spring and Brookeville meetings. One attendee remarked that her two-hour sermon was "a very pointed discourse, delivered in most beautiful language" that resulted in "no disorder." Only two or three Quakers showed up at the Brookeville meeting to hear her speak.

Nonetheless, some Friends are believed to have come to the aid of slaves on the run. The Hallowells, the Gilpins, and the Stablers may have risked the law and the wrath of neighboring slave owners to quietly aid passengers on the Underground Railroad making their way north. It is very possible that they worked with a young married Sandy Spring woman who had close connections with the Underground Railroad cell that worked in and around Washington—Emily Edmonson Johnson.

The Johnsons were not completely removed from sectional tensions over slavery and the everyday hostilities showered on both free blacks and slaves. The year before Emily married Larkin Johnson, Francis Valdenar, the man who had sold her and her siblings to Joseph

Bruin, attended a meeting of the Montgomery County Slaveholders' Association to elect delegates to a statewide convention. Two months later the state convention proposed expelling all free blacks from the state and prohibiting all future manumissions. The General Assembly of Maryland rejected their proposal.

----•◦•----

At the Republican National Convention in Chicago in May 1860, party operatives wrestled with the difficult task of nominating a candidate who could pass the antislavery litmus test while still attracting voters from the center. To the shock of William Seward, the acknowledged leading candidate going into the convention, and Salmon Chase, the "attorney for the fugitive slave" who believed he had a good chance of stealing that nomination from Seward, operatives for a still largely obscure favorite son from Illinois maneuvered his nomination. Abraham Lincoln, a powerful voice against the extension of slavery, could also appeal to "western" states like Illinois. And he was too recently reactivated as a politician to bring a history of "ultra" or "radical" votes to the table. Lincoln made it clear that the Constitution protected the rights of the states to govern their own affairs.

Lincoln garnered only 40 percent of the popular vote and lost every slave state, but easily won enough electoral votes to give him the presidency. The conservative *New York Herald* would later describe that election as the "day a sectional party, born of fanaticism, and nurtured for thirty years by a violent agitation which pervaded the lecture room, the schoolhouse, the pulpit and the family hearthstone, was elevated to power."

While the ultra abolitionists were troubled that the president-elect respected the sanctity of the Southern states to decide whether they would remain slave under the Constitution, the South was in an uproar. Its worst nightmare had come true: a Black Republican had won the White House. For most, any hope of extending slavery ended with that election, and discussions swiftly shifted to disunion.

By the end of January of 1861, two months before Lincoln's inauguration, secession fever had triumphed in the cotton states, and an exodus of Southern senators and congressman prepared to leave Washington. Mrs. Jefferson Davis graciously invited her highly skilled dressmaker to leave Washington with her, but Mrs. Elizabeth Keckley, a free woman of color, demurred. Robert Toombs and his wife packed their many belongings in a coach—Mrs. Toombs had been one of the most elaborate hostesses in Washington—to begin their long journey South. But their trip was delayed. The Toombs' enslaved coach driver, very likely the same man who had attempted to escape with William Chaplin in 1850, had run away.

Much of the Upper South was still undecided on whether to leave the Union or stay. The *Charleston Mercury*'s Washington correspondent reported that with Jefferson Davis, Robert Toombs, and Judah Benjamin gone from Washington, "the remaining Southern States will be utterly powerless. How they can consent to stay in the Abolition Union, I cannot tell; yet I fear they will do so."

In February 1861 the newly established Confederate government held a convention in Montgomery, Alabama, where delegates drafted a temporary constitution. Their document was modeled on the Constitution of the United States but omitted the troubling phrase "a more perfect Union." The Confederate constitution also declared each state sovereign and independent and guaranteed that slavery could be exported into any lands the Confederacy might acquire.

On January 1, 1861, even before Mississippi and Louisiana had voted on secession, a crush of Montgomery County residents came together at Rockville Courthouse to vote on whether Governor Hicks should summon the General Assembly to hold a convention on the question of secession. Those who supported secession pushed for the convention. To the relief of those who favored the Union, the resolution was defeated in a near tie vote of 133–131. The *Montgomery County Sentinel*, then strongly sympathetic to the South, knew just who to blame. "The attendance upon this meeting of so large a number of

Quaker Friends is significant," the paper noted, because the wishes of the proslavery people of Montgomery were "controlled and silenced by a class of men whose very religion is opposed to negro slavery." One member of that class, Henry Stabler, objected strongly to that paper's characterization and canceled his subscription to the *Sentinel*.

Many of Washington's older families favored the South, but there were many voices in the capital that strongly supported the Union. Georgetown's Southern sympathizers were particularly passionate. Robert Dodge, the brother of Francis Dodge Jr., who had owned three slaves on the *Pearl*, made it clear that he was a Unionist. His stables and warehouses were set on fire. Lumberyards, a grocery store, and even a few private homes belonging to other Unionists were torched. The Georgetown council offered a reward of three hundred dollars for anyone who helped to apprehend the busy arsonists.

In a surprising move for a town that was a part of the District of Columbia, the city council of Georgetown was persuaded to sponsor a debate on the issue of disunion. On January 31, 1861, amid competing marching bands playing "Hail Columbia," "Yankee Doodle," and "Dixie," residents packed Forrest Hall. Proposed resolutions were greeted with shouts, hisses, and applause and then just as quickly discarded. One resolution, emblematic of the tumult of feeling, set forth the proposition that "while we oppose secession as unconstitutional, we equally oppose coercion as incompatible with the spirit of our institutions." If there was any winner in the debate, it was likely the side for disunion. A reporter for the *Washington Evening Star* pointed out that as the meeting ended, the cheers for South Carolina's palmetto flag rang out the loudest.

With the help of Allan Pinkerton, the most experienced and competent detective in railroad security and an Illinois operative on the Underground Railroad who had worked with John Brown to move fugitives north, Lincoln safely arrived in Washington for his inauguration. On March 4, 1861, two weeks after Jefferson Davis had been inaugurated president of the Confederacy, Lincoln joined President

Buchanan in an open carriage to ride from the Willard Hotel to the East Portico of the Capitol for his swearing in. Tensions were high and streets were rife with rumors that the capital was in imminent danger of attack. Lincoln insisted on the open carriage to dispel the lingering uneasy feeling left by his clandestine entry into the city, and the Avenue was well guarded. A *Baltimore Sun* reporter wrote that "I have seen today such a sight as I could never have believed possible at the capital of my country. An inauguration of a President surrounded by an armed soldiery, with loaded pieces and fixed bayonets."

Congressmen and senators awaited the inauguration on the steps of the Capitol, where a scaffold surrounded the iron support for the new dome. Among the politicians there was the sullen, dark-haired and full-bearded Senator Wigfall of Texas, still living at Wormley's boardinghouse. He had lingered in Washington while the Texas legislature wrangled over its articles of secession, even in the face of a move in the Senate to have him expelled for disloyalty. He would soon leave Washington for the Confederacy, taking an eyewitness account of Lincoln's inauguration that would play well at dinner parties in Montgomery, Alabama.

The skeletal eighty-four-year-old Roger Taney, Chief Justice of the Supreme Court, waited to swear in the sixteenth president of the United States. While some of the Southern justices resigned, including Justice John Archibald Campbell of Alabama, Taney remained on the bench of the Supreme Court until his death in 1864.

In a carefully crafted inaugural address, Lincoln repeated that he had "no purpose, directly or indirectly, to interfere with the institution of slavery in the States where it exists." He offered nothing new when he said, "I believe I have no lawful right to do so, and I have no inclination to do so." He affirmed that he would uphold the Constitutional clause that fugitives from "service," who fled to other states would not be protected but cautioned that no free blacks should be in danger of being caught up as runaways. Even with that qualification, it was not a statement that would endear him to abolitionists.

Still, Lincoln pointed out that the only substantial dispute between the North and the South was that "one section of our country believes slavery is *right* and ought to be extended, while the other believes it is *wrong* and ought not to be extended." But there was nothing in the Constitution that settled this issue, Lincoln acknowledged, and it was an issue that must be settled by majority opinion.

Lincoln also addressed the South directly. "In *your* hands, my dissatisfied fellow-countrymen, and not in *mine,* is the momentous issue of civil war. . . . *You* have no oath registered in heaven to destroy the Government, while I shall have the most solemn one to preserve, protect, and defend it." The new president closed in the hope that the Union would hold if Americans were touched by the "better angels of our nature."

Neither angels nor goodwill descended, and Washington braced for war. On April 6, Patent Office examiner Horatio Nelson Taft, whose children played nearly daily with Lincoln's sons, wrote in his diary that "[t]he City is again threatened and a *"Coup d'État"* may be attempted in a few days." Taft cleaned his gun, but like everyone, got on with his usual affairs, including the hire of a new slave. Taft set off to pay twenty-four dollars to a Mrs. Smith, who lived near the Navy Yard, for the yearly hire of her "slave girl Larney." He returned with her to the family home at Franklin Square, between Twelfth and Thirteenth Streets near I Street, NW. The next day, Taft recorded in his diary that "Larney (the black chattel) is crouched behind the stove keeping comfortable, a basket of *young chickens* is in the corner by her." That he would define her so casually as "the black chattel" reflects on the general comfort with slavery among Washington's white middle class.

At 4:30 A.M., on Friday, April 12, 1861, a little over a month after Lincoln's inauguration, General Pierre Gustave Toutant-Beauregard ordered Confederate troops to open fire on Fort Sumter, in South Carolina. Word of the attack reached Washington that afternoon, and crowds began to surround the outdoor newspaper notice boards where the latest telegraphic reports were posted. Nothing could have created a greater purpose or more unity in the North, and volunteers thronged enlistment stations.

Jacob Dodson, a six-foot-tall free black Washington resident immediately offered to raise a contingent of three hundred black troops. Some fifteen years earlier, Dodson had crossed a still uncharted Sierra Nevada with the earlier Republican presidential contender John Charles Fremont and Kit Carson. The report on the expedition prepared for the government stated that Dodson, "a free young colored man of Washington City . . . performed his duty manfully throughout the voyage." Secretary of War Simon Cameron politely but firmly declined his offer, informing him that they had no plans to enlist colored troops.

By April 22, government departments had instituted a loyalty oath or, as some called it, the "strong oath." Michael Shiner, a black man who worked at the Navy Yard, wrote in his diary that a justice of the peace "administered the oath of allegiance to the mechanics and labouring class of working men without distinction of colour for them to stand by the stars and stripes and defend for the Union." The commander of the yard could not take that oath. He offered his formal farewells, and then departed to join the Confederacy.

Soldiers were squeezed into accommodations wherever space could be found in the city, including the Senate chamber of the Capitol, the U.S. Treasury Building, the Patent Office, Georgetown College, and even the White House. New camps and temporary buildings were thrown up, including one on Sixteenth Street's Meridian Hill, where some had once argued that a new prime meridian should run. As federal soldiers marched in, some Washington residents marched over the bridges to Virginia to join the Confederacy. Half of the students at Georgetown decamped to go south. Some left the city simply out of fear of attack.

By May 1861, Washington was bursting with new recruits and office seekers; carriages, carts, horses, and hustlers added to the usual mix of animals that either ran loose or were herded through streets that were muddy when it rained and dusty when it was dry. The Twelfth Regiment from New York set up camp in Franklin Square, and the Taft family became used to their constant drilling. The Seventh Regiment camped near the statue of George Washington on Pennsylvania Avenue in Foggy Bottom, while fifteen hundred members of the largely Catholic Sixty-Ninth Regiment from New York marched through Georgetown to reach their quarters at Georgetown College.

Federal troops had moved quickly to secure the bridges that connected Virginia to the District of Columbia. By May 1861, troops were occupying Alexandria. Slave trader Joseph Bruin fled farther south into Confederate territory.

As confident Northern regiments marched down the Avenue followed by endless lines of supply wagons, it seemed unthinkable that the rebels inching northward could hold out against such a force. Washingtonians took excursions around the city to visit the encamped troops, often stopping for supper at Willard's or ice cream at Gautier's. When the first secession flag was captured in northern Virginia, it was proudly raised high at Willard's Hotel, where anyone looking for the latest news or gossip would gravitate. Mary Todd Lincoln took her carriage to the Capitol grounds to watch a Massachusetts regiment drill on the east lawn.

Julia Ward Howe, the wife of Samuel Gridley Howe, was a guest at Willard's with her husband in 1861. In their visit to the troops, they listened to the men sing "John Brown's Body." She returned to Willard's to pen new lyrics to the old melody that would become the "Battle Hymn of the Republic." In most of today's renditions the words read "Let us live to make men free." Julia Ward Howe, a long-standing abolitionist whose husband had become equally radical, had written, "Let us die to make men free."

Skirmishes broke out across the Potomac in Virginia and along the C&O Canal. But to many these initial forays into war seemed more exhilarating than alarming. Troops continued to parade in their encampments to the delight of spectators. After a parade at Camp Cameron the soldiers of the Seventh New York performed "gymnastic exercises equal to a circus performance."

Lincoln's election proved a boon for a former operative in Washington's Underground Railroad. In the first year of his administration, the president granted a pardon to Dr. William Boyd, a white man who had served two years of a fourteen-year sentence of hard labor in the District of Columbia penitentiary. Boyd had been captured while assisting a number of slaves' escapes. But for his capture, Boyd would have remained one of the many unnamed black and white operatives who had helped slaves flee.

And while Washington was growing accustomed to preparing for war, residents continued to go on with their own lives, though conversations in black and white homes across the city remained preoccupied with the topic of secession. Couples still married, children were born, and residents died of consumption, scarlet fever, and typhoid fever. In May 1861 Emily Edmonson Johnson's twenty-year-old niece Kate Brent married a young man from Sussex, Delaware, named James H. Paynter, in her parents' home at Eighteenth and L Streets, NW. The Washington correspondent of the *Christian Recorder*, the official organ of the African Methodist Episcopal Church based in Philadelphia, described the "brilliant wedding" in the Brent home as "more than usually solemn and touching." Kate Brent was the oldest of the eight living Brent children. John and Elizabeth Brent had lost their twins, Joseph and Mary, born about a year after the *Pearl* escape. Both children were missing from the 1860 U.S. Census. Then two more children were born: Rebecca and Calvin Stowe, apparently named for the husband of Harriet Beecher Stowe.

The family celebrated the happy wedding "until the wee hours of the morning feasting on the delicacies of the season," with excellent food likely provided by James Wormley. Shortly after the end of the war, Wormley's son, Gerrit Smith Wormley, named for the New York abolitionist, married the bride's younger sister Amelia.

The Brent home filled with family and friends. Emily and Larkin were sure to have driven in from Sandy Spring, and it is possible that some of Paynter's family had made the journey from Delaware. Emily was possibly pregnant at the time; her first child, Ida Johnson, was born in 1862.

Emily's sister Evaline and family came to the wedding from their home right around the corner at 1011 Eighteenth Street, NW. She and her husband, William Ingraham, had three young daughters all under the age of twelve. Ingraham was a messenger at the Coast Survey, a federal agency mandated to chart every inch of coastal land in the United States. His was one of the most prestigious jobs that a black man could attain in the government.

The City Directory listed thirty-six-year-old Martha Edmonson, likely a widow at this time, on Eighteenth Street between K and L Streets, next door to the Ingrahams. Like her sister and brother-in-law, she was listed as owning $1,500 in real estate. Martha's property, together with personal income of $150, was impressive for a former slave. Not one of the white men listed just above her in the census—two cooks, a baker, and a gardener—claimed to own either real estate or personal property. A year later, Martha married Levi Pennington, a waiter, and she would soon be described as a confectioner in the city directories.

Another of Emily's sisters, Eliza Orme, who was once owned and then freed by Secretary of the Treasury Robert Walker, lived nearby on M Street near Nineteenth, just two blocks south of the Miner school. She and her husband, Dennis, had two children, fifteen-year-old Samuel and thirteen-year-old Mary. Orme was also employed as a messenger at the Coast Survey. Richard Edmonson, whose freedom had been purchased almost immediately after he was captured on the *Pearl*, and his wife, Martha, now had six children and lived close to Eliza and Dennis Orme on M Street. Their oldest, twenty-one-year-old Georgiana Edmonson, was listed in the 1860 U.S. Census as working as a live-in servant in the home of Thomas P. Morgan, a fertilizer manufacturer, with real estate holdings of $21,000 and personal income of $5,000. The census indicated that Georgiana could read and write, skills not yet widespread among the white working class or the new immigrants.

Ephraim, for whom Emily had traveled north twice to raise money for his freedom, had married Mary Bannister the year before and the young couple lived with Paul and Amelia on Twentieth Street. Neither Samuel nor John Edmonson was at the wedding. Samuel and his growing family were either in England or in Australia, and John was lost to slavery in the South.

———◦※◦———

Even before the first battle of the Civil War took place, a significant number of runaway slaves made their way to federal encampments in the South or managed to cross the bridges into the District of Columbia. Lincoln had pledged on his oath to uphold the Constitution, which included a clause that provided for the return of runaway servants. He was also desperate to keep slave owners in the border states calm and firmly attached to the Union. But the steadily increasing march of fugitive slaves made it clear the enslaved viewed things differently.

Not long after the bombing of Fort Sumter, the portly and often abrasive Gen. Benjamin Butler of Massachusetts was commanding the federal holdout at Fortress Monroe in Virginia when three slaves slipped across Union lines to take refuge. The men had been building Confederate fortifications and belonged to a Confederate officer, who approached the fort under a white flag to demand the return of his property. Butler refused. The men had been actively working to support the rebel forces, and Butler cleverly declared them "contraband" property of war. He suggested to their owner that he would gladly return the runaways if he would take "a solemn oath to obey the laws of the United States." The officer left without his slaves, and an exception to the Fugitive Slave Act was created. Thousands of slaves began to pour into federal encampments and a new branch of the Underground Railroad soon opened when men returned to collect their wives and children and bring them across the lines to live with them.

On Saturday, July 20, 1861, as regiment after regiment filed across the Potomac River to Virginia, rumors flew through the capital that the federal forces would engage the Confederates the next day. Sabbath or not, Washingtonians packed up picnic baskets and rented every available horse and carriage, determined to watch the war. William Russell, the sharp-tongued *London Times* reporter, observed that "the French cooks and hotel-keepers . . . have arrived at the conclusion that they must treble the prices of their wines [and] of the hampers of provisions which the Washington people are ordering to comfort themselves at their blood Derby." Excited residents crossed the Potomac River on the Long Bridge at the foot of Fourteenth Street or took the path along the aqueduct bridge in Georgetown.

The picnicgoers would have been shocked had anyone suggested to them that the battle they were about to witness had anything to do with ending slavery. One of them might have accurately retorted that if that was the purpose of this war, why hadn't the federal troops begun by freeing the slaves of Washington, D.C.? But there was no doubt that the conflict over slavery had caused the split. They had only to read the speeches of the late John Calhoun or Jefferson Davis and the other Confederate leaders to know that.

Washington residents mixed with congressmen and senators, gangs of reporters, and a daguerreotypist named Mathew Brady, lugging his heavy equipment to capture a permanent image of the war. They anticipated a quick return to the city after the battle to join in the victory celebrations. Back in Washington, Senator Charles Sumner of Massachusetts, who had rejoined the Senate, buttonholed anyone in hearing range to announce that the war was all but won. All the early reports from the battlefield agreed with him.

But the grim-faced men straggling back to Washington that evening told a different story. The battle had turned against the federal troops, and they had fallen apart and fled. Sightseers and soldiers ended up entangled on the Virginia roads and bridges. Senator Henry Wilson of Massachusetts fruitlessly screamed at retreating troops to turn around, regroup, and face the enemy. The streets of Washington and Georgetown that evening were clogged with the chaos of retreat and the smell of fear. A number of the three-monthers continued on their retreat until they reached home. Fortunately for the Union troops, the victorious Confederates were either too exhausted or too stunned to pursue them into Washington. Whatever illusions people had held about the length of the war were shattered. It would be protracted, and it would be bloody.

Three months later, Congress codified Butler's contraband policy in the first Confiscation Act, which authorized the taking of all property, including slaves, used to fuel the Confederate military engine. The act specifically stated that contraband slaves would be freed. General John C. Fremont, the head of the western division of the army, took a much larger stab at emancipation. To hearty applause from abolitionists frustrated by Lincoln's refusal to declare the war a battle to end slavery, he declared martial law in the state of Missouri and freed all slaves owned by Southern sympathizers, whether they were being used for the war effort or not. Lincoln, determined to keep control of such political matters and to move cautiously, overruled Fremont and removed him from his post. He was adamant that nothing should destroy the loyalty of the border slave states.

Abolitionists came to the defense of Fremont. In the *Independent*, now edited by Henry Ward Beecher, Harriet Beecher Stowe joined her brother in advising Lincoln to make the war a righteous one and declare that slavery was finished. Even the *New York Times* complained that "[I]t has been said that the war has nothing to do with Slavery, but no one will pretend that Slavery has nothing to do with the war. . . . The most natural way to put an end to a controversy is to remove the cause of it." The *Times*, certainly not an "ultra" publication, felt a need to reassure its readers that they would not be inundated with newly freed slaves. It added that the "general abolition of Slavery in the Southern States would not be attended with the much and justly dreaded evil of a large and free negro population in juxtaposition with the whites, except for a very brief period." Somehow, the paper explained, the laws of supply and demand would replace blacks with whites in the middle and border states and send the blacks in the Lower South off to "Mexico, the West Indies and other tropical regions."

After the disaster at Bull Run, the prim and self-absorbed General George McClellan replaced the lackluster McDowell as commander of the Army of the Potomac. Seeking better intelligence, McClellan turned to an old acquaintance from Illinois, already involved in security issues in the capital: Allan Pinkerton, who operated under the *nom de guerre* of Major E. J. Allen.

The Confederate troops set up winter quarters in Manassas, Fairfax, and Falls Church, Virginia, while McClellan waited for better weather, fewer rebel troops, and ideal battle conditions. Good news finally arrived from the coast of South Carolina. In November 1861 Captain Samuel du Pont captured Port Royal, an area that stretched across the Sea Islands and inland to include the attractive town of Beaufort, just south of Charleston. William Wormley, son of James Wormley, was an eyewitness to the action as Captain du Pont's personal servant. He jokingly wrote a friend that he had planted a "Fort Wormley" flag over a captured fort.

Back in Washington, the prudent General McClellan continued to resist moving against the Confederates still encamped in Manassas. During those winter months, with the war seemingly suspended, the only shots fired were ones of words as the abolitionist campaign made its way to a public forum in Washington. Joseph Henry, the director of the Smithsonian and one of the leading physicists of his day, reluctantly agreed to allow his institution to host a series of lectures on slavery during the winter of 1861–62. Had former Rep. Mason, the author of the Fugitive Slave Law, still been a member of the board of trustees for the Smithsonian, no such lectures would have taken place.

To the amusement of many in the lecture audiences, Henry required each speaker to read a disclaimer to clear the institution of any responsibility for their fiery statements. Some of America's leading abolitionists—journalist Horace Greeley, preacher Henry Ward Beecher, and Garrisonian orator Wendell Phillips—took to the podium in the red sandstone building on the Mall. On the evening of January 3, 1862, President Lincoln, Secretary of the Treasury Salmon Chase, and other members of the administration accepted an invitation to attend Greeley's lecture. Lincoln sat on the platform behind the podium. As Greeley thundered that the war had one purpose—to free the slaves—he pointedly turned to stare at the president sitting directly behind him. Lincoln turned to Homer Byington, the *Tribune's* correspondent, to ask, "What in the world is the matter with Uncle Horace? Why can't he restrain himself and wait a little while?" It was a revelatory comment, suggesting that Lincoln fully believed that the war would end slavery, but only when the time was right. Lincoln wasn't only concerned about retaining the loyalty of the border states. As the editorial in the *Times* strongly implies, most of the North was very concerned about what to do with the "Negro problem" after abolition.

Frederick Douglass, the greatest antislavery orator of them all, was not invited to speak at the Smithsonian lecture series. Joseph Henry could be pushed, but only so far. Douglass delivered his own landmark speech on the war in the National Hall on Market Street in Philadelphia that became his famous "Iron Hand" address. Douglass urged the federal government to "meet, fight, dislodge, drive back, conquer, and subdue the rebels," but he charged that the army was missing a necessary and crucial component—"the iron hand of the black man."

In December 1861 Congress was engulfed with resolutions and bills about war, drunken troops, and slavery. One resolution raised the issue of the ill treatment of fugitive slaves who were being swept up on the streets of Washington and placed in the Blue Jug. On December 4, Senator Henry Wilson of Massachusetts presented a resolution to remedy the crowded and uncomfortable conditions at the D.C. jail. Wilson submitted a thorough investigative report by E. J. Allen, who reported that sixty alleged fugitives were being held in the jail. Allen Pinkerton, using his *nom de guerre*, was keeping his hand in the antislavery cause. The detective reported that some were jailed because they had been picked up on the streets of Washington and assumed to be fugitives of loyal slaveholders from Maryland. Many, however, claimed that they had left hostile territory and were attached to various federal regiments. A large number of the detainees were slaves whose owners had jailed them because they feared they were flight risks.

Senator Sumner raised the issue of discrimination in his own state stemming from the *Dred Scott* decision. He reported that a black man in Boston had been blocked from applying for a patent because he was not a citizen. A few years earlier, Frederick Douglass had been informed that he was not entitled to a passport because he, too, was not a citizen, though his fame was sufficient that it was an unnecessary document for him. Congress quickly passed a resolution that removed any hindrance to obtaining such documents based on race.

TWELVE

Freedom in the District of Columbia

I n December 1861 the city swarmed with "stubborn mules refusing to go, drivers swearing, soldiers marching, drums beating, [and] bands playing." The wide sidewalk that straddled the northern side of Pennsylvania Avenue was filled with "officers and privates, citizens & congressmen, negroes & newsboys, all hurrying with no respect of the custom to move "to the right."

In the midst of apparent chaos, antislavery congressmen and senators returned to the issue that had once been the center of abolitionist activism: ending slavery in the District of Columbia. With the Confederate legislators gone, it should now be possible to quickly pass legislation that would finally put an end to slavery in the nation's capital. But even with the Southerners gone, it was not an easy task. The loyal slave states had no interest in freeing slaves anywhere and, in the case of Maryland, there was a realistic fear that they would be in danger of losing their own slaves to a slave-free Washington. A surprisingly large number of Northerners wanted no part of emancipation.

On December 16, Senator Henry Wilson of Massachusetts introduced Senate Bill 108 to provide for the "immediate, preemptory, and absolute" freedom of all persons of African descent who were enslaved in the federal District. It differed substantially from Lincoln's earlier proposed legislation to end slavery in the capital. Wilson's act called for an immediate, not a gradual, emancipation. It also abandoned President Lincoln's proposed provision that required approval of the white male residents of the District of Columbia. But the bill retained his provision that slave owners would be paid compensation for the emancipation of their slaves: it allocated one million dollars to pay them for the loss of their property.

The bill was sent to committee for further work and was reported back to the Senate in March 1862. It had been amended to provide that only those slave owners who were willing to take a loyalty oath to the Union would receive compensation. Senator Garrett Davis, of Kentucky, proposed an amendment that required all slaves freed under the act to be forcibly colonized outside the limits of the United States. When Senator James R. Doolittle, of Wisconsin, replied that he could never support a bill that required mandatory colonization, Davis shot back that he "was better acquainted with the Negro nature than the senator from Wisconsin." He added that in "ninety-nine cases out of one hundred, freedom ruined industrious slaves." Davis told his colleagues that the state of Kentucky held about 225,000 slaves within its borders and, if they were ever to be emancipated, they would not be allowed to remain there.

Doolittle succeeded in eliminating the forcible colonization clause, but funds would still be available, at a maximum of $100 per person, for any slaves freed by the bill who voluntarily chose to emigrate. But there was still general opposition to the act. Senator Waitman T. Willey, a loyal Virginian from the northwestern section of Virginia, the area that would soon become the state of West Virginia, rose to condemn the entire bill. He spoke, he said, on behalf of two hundred loyal Virginians who were imprisoned in a Richmond dungeon for fighting for the Union.

The following day, as heated debate on the emancipation bill continued, smoke began to fill the Senate chamber, but the legislators remained calm. The smoke signaled that the army bakeries in the basement, which served bread to the troops scattered all over the city, had fired up their ovens and had again "smoked out" the Senate. The session was adjourned, but not before Senator William Fessenden, of Maine, angrily asked what had become of their resolution to move the bakeries out of the Capitol. He was informed that the House of Representatives had refused to pass it on the grounds that such a move might appear unpatriotic. Someone suggested that the bakeries be immediately moved to the basement of the House of Representatives.

When the Senate returned, it passed the amended bill for emancipation in the District of Columbia on a vote of 29–14. The House of Representatives soon followed with a vote of 92–38. The bill now only needed the signature of the president to be made law. Many Unionists in the border states hoped that Lincoln would veto such a radical bill to maintain their loyalty. But opposition to the bill was not restricted to Maryland and the other slave states. Although the bill had mustered enough votes to pass, twenty-two Northern representatives had voted against it. The *New York Times* declared the bill ill-timed, the colonization funding useless, and the provision for immediate emancipation, instead of a gradual program, "mischievous." Even before the act was signed, the *New York Herald* was calling it a disaster. It complained that it had "produced irreparable domestic confusion, breaking up, in many instances, family relations that had subsisted undisturbed for years, and severing associations that were endeared by affections that can be appreciated only by those who have reared their own servants."

What looked to be the coming of emancipation in the District of Columbia signaled to Charles Price that it might be a good time to move farther south. But he saw a business opportunity before he left. He advertised that he wished "to purchase a few likely young Negroes, of both sexes, for Louisiana, to settle a plantation." Price was giving slave owners in the District of Columbia one last chance to sell.

On the lovely spring day of April 16, 1862, Abraham Lincoln signed the bill that immediately freed the enslaved people of the District of Columbia. Secretary of the Treasury Salmon P. Chase, who claimed to have had a significant influence on the monster petition of 1828 from District residents asking for the end of slavery, was now authorized to pay out funds totaling nearly one million dollars to compensate loyal slave owners for losing their valuable property. While the slaves in the District of Columbia were freed as of April 16, the process of compensating the owners would stretch out for many months. Three commissioners appointed by the president to oversee the hearings met together for the first time at city hall nearly two weeks later. Republican Daniel Goodloe, an abolitionist and journalist from North Carolina who had lived in Washington for some time and briefly edited the *National Era* for Gamaliel Bailey, was appointed chairman of the commission. Goodloe had spent a significant amount of time studying issues related to slavery, and wrote a pamphlet about its impact on the economy of the South in 1846. More to the point, in August 1861, he wrote a tract called *Emancipation and the War! Compensation Essential for Peace and Civilization*, which proposed a nationwide compensation program. He estimated that it would take an average of three hundred dollars per slave to accomplish that purpose, the very same figure settled on by Congress for the District of Columbia. It's not surprising that he was considered to be a suitable chairman for the commission.

Some slave owners did not file for compensation because they would not sign a loyalty oath. But 966 slave owners, who filed claims seeking compensation for 3,100 slaves, were willing to sign the oath. They had to then wait to be summoned to the Grand Jury Room at city hall for a hearing to determine whether they were entitled to compensation and, if so, what amount they were entitled to receive.

The hearings got under way later that summer and owners brought their former slaves to city hall. The newly freed slaves were willing to cooperate because they would receive a certificate of freedom, an important protection against imprisonment in the Blue Jug as runaway slaves. But the commissioners were faced with the intriguing question of how they would determine each slave's value. They could hardly rely on the word of the owners, all of whom had a strong motive to overestimate the value of their former slaves—who were undoubtedly the finest cooks, the most skilled bricklayers, the fastest blacksmiths in all of the District of Columbia, or, as a number claimed, the most loyal of servants.

For a more objective estimate, the commissioners hired Bernard Campbell, the slave trader who had taken over Hope Slatter's pen on Pratt Street, in Baltimore, to evaluate the value of the slaves. Campbell arrived in Washington still bearing angry marks on his face from an insurrection in his own slave pen. In late May sixty enslaved men, who had been stored in Campbell's pen by their owners, refused to leave the walled yard to be locked down in their quarters for the night. Twenty-one Baltimore law enforcement officers arrived to quell the disturbance and were met with flying "sticks, pieces of iron, stools, benches and buckets." They were pulled into hand-to-hand combat, and Campbell was knocked down with a strong blow to the back of his head. The slave trader lost his bowie knife in the melee and was lucky not to lose his life. But the city eventually provided enough force to subdue the men, and Campbell went to Washington to straighten out the evaluation process by first rejecting the naïve idea that a slave's alleged loyalty was of any value. After some time, the commissioners became sufficiently experienced so that they were able to evaluate the value of the slaves without the presence of a slave trader.

In the end, the commissioners denied thirty-six petitions, primarily based on evidence of the peititioner's disloyalty. Jacob Smoot's petition for compensation for eight slaves brought into the District of Columbia after federal troops had occupied his Fairfax farm was rejected when witnesses testified that he had supported Virginia's secession and even voted in favor of it. Several claimants were able to successfully rebut witnesses who testified that they were disloyal. The loyalty of widow Lucinda Matthews, of Georgetown, was called into question because she had two sons fighting for the Confederacy. But when Matthews presented her recently deceased husband's will showing that he had cut his rebel sons out of any inheritance until they laid down their arms and abandoned the rebellion, she received her compensation.

At least two fugitives from the *Pearl* were freed by the District of Columbia Emancipation Act. Sarah Jane O'Brien filed a claim for Eleanora Bell and her six-month-old child, Caroline. O'Brien was the daughter of Susannah Armistead, the widow who had steadfastly maintained that she owned the eleven members of the Bell family. She explained that Eleanora Bell had been a gift from her mother and that Caroline was Eleanora's mulatto offspring. The land records of the District of Columbia confirm that on February 20, 1862, "in consideration of love and affection for my daughter Sarah J. O'Brien," Susannah Armistead gave her "Nora Bell, a slave for life." In her petition for compensation, O'Brien described Eleanora as a woman of "dark color, 5'3" or 4" tall . . . very healthy and a good worker." O'Brien claimed $1,200 for the two Bells but received $394 for Eleanora and just under $44 for her daughter. (Every claim was reduced to just under 44 percent of the assessed value.)

Those same land records show that Armistead gave another enslaved woman named Caroline to a different daughter, again for the consideration of her love and affection and $1. She was very likely Eleanora's sister, another veteran of the *Pearl*. There is no information indicating in which city or state Armistead's daughter lived but there is no record of Caroline Bell receiving her freedom in Washington.

The second fugitive of the *Pearl* to be freed by the Emancipation Act in Washington, D.C. was Hannibal Rosier, owned by Ariana Lyles, a wealthy woman who claimed compensation for him, three members of his family, and nine other slaves. She received $197 for Rosier. Several other slave owners who submitted claims, including manufacturer Andrew Hoover and grocer Benjamin Middleton, had had slaves on the *Pearl* fourteen years earlier but their claims were submitted for other people. Francis Dodge Jr., who sent the steamboat *Salem* after the *Pearl*, did not file a petition for compensation. He had been hit particularly hard by the financial crisis of 1857 and had been forced to sell his impressive Georgetown mansion. He likely had sold any slaves he still owned at that time.

Other residents closely associated with the escape filed claims, including Thomas Orme, the policeman who guarded Drayton, and Thomas Carberry, the former mayor who served on the grand jury that indicted the two captains. Thomas Blagden, the wealthy man who had loaned money to the Bells to redeem family members before they could be sold south, presented a compensation claim for three slaves, one of whom was named Charles Bell. He may have been related to Daniel Bell's family, but he was not listed as one of the passengers of the *Pearl*. Joseph H. Bradley, Samuel Edmonson's former employer and prominent attorney who had represented members of the Bell family in their petitions for freedom, made a claim for one slave. He received $219 in compensation for a woman named Louisa Carter.

Joseph C. Willard, who later enlisted as an officer in the Union army, and his brother Henry filed claims for five slaves. Francis P. Blair Sr., who hosted the founding meeting for the Republican Party at his estate in Silver Spring, Maryland, claimed compensation for two women, and he continued to retain slaves in Maryland, where slavery remained legal. George Washington Young, a descendant of Notley Young, who had once owned the vast swath of land that included the wharf area at the foot of Seventh Street, was awarded $17,771.85 for sixty-nine slaves, the highest amount of compensation paid to any one individual. Other descendants of Young presented claims for more than twenty other slaves. Clark Mills, who sculpted the statue of Andrew Jackson and was finishing up the casting of the statue for the top of the new Capitol dome, designed by Thomas Crawford, received compensation for eleven slaves. One can only wonder how many enslaved hands had played a part in the creation of the statue called *Freedom*. One who certainly did was Philip Reed, who continued to work as a free man for Mills in his studio on the Bladensburg Road inside the District of Columbia border. As a slave, he had been the one worker who could figure out how to dismantle the plaster prototype of the statue sent from Italy. Mills received $350 in compensation for Reed's freedom.

The Sisters of the Visitation near Georgetown University received

$4,073.40 for twelve members of the Tilghman family. Ignatius Tilghman, who claimed to be free, also applied for compensation for his own family. In the end the compensation awarded to the sisters for the Tilghman family was reduced by $298.75, the amount that Tilghman had paid for his own freedom. Tilghman received nothing.

A small number of black slave owners claimed compensation for emancipating slaves under the act. They were, in the main, freeing family members of the same surname who had been purchased but not technically freed. There were good reasons why some families did not rush to register family members they had managed to purchase. The city council still retained laws requiring good behavior bonds for free blacks, and struggling families could do without more—patently unfair—financial responsibilities even if they were randomly enforced. In a perverse kind of justice, these black slave owners were able to recoup some of the money that they had likely paid to free their loved ones.

On July 12, 1862, a supplementary act was passed to allow former slaves to come forward to obtain free papers in cases where their owners had not filed for compensation for a variety of reasons. Former slave Phillip Meredith requested a certificate of freedom under these provisions. He reported that his former owner was General Robert E. Lee, "late of Arlington Heights."

The business of the commission was done. Most of the freed slaves continued to carry on with their lives much the same as they always had—except they would now keep their own earnings, and they knew that they could never be forcibly severed from their families and homes and sold as chattel. According to the commissioners' report, some freedmen left the city immediately and headed north, while others set off to work for military units.

Critics of the act from Maryland were correct in one respect. The rate of runaways leaving Maryland quickened. On May 2, 1862, the *Montgomery County Sentinel* reported that "we hear everyday [*sic*] of Negroes running away to Washington which is the abolition paradise." Other newspapers reported clusters of slaves, some as large as fifty, making their way into the District of Columbia from Prince George's County, Maryland, in the hope of finding freedom.

More and more fugitives came from Virginia as well, and many ended up in the Old Capitol Prison on First Street, where Joseph Bruin, the slave trader from Virginia who had purchased the Edmonsons, was also incarcerated after having been apprehended in Loudoun County, Virginia. The authorities used the row of houses owned by Duff Green, the proslavery activist from Kentucky, to house more contraband. One of those houses had once been leased to Mrs. Sprigg, whose boarders had included antislavery forces like Joshua Giddings, Theodore Weld, Joshua Leavitt, Ezra Stevens, and the future president of the United States Abraham Lincoln. Contraband were also being housed in Alexandria, and a camp was built on Arlington Heights, the former home of General Robert E. Lee. Those facilities were often wretched. Black churches and many black women, some who were to become famous, reached out to help the contrabands in the Washington area. Elizabeth Keckley, whose skilled dressmaking fingers now served Mary Todd Lincoln, began collecting relief materials organized for the refugees from slavery and enlisted the first lady as a supporter.

Harriet A. Jacobs, a former slave who had completed an autobiography detailing seven harrowing years when she hid in an attic from her owner, visited contraband facilities and wrote an account of rampant disease and dangerous overcrowding in the camps, where she witnessed barely clothed contraband living with no bedding. She would return to establish the Jacobs Free School in Alexandria to teach literacy to the freedmen. Sojourner Truth would also teach at the Freedman's Village at Arlington Heights.

A Proposal to Free the Slaves

In Sandy Spring, Maryland, Emily and Larkin tended their farm and nurtured their growing family. Larkin sold a parcel of his land to a Sandy Spring man of color and then purchased another smaller lot in the area. The family most likely worshipped at the Sharp Street Methodist Church in Sandy Spring, which had been established in 1822 with help from members of the Quaker community. While the Quakers may have been the black community's most constant supporters in the area, few blacks were drawn to the silent worship of the Friends.

In March 1862, the Tenth Regiment of Massachusetts Volunteers made a foray into Montgomery County accompanied by two local runaway slaves who had joined their camp. The *Montgomery County Sentinel* reported that the runaways took the soldiers to their owners' farms, where they demanded money; one demanded to collect his clothes. The soldiers visited a number of other farms in the area, including the one that belonged to Francis Valdenar, where the proslavery *Sentinel* reported that no harm had been done. The men did move on to another farm, where they shot about a dozen turkeys and made off with a number of chickens. A week later, pro-South forces in the county took their revenge. A Confederate flag was hoisted to fly over the Rockville Courthouse.

On July 7, a frustrated President Lincoln journeyed by steamboat to General George McClellan's headquarters at Harrison's Landing in Virginia and returned convinced that Richmond was in no imminent danger from Union troops. Historian Allen C. Guelzo suggests that it may well have been that on the return from his dismal visit in Virginia that Lincoln began to formulate an emancipation plan under the war powers provisions. And he may also have been influenced by the fact that just three months earlier, he had signed legislation that freed more than three thousand slaves in the nation's capital, and the sun still rose the next day, servants continued to prowl the Center Market to fill boardinghouse tables with canvasbacks and terrapins, and the border states remained in the Union. That success may well have bolstered Lincoln's resolve to take the most radical step ever taken by an American president: the emancipation of nearly four million slaves. It was an act that transformed the war, even if the vast majority of those slaves were still within the bounds of the Confederacy.

But something else might have given Lincoln heart while he was writing the first draft of the Emancipation Proclamation. The log of the Library of Congress shows that, on June 16, 1862, Lincoln or a member of his staff checked out Harriet Beecher Stowe's *Key to Uncle Tom's Cabin*. As Lincoln was writing the document that would end slavery in the United States forever, he may well have been fresh from reading Stowe's many detailed accounts of slavery, including the story of the Edmonson family and the escape on the *Pearl*. Harriet Beecher Stowe's nonfiction account of slavery was returned to the Library of Congress on July 29, 1862.

On July 21, 1862, at a special cabinet meeting, Lincoln read aloud, from handwritten notes, his proposed proclamation, which stated that on the first of January 1863, "all persons held as slaves within any state or states, wherein the constitutional authority of the United States shall not then be practically recognized, submitted to, and maintained, shall then, thenceforward, and forever, be free." Maryland, the other border states, and Southern lands already under the control of the North would not be affected.

Secretary of State William Seward advised Lincoln to delay issuing the order until the army had managed to win a significant battle so that it would not look like the desperate last effort of a collapsing military. Seward, who had come to be seen as a conservative influence on Lincoln and was much distrusted by the radicals, had played an earlier role in the Underground Railroad in his home state of New York. There is evidence that he kept his hand in while he was a member of Lincoln's cabinet. The Seward family papers make reference to a meeting after the war between Seward and James Wormley, who operated the boardinghouse that housed both Union generals and Confederate senators, that links both men to the Underground Railroad in Washington. After Seward had introduced Wormley to other guests in his home, he told them that "Wormley and I went into the emancipation business a year and a half before Mr. Lincoln did, down on the James River." Wormley is said to have catered the government vessels that took the Lincolns and other dignitaries to war sites.

Seward then turned to the well-respected postwar hotel owner and asked, "How was it Wormley—how many slaves did we take off on our steamer?"

"Eighteen," Wormley replied.

Lincoln decided to wait for that military victory before issuing his proclamation, but he continued to prepare for the day when it would be issued. He stubbornly held on to the belief that emancipation would be more palatable to white America if it included a program for voluntary colonization. To that end, on August 14, 1862, the president invited a committee of black men from the District of Columbia to meet with him at the White House: Benjamin McCoy; Edward M. Thomas; Cornelius Clark; John F. Cook, the son of the now deceased founder of the First Presbyterian Church; and John T. Costin, a black descendant of Martha Custis Washington, arrived to listen to what the president had to say.

Lincoln candidly told the men that he believed that free blacks would never be accepted in this country, offering much the same argument used by the American Colonization Society for forty-five years. He asked these men to help put together a contingent of "tolerably intelligent" black men who, with their families, would voluntarily emigrate to a colony in Central America. But Lincoln had also told the men that but for their presence in the country, there would be no war. William Lloyd Garrison's biographer, Henry Mayer, observes that such a startling statement was "both a perverse way of recognizing the abolitionist argument that slavery lay at the root of the controversy and an offensive suggestion that black removal would resolve it." Douglass and Garrison were furious when they heard about the meeting, and Garrison contemptuously called Lincoln the "President of African Colonization."

On September 22, after the Battle of Antietam blocked the South from a victory in Maryland, Lincoln issued a document that would become known as the "preliminary" Emancipation Proclamation. Radical abolitionists were guardedly pleased. Frederick Douglass thought the document too legalistic and wished that Lincoln had condemned slavery as immoral. Slave owners, particularly those living near federal troops, were outraged and jittery. The *National Republican* reported that a fugitive slave who had made his way into a Union encampment near Culpepper, Virginia, reported that the proclamation was "well-known among all the negroes, and it produces the most startling effect." He said that seventeen Negroes, mainly free, had been caught by the Confederate authorities with newspapers that contained the full text of the preliminary Emancipation Proclamation. He reported that they were charged with plotting the uprising of the entire colored population; all seventeen were hanged.

Critics claimed that the proclamation would split the army and diminish support for the war from whites in the North. The Abraham Lincoln who doggedly continued to push both compensated emancipation and colonization had quite suddenly become the ultimate "ultra." Lincoln remarked to a friend that emancipation "will be pushed with all the power left in the federal arm" and that his policy would become "more radical than ever," adding that the war will become "one of subjugation and extermination." As a measure of his new resolve, Lincoln dismissed General McClellan immediately after the fall congressional elections. But the more conservative Republicans were right about one thing: the proclamation created a backlash in the North. Republicans lost a number of seats in those elections, and many wondered if Lincoln could win reelection.

A Promissory Note for Freedom and the Death of the Family Patriarch

Antietam did not, unfortunately, signal a significant turnaround for the Union, and the number of dead and injured continued to mount. In December 1862, General Ambrose E. Burnside's attempt to dislodge

Confederate troops in Fredericksburg collapsed in a debacle that produced more than twelve thousand federal casualties and less than half that amount for the Confederacy. The wounded were transported by steamboat for the five-hour journey up the Potomac River, unloaded at the Seventh Street wharf, transferred to waiting ambulance carts, and then delivered to one of the forty-one hospitals scattered around the District of Columbia. One of the nurses awaiting the wounded at the Union Hotel in Georgetown was Louisa May Alcott, whose uncle had been involved in the Boston support committee for Drayton and Sayres. From an upstairs window, she watched a column of some forty carts approaching the hotel and first thought they were delivering produce from the market. Instead, they were filled with the dying and wounded. With the help of the "colored sisters," who arrived to help care for the men, she got to work. On the other side of Rock Creek, Myrtilla Miner's school was also turned into a hospital, one to treat contraband who had come down with smallpox.

As the New Year approached, supporters and detractors alike anxiously waited to learn if Lincoln would sign the final Emancipation Proclamation in the face of continuing battle losses. On December 29, Lincoln assembled his cabinet for yet another reading of the proclamation with one significant and, to many, startling addition; he had decided to arm the newly freed slaves. At the time that the proclamation was signed, some contraband and a few contingents of black soldiers were already in place. Now the enlistment of black men would be government policy.

Lincoln also agreed to add a closing statement to the proclamation, drafted by Salmon Chase, which spoke to Frederick Douglass's initial criticism that the document was devoid of any comment on justice or morality. Invoking the "considerable judgment of mankind" and the "gracious favor of Almighty God," the proclamation was declared an "act of justice, warranted by the Constitution, upon military necessity."

On New Year's Day, supporters of emancipation across the country gathered in black churches, white churches, halls, and homes, to await the news that the president had signed a document that would declare about three million slaves free (some five hundred thousand would remain in slavery in Maryland and the other loyal slave states). In Washington, the long-standing free black community, the former slaves freed nine months earlier, and the continually arriving contraband did the same. Contraband at the Twelfth Street camp, located on the circle later named for Union General John A. Logan, had gathered to cheer and march well into the night before in anticipation. The next day, a tired crowd packed tightly into the camp's chapel to wait for news of the signing.

But the signing was delayed. Lincoln had detected a clerical mistake in the document and, while a new version of the proclamation was prepared, he hosted the annual New Year's Day reception at the White House. At 2:00 P.M., he returned to his desk, where the corrected document was waiting for him. His hand, still tired from the reception line, shook as he picked up his pen to sign the order that would dwarf all earlier emancipation programs in the North and, more recently, in the District of Columbia. Lincoln finally managed to affix his name to the document, and word sped across the telegraph wires as far west as St. Louis, Missouri, where the wires stopped. From there the news of emancipation traveled by steamboat, Pony Express, and foot.

In Washington, the black community celebrated, and their churches offered special prayers for a new day in America. Word of its signing passed swiftly through the contraband camps. The superintendent of the Twelfth Street camp read the proclamation to an uproar of joy from the assembled crowd, although some of the excitement dissipated when he read out the names of the occupied territories where the proclamation would not apply.

In the North, cheers rang out in the Boston Music Hall, where Harriet Beecher Stowe was in the balcony. Stowe wept as hats flew in the air and people embraced. When the jubilant crowd learned she was there, they called her forward to take a bow. Frederick Douglass celebrated at the packed Tremont Temple in that same city. In the Shiloh Presbyterian Church in New York City, crowds listened to a speech by Henry

Highland Garnet, who had turned back to America after considering a life in Africa. William Lloyd Garrison, always one of Lincoln's fiercest critics, announced that with the Emancipation Proclamation they "had come from midnight darkness to the bright noon of day."

But there were those in the North who condemned the proclamation. The *New York Herald* derided Lincoln for only freeing slaves in territory where they could not be free and leaving slavery intact only in areas where he had the power to free them. It was certainly true that the proclamation only freed those slaves who were inside Confederate lines, but those lines were constantly shifting—and so were the slaves within them. Historian Allen Guelzo, citing William Seward, states that the Emancipation Proclamation likely freed two hundred thousand and even as many as four hundred thousand before the end of the war. In Mississippi alone, twenty thousand slaves in Confederate-controlled land poured into contraband camps around New Orleans and other Union-occupied sites. Many families in Washington and Maryland, including the Edmonsons and the Bells, waited anxiously for word that loved ones who had been sold south over the years were among the thousands fleeing the Confederacy to make their way to freedom.

There was some truth in the predictions that there would be backlash to the proclamation. Some soldiers refused to fight after the Emancipation Proclamation was issued, and there was an increase in racial attacks on black people. In Washington, as federal soldiers who had been convalescing in the city marched back to war, hateful words and rocks flew through the streets. But the army held. Two days after the proclamation was signed, the Union drove back the Confederates in Tennessee. When Lincoln wired his thanks to General William Rosencrans, he reported that "had there been a defeat instead, the nation could hardly have lived over."

More and more black refugees from the South poured into Washington. On March 14, 1863, the *Christian Recorder* published an appeal from the Contraband Relief Association under the signature of its president,

Elizabeth Keckley, asking that donations be sent to Mr. Wormley at his home on I Street in Washington. She asked that ministers appeal to their black congregations to help them relieve "the wants of those destitute people, but also to sympathize with, and advise them. . . ."

On April 16, 1863, crowds of well-dressed black people gathered on the White House lawn to celebrate the first anniversary of the end of slavery in the nation's capital, but it is unlikely that any of the Edmonson attended. Paul Edmonson, a remarkable husband and father, died that same day, and the family was in mourning. Death certificates were not used at the time, and Washington's newspapers only listed the deaths of important white people. But Edward Young, Paul Edmonson's seventeen-year-old grandson, wrote on the inside cover of a notebook that his grandfather died on April 16, 1863, at the impressive age of eighty-four. The once enslaved Paul Edmonson, who had owned his own forty-acre farm in slave territory, raised a truly noteworthy family, and traveled to New York to help free his daughters had lived long enough to see the promise of freedom extended to slaves throughout the rebellious South, including his son John. Paul left his wife property, the proceeds of the sale of his farm, and a loving family. In the City Directory published the next year, his widow was listed as "Amelia Edmondson [sic], (col'd), wid Paul." She was still living at the same address on Twentieth Street with her son Josiah.

As the war ground on, many more soldiers died, and black men were among them. Even before the Emancipation Proclamation, which gave specific authority to enlist black soldiers, some had served with regiments formed in the loyal slave state of Missouri; in New Orleans, where General Butler had put into service the First Regiment Louisiana Native Guards; and in the occupied Sea Islands. Now, with official sanction, Northern states were beginning to form black regiments that would rely on white officers to lead them. Massachusetts authorized the formation of the legendary Fifty-fourth Massachusetts Regiment of black troops, led by Robert Gould Shaw, the son of prominent abolitionists in Boston. That regiment would soon be followed by the Fifty-fifth. High-profile African-Americans, including Frederick Douglass, Henry Highland Garnet, Jermain Loguen, and John Mercer Langston fanned out across the North as paid recruiters. Douglass's two sons enlisted in the 54th, as did many men of color from New Bedford, Massachusetts.

William Bush, the last friend seen by Daniel Drayton before his suicide, saw a number of his family answer the call to serve. His son-in-law William H. W. Gray, served with the Fifty-fourth and became a first sergeant. Bush's daughter, Martha Bush Gray, joined him in the South to nurse the sick and wounded men of the Fifty-fourth and the Fifty-fifth Massachusetts. In a letter she wrote from the field, she noted that in addition to her husband, she had nursed "two cousins, and no less than seven young men that I have taught in the Sabbath School . . . [and] three young men who boarded with my family."

Frederick Douglass considered the arming of black men to be one of the most significant steps taken in the war effort, a step that would overturn the *Dred Scott* decision. However, a disappointed Douglass never received the military commission that he wanted and believed was his due. And he had a new wrong to right: black soldiers were paid almost half of what white soldiers received, apparently on the presumption that they would be serving only in support roles. It would take a year to remove some of the disparity in pay, though it would never be completely equalized during the war.

In May 1863 recruitment began for the First District Colored Volunteers in the city whose slaves were the first to be freed. A notice went out across Washington announcing that "a meeting will be held in Asbury Chapel, corner of 11th & K Streets, on Monday evening next, May 4th, 7:30 o'clock, to organize, and make arrangements to visit the President and receive his orders." One hundred men enlisted that night at Asbury, and recruitment continued at the First Presbyterian Church, where Oberlin-educated John Cook Jr., the son of the late John Cook, was the pastor. Israel Bethel A.M.E. Church, at South Capitol Street, near Independence Avenue, became a major recruiting station and contributed more than just its young men: it would send its pastor, Henry

McNeal Turner, to be the regiment's chaplain—the first black chaplain ever appointed by the U.S. Army.

Most of Emily's brothers were beyond the age of enlistment, but some of their sons were just old enough. On the first day enlistment opened, eighteen-year-old Richard Edmonson—five feet three, with black eyes and hair—signed up for a three-year stint as a drummer for the regiment. His military records at the National Archives carefully note that he had been born free before April 19, 1861, a distinction that entitled him to equal pay with white soldiers. A legal technicality that continued to frustrate Douglass, pay equality was limited to those black soldiers who were free before April 19, 1861; this distinction remained in place until after the end of the war.

Black soldiers would face far more dangerous disparities. Jefferson Davis issued an order refusing to exchange captured colored troops for captured Confederate men, because the former were viewed as stolen property. Captured black soldiers were returned to slavery, and many were executed immediately rather than taken prisoner.

The District of Columbia regiment was taken to Analostan Island, today's Roosevelt Island, across from Georgetown and well out of view of hostile white eyes. There, in what the army called Camp Greene, the black soldiers began training under Colonel William Birney, the son of James Birney, the former slave owner and presidential candidate on the Liberty Party ticket who had enlisted Gamaliel Bailey to work on his abolitionist newspaper in Cincinnati. Gamaliel Bailey died before the Civil War began, but his son, Marcellus, served for a period as a second lieutenant with the District of Columbia's regiment.

In spotless uniforms and proud bearing, the men could be seen marching in full formation across the Avenue, and moving through the city to attend church and spend time with their families. They encountered a good share of hostile taunting that sometimes escalated into physical attack from whites who saw no place for them in the uniform of the U.S. Army. However, the taunts ceased when they appeared on Washington streets carrying arms.

The number of black recruits rose daily. On June 30, 1863, to handle the increasing numbers, the War Department issued orders forming the "Bureau of Colored Troops," which transferred all but the Massachusetts regiments to serve under the umbrella of the United States Colored Troops. The Washington volunteers were renamed the First Regiment U.S. Colored Troops. Before they were shipped out to Portsmouth, Virginia, in July, the women of the Fifteenth Street Presbyterian Church presented them with a "beautifully wrought banner."

Soon after their arrival, Company B of the First Regiment—Richard Edmonson's company—marched through the city of Norfolk, giving stunned residents of that city their first sighting of armed black soldiers. Their white commander, Second Lt. A. L. Sanborn, became the target of insults shouted from the sidewalk by Dr. D. M. Wright, a wealthy physician of the city. In one account of the incident, Sanborn stopped the company to warn Wright that he would be arrested if he continued. In another account, he directed two of the black soldiers to take hold of Wright. In either case, the Virginian then pulled out a gun and shot Sanborn dead. Wright was convicted of murder by a military tribunal and sentenced to die. President Lincoln gave him a week's reprieve to study the case but chose to not commute the sentence. After an abortive attempt to escape jail dressed in his daughter's clothes, Wright was hanged.

Frederick Douglass extended his recruiting to the occupied land along the Mississippi River, and former slaves from that area would soon fill twenty regiments of colored troops. More blacks were already serving in the navy. In the end, some two hundred thousand black men served in the Civil War.

On July 15, 1863, in the same month that her grandson arrived in Virginia with his regiment, Amelia Edmonson purchased Lot 7, in the subdivision of Lot 1 of Square 161, located on L Street between Eighteenth Street and Connecticut Avenue. She paid $119.80 in cash and signed promissory notes for $59.90 each, one due in six months and the other in twelve. Amelia's land was diagonally across the street from her daughter Elizabeth Brent and just a block north of daughters Martha and Eveline. Her son Ephraim and his family had already been living there for two years, likely as renters. In 1864, to help finance the new purchase, the family sold the only other land they owned, Lot 4 in square 313, for $575.

Amelia's two youngest children did not always live in her new home with her. The 1860 U.S. Census shows that Louisa and Josiah, along with their cousin, John S. Brent, were working as live-in servants in the home of a navy admiral. Josiah also worked as a hostler, most likely taking care of military horses.

More Edmonson grandsons began to march off to war. On November 11, 1863, nineteen-year-old Ephraim Edmonson enlisted in the Second Regiment U.S. Col'd Infantry in Arlington, Virginia, for a three-year stint. Ephraim was described as five feet seven, with a black complexion, born in Washington, D.C., around 1844. He was undoubtedly the son of Ephraim, who had joined his brothers and sisters on the *Pearl*, though he was likely a son from an earlier marriage. A few years after Ephraim was redeemed from slavery and returned to Washington, he married Mary Bannister. According to Civil War records, Ephraim Edmonson was serving as a substitute for Gilbert Joy, the husband of his aunt, Louisa Edmonson.

John Sommerfield Brent, the son of John and Elizabeth Brent, was drafted in May 1863. However, at that time he was working in a hotel in Chicago, and he and his young wife were expecting their first child. Brent managed to provide a substitute named John Hill to fulfill his draft requirements. A year later, when he returned to Washington, he enlisted in Company C of the Massachusetts Fifth Cavalry (Col'd), which was credited to the town of Cambridge, Massachusetts, and received an enlistment bounty of three hundred dollars. He was described as five feet seven and a half, with black eyes, black hair, and a yellow complexion; his records indicate that he had originally been drafted the year before.

Brent traveled north for his training along with Franklin Jennings, the son of Paul Jennings, who produced the White House memoir describing the British attack on Washington and then became involved with Underground Railroad activists. Jennings, five feet six, with a copper complexion, brown eyes, and black hair, was born in Orange County, Virginia, where the Madison family home was located. He received twenty-five dollars from his hundred-dollar bonus when he enlisted. Both men were described as having been free as of April 19, 1861.

Like the Fifty-fourth's legendary Robert Gould Shaw, Major Charles Francis Adams of the Fifth Cavalry came from an illustrious family, one even more renowned than the Shaws. The major's father, an earlier unsuccessful candidate for the vice presidency of the United States, was the ambassador to Great Britain during the Civil War. His grandfather John Quincy Adams, the sixth president of the United States, led the assault on the oppressive antislavery gag rule in the House and successfully argued the case for the *Amistad* mutineers at the Supreme Court. His great-grandfather John Adams was a founding father and the second president of the United States. Unlike Shaw, Adams survived the war.

Brent and Jennings's regiment was deployed to Fortress Monroe, the site where fugitives from slavery had first been accepted as contraband of war. In June 1864 they were sent to City Point, Virginia, the bustling Union landing wharf for troops and goods. Under the leadership of General Benjamin Butler, they moved out to attack part of the ring of defenses around Richmond at the Battle of Chaffin's Farm. Confederate troops led by General Robert E. Lee rallied to protect their defensive structures but, after some forty-five hundred casualties, black and white Union soldiers prevailed.

Brent and his unit went on to Petersburg, Virginia, where they joined other black and white regiments to take part in one of the longest and bloodiest sieges of the war. Brent should have joined up with his brother-in-law James Paynter whose marriage to Kate Brent had been so happily described in the *Christian Recorder* in 1861. But Paynter, serving in Company F of the Eighth Infantry Regiment since August 14, 1863, had been hospitalized at the General Hospital for colored troops in Beaufort, South Carolina, since February 1864, and remained so until October. He was released just in time to be wounded in a skirmish on the Darbytown Road outside Richmond on October 13, 1864, and spent the next two and half months in the Augur General Hospital in Alexandria, Virginia. Like the other long-standing free black soldiers, Paynter's records were carefully marked that he was free on or before April 19, 1861.

Lincoln gained sustenance from the men in the field, and they from him. He traveled from Washington by steamboat to visit the Petersburg front and meet with General Ulysses S. Grant, the man on whom he now pinned his hopes. As Lincoln began the short return journey to the wharf at City Point, he came upon a black brigade, who sent up cheers for the "Liberator." Historian Doris Kearns Goodwin reports that Lincoln was moved to tears and "could hardly reply." John Brent may have been among the men who cheered the president that day.

The siege of Petersburg stretched out for more than nine months, but Brent would leave the area shortly after Lincoln's visit in June. The Fifth Massachusetts was transferred to a prisoner-of-war camp at Point Lookout, just behind Cornfield Harbor, in southern Maryland. For ten months, John Brent served in close view of the spot where his four uncles and two aunts had been captured as fugitives onboard the *Pearl*.

Lincoln was now facing a difficult reelection campaign. The Copperheads, as the peace Democrats were called, had turned to George McClellan, the former general, to lead their ticket. The former general continued to voice his commitment to keep the Negro out of the war he vowed to end. In an extraordinary reversal of fortune, the troops who had once worshipped McClellan cast their vote for Abraham Lincoln, as did much of the North. Lincoln won all but three states—New Jersey, Delaware, and Kentucky. Even New York went for Lincoln, as did the border slave state of Maryland. Of course, it helped the Republicans that only Marylanders willing to take a loyalty oath to the Union were allowed to vote.

In that same election, Maryland voted to amend their constitution to end slavery. Baltimore County led the vote in favor of emancipation, which was supported in the northern and western counties. Montgomery County, where the Edmonsons had grown up and where Emily and Larkin still lived, voted overwhelmingly against it, aligning itself with the southern counties. The Quakers and any others in the county ready to abolish slavery were outnumbered. But the amendment passed, and the state of Maryland abolished slavery.

In December 1864 Myrtilla Miner returned to Washington with hopes to reopen her school now that the end of the war was in sight. But when her train arrived in Washington, Miner failed to disembark as expected; her friends found her deathly ill inside one of the cars. Like Mary Edmonson, she had contracted tuberculosis, which had already progressed to end stage. She died two weeks later, at the age of forty-nine, and was buried in Georgetown's Oak Hill Cemetery, not far from Gamaliel Bailey.

In February 1865 Robert E. Lee was still tied down in the defense of Petersburg as General William T. Sherman marched to the sea from Atlanta. A desperate Lee joined a very small chorus of Southern voices who urged the government to enlist black soldiers, even if it meant granting them freedom. The South was now considering the radical step of freeing black men to fight for the Confederacy. "The Negroes, under proper circumstances, will make efficient soldiers," Lee wrote, adding "[t]hose who are employed should be freed. It would be neither just nor wise . . . to require them to serve as slaves." Most Confederate leaders were appalled by the proposal. In the end, several companies of blacks were formed and began minimal training, but they would never be sent into battle. There is little evidence that any slaves fought as regular soldiers, though they were certainly used to perform manual labor for the Confederate forces. Many were hired out by their owners, including two who belonged to President James Buchanan's secretary of the treasury, Howell Cobb, of Georgia. Cobb hired out two of his slaves to the Confederacy. The signed contract included an appraisal for the value of each man and a pledge to compensate the owner should his property be killed.

John Brent's regiment was called back to Petersburg, and, as the exhausted Army of Virginia retreated further south, they marched toward Richmond. After advising Jefferson Davis and the civilian government to evacuate Richmond immediately, the Confederates abandoned the city. As John Brent's Fifth Massachusetts reached the capital, other regiments were coming together to enter the city. The Fifth led one procession of infantry into Richmond with drum and fife making for a "grand, triumphal march."*

At the extraordinary sight of black soldiers in Richmond, black residents poured into the streets in waves of welcome. An older black woman approached a number of the soldiers to ask if they knew of her son, who had been sold to Robert Toombs when he was very small and then taken off to Washington. After the war broke out, she had gone to see Toombs, who served as the first secretary of state for the Confederate States of America and then as a brigadier general. He told her that her son had run away and the last he had heard, he was living in Ohio. He may have been the carriage driver who had fled just as Toombs was trying to leave Washington. The woman was sent to talk with Garland H. White, the chaplain of the Twenty-eighth USCT, to see if he could help her. After she had told her story to Chaplain White, and he had answered her questions about his own background, the woman realized she was talking with her own son. White had been

---

* According to pension papers filed by his family, John S. Brent "was at the fall of Richmond and bore the flag on that memorable occasion when the Union soldiers entered that last stronghold of the Confederacy."

one of the two runaways captured after William Chaplin's carriage had been stopped in 1850, later escaped to Canada, and returned to serve with the Union army.

Lee retreated to a small town called Appomattox Courthouse, and Grant's army followed as droves of hungry and weary rebels either crossed over into Union lines or began walking home. Six days after Richmond fell, Lee submitted to a complete surrender and then asked Grant to feed his hungry men.

As Washington exploded in celebration at the news of Lee's surrender, Lincoln appeared at an open window overlooking a massive crowd that had gathered on the White House grounds below. A visibly aged but relieved president voiced his strong desire that the vote be extended to those blacks in Louisiana who had served their country in the war and to all literate men of color. John Wilkes Booth, listening in the crowd to the president's speech, turned to his companions and said that this would be the last speech that Lincoln would ever make.

On Good Friday of April 14, as Washington residents continued to wildly celebrate the end of the war in the streets and bars of the city, the president and his wife arrived at Ford's Theatre on Tenth Street to enjoy a production of *Our American Cousin*. After the production began, Booth quietly entered the box, pulled out a small derringer pistol, aimed it at the base of Lincoln's head, and pulled the trigger.

The president of the United States died the next day in a dark room in a rooming house across the street from the theater. He lost his life in a war that ended slavery as surely as the 630,000 soldiers, including 43,000 men of color, who had died in battle or in the hospitals. At times Lincoln had seemed implacably indifferent to slavery. While he was secretly drafting the Emancipation Proclamation, he wrote a letter to Horace Greeley's newspaper stating that if he could end the war by freeing all the slaves he would, and if he could only end the war by freeing none of the slaves he would do that. But the one thing he would not consider doing, though he was urged by many to do so, was end the war by allowing slavery to extend into the new territories, a concession to the South that would guarantee the continuation of slavery for many years to come. That unfaltering stand led to a Civil War that did, in the end, break the yoke of slavery in America.

THIRTEEN

Emily and Samuel Return to Washington; John Is Found

Washington struggled to return to normalcy after the war. With peace at hand, some who had come to Washington for war-related jobs returned home. But few of the black refugees from the former Confederacy had any desire to return. A special census taken in 1867 showed a 60 percent increase in the white population since the U. S. Census of 1860, while the black population had increased by nearly 300 percent. The enormous wear on the city over four years had left it overcrowded and crumbling. Historian Constance McLaughlin Green describes Washington at this time as in high disrepair, with rampant outbreaks of dysentery and typhoid fever caused by inadequate sewerage systems, roads ripped to pieces, and widespread unemployment. Horace Greeley of the *New York Tribune* joined the chorus in disparaging Washington. "The rents are high, the food is deplorable, the dust is disgusting, the mud is deep and morals are deplorable," he wrote. Some voices would begin to call for the capital to relocate farther west.

There were a number of improvements in the city for the black community, but some, like the right to vote, would prove to be transitory. The most important improvement was a publicly funded school system for black children, which employed black teachers who were some of the most talented educators in the country, largely because they were unemployable elsewhere because of their color. The black school board did not forget those who had worked for freedom. Schools in Washington, D.C., were named for many who had dedicated themselves to that end, including Frederick Douglass, Joshua Giddings, Charles Sumner, Robert Gould Shaw, Myrtilla Miner, and John Cook, whose son was appointed as the first superintendent for the black public school system.

And if the black community thought they would be welcomed into the full panoply of freedoms after the war, they were quickly disabused of that notion. When the Grand Review of troops marched down Pennsylvania Avenue in May 1865 to celebrate the end of the war, not one of the regiments in which the Edmonsons, Jenningses, Brents, Paynters, and Youngs had served were invited to participate; it was a review that consisted solely of the white regiments.

Amelia Edmonson left her home on Twentieth Street and moved into the brick house she had purchased three years earlier on L Street, just west of Connecticut Avenue. On July 7, 1866, she prepared the first of two wills. In the first one, she left her home to nine of her children: Ephraim, Elizabeth, Eliza, Eveline, Martha, Emily, Louisa, Richard, and Josiah, as well as to two of her grandchildren: Singleton Little and Caroline Little. There is no information that explains how the two children are linked to the family, but their mother may have been Henrietta, an older sibling of Mary and Emily's who died. Amelia stated in the first will that she had not included Hamilton, Samuel, or John because she did not know where they were, and she feared that if they could not be located, the distribution of the proceeds of her estate would be held up. Slavery had disrupted her family and flung three of her children far from home.

But Amelia added a paragraph at the bottom of that will saying that she had finally heard from two of her sons, Hamilton and John, and that Samuel had come home with his wife and children. City directories show that Samuel was living in his mother's L Street home in 1868, and that he was working as a waiter or porter in various hotels, identified in one directory as the Willard. Samuel had fled slavery and traveled to extraordinary places but, like Emily, he too had come home.

There is no evidence that John Edmonson ever returned to Washington. A forty-five-year-old man of that same name, described as a Maryland-born farmer, appears in the 1870 U.S. Census as a resident of Bellevue, Louisiana, in Bossier Parish, in the northwest corner of the state, about seventeen miles from Shrevesport. There is no other listing anywhere in that census which describes a John Edmonson who fits the profile of Paul and Amelia's son. John had likely been sold from the New Orleans slave pen, where he had been taken with his brothers and sisters, to a planter who lived in Bossier Parish. He was married to forty-year-old Mary Edmonson, who had been born in Arkansas, and the couple had four children. Lillie, the oldest, was eighteen years old in 1870, indicating that John and Mary Edmonson had been together at least since 1852. John Edmonson then disappears from the U.S. Census. He may have died in Louisiana without ever seeing his family again.

Ephraim and Richard, along with their families, remained near Amelia and other members of the family. Both men were described in city directories either as coach drivers or hackmen. The younger Ephraim Edmonson does not appear anywhere in the census data or city directories after the war. On November 24, 1863, he had been admitted to the General Hospital in Washington, D.C., and remained there through January and February. His records cease at that point.

A few months after the fall of Richmond, John Brent and Franklin Jennings accompanied the Fifth Massachusetts to Clarksville, Texas. At the end of hostilities in Virginia, their regiment had suffered relatively few fatalities on the battlefield: 7 died in battle and 116 died of disease. On August 14, 1865, Brent was discharged from the army holding the rank of corporal and made his way home through New Orleans, stopping to visit his uncle Hamilton (Edmonson) Taylor.

After the war, Brent was employed as a coach driver in Washington by Henry Adams, the brother of Charles Francis Adams, one of the officers in his Fifth Massachusetts regiment. Following in his father's footsteps by holding a respected position in the black community, John Brent Jr. would become the first black man appointed as a fireman in the District of Columbia. After his death on March 24, 1917, he was buried at Arlington Cemetery.

When Edward Young returned from the Civil War, he put the notebook he used to record the death of his grandfather to other purposes. The front cover reads "The Log Book of the 1st U.S. Co. B Band of Washington City, dated June 18, 1866." The notebook implies that Young was enlisted in the First U.S. Colored Troops, but his name is not included in the regiment's Civil War records located at the National Archives. It is possible that his records were lost. On an inside page of that notebook, Young wrote the names of the "1st Relief Base Ball club of the City of Washington." There were enough players to fill two teams. Young was the catcher for the first team and Richard Edmonson covered second base. Calvin Brent, a budding architect, played second base on the second team along with another Edmonson identified as "S." After living away from America for fifteen years, it is very possible that Samuel Edmonson wanted to try what was becoming America's most popular sport. At forty, there's no reason why he wouldn't have been able to play.

The four older married Edmonson sisters—Eveline, Eliza, Martha, and Elizabeth—continued to live with their families, in homes their husbands owned, not far from one another. They raised their children well. Elizabeth's son Calvin Brent became one of Washington's first black architects. Some of his designs still stand today: homes at 1700 V Street and 1737 S Street, both in northwest Washington; and two churches, Mount Jezreel Baptist, at Fifth and E Streets, SE, on Capitol Hill, and the Third Baptist Church, at 1546 Fifth Street, NW. Brent took his cousin Edward Young on as an apprentice, and some of Young's architectural drawings are in the possession of descendants who attend St. Luke's Episcopal Church at Fifteenth and Church Streets, NW, a Gothic structure that was modified by Calvin Brent.

In 1869 Emily and Larkin sold their six-and-a-quarter-acre farm, in Sandy Spring for $375.01 and, like Paul and Amelia before them, moved into Washington, D.C., with seven-year-old Ida, six-year-old William, and two-year-old Emma. They purchased two large contiguous lots of land, numbered 16 and 19, in Section 9 of Barry's Farm for $1,200. The U.S. Bureau of Refugees, Freedmen, and Abandoned Lands (more popularly known as the Freedmen's Bureau), which was formed to assist in the transition from slavery to freedom, had purchased this 375-acre farm in southeast Washington, on the east side of the Anacostia River, in 1867. It was divided into lots and sold to freedmen together with sufficient timber to build their houses. Eager first-time homeowners bought lots in Barry's Farm, and after working all day made their way to their own piece of land to build their homes by the light of lanterns and candles.

The streets in the neighborhood, which came to be known as Hillsdale, were named for antislavery notables including Senator Charles Sumner, of Massachusetts, and the equally radical Thaddeus Stevens, of Pennsylvania. Many of those street names have since been changed. The Government Hospital for the Insane, known today as St. Elizabeth's—for the land tract once owned by Thomas Blagden, the man who had helped purchase the freedom of Bell family members—stretched out to the south.

Emily and Larkin's land faced Howard Avenue and partly backed up to the Anacostia River. To finance their sizable purchase and build their home, Larkin and Emily took out a loan from Gerrit Smith Wormley (named for the wealthy abolitionist who had financially contributed to Washington's Underground Railroad cell), who was married to Emily's niece Amelia Brent. For collateral, the couple put up two horses, one with a white star on its forehead; a two-horse wagon and double harness; an ambulance wagon for two horses; a one-horse wagon and harness; and three plows. Larkin's ambulance wagon suggests that he may have been one of the many drivers who transported the wounded during the Civil War to hospitals around Washington, D.C., perhaps while his Sandy Spring farm was idle. In 1880 the U.S. Census reports that he was employed as a gardener, possibly on the extensive grounds of nearby St. Elizabeth's.

Emily and her family would never move again. Their son William may have died, as he disappears from the census records by 1880, but Emily and Larkin had another child, Robert, born in 1871. The Johnson children likely attended the Hillsdale public school, which opened the same year Robert was born. The Johnsons were respected members of their community. At a Hillsdale Civic Association meeting held on September 26, 1921, a number of senior residents came together to make a list of the couples who had built their community. The names of Mr. and Mrs. Larkin Johnson are on that list.

Frederick Douglass, Emily's old friend, moved to Washington in 1870 to publish the *New National Era*. In 1877, after his appointment as U.S. marshal for the District of Columbia, Douglass purchased a substantial home not far from Emily and Larkin in Anacostia. Years later, one of Emily's granddaughters wrote that "Grandma & Frederick Douglass were like sister and brother—great abolitionists. I sat on his knee in his office in the house that is now a museum in Anacostia where we were born." A descendant of Emily, Dr. Marian Holmes, recalls being told that Harriet Beecher Stowe came to Anacostia to visit the former slave she sponsored at Oberlin College, and the two women walked together to Douglass's house to pay their respects.

On May 2, 1873, Amelia Edmonson revoked her earlier will and prepared a new one in which she left her home at 1741 L Street, NW, to her youngest son, Josiah Edmonson, for life. After his death, the house would revert to her daughter Louisa Edmonson Joy. She left twenty dollars to each of her more established children and said, "I thank God, however, that I am now entirely free of debt."

After living as a free woman for twenty years, Amelia Edmonson died on November 4, 1874, at the age of ninety-two, of ulceration of the stomach, which had lasted four months. Her death certificate states that she was buried in the Mount Pleasant Plains Cemetery (originally named the Colored Union Benevolent Association), on Adams Mill Road in northwest Washington. Amelia's son-in-law Dennis Orme, the named executor of Amelia's first will, predeceased her and became the first person buried in that cemetery in March 1871. The cemetery trustees had purchased the land from Charles Francis Adams, an officer in John Brent Jr.'s Fifth Massachusetts Cavalry. It had been part of the land associated with the Adams Mill on Rock Creek, which runs just below the cemetery. Some years later, the National Zoo bought a portion of the cemetery and disinterred some of the remains, removing them to Woodlawn Cemetery; but not all were moved, and there are no records to indicate which were. Five years later, Amelia's son Richard, who had been taken to New Orleans with his brothers and sisters even though his freedom had been purchased, died of hepatitis at the age of fifty-nine; he also was buried in Mount Pleasant.

Larkin Johnson died of pneumonia in his Howard Street home on February 26, 1885. Ten years later, on September 15, 1895, Emily C. E. Fisher Johnson died, just seven months after the death of her friend and neighbor Frederick Douglass. The death certificate listed the primary cause of her death as "Insolation," or heatstroke. It stated that the most immediate cause of Emily's death was exhaustion. She was buried in Hillsdale Cemetery, where Larkin had been laid to rest.

Emily's death certificate left the family a surprising link to their African roots. Someone in her family reported that Paul Edmonson was a "Madagascian," indicating that he was born in Madagascar. Her mother, Amelia, was described as American-born. It is conceivable that Paul Edmonson was born in Madagascar and brought to the United States at a very young age, before the ban on the African slave trade took effect. The U.S. Census of 1880 reports that both of Emily's parents were born in Maryland, but that might be inaccurate. It is also possible that her father was born to a parent from Madagascar who passed on enough of that native culture that Paul Edmonson became known as an honorary Madagascan. In any case, it is a fascinating clue into the background of a family that survived and prospered against enormous odds.

Emily's brother Samuel had moved to Anacostia in the District of Columbia where he purchased land in Barry's Farm—Lot 6 and Lot 20, the last of which was located immediately next to Larkin and Emily. He lived in Anacostia, at 117 Howard Avenue, until his death in 1907, when he was just over eighty years old. His wife and children all predeceased him, and his 1905 will directed that all of his property be divided among his three grandchildren. In addition to the two lots, he left them a covered, four-wheel coach and a piano. Even more important, he passed along a good deal of information to John Paynter, his nephew, who credits him with providing many of the details on the story of the *Pearl*.

Emily and the rest of her remarkable family left their children and their children's children a legacy to be cherished. The Edmonsons— Mary and Emily in particular—were participants in an antislavery movement that built the resolve to end slavery and to prevent its spread into the territories. That movement began when the enslaved resisted slavery by running away, sabotaging production, planning insurrections, and bearing witness against the horrors of what was idly referred to as the "peculiar institution." It included both black and white abolitionists who led a constant attack in pulpits, schools, newspapers, voting booths, and communities across America, even as they were vilified. The movement embraced the black and white operatives on the Underground Railroad who were complicit in the theft of the "capital" that was so essential to the slave economy. Even when an escape failed, as it did for the fugitives who boarded the *Pearl* in 1848, their willingness to risk all for freedom pricked more consciences and channeled more votes against the evil of slavery. Throughout their journey, the Edmonsons never ceased struggling to free themselves, keep their faith, raise their families, and move their lives forward.

With the battle won against slavery, black America faced an arduous and lengthy campaign for equality. It would take a civil rights movement—with remarkable parallels to the antislavery movement—to force the passage of a Civil Rights Act that would begin to end discrimination and eliminate the entrenched and rigid system of segregation that had replaced slavery in the South, and the more subtle forms of discrimination in the North. The descendants of the Edmonsons and of many of the fugitives of the *Pearl* played a part in that struggle and continue to promote the ongoing campaign for better opportunities across America for their young people.

Epilogue

As the story of the *Pearl* becomes better known, more information about other fugitives should come to light. Public records reveal further details of some of the more well-known fugitives on the *Pearl*. Daniel Bell died in 1877. He filed a will that states his daughter, Eleanora, who had been freed in 1862 under the Emancipation Act in the District of Columbia, had died; and so had Harriet, the young girl for whom James Mandeville Carlisle had filed an injunction to keep her from being taken out of the city. His son Daniel Bell Jr. was acknowledged in the will, but there were no details regarding his whereabouts.

Information about that son did come to light. A few years later, in 1883, Mary Bell wrote a letter to request that $75.55 be taken from her late husband's estate for the purpose of sending it to her son Daniel in Natchitoches, Louisiana. The 1870 U.S. Census reveals that a thirty-four-year-old Daniel Bell was a literate bartender in that city, possessed $300 in personal property, and had been born in Washington, D.C. He and his thirty-six-year-old wife, Louisa, also literate, had six children between the ages of one and thirteen. The older ones were attending school. Like John Edmonson, Daniel Bell had undoubtedly been sold to a slave owner in Louisiana, and like many of the large numbers of slaves sold south, found it impossible to make the long trek back to Washington. They had new homes now.

Pearl veteran Alfred Pope, of Georgetown, was freed one year after the death of his owner and uncle, John Carter, in 1851, pursuant to a will drafted in 1844. Carter had added a codicil to the will that promised the same freedom to Pope's wife, Hannah. Hannah Pope, a member of Mt. Zion Church before 1848, had been owned by Brittania Kennon, a descendant of Martha Custis Washington, and lived at the Tudor Place mansion near Carter's home. Kennon later recalled that she had sold Hannah to Carter at his request so she could spend more time with her husband, Alfred. The former fugitive of the *Pearl* went on to become a well-respected landowner, builder, and businessman in Georgetown—certainly an elite in the town's black community and a well-respected figure in the white one. In 1870 Pope was asked to speak on behalf of the community at a congressional hearing on the question of whether Georgetown should give up its municipal identity and merge completely with Washington City, which it eventually did.

Pope owned nearly half a city block in Georgetown and in 1875 sold part of that land, just around the corner from the family's impressive and substantial home at the southwest corner of Twenty-ninth and O Streets, to the Mt. Zion Church for $2,500 for a new building. The fine brick church constructed on that site still serves the congregation today. Pope's involvement in the 1848 attempted escape on the *Pearl* was unknown to members of the church until 1998, when this research on the *Pearl* affair began.

Professor Kathleen M. Lesko of Georgetown University interviewed Alfred and Hannah Pope's ninety-year-old granddaughter, Hannah Pope Williams, for the book *Black Georgetown Remembered: A History of Its Black Community*, published in 1999. Mrs. Williams told Lesko that Hannah Pope's father was the brother of Brittania Kennon, who had sold her to John Carter. She said her grandmother told her that some years after the Popes had settled into their own home in Georgetown, Britannia Kennon summoned Hannah Pope to her Tudor Place mansion, where she had once lived as a slave, and instructed her to bring her children. Apparently, Kennon wished to see her nieces and nephews.

In 1872 the trustees of Myrtilla Miner's school, which had come under the authority of the Colored Public Schools, sold the building at Dupont Circle for $40,000, a figure that was ten times higher than what they had paid for it. A new school was erected at Seventeenth and Church Streets, NW, and the Miner Normal School opened its doors to train teachers for the black children of the District. In 1914 it moved yet again, this time into a new building on the campus of Howard University, overlooking Georgia Avenue, where it served as the Miner Teachers College. Until the Supreme Court outlawed segregated schools in 1954, the Wilson Teachers College served the same purpose for the white students of the District of Columbia. The two schools merged to become the District of Columbia Teachers College. That institution has now been incorporated into the University of the District of Columbia. The Miner building remains on Howard's campus.

In today's Alexandria, the two slave pens on Duke Street have survived in large part. During the war, Bruin's slave pen was used as a hospital by federal troops and also briefly housed the county courts when rebels operated dangerously near the Fairfax Courthouse. Bruin had fled Alexandria when Union soldiers approached but was captured in May 1862. He was held in the Old Capitol Prison in Washington for six weeks and then released. His slave-trading business had not been against the law. Shortly after the war ended, Joseph Bruin filed suit to reclaim the Alexandria slave pen that had been confiscated by the federal government and then sold. In an order signed by Chief Justice of the Supreme Court Salmon Chase, his property was returned to him. Today, Bruin's slave pen is a real estate office at 1707 Duke Street.

The Price & Birch slave pen, which had once belonged to the notorious slave traders Franklin & Armfield, was also confiscated during the war. It was used, at varying times, as a prison, a contraband quarters, and a hospital for black soldiers. What is left of that slave pen, at 1315 Duke Street, is now the headquarters of the Northern Virginia Urban League, which is converting the basement into a historical and cultural museum to honor the victims of America's internal slave trade.

———

Today's Edmonson descendants have embraced their family's story and proudly share it through their many communities. Paynter's 1930 book, *The Fugitives of the Pearl,* was carefully handed down through the generations of most, but not all, of the Edmonson descendants. Paul Johnson, a direct descendant of Paul and Amelia Edmonson through their daughter Eveline Edmonson Ingraham, was a senior executive in the federal government when a cousin lent him Paynter's book in the late 1970s. His parents had come of age at a time when many black parents thought it best not to discuss slavery with their children. But they soon made up for lost time. Johnson and his wife, Amy, became involved in sharing his family's story with community and youth groups. Until their retirement to Virginia a few years ago, the couple belonged to Asbury Church on Eleventh Street where their family worshipped so many years ago. Both of Paul and Amy Johnson's daughters now live in Montgomery County, not far from where Paul Edmonson owned a forty-acre farm.

Other members of the family kept the story alive. Dr. Marion Holmes, a direct descendant of Emily Edmonson and now a retired administrator in the Philadelphia school system, once worked with students in Philadelphia to construct a small-scaled replica of the schooner named the *Pearl*. Diane Young, a descendant of John and Elizabeth Brent through architect Calvin Brent, is a teacher in the Montgomery County School System. When this writer was giving a slide presentation on the story of the *Pearl* to social study teachers several years ago, she found

Young standing by her side shaking when the lights came up. "That's my family," she whispered. "That's my family." Young teaches in the same county where Emily and Mary grew up. She has devised a character development program for her middle school.

Diane Taard and her daughter Kirby, who explored her family's history for school projects in her District of Columbia public schools, are descended from Martha Edmonson Young Pennington and her son, Civil War veteran and architect Edward Young. One evening at their home just off Sixteenth Street in northwest Washington, Mrs. Taard placed a notebook on her dining room table that had belonged to Edward Young, and revealed the date of Paul Edmonson's death for the first time as well as the formation of a black veterans' baseball team. Kirby Taard grew up in a home with a copy of a daguerreotype of Mary and Emily on her bedroom wall.

Stephan Gilbert, a specialist at the Bureau of Labor Statistics and a direct descendant of Emily's, presented a talk on his family at the annual Black History event at the Bureau of Standards in the Department of Labor in 2002. Gilbert was told to expect the usual fifteen or twenty people to attend. More than two hundred people arrived with others straining to hear from the hallway. Gilbert's mother, who had been raised by Emily's eldest daughter, Ida Berry, proudly listened to her son detail her family's story.

Until recently, the events surrounding the attempted escape on the *Pearl* were missing from the history texts taught to America's children. Even in Washington, D.C., little was taught about these events until 1983, when the story was included in the splendid textbook, the *City of Magnificent Intentions: A History of the District of Columbia*, written by historians who created a new template for teaching history: an inclusive one.

In June 2002, a group of students from the Washington area took a five-day trip down the Potomac to retrace the journey of the *Pearl*. Under the direction of Carl Cole, of the Potomac Heritage Partnership, whose family has been a part of the African-American community around the

Navy Yard since the end of the nineteenth century, and Joe Youcha, of the Alexandria Seaport Foundation, the students set sail, stopping along the way to share the story of *Pearl* with other students. Edmonson descendants Paul Johnson, with his wife, Amy, and Diane Young, with her daughter, Dawne, were waiting to greet them in a small group that had gathered on the bank of the St. Mary's River, not far from Cornfield Harbor. When the ceremonies ended, the Edmonson descendants drove to Cornfield Harbor and stood on a bridge stretching over a creek flowing into the harbor. There, they quietly looked out over the water where a crowded schooner once sought shelter during a fateful journey in search of freedom.

Acknowledgments

The story of the *Escape on the Pearl* has been greatly enriched by the wholehearted support of Edmonson descendants Imogene F. Gilbert, Stephan Gilbert, Marion Holmes, Paul and Amy Johnson, Diane and Kirby Tardd, and Diane Young, all of whom contributed whatever information and materials they had in their possession that relate to their family. I would also like to especially thank Paul and Amy Johnson for their many kindnesses, including a meticulous review of my manuscript.

Carter Bowman and Janet Ricks of the history committee at Mt. Zion United Methodist Church and Lonise Robinson, the historian of Asbury United Church—both churches attended by fugitives of the *Pearl*—have provided ongoing support, guidance, and access to their church histories and records. Janet and her husband, Vernon Ricks, longtime activists for equal rights with many community organizations, including the NAACP, share their name both with two fugitives on the *Pearl* and my husband and me. They have become friends.

The genesis of this book stems from two articles on the *Pearl* escape that appeared in the *Washington Post*. The first, published on August 12, 1998, edited by Michael Farquhar, outlined the story of the escape on the

Pearl. In 2002, former editor of the *Washington Post Magazine* Glenn Frankel commissioned a story that focused on the lives of Mary and Emily and the history of the Edmonson family. Magazine editor Tom Shroder helped shape that article, and story editor David Rowell skillfully guided it through the writing process.

A work of history is in many ways a community project. In addition to the descendants of the Paul and Amelia Edmonson family, I am deeply grateful to the dozens of people who have aided me in my own voyage of discovery. Historian Mary Beth Corrigan performed a critical reading of the manuscript and provided particularly insightful suggestions. Other historians—Carroll R. Gibbs, Stanley Harrold, Kathleen M. Lesko, and Michael Winston—have gone out of their way to provided information, materials, support, and advice. Writer Kathryn Grover graciously fielded questions relating to her book on the New Bedford abolitionist community and author Harold T. Pickett did the same on the history of the John Wesley A.M.E. Zion Church.

Frank Newton, of the Richardson Maritime Museum, offered his invaluable knowledge of the history of sailing in the Chesapeake area, his insightful research into the Frenchtown Landing on the northern part of the bay, and a very helpful critical read of the manuscript. Carl Cole did the same for Washington and its waterfront and, with Ned Chalker of the National Maritime Heritage Foundation, helped organize a memorable voyage on a schooner that left the Seventh Street wharf and arrived at Cornfield Harbor at the mouth of the Potomac River. Through the generosity of the foundation and with the capable and knowledgeable crew of Lisa Finney, Gary Knight, Bill Ross, and Roger Staiger assisting Captain Chalker, I was able to trace the path of the *Pearl*. Anthony Cohen of the Menare Foundation was one of the first activists for the study of the Underground Railroad to support the writing of this book and generously provided materials, advice, and encouragement. Jenny Masur, coordinator of the National Capital Region Underground for the National Park Service, has regularly done the same.

I very much appreciate the support provided by Frieda Wormley and Donet Graves who gave me access to the private archives of the Wormley family and also pointed me to other nineteenth-century sources.

Many librarians, archivists, and curators aided in the research for this book. Robert Ellis and others at the National Archives helped me navigate the court records and other documents that greatly contributed to this story. I am also indebted to Karen Blackman-Mills, Jerry McCoy, Faye Haskins, former staff member Susan Malbin, and many others at the Washingtoniana Division of the Martin Luther King Jr. Memorial Library; Ida E. Jones of the Moorland-Spingarn Research Center; former librarian Gail Redmann and current staff Ruele Skelsen, Richard Evans, and David Songer of the Historical Society of Washington; Pat Anderson at the Jane C. Sween Library of the Montgomery County (Maryland) Historical Society; Archivist Roland M. Baumann of the Oberlin College Archives; David Stratton of the Salem (Ohio) Historical Society; Wendy Kail of Tudor Place Historic House and Gardens; Lee Langston-Harrison of James Madison's Montpelier; Pamela J. Cressey, City Archaeologist for the City of Alexandria, Virginia; Sarah MacLennan Kerr of the Oberlin Historical and Improvement Organization; Laura Blanchard of the Historical Society of Pennsylvania; Christopher Densmore of Swarthmore College; Mike Klein of the Geography and Map Room of the Library of Congress; Ann Wakefield of the Notarial Archives of New Orleans; Jeffrey Ruggles and Heather Beattie of the Virginia Historical Society; and Maya Davis and other staff members of the Maryland State Archives.

I also would like to thank the staffs at the Library of Congress, the University of Maryland's McKeldin Library, the Pennsylvania State Archives, the Harriet Beecher Stowe Center, the Maryland Historical Society, the Massachusetts Historical Society, the Recorder of Deeds Office of Washington, D.C., the Montgomery County Courthouse in Rockville, Maryland, the Lauinger Library of Georgetown University, the New-York Historical Society, the Madison County Historical Society in New York, the Schomburg Center for Research in Black Culture of the New York City Library, the Utica Public Library, the Northern Virginia Urban League (located in a building that once housed a slave pen in Alexandria), the Sandy Spring (Maryland) Museum, the Enoch Pratt Free Library in Baltimore, Maryland, the Cortland County Historical Society in New York, the City Archives of the New Orleans Public Library, the Historic New Orleans Collection–William Research Center, and the Alexandria (Virginia) Library. Additionally, the Godfrey Memorial Library of Middletown, Connecticut, offers a Scholar Online Portal that was particularly helpful for accessing nineteenth-century newspapers.

Madison County, New York, proved a rich resource in supportive scholars and historians willing to aid this project. The contributions of documents and information from Norm Dann, Russ Grills, Hugh Humphreys, and Dot Willsey on the abolitionists of Madison County and the story of the 1850 convention to protest the Fugitive Slave Act proved invaluable. Barbara Bartlett of the Lorenzo State Historic Site was the key facilitator who brought us all together, while Betsy Kennedy and the staff of the Cazenovia Public Library, and Donna D. Burdick, the historian of Peterboro, New York, went out of their way to provide me with much information. Closer to home, Leslie Garcia of the *Washington Post Magazine* helped me enormously in locating many of the images, and Irene Ousley provided the author's photograph.

A very special thanks is due Ralph Clayton, the author of the definitive book on the Baltimore slave trade—*Cash for Blood*—in which he painstakingly records the names of each transportee to the Lower South taken from ships' manifests. Clayton also provided materials relevant to my book and personally escorted me on a tour of the Baltimore waterfront where the slave trade was centered. He also very kindly read and corrected my manuscript, for which I am grateful. I am also indebted to Ann Hagedorn for her insightful input.

I would also like to thank the esteemed Dr. Dorothy Height of the Council of Negro Women who spread the story of the *Escape on the Pearl* far and wide after it appeared in the *Washington Post Magazine*.

Over the course of writing this book, I've enjoyed the support of friends too numerous to name here but they know who they are and I thank them all. But I would be remiss if I didn't specifically thank two of my oldest and closest friends, Karen Lord and Ellie Rider, who were always there.

Warm thanks are much due to my supportive agent, Alice Martell, my excellent and patient editor at William Morrow, Henry Ferris, and Peter Huffard, assistant editor, for all of his help. Last, and very important, my husband, Tom, my son, Christopher, and my daughter, Molly, have supported and encouraged me throughout this whole process and have come to know the Edmonsons of the nineteenth century and their descendants today as a family to respect and admire.

Appendix A—The Edmonson Farm

Land records of this era make it very difficult to place the exact location of Paul Edmonson's farm or any other parcel of land. Generally, the records trace title back to early, and very large, colonial patents (grants), in which the parcel of land being recorded was originally contained. The land is then described in measurements of rods and perches and defined in proximity to rocks, trees, and lines on adjacent parcels of land. But rocks are moved and trees are felled. And, without a map of these contiguous parcels, it is very difficult to exactly place a particular piece of land.

But we are fortunate in the case of Paul Edmonson's farm. The land record book for the first thirty-five acres he purchased state that his land borders "the 6th line of Lot Number two in the division of the real estate of Jeremiah Beall. . . ." That language implied that Beall's land had been divided subject to a court ruling, which suggests that more details might exist that could help locate the Edmonson farm. They did. Equity court records, located at BS 8/599 in the Montgomery County Courthouse in Rockville, Maryland (recorded 1838), reveal that Beall's land was divided into three district lots in 1823. These court records contain a folded map attached to the page clearly outlining the Beall tract, including the sixth line of Lot 2. (Lots were often jagged and each straight line contained in the perimeter was numbered until the entire parcel was completely outlined).

Using a map showing the location of all the old patents, which was produced by the Montgomery County History Society, the map of the Beall land fits as neatly as a puzzle piece with its jagged lines matching the same jagged lines of the original patent. It is situated just east of Brookeville Road and south of Norbeck Road, within the two patents cited in the land records, generally as it was described in Harriet Beecher Stowe's *The Key to Uncle Tom's Cabin*. Edmonson's farm, including his second purchase of twenty contiguous acres, can be traced from that sixth line of Lot 2 as a long and narrow stretch of land running southeast to northwest and almost wholly contained within today's Leisure World, one of the country's first modern retirement communities. At least one descendant of Paul and Amelia Edmonson has been a resident of that development.

Appendix B—The Fugitives

Initial reports on the capture of the *Pearl* stated that seventy-seven fugitives were found onboard: thirty-eight men and boys, twenty-six women and girls, and thirteen children. On April 17, Hampton Williams, the posse leader and justice of the peace, prepared a partial commitment order requesting that the U.S. marshal jail sixty-seven escapees belonging to thirty-seven different owners. The following day, a supplemental commitment order was issued to jail an additional ten fugitives, bringing the total to seventy-seven fugitives. However, when bail was set for Drayton and Sayres a few days later, the amount was fixed at $76,000 based on $1,000 per fugitive. That change may reflect the fact that Alexander Hunter was originally listed as having two slaves on the *Pearl*, Daphne Paine and a child, but future reference to the child was subsequently dropped from the list. It is not known why.

When the grand jury met six weeks later, it issued a presentment of charges against the captains that listed forty-one named owners, though a few of those names had changed from the commitments, and seventy-four unnamed fugitives. Again, no reason was provided.

However, it is not explained by the fact that several of the owners were from Virginia, because Drayton's supporters were involved in lobbying Virginia owners to waive their rights to the fines due to them under the convictions.

The following list of *Pearl* fugitives is compiled from the indictments, trial documents, and final disposition of the cases in the court docket book, which show that Daniel Drayton and Edward Sayres were pardoned by the president. The number of cases at the time those pardons were issued was reduced yet again, this time to seventy-three. For unexplained reasons, Elizabeth Dick was listed as owning one slave, not two as the commitment had stated. It is possible that one of the men who had originally been claimed as her property was, in fact, found to be free.

FUGITIVES	OWNERS	COURT DOCKET #
MARY BELL—MOTHER	SUSANNAH ARMISTEAD	41–51
JOHN		
THOMAS		
ELEANORA		
HARRIET		
ANDREW		
GEORGE		
DANIEL (JUNIOR)		
CAROLINE		
MARY ELLEN		
CATHERINE		
BRENT, JANE	DR. N.P. CAUSIN	56
BROOKE, JOHN B.	JOSEPH DOWNING	66

FUGITIVES	OWNERS	COURT DOCKET #
CALVERT, JOHN	REV. OBADIAH BROWN	52
CHASE, AUGUSTUS	VINCENT KING	77
CRAIG, GEORGE	ELIZABETH LEWIS (NALLY, AGENT)	81
CROWLEY, PHILIP	OWNED BY RACHEL HARRISON (COMMITMENT LISTED WILLIAM HARMON)	72
DAVIS, MIMA/JEMIMA	MARY WATERS	109
DAY, MARY/MINNEY	CHARLES FLETCHER	68
DODSON, MARY KING, MARY KING, LEONARD FOREST, JOSEPH	JONATHAN Y. YOUNG	104–107
EDMONSON SIBLINGS EPHRAIM RICHARD JOHN SAMUEL MARY EMILY	REBECCA CULVER— FRANCIS VALDENAR ACTING AS TRUSTEE	108 110–114
ELLEN——NO SURNAME GIVEN	EMILY CORCORAN	59

FUGITIVES	OWNERS	COURT DOCKET #
GRAHAM, HENRY	SAMUEL BRERETON	53
GROSS, PERRY	SARAH CRANE	58
KING, EDWARD	W. KIRKWOOD	75
KING, PRISCILLA PRISCILLA (DAUGHTER) CLARISA (DAUGHTER)	FRANCIS DODGE JR.	62–64
MARSHALL MADISON ELIZABETH MATHEW	IGNATIUS MUDD	96–98
PAINE, DAPHNE	ALEXANDER HUNTER	73
PITTS, MADISON	GEORGE C. HARVEY	69
POPE, ALFRED	JOHN CARTER	55
QUEEN, PRISCILLA TWO CHILDREN	WILLIAM UPPERMAN	101–103
RIX (RICKS), JOHN	B. F. MIDDLETON	100
RIXX (RICKS), PETER	THOMAS CONNELLY	57
ROSIER, HANNIBAL AUGUST NAT	ARIANA LYLES	83–85

FUGITIVES	OWNERS	COURT DOCKET #
RUSSELL, GRACE	DR. THOMAS TRIPLETT	94
SHAKLIN/SHAALKIA, GEORGE	W. FROZEL	67
SMALLWOOD, HENRY	W. JACKSON (DECEASED)	76
STEWART (STEWARD), MARY ELLEN (HELEN)	DOLLEY MADISON	95
TURNER, SAMUEL	CHARLES LYONS	78
WASHINGTON, MINERVA— MOTHER LOUISA (DAUGHTER) MARIA (DAUGHTER) MELVINA (DAUGHTER)	JOHN H. SMITH	87 AND 91–93
YOUNG, MADISON	JAMES IRWIN	74
NEWMAN/TRUMAN	L. STORM	86
WILLIAM	MATILDA ANN BEALL (APPEARED FIRST AS MR. BELL)	54
SAM OR WILLIAM	ELIZABETH DICK	60
ISAAC	ANN MCDANIEL	61
JOE AND FRANK	ANDREW HOOVER	70–71

FUGITIVES	OWNERS	COURT DOCKET #
JANE KITTY	MARGARET LAIRD (INITIALLY LISTED AS BELONGING TO ELIZABETH DICK)	79–80
MARY ANN—MOTHER CHARLES (SON) JOHN (SON)	JOHN J. STULL	88–90
UNNAMED RUNAWAY WHO MAY BE GABRIEL CAMPBELL	OWNER LETITIA LENHAM (FIRST APPEARED IN COURT DOCKET RECORDS)	82
UNNAMED RUNAWAY	OWNER HENRY MONCURE (FIRST APPEARED ON GRAND JURY PRESENTMENT)	99

Notes

As discussed in the introduction, many of the details about the Edmonson family and their role in the escape stem from John Paynter's two invaluable biographical works: "The Fugitives of the Pearl," *Journal of Negro History* 1 (July 1916): pp. 243–64, and *Fugitives of the Pearl* (Washington, D.C.: The Associated Publishers, Inc., 1930), his partially novelized account of the same material. Paynter, a descendant of the Edmonsons was able to speak with family members close to the event. In the 1916 article, he specifically says that he interviewed Samuel Edmonson personally, and other members of his family undoubtedly passed down the details of the events described in this work.

Harriet Beecher Stowe also provides extremely important material on the family and their involvement in the escape. She met with Mary, Emily, and their mother, and also noted that someone at Oberlin, likely a member of the Cowles family, had interviewed the sisters about the event and sent her the details. Shortly after meeting the sisters in New York City, Stowe sponsored a fund-raising campaign to finance their education and wrote a brief *History of the Edmonson Family* (no date, printed for private distribution; copy courtesy of the Harriet Beecher Stowe Center in Hartford, Conn.). Stowe then included an expanded story of the Edmonsons in her nonfiction follow-up to *Uncle Tom's Cabin*, *The Key to Uncle Tom's Cabin* (1853; New York: Kennikat Press, 1968).

The third essential biographical source for the book is the *Personal Memoir of Daniel Drayton, for Four Years and Four Months a Prisoner (for Charity's Sake) in Washington Jail, Including a Narrative of the Voyage and Capture of the Schooner Pearl* (1854; New York: Negro Universities Press, 1969). This work was actually written by Richard Hildreth, the Boston abolitionist and attorney who was at Drayton's side during the extensive trials in Washington after the capture of the *Pearl*. It is not surprising that the book gives a detailed and clear summation of the legal aspects of the story. Horace Mann's Papers at the Massachusetts Historical Society provide extensive insight into Mann's involvement and the trial itself, as does his book *Slavery: Letters and Speeches* (1851; Negro Universities Press, 1969).

There are three other very important resources on events related to the *Pearl*. Catherine M. Hancett's "What Sort of People & Families: The Edmonson Sisters," *Afro-Americans in New York Life and History* 6, no. 2 (1982), provides especially helpful background for Mary and Emily's stay at Central College. The Black History Miscellaneous Papers, in the Manuscript Division of the Library of Congress, contain correspondence of the Boston Committee in Support of Drayton. And the papers of constitutional law scholar and abolitionist Lysander Spooner, at New-York Historical Society, unveiled the only detailed report of how Drayton came to be involved in the escape and the surprisingly bitter dispute between Drayton and Charles Cleveland, the man who proposed him for the trip and was assigned to support the Drayton and Sayres families while the men were in jail.

Among the many sources of Washington history, I have particularly relied on the following texts for background on Washington, D.C.: Letitia Woods Brown, *Free Negroes in the District of Columbia*

1790–1846 (New York: Oxford University Press, 1972); Elizabeth Clark-Lewis, ed., *First Freed: Washington, D.C., in the Emancipation Era* (Washington, D.C.: Howard University Press, 2002); Mary Beth Corrigan, "The Ties That Bind: The Pursuit of Community and Freedom Among Slaves and Free Blacks in the District of Columbia, 1800–1860," in Howard Gillette Jr., ed., *Southern City, National Ambition: The Growth of Early Washington, D.C.* (Washington, D.C.: The George Washington University Center for Washington Area Studies, 1995), 70–73; Jane Donovan, ed., *Many Witnesses: A History of Dumbarton United Methodist Church, 1772–1990* (Washington, D.C.: Dumbarton United Methodist Church, 1998); Constance McLaughlin Green, *A History of the Capital, 1800–1950* (Princeton, N.J.: Princeton University Press, 1962); Constance McLaughlin Green, *The Secret City: A History of Race Relations in the Nation's Capital* (Princeton, N.J.: Princeton University Press, 1967); Louise Daniel Hutchinson, *The Anacostia Story: 1608–1930* (Washington, D.C.: Smithsonian Institution Press, 1977); Kathleen M. Lesko, Valerie Babb, and Carroll R. Gibbs, *Black Georgetown Remembered: A History of Its Black Community* (Washington, D.C.: Georgetown University Press, 1999); Pauline Gaskins Mitchell, "The History of Mt. Zion United Methodist Church and Mt. Zion Cemetery," *Records of the Columbian Historical Society* 5:1984, 103–118; and Mary Tremain, *Slavery in the District of Columbia: The Policy of Congress and the Struggle for Abolition* (1892; New York: Negro Universities Press, 1969).

On the Underground Railroad in the Washington, I was fortunate to have the following excellent recent works: Stanley Harrold's invaluable *Subversives: Antislavery Community in Washington, D.C., 1828–1865* (Baton Rouge: Louisiana State University Press, 2003); Josephine Pacheco, *The Pearl: A Failed Slave Escape on the Potomac* (Chapel Hill: University of North Carolina Press, 2005); Hilary Russell, *The Operation of the Underground Railroad in Washington, D.C., c. 1800–1860: Final Research Report* (Washington, D.C.: Historical Society of the District of Columbia, 2001); and Hilary Russell, "Underground Railroad

Activists in Washington, D.C.," *Washington History* 13, no. 2 (2001–2002): 28. Two African-American conductors on the Underground Railroad provide a firsthand account of their involvement in slave escapes from Washington, D.C. They are the indispensable recordings of William Still, *Underground Railroad* (1872; Chicago: Johnson Publishing Company, Inc., 1970); and Thomas Smallwood's *A Narrative of Thomas Smallwood (Coloured man)*, ed., Richard Almonte (Toronto: Mercury Press, 2000). Another valuable source was C. J. Lovejoy, *Memoir of Rev. Charles T. Torrey, Who Died in the Penitentiary of Maryland, Where He Was Confined for Showing Mercy to the Poor* (1847; New York: The Negro Universities Press, 1969). Though focused on New Bedford, Massachusetts, Kathryn Grover's *The Fugitive's Gibraltar: Escaping Slaves and Abolitionism in New Bedford, Massachusetts* (Amherst: University of Massachusetts Press, 2001) proved immensely helpful on details related to the *Pearl* escape.

On the Underground Railroad in general, in addition to indispensable William Still, *Underground Railroad* (1879; Chicago: Johnson Publishing Company Inc., 1970), the main sources are: David Blight, ed. *Passage to Freedom, the Underground Railroad in History and Memory* (New York: Smithsonian Books, 2006); Charles L. Blockson, *The Underground Railroad* (New York: Hippocrene Books, 1994); Fergus M. Bordewich, *Bound for Canaan: The Underground Railroad and the War for the Soul of America* (New York: Amistad, 2005); William Arthur Breyfogle, *Make Free: The Story of the Underground Railroad* (New York: J. B. Lippincott, 1858); Henrietta Buckmaster, *Let My People Go* (New York: Harper and Brothers, 1941); John Hope Franklin and Loren Schweninger, *Runaway Slaves: Rebels on the Plantation* (New York: Oxford University Press, 1999); Larry Gara, *The Liberty Line: the Legend of the Underground Railroad* (Lexington: University Press of Kentucky, 1961); and Ann Hagedorn, *Beyond the River: the Untold Story of the Heroes of the Underground Railroad* (New York: Simon and Schuster, 2003).

In addition to the texts already listed, I relied on the following texts for details on slavery, tobacco, and the antebellum free black community:

Herbert Aptheker, *American Negro Slave Revolts* (New York: Columbia University Press, 1943); Ira Berlin, Marc Favreau, and Steven F. Miller, eds., *Remembering Slavery: African Americans Talk About Their Personal Experiences of Slavery and Freedom* (New York: New Press; Washington, D.C.: Library of Congress, 1998); Ira Berlin and Leslie S. Rowland, eds., *Families and Freedom: A Documentary History of African-American Kinship in the Civil War Era* (New York: New Press, 1997); Ira Berlin, *Many Thousands Gone* (Cambridge, Mass.: Harvard University Press, 1998); Ira Berlin, *Slaves Without Masters: The Free Negro in the Antebellum South* (New York: The New Press, 1974); John W. Blassingame, ed., *Slave Testimony: Two Centuries of Letters, Speeches, Interviews, and Autobiographies* (Baton Rouge: Louisiana State University Press, 1977); T. H. Breen, *Tobacco Culture: The Mentality of the Great Tidewater Planters on the Eve of Revolution* (Princeton, N.J.: Princeton University Press, 1985); Leonard P. Curry, *The Free Black in Urban America, 1800–1850* (Chicago: University of Chicago Press, 1981); David Brion Davis, *Inhuman Bondage: The Rise and Fall of Slavery in the New World* (New York: Oxford University Press, 2006); James Oliver Horton and Lois E. Horton, *Slavery and the Making of America* (New York: Oxford University Press, 2005); Ivor Noël Hume, *The Virginia Adventure: Roanoke to James Towne* (Charlottesville: University of Virginia Press, 1994); Allan Kulikoff, *Tobacco and Slaves: The Development of Southern Cultures in the Chesapeake, 1680–1800* (Chapel Hill: University of North Carolina Press, 1986); Edmund S. Morgan, *American Slavery, American Freedom: The Ordeal of Colonial Virginia* (New York: W. W. Norton & Co., 1975); Philip D. Morgan, *Slave Counterpoint: Black Culture in the Eighteenth-Century Chesapeake and Lowcountry* (Chapel Hill: University of North Carolina Press, 1998); Stephen B. Oates, *The Approaching Fury: Voices of the Storm, 1820–1861* (New York: HarperCollins, 1997); James Brewer Stewart and Eric Foner, eds., *Holy Warriors: the Abolitionists and American Slavery* (New York: Hill and Wang, 1996); and Henry Irving Tragle, Comp., *The Southampton Slave Revolt of 1831: A*

Compilation of Source Material (Amherst: The University of Massachusetts Press, 1971).

On the slave trade in particular, the sources I most relied on are: Frederic Bancroft, *Slave Trading in the Old South* (1931; Columbia: University of South Carolina Press, 1996); Ralph Clayton, *Cash for Blood: The Baltimore to New Orleans Domestic Slave Trade* (Bowie, Md.: Heritage Books, 2002); Mary Beth Corrigan, "Imaginary Cruelties? A History of the Slave Trade in Washington, D.C.," *Washington History* 13, no. 2 (2001–2002): 4; Steven Deyle, *Carry Me Back: The Domestic Slave Trade in American Life* (New York: Oxford University Press, 2005). Robert H. Gudmestad, *A Troublesome Commerce: The Transformation of the Interstate Slave Trade* (Baton Rouge: Louisiana State University Press, 2003); Walter Johnson, *Soul by Soul: Life Inside the Antebellum Slave Market* (Cambridge, Mass.: Harvard University Press, 1999); Solomon Northup, *Twelve Years a Slave*, ed. Sue Eakin and Joseph Logsdon (Baton Rouge: Louisiana State University Press, 1968); Michael Tadman, *Speculators and Slaves: Masters, Traders, and Slaves in the Old South* (Madison: University of Wisconsin Press, 1989); Hugh Thomas, *The Slave Trade* (New York: Simon & Schuster, 1997). Additionally, historian T. Michael Miller's memorandum, "An Overview of the Dwelling at 1707 Duke Street, Joseph Bruin and His Slave Pen," prepared for Pamela Cressey, Director, Alexandria Archaeology Center, provides a detailed history of the Bruin slave pen; and Janice G. Artemel and Elizabeth A. Crowell's "The Alexandria Slave Pen: Archaeology of Urban Captivity," prepared for the Middle Atlantic Archaeological Conference, held in Lancaster, Pennsylvania (April 1987), provides details on the Franklin & Armfield slave pens.

I have also found the following sources on the history of black America and the movement to end slavery and the coming of freedom very helpful: Frederick Douglass, *Life and Times of Frederick Douglass* (1892; Toronto: Collier-MacMillan Ltd, 1962); John Hope Franklin and Alfred A. Moss Jr., *From Slavery to Freedom*, 6th ed. (New York: Alfred A. Knopf, 1988); Allen C. Guelzo, *Lincoln's Emancipation*

Proclamation: The End of Slavery in America (New York: Simon & Schuster, 2004); Steven Hahn, *A Nation Under Our Feet: Black Political Struggles in the Rural South from Slavery to the Great Migration* (Cambridge, Mass.: Harvard University Press, 2003); Stanley Harrold, *Gamaliel Bailey and Antislavery Union* (Kent, Ohio: Kent State University Press, 1986); Paxton Hibben, *Henry Ward Beecher: An American Portrait* (New York: The Press of the Readers Club, 1942); Carleton Mabee, *Black Freedom: The Nonviolent Abolitionists from 1830 Through the Civil War* (New York: Macmillan Company, 1970); Henry Mayer, *All on Fire: William Lloyd Garrison and the Abolition of Slavery* (New York: St. Martin's Press, 1998); William S. McFeely, *Frederick Douglass* (New York: Simon & Schuster, 1991); William Lee Miller, *Arguing About Slavery: The Great Battle in the United States Congress* (New York: Alfred A. Knopf, 1996); Benjamin Quarles, *Black Abolitionists* (New York: Da Capo Press, 1991); Milton Rugoff, *The Beechers: An American Family in the Nineteenth Century* (New York: Harper & Row, 1981); Benjamin P. Thomas, *Theodore Weld: Crusader for Freedom* (New Brunswick, N.J.: Rutgers University Press, 1950); Ronald G. Walters, *The Antislavery Appeal: American Abolitionism After 1830* (Baltimore: Johns Hopkins University Press, 1976); and Bertram Wyatt-Brown, *Lewis Tappan and the Evangelical War Against Slavery* (Cleveland: The Press of Case Western Reserve University, 1969).

Hugh C. Humphreys's monograph, *"Agitate! Agitate! Agitate!" The Great Fugitive Slave Law Convention and Its Rare Daguerreotype* (New York: Madison County Historical Society, 1994), rediscovered a largely lost but important episode in the antislavery movement. The monograph is in print and available from the Madison County Historical Society (New York).

Many of the materials about Oberlin were found in the rich archives at Oberlin University. The Cowles Papers invaluably preserve the correspondence from Harriet Beecher Stowe about the Edmonsons as well as letters from the Edmonsons. Robert Samuel Fletcher's *A History of*

Oberlin College: From Its Foundation Through the Civil War (New York: Arno Press, 1971) provides detailed background on the college. Ellen Lawson and Marlene Merrill do the same for the black students at Oberlin in "The Antebellum 'Talented Thousandth': Black College Students at Oberlin Before the Civil War," *Journal of Negro Education* 52, no. 2 (1983).

The main sources for Myrtilla Miner and her Washington school are the Myrtilla Miner Papers in the Manuscript Division of the Library of Congress, which provide an in-depth account of the school. I've also relied on Philip S. Foner and Josephine Pacheco's *Three Who Dared: Prudence Crandall, Margaret Douglass, Myrtilla Miner—Champions of Antebellum Black Education* (Westport, Conn.: Greenwood Press, 1984), and Ellen M. O'Connor's *Myrtilla Miner: A Memoir* (New York: Arno Press, 1969). This appears to have partly incorporated an address published as *The School for Colored Girls, Washington, D.C.* (Philadelphia: Merrihew & Thompson's Steam Power Press, 1854). Gerrit Smith Wormley, the son of Amelia Brent Wormley, who attended the school, wrote "Myrtilla Miner" in the *Journal of Negro History* 5, no. 4 (October 1920), for which he interviewed former students.

The following books on Montgomery County and the state of Maryland were essential. They are: Barbara Jeanne Fields, *Slavery and Freedom on the Middle Ground: Maryland During the Nineteenth Century* (New Haven: Yale University Press, 1985); Jerry M. Hynson, *Free African Americans of Maryland 1832* (Westminster, Md.: Willow Bend Books, 2000); and Richard K. MacMaster and Ray Eldon Hiebert, *A Grateful Remembrance: The Story of Montgomery County, Maryland* (Rockville, Md.: Montgomery County Government and the Montgomery County Historical Society, 1976).

For background on the Civil War, I have depended on Ernest B. Furgurson, *Freedom Rising: Washington in the Civil War* (New York: Alfred A. Knopf, 2004); Margaret Leech, *Reveille in Washington* (New York: Harper & Brothers, 1941); James McPherson, *Battle Cry of Free-*

dom: The Civil War Era (New York: Ballantine Books, 1988); Mary Mitchell, *Divided Town: A Study of Georgetown, D.C., During the Civil War* (Barre, Mass.: Barre Publishers, 1968); P. J. Staudenraus, ed. *Mr. Lincoln's Washington: The Civil War Dispatches of Noah Brooks* (South Brunswick, N.J.: Thomas Yoseloff, 1967); Noah Andre Trudeau, *Like Men of War: Black Troops in the Civil War, 1862–1865* (Boston: Little, Brown and Company, 1998).

I was extremely fortunate to have C. R. Gibbs, *Black, Copper, and Bright: The District of Columbia's Black Civil War Regiment* (Silver Spring, Md.: Three Dimensional Publishing, 2002). Gibbs details the formation and history of the black regiment with its close links to the Edmonson family and charts the people who recruited and supported them.

Two of the historic black churches of Washington closely linked with this story—Asbury United Methodist Church and Mt. Zion United Methodist—have generously assisted me by providing access to their archives.

As can be seen from the frequent quotes through all of this book, nineteenth-century newspapers and, most important, those of an abolitionist persuasion, provide rich information on the "first draft of history" as well as the passions and everyday life of the era. The *Congressional Globe*, published by Francis Blair, was the official record of the proceedings of Congress; it would later become the *Congressional Record*. Also, Jefferson Morley's "Through the Perilous Fight: The Scandalous History of Francis Scott Key and Washington's First Race Riot," *Washington Post Magazine* (February 6, 2005), provides an in-depth report on the Snow Riot of 1835.

ONE
Two Young Girls Join an Audacious Escape

8 Washington Gas Light Company: Sarah Pressey Noreen, *Public Street Illumination in Washington, D.C.: An Illustrated History* G.W. Washington Studies, no. 2 (Washington, D.C.: George Washington University, 1975): 8–12.

10 purchased his first twenty acres: Montgomery County Land Records, BS 7, 414–15, Montgomery County Courthouse, Rockville, Maryland.

10 cultivated oats, corn, and Irish potatoes: The U.S. Census, Agricultural Schedule, Berry Division, Montgomery County, Maryland.

10 a young slave named Amelia: Microfilm copy of Wills of Montgomery County, The Montgomery County Historical Society, Rockville, Maryland.

11 writ *de idiota inquirendo*: filed on February 19, 1827 (March Term) in Chancery Court, Equity Records, Montgomery County Courthouse, Rockville, Maryland.

12 both men's names were logged: Entry 427, Runaway Docket, Baltimore City and County Jail, Maryland State Archives.

13 Moroccan walking "slips" (and other items for sale): *Washington Daily National Intelligencer*, April 14–22, 1848.

13 "written much more nearly to the life . . .": *Boston Chronotype*, April 29, 1848.

15 sold his future share: Montgomery County Land Records, STS 1(544–45), Montgomery County Courthouse, Rockville, Maryland.

15 scattering of buildings along the river: Nicholas King, "1790 Map of Notley Young's River Farm," Geography and Map Room, Library of Congress.

16 some of whom he hired: William C. Allen, "History of Slave Laborers in the Construction of the United States Capitol," Office of the Architect of the Capitol, May 9, 2005.

16 "rather lonely" White-house wharf: *Personal Memoir of Daniel Drayton, for Four Years and Four Months a Prisoner (for Charity's Sake) in Washington Jail, Including a Narrative of the Voyage and Capture of the Schooner Pearl* (1854; New York: Negro Universities Press, 1969), 29.

16 ". . . below the Long Bridge": *Washington Daily Union*, April 19, 1848.

17 Caleb Aaronson . . . would later issue a statement: *Baltimore Sun*, April 24, 1848.

17 "to retrieve the slaves under some ruse . . .": Kathryn Grover, *The Fugitive's Gibraltar: Escaping Slaves and Abolitionism in New Bedford, Massachusetts* (Amherst, Mass.: University of Massachusetts Press, 2001), 192.

18 six feet of head room: *Baltimore Sun*, July 29, 1848.

18 "draw but little water": Drayton, *Personal Memoir*, 8.

19 "the African Church": *The Georgetown Directory for the year 1830* (District of Columbia: printed by Benjamin Homans), 21.

19 Brent was a preacher: Records of the Mt. Zion United Methodist Church, Washington, D.C.

19 Brent is also credited: Paul E. Sluby, Jr., *Asbury, Our Legacy, Our Faith*

1836–1993: The History of the Asbury United Methodist Church, Washington, D.C.
2nd revision (Washington, D.C.: n.p., 1999), 19.

21 another account of that incident: Charles Cleveland to Wendell Phillips, 18
February 1854. Spooner Papers, New-York Historical Society.

22 Frenchtown where the family was stranded: Francis E. Newton, "Long Lost
Frenchtown, Maryland: A Secret Station on the Underground Railroad," unpublished paper, November 2002. Mr. Newton, president of the Richardson Maritime Museum, clearly established for the first time that the *Pearl*'s destination
was Frenchtown, Maryland and not Frenchtown, New Jersey.

22 "sail between Philadelphia and Washington": Charles Cleveland to Wendell Phillips, Francis Jackson, and Lysander Spooner, 18 February 1854. Spooner Papers,
New-York Historical Society.

23 "gentleman of Washington": Ibid.

23 "see what could be done": Drayton, *Personal Memoir*, 24.

23 ". . . not less than 75" enslaved Washingtonians: William Chaplin to Gerrit
Smith, 25 March 1848. Gerrit Smith Papers, Library of Congress.

24 John Greenleaf Whittier poem: John G. Whittier, *The Branded Hand* (Philadelphia, 1845). Rare Book and Special Collections Division, Library of Congress.

24 "according to the arrangement . . .": Drayton, *Personal Memoir*, 25.

24 "chose to receive on board": Ibid.

25 "inexperienced as a child": Ibid.

26 Sayres and Drayton quarreled: Statement or testimony of Chester English, Key
Family Papers, Rare, Manuscript, and Special Collections Library, Duke University.

26 ". . . those elements of character . . .": *Albany Patriot*, February 23, 1848.

27 "to the whole family of man . . .": *Washington Daily Union*, April 20, 1848.

27 58 out of the city's 5,893 dwellings: *Washington Daily National Intelligencer*,
April 17, 1848.

27 "given the character of [the French] . . .": *Georgetown Advocate*, April 15, 1848.

27 a performance of the Ethiopian Serenaders: Abraham Lincoln to Mary Todd
Lincoln, July 2, 1848, in Roy Basler, Marion Dolores Pratt, and Lloyd A. Dun-
lap, eds., *The Collected Works of Abraham Lincoln* (New Brunswick, N.J.: Rutgers
University Press, 1953), vol. 1:495–96. The concerts were advertised as taking
place between January 8 and 17, 1848.

27 "the monsters of iniquity": *Cleveland Daily True Democrat*, April 19, 1848.

27 "like so many venomous serpents": *Baston Weekly Chronotype*, April 23, 1848.

28 "The Revolution in Europe.": *Washington Daily National Intelligencer*, April 12, 1848.

28 Later that evening: Chester English, Key Family Papers, Duke University.

28 "unusual nature of the business . . .": Drayton, *Personal Memoir*, 30.

TWO

Washington's Underground Railroad

32 "$150 REWARD . . . Ran away . . .": *Pennsylvania Intelligencer*, March 24, 1826.

34 Some details of: Seth Gates to Joshua Giddings, 5 December 1848, Joshua Giddings Papers, Ohio Historical Society.

34 Mr. Cartwright, the "colored minister": C. J. Lovejoy, *Memoir of Rev. Charles T. Torrey, Who Died in the Penitentiary of Maryland, Where He Was Confined for Showing Mercy to the Poor* (1847; New York: The Negro Universities Press, 1969), 90.

36 Mt. Zion's Georgetown cemetery: Pauline Gaskins Mitchell, "The History of Mt. Zion United Methodist Church and Mt. Zion Cemetery," *Records of the Columbian Historical Society* 51 (1984): 103–18.

36 "in consideration of good will . . .": Registration no. 2,226, Dorothy Provine, compiler and editor, *District of Columbia Free Negro Registers, 1821–1861* (Bowie, Md.: Heritage Books, 1996).

37 "[I]f we cannot summon virtue . . .": *Albany Patriot*, January 5, 1848.

38 a decent wage of $1.20 per day. Payroll Records of the United States Navy Yard. RG 71, National Archives.

39 "a husband and father . . .": *Albany Patriot*, March 22, 1848.

39 "expedition had principally originated in the desire . . .": Drayton, *Personal Memoir*, 28.

41 "handsome mulatto": transcription by Lee Langston-Harrison, the curator at James Madison's Montpelier, of Mary Cutts's unpublished memoirs (Mary Estelle Elizabeth Cutts Papers. Schlesinger Library, Radcliffe College). No last name was provided in this memoir, but the Paul is believed to be Paul Jennings. This memoir also states that "Paul . . . signed for his freedom and having sufficient money moved to New York. . . ." She went on to say that when his funds were exhausted, he requested permission to return to Montpelier and "his journey to New York was never mentioned!"

41 first memoir of a servant's life: Paul Jennings, "A Colored Man's Reminiscences of James Madison," and "Commentary: The Washington of Paul Jennings—White

House Slave, Free Man, and Conspirator for Freedom," by G. Franklin Edwards and Michael R. Winston, *White House History* 1, no. 1 (1983), 46–63.

41 "As for our enemy at home . . .": Gaillard Hunt, ed., *The First Forty Years of Washington Society in the Family Letters of Margaret Bayard Smith* (1906; New York: Frederick Ungar Publishing Co., 1965), 90.

41 ". . . acted as became patriots": *Washington Daily National Intelligencer*, August 24, 1814.

41 some enslaved blacks: John Hope Franklin and Loren Schweninger, *Runaway Slaves* (New York: Oxford University Press, 1999), 28.

41 "Clear out! Clear out!": Jennings, *A Colored Man's Reminiscences*, 48.

43 "*I have paid $120 . . .*": Signed statement of Daniel Webster, Washington, March 19, 1847. Moorland-Spingarn Research Center, Howard University, Washington, D.C. While Webster states that the freedom papers were recorded in the records of the District of Columbia, Jennings's name is not listed in the Register of Free Blacks in Washington, D.C. Jennings may not have found it necessary to record his papers, because he was so well known in the city from his association with the Madisons and then with Daniel Webster. Again, a powerful white name could act as protection.

43 "last red cent": *Albany Patriot*, March 15, 1848.

44 Stewart "made tracts down the street": Ibid.

44 "deep desire to be of help . . ." John H. Paynter, *Fugitives of the Pearl* (Washington, D.C.: Associated Publishers, June, 1930), 34.

44 an excited and anxious William Chaplin: John Wallace Hutchinson, *Story of the Hutchinsons (Tribe of Jesse)* (Boston: Lee and Shepard, 1896). Stanley Harrold, in *Subversives*, points out that Hutchinson wrote two different accounts of the singers' meeting with the abolitionist, of which only the second one, cited here, was published. In the earlier account, the name of the man accompanying Bailey was given as Wilson, but that may have been a precaution. In the later 1896 account, the abolitionist was named as Chaplin and the meeting was described as taking place on Sunday, shortly after the *Pearl* left Washington.

48 A black man named Antonio: Ira Berlin, *Many Thousands Gone* (Cambridge, Mass.: Harvard University Press, 1998), 30.

48 instructed his agent: Donald G. Shomette, *Tidewater Time Capsule: History Beneath the Patuxent* (Centreville, Md.: Tidewater Publishers, 1995), 34.

49 "naturally inclin'd to love neigros [sic]": Governor Charles Calvert to Lord Calvert, 27 April 1664. Calvert Papers, Maryland Historical Society.

51 to 12.8 percent in 1850: Barbara Jeanne Fields, *Slavery and Freedom on the*

Middle Ground: Maryland During the Nineteenth Century (New Haven: Yale University Press, 1985), 12.

51 from 100,000 in 1810: Ira Berlin, *Slaves Without Masters: The Free Negro in the Antebellum South* (New York: The New Press, 1974), 15.

51 the free black population increased dramatically: Letitia Woods Brown, *Free Negroes in the District of Columbia 1790–1846* (New York: Oxford University Press, 1972), 11.

51 "little fellow went about . . .": Eunice Tripler, *Some Notes of Her Personal Recollections* (New York: The Grafton Press, 1910), 44–45.

52 While visiting a slave pen in Baltimore: Ethan Allen Andrews, *Slavery and the Domestic Slave-Trade in the United States* (New York: Books for Libraries Press, 1971), 78.

53 "[m]ost of those he'd known since childhood": Joan Steinau Lester and Eleanor Holmes Norton, *Fire in My Soul: The Life of Eleanor Holmes Norton* (New York: Atria, 2002), 7–8.

56 Armistead signed manumission papers: Registration No. 1312, Provine, *District of Columbia Free Negro Registers*.

57 "robust, worthy, industrious man": *New York True Wesleyan*, September 23, 1848.

57 ". . . Seventh Street on the Avenue": Ibid.

57 "trusty friend" his property: named Thomas Blagden: Ibid.

58 inventory of his property: Robert Armistead probate records, the Orphans Court of the District of Columbia Circuit Court, RG 21, National Archives.

59 ". . . the legality of her title to freedom": Mary Bell's Certificate of Freedom issued by the Registrar of the City of Washington in 1843. Bell Trial Records.

59 petitions for freedom for two Bell daughters: *Mary Bell* v. *Susan Armistead* and *Eleanor Bell by William Simms, her next friend*, v. *Susan Armistead*, Trial Records of the United States District Court for the District of Columbia, 1838–61, RG 21, National Archives. Eleanor Bell was a minor, and William Simms was the adult who represented her in the legal suit.

59 petition . . . for Harriet's freedom: *Harriet Bell, by her next friend Daniel Bell* v. *Susan Armistead*, Trial Records of the United States District Court for the District of Columbia, 1838–61, RG 21, National Archives. In this case, Harriet Bell's father represented her best interests.

59 ". . . she may be lost in irredeemable slavery": petition for injunctive relief, Chancery Case #0421, United States District Court for the District of Columbia, RG 21, National Archives.

60 Edward Clarke's death signaled the end: Harriet Beecher Stowe, *The Key to Uncle Tom's Cabin* (1853; New York: Kennikat Press, 1968), 158. Stowe does not name Clarke, but indicates that the family had been protected by a white official until his death, and that man was very likely Clarke.

61 a "warm-hearted" Washington resident: *Albany Patriot*, July 16, 1847. The unsigned article was likely written by William Chaplin.

61 "the wind being dead in our teeth . . .": Drayton, *Personal Memoir*, 31.

THREE
Slavery in the Washington Area

63 "habit of frequenting the ball-room . . .": *Cleveland Daily True Democrat*, February 28, 1848.

63 "this hegira of the servants": *Washington Daily National Intelligencer*, April 19, 1848.

64 "monster petition": The petition was referred to the Committee for the District of Columbia on March 24, 1828, and seven years later it was ordered to be printed on February 9, 1835, on the motion of Rep. Henry Hubbard, of New Hampshire.

64 A congressional committee concluded: William Lee Miller, *Arguing About Slavery: The Great Battle in the United States Congress* (New York: Knopf, 1996), 107.

65 "[m]any of the African race . . .": Minutes of the Twenty-first Biennial American Convention for Promoting the Abolition of Slavery, and Improving the Condition of the African Race, Daniel A. P. Murray Collection, Rare Book and Special Collections Division, Library of Congress.

65 called for black revolution: *David Walker's Appeal to the Coloured Citizens of the World* (University Park: Pennsylvania State University Press, 2000).

65 Washington "was palsied by public indifference": *Liberator*, January 1, 1831.

65 William Wormley . . . agreed to act: Hilary Russell, *Operation of the Underground Railroad in Washington, D.C., C. 1800–1860: Final Research Report* (Washington: Historical Society of the District of Columbia, 2001).

66 a bloody insurrection: Henry Irving Tragle, *The Southampton Slave Revolt of 1831: A Compilation of Source Material* (Amherst: The University of Massachusetts Press, 1971), 3–25.

67 ". . . dangerous portion of its population": Inaugural meeting of the American

Colonization Society, 1816. Papers of the American Colonization Society, Manuscript Division, Library of Congress.

67 "insubordination and disregard of authority . . .": Robert H. Gudmestad, *A Troublesome Commerce: The Transformation of the Interstate Slave Trade* (Baton Rouge: Louisiana State University Press, 2003), 7.

67 "is willing to go to Liberia": Microfilm copies of the Montgomery County Census for Free Blacks of 1832. Maryland Historical Society.

68 "a negro man named Paul": V:100, Montgomery County Land Records, Montgomery County Courthouse, Rockville, Maryland.

69 "Slave Market of America": Rare Book and Special Collections Division, Library of Congress.

71 "A young man, about to disenthrall . . .": Cook Family Papers, Moorland-Spingarn Research Center, Howard University.

72 abolitionist pamphlets turned up: *The trial of Reuben Crandall, M.D., charged with publishing and circulating seditious and incendiary papers, &c., in the District of Columbia, with the intent of exciting servile insurrection.* Washington City, printed for the proprietors, 1836. Available online at http://hdl.loc.gov/loc.rbc/rbcmisc.lst0090.

73 run by Maria Wormley: the collected papers of the Wormley Family, held by Mrs. Frieda Wormley.

74 In 1837, and then again: Mary Tremain, *Slavery in the District of Columbia: The Policy of Congress and the Struggle for Abolition* (1892; New York: Negro Universities Press, 1969), 90.

75 "Whether France will sustain a Republic . . .": *New York Tribune*, April 18, 1848.

75 "short, stout and stubborn": Paynter, *Fugitives*, 68.

75 Diggs, freed in 1844: Provine, *District of Columbia Free Negro Registers*. The 1850 U.S. Census lists him as "Judson Digges."

75 "gone tearin' down" to the wharf: Paynter, *Fugitives*, 104.

76 questioned on Sunday "forenoon": *Cleveland Daily True Democrat*, April 24, 1848.

76 escapee from Washington named Anthony Blow: William Still, *Underground Railroad* (1872; Chicago: Johnson Publishing Company, Inc., 1970), 46–47.

77 Major Hampton C. Williams: *The Georgetown Advocate* of April 29, 1848, listed the posse as: Major H. C. Williams captain; volunteers, viz: Messrs. Thomas K. Wilson, Wm. Denham, Marcellus Dashields, W. A. Waugh, J. H. Craig, Caleb L. March, John G. Anderson, John B. Lewellin, J. D. Hoover, H. C. Dean,

Jeremiah Lockerman, Samuel Anderson, Andew Hoover, John Dewdney, Wm. Dawson, W. H. Craig, Geo. S. R. Morgan, H. Ridgway, ?? Bruce, Stephen Cassin, Jr., J. S. Marll, John Knight, H. W. Blount, John Mankin; James Ellis, Thos. Orme, John Whalan, Joshua Hilton, Joseph Marll, John Ross, R. Ballenger, W. N. Nicholls, John Essex (boy).

77   the posse on the *Salem* realized: *Washington Daily Union*, April 19, 1848.

78   "Niggers, by God": Drayton, *Personal Memoir*, 32; styled as "G-d" in the original.

78   saw the captain "groping around": *Baltimore Sun*, July 29, 1848.

78   The Thomas Orme who kept Drayton: Richard K. MacMaster and Ray Eldon Hiebert, *A Grateful Remembrance: The Story of Montgomery County, Maryland* (Rockville, Md.: Montgomery County Government and the Montgomery County Historical Society, 1976), 80–81.

79   "the most effectual means . . .": Ibid., 31.

79   "armed to the teeth with guns, pistols . . .": Drayton, *Personal Memoir*, 34.

80   "Do yourselves no harm . . .": Paynter, *Fugitives*, 89.

81   "only a mite . . .": *Baltimore Sun*, July 29, 1848.

81   "very insolent tone": Drayton, *Personal Memoir*, 35.

81   ". . . a prisoner in that way": *Baltimore Sun*, July 29, 1848.

81   "The first volume of Lynch": *New York Tribune* (n.d.), in *Boston Chronotype*, April 29, 1848.

81   "committed the highest crime, next to murder . . .": Drayton, *Personal Memoir*, 37.

82   ". . . torn in pieces by a mad bull": Ibid., 38.

82   "so much attached to the Bourbons . . .": *Albany Patriot*, April 19, 1848.

83   "much excitement" was generated: *Washington Daily Union*, April 19, 1848.

83   "has been entirely successful": *Baltimore Sun*, April 19, 1848.

83   "a bold stroke . . .": *Washington Daily Union*, April 19, 1848.

83   "a horde of idle, unprincipled, soulless fanatics . . .": Ibid.

84   "the songs of the slave . . .": Frederick Douglass, *My Bondage and Freedom* (New York: Miller, Orton & Mulligan, 1855), 77.

85   unarmed because Williams was confident: *Washington Daily Union*, April 19, 1848.

85   "Hasn't she got good spunk?": Stowe, *Key to Uncle Tom*, 159.

85   "the colored population are in anguish . . .": *Cleveland Daily True Democrat*, April 25, 1848.

86 he saw the Edmonson sisters marching: Paynter, *Fugitives*, 111.

86 "Negroes Wanted": *Washington Daily National Intelligencer*, April 28, 1849.

87 where Gannon owned land: Gannon's will shows that he owned Square 564, lots 10 and 11; Last Will and Testament of James Gannon, Archives of the District of Columbia.

87 Dr. Jesse Torrey of Philadelphia: Jesse Torrey, *A Portraiture of Domestic Slavery* (Philadelphia: Published by the author, printed by J. Bioren, 1817). See also W. B. Bryan, "A Fire in an Old-Time F Street Tavern and What It Revealed," *Records of the Columbia Historical Society* 9: 198–215.

87 "a procession of men, women and children . . .": Torrey, *Portraiture of Domestic Slavery*, 331–34.

88 ". . . the greatest curiosity to be seen . . .": *Evening Journal*, May 7, 1848; quoted in *Albany Patriot*, May 17, 1848.

89 "two stories high . . .": Solomon Northup, *Twelve Years a Slave*, ed. Sue Eakin and Joseph Logsdon (Baton Rouge: Louisiana State University Press, 1968), 22–23.

90 "Damn the law!": Drayton, *Personal Memoir*, 40; styled as "D—n" in the original.

90 Shouting "Lynch them!": Drayton, *Personal Memoir*, 40.

90 "Shoot him! Knock his damned brains out! . . .": *Boston Whig*, April 18, 1848, as reported in the *Liberator*, April 28, 1848. According to historian Stanley Harrold, the writer is Jacob Bigelow.

91 " anything but attractive.": Rev. Page Milburn, "Fourth Ward," *Records of the Columbia Historical Society* 33–34, (1932): 61.

92 "bank of a small stream . . .": Paynter, *Fugitives*, 119–24.

FOUR

Waves in Congress

93 to introduce a resolution: *Congressional Globe*, 30th Cong., 1st sess.: 641.

96 "a peculiar species of slave trade . . .": Abraham *Lincoln: Speeches and Writings*, 1832–1858 (New York: The Library of America, 1989), 313.

97 face-to-face with a slave coffle: Stewart, James Brewer, *Joshua R. Giddings and the Tactics of Radical Politics* (Cleveland: Press of Case Western Reserve University, 1970), 41.

97 Giddings became directly involved: *Cleveland Daily True Democrat*, January 24, 1848.

98 "... so close a vote on any question ...": *Albany Patriot*, February 2, 1848.

98 Duff Green, the strident proslavery activist: Stanley Harrold, *Subversives: Antislavery Community in Washington, D.C., 1828–1865* (Baton Rouge: Louisiana State University Press, 2003), 110.

98 Giddings quickly raised the money: *Cleveland Daily True Democrat*, February 16, 1848.

98 Ezra Stevens ... reported: *Cleveland Daily True Democrat*, January 24, 1848.

99 "that no man should enter ...": *Baltimore Sun*, April 20, 1848.

100 "never heard of a more outrageous ...": *New York Herald* in *National Anti-Slavery Standard*, May 4, 1848.

101 "Capture of Runaway Slaves ...": *Washington National Daily Intelligencer*, April 19, 1848.

101 [t]oo much credit cannot be given ...": *Washington Daily Union*, April 19, 1848.

101 "the negroes were deluded ...": *Baltimore Clipper*, cited in *Georgetown Advocate*, April 29, 1848.

102 "men, women, and children born and raised ...": *Baltimore Sun*, April 19, 1848.

102 "... one negro boy named Andrew ...": *Washington Daily Union*, April 19, 1848.

103 Susannah Armistead paid Dodge $282: Josephine Pacheco, *The Pearl: A Failed Slave Escape on the Potomac* (Chapel Hill: University of North Carolina Press, 2005), 164–65.

103 [t]he jail and surrounding premises are crowded ...": *Baltimore Sun*, April 20, 1848.

104 informed of the escape by "a friend": Joshua R. Giddings, *A History of the Rebellion, Its Authors and Causes* (New York: Follet, Foster, and Co., 1864), 272–73.

104 "they had friends who would see ...": *Cleveland Daily True Democrat*, April 25, 1848.

105 "the respectable, quiet, unoffending injured citizens ...": *Baltimore Sun*, April 20, 1848.

105 "lay violent hands upon me": *Congressional Globe*, 30 Cong. 1st sess., April 24, 1848:664.

105 "phrenological development bespoke ...": Giddings, *History of the Rebellion*, 279.

105 "things had come to a pretty pass": Drayton, *Personal Memoirs*, 45–46.

106 "I wanted *liberty*, wouldn't you, sir?" *Cleveland Daily True Democrat*, April 26, 1848.

107 John Brent was trusted: Paynter, *Fugitives*, 37.

107 registered at city hall: Registration no. 1990, Provine, *District of Columbia Free Negro Registers*.

107 then recorded her freedom: Registration no. 2304. Ibid.

108 the astonishingly high sum of seventy-five dollars: Receipt for contribution to Daniel Bell, 2 November 1848. Alexander Taverns Papers, Historical Society of Washington, D.C.

108 a select party at the Assembly Rooms: Invitation sent from Washington City, 26 January 1846. Ibid.

108 "beautiful girl of eighteen . . .": *Albany Patriot*, May 24, 1848.

109 part of which she sold: 788, 361 and 789, 489 (1875) Land Records, Recorder of Deeds, District of Columbia.

109 Alfred Pope was said to bear: Mary Beth Corrigan, Servant and Slave Biographies prepared for Tudor Place Historic House and Gardens, Washington, D.C., 2003.

110 Elizabeth Dick died eleven years later: Last will and testament of Elizabeth Dick, Archives of the District of Columbia.

110 "was of the number who ran off . . .": *Washington National Daily Intelligencer*, November 27, 1849.

110 Calvert was committed to the jail: Jerry Hynson, *District of Columbia Department of Corrections Runaway Slave Book, 1848–1863* (Westminster, Md.: Willow Bend Books, 1999).

111 "did not believe in distinction . . .": John W. Cromwell, "First Negro Churches in Washington," *The Journal of Negro History*, 7, no. 1 (January, 1922):76.

112 "Mr. Begelow . . . I hop yu . . .": Stowe, *Key to Uncle Tom*, 171–73.

113 letter signed "A Volunteer": *Albany Patriot*, May 17, 1848.

113 Palfrey presented a resolution: Congressional Globe, 30 Cong., I session, April 20, 1848: 641.

113 "a very faithful man": *New York Tribune*, April 18, 1848.

113 "possessed before the universal world . . .": *Cleveland Daily Time Democrat*, April 28, 1848.

114 carrying a "bowie-knife": *New York Express*, quoted in the *Cleveland Daily Time Democrat*, May 19, 1848.

114 "public indignation had been increased . . .": *Washington Daily Union*, April 20, 1848.

114 "an almost boyish brightness . . .": Grace Greenwood, "An American Salon," *The Cosmopolitan* 8 (November 1889–April 1890): 440.

114 "one of the most splendid buildings . . .": Pamela Scott and Antoinette J. Lee, *Buildings of the District of Columbia* (New York: Oxford University Press, 1993), 192.

116 "no change, of course, will be made . . .": *Albany Patriot*, February 23, 1848.

116 Bailey reported that "a coffle of slaves . . .": *Washington National Era*, September 2, 1847.

117 "take part in any movement . . .": *Washington National Era*, April 27, 1848.

117 "not less than three thousand . . .": *Baltimore Sun*, April 20, 1848.

117 the southern façade of the Patent Building: *Baltimore Sun*, April 20, 1848. (The eastern façade of the Patent Office that faced the *National Era* had not been constructed at that time.)

118 "to accomplish by force . . .": *New York Herald*, April 21, 1848.

119 "You are demanding from me . . .": Report of John Smith the Younger of May 1, 1848, for the *New York Tribune*, excerpted in *Washington National Era*, May 4, 1848.

120 "Down with the *Era!*": *New York Herald*, April 21, 1848.

121 "we cherish an instinctive abhorrence . . .": *Washington National Era*, April 20, 1848.

121 "fearful acts of lawless and irresponsible violence . . .": Handbill in Historical Society of the District of Columbia.

121 unrest could be used to agitate: *New York Express* (undated), quoted in the *Cleveland Daily Time Democrat*, April 27, 1848.

122 no question where Polk stood: William Dusinberre, *Slavemaster President: The Double Career of James Polk* (New York: Oxford University Press, 2003), 121.

122 the mob was rightfully provoked: James Polk, *The Diary of a President, 1845–1849, covering the Mexican War, the acquisition of Oregon, and the conquest of California and the Southwest* (New York: Longmans, Green & Co., 1952), 320.

123 "but what if the proprietor . . .": *Baltimore Sun*, April 21, 1848.

123 On Thursday, Rep. John Palfrey: *Congressional Globe*, 30th Cong., 1st sess.: 649–656.

124 In the Senate that same day: Ibid., 656.

124 "a debate of a most exciting . . .": Ibid.

124 "[T]here is but one question . . .": Ibid., 501–502.

125 "Honorable Senators talked of lynching Mr. Hale": *New Orleans Times Picayune*, May 2, 1848.

126 "the District was forgotten": *Utica Liberty Press*, May 4, 1848.

FIVE
The Fate of the Edmonsons

127 "eclipse even Lord Chesterfield himself": *New York Independent*, April 18, 1850.

128 "they became comparatively quiet . . .": *Washington National Era*, April 27, 1848.

129 "[i]n a certain sense . . .": Ibid.

129 "dreary" place, "marked by the frowns . . .": *New York Independent*, April 18, 1850, quoting the Washington correspondent of the *Cleveland Daily True Democrat*.

129 a "trader in Negroes": T. Michael Miller, "An Overview of the Dwelling at 1707 Duke Street, Joseph Bruin and His Slave Pen," memorandum, Alexandria Archaeology center. Miller is citing *Terrett v. Terrett* (1851), a legal suit in which Bruin was involved.

130 "cash for negroes": Ibid.

132 Slatter had completed sixty shipments: Ralph Clayton, *Cash for Blood: The Baltimore to New Orleans Domestic Slave Trade* (Bowie, Md.: Heritage Books, 2002), 98–101.

132 "deliver the above named slave . . .": *Drayton v. U.S.*, Trial Records of the United States District Court for the District of Columbia, 1838–61. RG 21, National Archives. The initial criminal charge was entitled *U.S. v. Drayton*, but all of the lower court records were transferred to the appellate case (*Drayton v. U.S.*).

133 "Friend [Thurlow] Weed": *Albany Evening Journal*, reprinted in the *Albany Patriot*, May 3, 1848.

133 a position associated with Bigelow: Harrold, *Subversives*, 134n.

133 "wives were there to take leave . . .": Letter published in *Albany Evening Journal*, reprinted in *Albany Patriot*, May 3, 1848.

134 "with so much affect . . .": New York *True Wesleyan*, September 23, 1848.

134 "slight tinge of African blood . . .": Letter published in *Albany Evening Journal*, reprinted in *Albany Patriot*, May 3, 1848.

134 "Southern in every respect": Jane Donovan, ed., *Many Witnesses: A History of Dumbarton United Methodist Church, 1772–1990* (Washington, D.C.: Dumbarton United Methodist Church, 1998), 166.

134 "to view the heart-rending scene . . .": letter published in *Albany Evening Journal*, reprinted in *Albany Patriot*, May 3, 1848.

134 Ezra Stevens's account of this incident: *Cleveland Daily Tree Democrat*, April 28, 1848.

135 One of Turner's men called out: Kenneth S. Greenberg, *Nat Turner: A Slave Rebellion in History and Memory* (New York: Oxford University Press, 2003), 9.

135 conference voted 110–68 to suspend him: Donovan, *Many Witnesses*, 171–72.

135 "wonton and unprovoked attack": *Washington Daily Union*, May 7, 1848.

136 "mortified at being brought back . . .": Ibid.

136 writer wondered what "Henry" thought: letter published in *Albany Evening Journal* May 7, 1848, reprinted in *Albany Patriot*, May 17, 1848.

137 Henry Smallwood suddenly disappeared: Mt. Zion Church Records.

138 Amelia had always lived: Stowe, *Key to Uncle Tom*, 156.

138 more than thirteen hundred slaves: Clayton, *Cash for Blood*, 106–107.

139 Douglass wasn't the only influential abolitionist: Henry Mayer, *All on Fire: William Lloyd Garrison and the Abolition of Slavery* (New York: St. Martin's Press, 1998), 71–94.

141 "fast sailing coppered" ship: *American and Commercial Daily Advertiser* (Baltimore), May 4, 1848.

141 As required by law: Slave Manifests, Baltimore to New Orleans, RG 36, National Archives.

143 "ill health and circumstances . . .": *Albany Patriot*, May 24, 1848.

144 Joshua Giddings later said: Giddings, *History of the Rebellion*, 279.

144 "Humanity . . . Fraternity . . . Pity": *Albany Patriot*, May 24, 1848.

144 a "noble man" from New York: *Utica Liberty Press*, May 18, 1848.

147 "By the rivers of Babylon . . .": Paynter, *Fugitives*, 142–43

151 a resident population of 79,998: *Cleveland Daily True Democrat*, December 22, 1847.

152 1,396 bales of cotton: *New Orleans Times Picayune*, April 23, 1848.

153 "[y]outh and age—all colors, nationals . . .": *Cleveland Daily True Democrat*, January 28, 1848.

153 the demand for domestic slaves: Charles Wesley, "Manifests of Slave Shipments," *Journal of Negro History* 27 (April 1942): 156–72.

153 "Louisiana Ballroom—American Style": *New Orleans Daily Picayune*, April 20, 1848.

154 *quadroon*, which means one-quarter black: Mary Gehman, *The Free People of Color of New Orleans* (New Orleans: Margaret Media, Inc., 1994), 60–61.

154 "Richmond and Charleston combined": Frederic Bancroft, *Slave Trading*

in the Old South (1931; Columbia, S.C.: University of South Carolina Press, 1996), 315.

154 City authorities did try: Walter Johnson, *Soul by Soul: Life Inside the Antebellum Slave Market* (Cambridge, Mass.: Harvard University Press, 1999), 25.

155 "calkers, masons, butlers, coopers . . .": Bancroft, *Slave Trading*, 313–14.

155 the trade in "fancy girls": Johnson, *Soul by Soul*, 113.

156 "[t]he slave market was suffused with sexuality . . .": Ibid.

156 "at his old stand . . .": Bancroft, *Slave Trading*, advertisements opposite page 316. These advertisements are in the 1931 edition and are not included in the 1996 edition of the book.

157 Jonathan Wilson, also of Baltimore: See, Clayton, *Cash for Blood,* 57. Wilson's partnership with Donovan was dissolved in 1849, but Wilson continued to trade at 15 Esplanade.

157 He wrote that Theophilus Freeman: Northup, *Twelve Years a Slave,* 51–59.

158 "suits of coarse blue jean": Paynter, *Fugitives,* 149.

158 "subjected to examination . . .": Ibid., 150.

161 the disease caused backaches, high fever: Jo Ann Carrigan, *The Saffron Scourge: A History of Yellow Fever in Louisiana, 1796–1905* (Lafayette: University of Southwestern Louisiana, 1994), 55.

161 given a "positive assurance": *Salem (OH) Anti-Slavery Bugle,* November 17, 1848.

SIX

Trials and Tribulations

---

164 "To the Friends of Liberty . . .": "To the Friends of Liberty Throughout the United States," May 1848. Black History Miscellaneous Papers, Library of Congress.

166 "good health and good spirits": Charles Cleveland to Boston Committee in Support of Drayton, 11 January 1849. Black History Miscellaneous Papers, Library of Congress. The committee member was either Richard Hildreth or Henry Bowditch. Cleveland gives conflicting reports in his letter of May 29, 1848, and his statement of January 11, 1849.

167 "may think desirable": Samuel Sewell to Horace Mann, April 26, 1848. Horace Mann Papers, Massachusetts Historical Society.

167 "dictated more by a love for me . . .": Louise Hall Tharp, *The Peabody Sisters of Salem* (Boston: Little Brown, 1950), 203.

167 "bear it very well": Horace Mann to Mary Peabody Mann, 9 May 1848. Horace Mann Papers, Massachusetts Historical Society.

167 "a bold, stern, determined man . . .": "Captains Drayton and Sayres, Or the Way in Which Americans are Treated, for Aiding the Cause of Liberty at Home." Pamphlet published by the Eastern Pennsylvania Anti-Slavery Society in Philadelphia, 1848.

168 his "first antislavery impressions . . .": Salmon P. Chase to Samuel E. Sewell, 27 May 1848. Horace Mann Papers, Massachusetts Historical Society.

168 "we have no Gerrit Smiths in Philadelphia": Charles Cleveland to Horace Mann, 19 June 1848. Horace Mann Papers, Massachusetts Historical Society.

169 "dry as dust": *Boston Weekly Chronotype*, August 12, 1848.

169 "hardly conceive how beautiful": Horace Mann to Mary Peabody Mann, 20 June 1848. Horace Mann Papers, Massachusetts Historical Society.

170 David Hall, the local attorney: David A. Hall to Horace Mann, 22 June 1848. Horace Mann Papers, Massachusetts Historical Society.

171 "Horrors of the Slave Trade, etc.": *Baltimore Sun*, June 30, 1848.

172 Drayton "insists on seeing you this afternoon . . .": David A. Hall to Horace Mann, 3 July 1848. Horace Mann Papers, Massachusetts Historical Society.

172 "Here I am alone . . .": Horace Mann to Samuel Gridley Howe, 20 July 1848. Horace Mann Papers, Massachusetts Historical Society.

172 "abolitionists and they will not consent . . .": Horace Mann to Mary Peabody Mann, 23 July 1848. Horace Mann Papers, Massachusetts Historical Society.

172 the first of multiple trials: *Baltimore Sun*, July 28, 1848.

173 the "most horrid atrocity": Horace Mann, *Slavery: Letters and Speeches* (1851; New York: Negro Universities Press, 1969), 91–93; see also, *Baltimore Sun*, July 27, 1848. The newspaper claimed that Key had already reached his ceiling of fees.

173 Key had been raised with slaves: *The District of Columbia Free Register* shows that, in 1831, Francis Scott Key manumitted a forty-year-old mulatto named Romeo for one dollar, an indication that he may have freed him outright. There were a few more manumissions down the road, but they came at a cost. William Ridout, about twenty-six years old, paid $300 for his freedom, and a thirty-five-year-old woman named Nelly paid $200 for hers. As a teenager, Philip Barton Key's family moved from Georgetown into a home on C Street near Washington's Judiciary Square, where—his father now dead—Key continued to live at the time of the Drayton and Sayres trials.

173 drawn a "dirk" on Drayton: Mann, *Slavery*, 87n.

173 "other kinds of property were protected . . .": *Baltimore Sun*, July 28, 1848.

174   worth a considerable $30,000: U.S. Census for Population of 1850.

174   ". . . the 'underground railroad to freedom' ": *Drayton v. U.S.*, Trial Records of the United States District Court for the District of Columbia, 1838–61. RG 221, National Archives.

175   "in a condition to go . . .": Ibid.

175   an "utter stranger" to them: Mann, *Slavery*, 99–109.

177   "the living and dead . . .": Ibid., 116–117.

177   Bell's employment records: Payroll Records of the United States Navy Yard. RG 71, National Archives.

178   "a liar, a thief . . .": Mann *Slavery*, 82.

179   "patronage and custom in the city": Horace Mann to Mary Peabody Mann, 5 August 1848. Horace Mann Papers, Massachusetts Historical Society.

180   "a class of loafers . . .": Drayton, *Personal Memoir*, 99.

180   "tissue of misrepresentation . . .": *New York Tribune*, quoted in the *Salem (OH) Anti-Slavery Bugle*, September 1, 1848.

181   Senator John Hale introduced a petition: *Alexandria Gazette*, July 11, 1848.

182   "the most miserable of all his life": Paynter, *Fugitives*, 177.

182   he lived with his wife, Martha: Federal census of 1850, in which Bruin was listed under the name of "Brewen."

183   "liberality of the humane . . .": *Salem (OH) Anti-Slavery Bugle*, November 17, 1848. The originals of these letters have not been found. However, they were copied by a number of antislavery newspapers of the day, and then, five years later, copy of Bruin's letter was included in Stowe, *Key to Uncle Tom*.

184   "aged coloured man of tall and slender": James Pennington, *The Fugitive Blacksmith; or Events in the History of James W. C. Pennington, Pastor of a Presbyterian Church*, 2nd ed. (New York, London: Charles Gilpin, 1849).

184   "highly respectable lawyer": *Salem (OH) Anti-Slavery Bugle*, November 17, 1848.

186   "exemplary members of the Methodist Episcopal Church": *Salem (OH) Anti-Slavery Bugle*, November 17, 1848.

187   outnumbered European Methodists: David Nempton, *Methodism: Empire of the Spirit* (New Haven, Yale University Press, 2005), 4.

187   "for the purpose of laying the matter . . .": "The Case of the Edmondson Sisters," October 21, 1848. Anti-Slavery Collection of Samuel J. May, Cornell University.

188   "to sell, buy, or swap": William Chaplin letter to New York Anti-Slavery Society, of October 12, 1848, Anti-Slavery Bugle, November 17, 1848.

188 "Gay calico was brought in": Stowe, *Key to Uncle Tom*, 164.

189 Giddings wrote that he had been approached: Giddings, *History of the Rebellion*, 279.

190 ". . . the very highest character": *Salem (OH) Anti-Slavery Bugle*, November 17, 1848.

190 "replete with noble feeling . . .": *New York Evangelist*, quoted in *Washington National Era*, November 2, 1848.

190 Since his ordination in 1837: Paxton Hibben, *Henry Ward Beecher: An American Portrait*, (New York: The Press of the Readers Club, 1942), 17.

191 "we have not come here . . .": *Rochester North Star*, November 17, 1848.

192 "I know no names of Baptist": *Utica Liberty Press*, November 30, 1848.

192 "Suppose them so comely": Hibben, *Henry Ward Beecher*, 111.

192 "his sons are long ago": *Utica Liberty Press*, November 30, 1848.

193 "In sentiment and witty sarcasm . . ." *Rochester North Star*, November 17, 1848.

193 They had not collected the full amount: *New York Evangelist*, quoted in *Washington National Era*, November 2, 1848; *New York Tribune*, October 25, 1848; *Christian Advocate and Journal*, n.d., in the *National Anti-Slavery Standard*, November 30, 1848.

194 "rejoice to hear . . .": *Washington National Era*, November 2, 1848.

194 "While we should be sorry . . .": *Salem (OH) Anti-Slavery Bugle*, November 17, 1848. The *Bugle* was a Garrisonian publication.

194 "result of this effort . . .": William Chaplin to Gerrit Smith, 2 November 1848. Gerrit Smith Papers, Library of Congress.

195 "that white man we have seen . . .": Stowe, *Key to Uncle Tom*, 166.

195 "man of very different character . . .": Ibid., 165.

195 *Received of W. L. Chaplin* . . . : *Washington National Era*, November 30, 1848.

196 "You're free at last! . . .": Paynter, *Fugitives*, 191.

196 "Thank God! . . .": *Christian Advocate and Journal*, n.d., in *National Anti-Slavery Standard*, November 30, 1848.

196 "humanity, justice, and republican freedom . . .": *National Anti-Slavery Standard*, November 30, 1848.

198 "better fitted to bawl to a jury . . .": Drayton, *Personal Memoir,* 100.

199 "a young man, rather small but beautiful . . .": Horace Mann to Mary Peabody Mann, 2 December 1848, Horace Mann Papers, Massachusetts Historical Society.

199 "little too apt to wander . . .": Richard Hildreth to Horace Mann, 7 December 1848. Horace Mann Papers, Massachusetts Historical Society.

199 definition of larceny was "rotten": *Salem (OH) Anti-Slavery Bugle,* December 29, 1848.

199 Judge Crawford took the comments personally: *Washington National Era,* December 21, 1848.

199 "Pursuing hounds say he's mistaken": Ibid.

199 "to aid some of the poor . . .": Louis Tappan to Joshua P. Blanchard, 14 February 1849 and 15 May 1848. Black History Miscellaneous Papers, Library of Congress.

200 "Recent events, especially those: *New York Independent,* December 7, 1848.

200 "the traffic now prosecuted in this metropolis . . .": *Salem (OH) Anti-Slavery Bugle,* January 5, 1849.

201 "a bill was introduced": Appendix to the *Congressional Globe,* 30th Cong., 2nd Sess., February 23, 1849, 318.

202 Samuel Gridley Howe's report: *Slavery at Washington. Narrative of the Heroic Adventures of Drayton, An American Trader, in "The Pearl," Coasting Vessel, which was Captured by American Citizens, Near the Mouth of the Potomac, having on board Seventy-Seven Men, Women, and Children, Endeavouring* [sic] *to Escape from Slavery in the Capital of the American Republic, (in a Letter from Dr. S. G. Howe, U.S.) Together with The Proceedings Upon Captain Drayton's Trial and Conviction* (London: Ward and Co. and C. Gilpin, 1848).

202 "bitter anti-abolitionist feelings": James Mandeville Carlisle to Horace Mann, 30 March 1849. Horace Mann Papers, Massachusetts Historical Society.

203 "acting under the garb of philanthropy": *Baltimore Clipper,* reprinted in *Washington National Era,* May 17, 1848.

205 "[w]hatever may be the evils [of slavery] . . .": *Rochester North Star,* September 22, 1848. Five days after the Free-Soilers met in Virginia, the *Boston Whig* changed its name to the *Boston Republican* and advocated the doctrines of the Free-Soil Party.

206 "between slavery and freedom": James McPherson, *Battle Cry of Freedom: The Civil War Era* (New York: Ballantine Books, 1988), 61n.

206 "heartily co-operating with us . . .": *Rochester North Star*, September 29, 1848.

206 "Free soil, Free speech . . .": McPherson, *Battle Cry of Freedom*, 62n.

207 "is in exercise at the thought": William Chaplin to Gerrit Smith, 11 November 1848. Gerrit Smith Papers, Library of Congress.

208 "are here with us FREE": *New York Independent*, December 21, 1848.

210 "horrors of the Southern prison-house": *Little Falls (NY) Herkimer Freedman*, n.d., reprinted in *Rochester North Star*, December 8, 1848.

210 "you had far better all die . . .": Deirdre Mullane, ed., *Crossing the Danger Water: Three Hundred Years of African-American writing* (New York: Anchor Books, 1993), 119.

211 the sisters were living in Macedon: *Salem (OH) Anti-Slavery Bugle*, December 29, 1849.

211 "our friend" William R. Smith: *Washington National Era*, October 28, 1847.

211 "most exemplary industry . . .": *Rochester North Star*, October 26, 1849.

212 their admission records: Central College records, Cortland Historical Society of New York.

212 a "brother" to her: Myrtilla Miner to Harriet Beecher Stowe, 1 October 1853. Myrtilla Miner Papers, Library of Congress.

EIGHT
The Fugitive Slave Act and the Great Protest Meeting

215 "prejudicial to the interest of our city . . .": Constance McLaughlin Green, *The Secret City: A History of Race Relations in the Nation's Capital* (Princeton, N.J.: Princeton University Press, 1967), 46.

215 But the abolition of slavery: Tremain, *Slavery*, 92.

215 "produced nothing good or valuable": Irving H. Bartlett, *Daniel Webster* (New York: Norton, 1978), 248.

216 an ocean view with the schooner *Pearl*: C. Peter Ripley, ed., *The Black Abolitionist Papers* (Chapel Hill: The University of North Carolina Press, 1985), 1:197.

216 "bid a most cordial welcome . . .": Hugh C. Humphreys, *"Agitate! Agitate! Agitate!" The Great Fugitive Slave Law Convention and Its Rare Daguerreotype* (New York: Madison County Historical Society, 1994), 8.

216 A survey of documents: unpublished materials provided by Russ Grills, town historian of Cazenovia, New York.

218 called *Chaplin's Portfolio*: *Washington National Era*, November 1, 1849.

218 He left Washington: *The Case of William Chaplin* (Boston: The Chaplin Committee, 1851).

218 named Allen and Garland: *Washington Daily National Intelligencer*, August 18, 1850.

218 "a little slim, pale-faced, consumptive man": *Abraham Lincoln: Speeches and Writings, 1832–1858* (New York: The Library of America, 1989), 174.

219 Chaplin fired a pistol: *Washington Daily National Intelligencer*, August 10, 1850.

219 "forget that night of our extremest peril . . .": William Still, *Underground Railroad* (1872; Chicago: Johnson Publishing Company, Inc., 1970), 27.

220 "determined that the two hundred thousand . . .": Humphreys, *"Agitate!,"* 12.

220 Frederick Douglass, a veteran runaway: Minutes published in the *Rochester North Star*, September 5, 1850.

220 "were closely attached to Mr. Chaplin": *Rochester North Star*, September 5, 1850.

221 "the marvelous way . . .": *Cazenovia Republican*, December 10, 1885, as cited in Humphreys, *"Agitate!,"* 45.

221 "When the insurrection of the Southern slaves . . .": Philip S. Foner, ed., *Frederick Douglass: Selected Speeches and Writings* (Chicago: Lawrence Hill Books, 1999), 158–62.

222 "many abolitionists in the throng . . .": Humphreys, *"Agitate!,"* 22.

222 "We call on every man . . .": Ibid., 29.

223 Attacking it as a "witches cauldron": Ibid., 35.

224 Gilbert was wearing bloomers: *Madison County, New York Republican*, December 10, 1885.

225 when agents came to claim: Benjamin Quarles, *Black Abolitionists* (New York: Oxford University Press, 1969—Da Capo Reproduction), 62–63, 202–203.

226 town of Christiana, Pennsylvania : Thomas P. Slaughter, *Bloody Dawn: The Christiana Riot and Racial Violence in the Antebellum North* (New York: Oxford University Press), 1991.

227 "[t]he magnitude of the tragedy . . .": Humphreys, *"Agitate!,"* 37.

227 threw themselves into the fund-raising events: *Rochester North Star*, September 5, 1850.

227 two counts of larceny: *Washington National Era*, November 21, 1850.

228 In January, 1851, Chaplin was released: *National Anti-Slavery Standard,* January 9, 1851.

228 his "chains" weighed "so heavily . . .": William R. Smith to Gerrit Smith, 19 February 1851. Gerrit Smith Papers, Library of Congress.

229 "confidential agent": William R. Smith to Gerrit Smith, 22 March 1851.

229 "[i]nasmuch as the imprisonment of Drayton . . .": *National Anti-Slavery Standard,* January 16, 1851.

229 Frederick Douglass was so thoroughly impressed: *Rochester North Star,* June 26, 1851.

230 "TO WILLIAM L. CHAPLIN IN PRISON . . .": *Rochester North Star,* September 25, 1851.

231 "share the privilege": *Frederick Douglass' Paper* (renamed from *North Star*), October 2, 1851.

232 The same man who had owned Grace: Stowe, *Key to Uncle Tom,* 168–170.

233 the attractive young woman was "persecuted": John White Chadwick, ed., *A Life for Liberty, Anti-Slavery and Other Letters of Sallie Holley* (New York: Negro Universities Press, 1969), 170.

233n "People Called Quakers": Papers of the Continental Congress 1774–1783, Microfilm M247, roll 57, p. 337, National Archives.

234 were operating twenty-four hours a day: Johanna Johnston, *Runaway to Heaven: The Story of Harriet Beecher Stowe* (New York: Doubleday, 1963), 225.

235 "directly to the Rev. Henry W. Beecher's . . .": Stowe, *Key to Uncle Tom* 167.

235 "fine-looking mulatto girls . . .": Harriet Beecher Stowe, *History of the Edmonson Family* (no date, printed for private distribution), 2.

235 "bitter language against all slaveholders": Stowe, *Key to Uncle Tom,* 167.

235 "a woman of very strong character . . .": Johnston, *Runaway to Heaven,* 233.

236 partly based on Josiah Henson: Henson was far more complicated than the Uncle Tom of Stowe's book. After he was sent to Kentucky with other slaves from Maryland and then betrayed by his owner, he escaped to the North with his two children hidden in a rucksack on his back and two loaded guns stuck in his belt.

237 "had acquired the rudiments": Stowe, *History of the Edmonson Family,* 8.

237 negotiations with Valdenar: Samuel Rhoads to Myrtilla Miner, 1853 (month unclear). Myrtilla Miner Papers, Library of Congress.

237 "perfect their education . . .": Stowe, *History of the Edmonson Family,* 8.

238 "the insidious report . . .": *Washington Daily Union,* correspondence of December 12, 1850, in *National Anti-Slavery Standard,* December 26, 1850.

240 The Boston Committee unsuccessfully: Samuel E. Sewell to Horace Mann, 9 January 1850. Horace Mann Papers, Massachusetts Historical Society.

240 "gentleman visited the men once a week": *Washington National Era*, October 17, 1850.

240 Drayton was often discouraged: Daniel Drayton to Horace Mann, 30 July 1850. Horace Mann Papers, Massachusetts Historical Society.

240 "one of the most unreasonable . . .": Charles Cleveland to Horace Mann, 1 February 1851. Horace Mann Papers, Massachusetts Historical Society.

241 "full liberty to state publickly [*sic*] . . .": Charles Cleveland to Horace Mann, 16 February 1849. Horace Mann Papers, Massachusetts Historical Society.

241 plan proposed by Daniel Radcliffe: Charles Cleveland to Horace Mann, 1 February 1851, and 22 March 1851. Horace Mann Papers, Massachusetts Historical Society.

242 "comfortable during the next winter": *Washington National Era*, October 16, 1851.

242 ". . . Thanksgiving is at hand": *Washington National Era*, November 27, 1851.

242 a letter from "poor Drayton": Charles Cleveland to Horace Mann, 19 January 1852. Horace Mann Papers, Massachusetts Historical Society.

242 "disapproved of the act": *Washington National Era*, January 29, 1852.

244 "Pardoned by the President . . .": Docket Books for the District of Columbia Courts, RG 21, National Archives.

244 alarmed senator hurried to the office: Walter C. Clephane, *"Lewis Clephane: A Pioneer Washington Republican,"* *Records of the Columbia Historical Society*, 21:267. Drayton makes no mention of Clephane's involvement in his memoirs, but he may have been constrained by the fact that Clephane, a resident of Washington, D.C., might have been subject to prosecution.

244 door of the Blue Jug opened: Drayton, *Personal Memoir*, 118.

246 "indefatigable in his exertions . . .": *Washington National Era*, August 19, 1852.

246 "power of the President to remit . . .": *Washington National Daily Intelligencer*, August 13, 1852.

246 template of a "negro-stealer": *Washington Daily Union*, August 13, 1852.

246 "We know of no man . . .": *Washington National Era*, September 16, 1852.

246 Drayton credited only Charles Sumner: *Pennsylvania Freeman*, August 21, 1852.

246 "Capt. Drayton has behaved with great ingratitude . . .": Charles Cleveland to Horace Mann, December 1853 (no day). Horace Mann Papers, Massachusetts Historical Society.

247 Drayton's "labors with abundant success": *Liberator*, September 24, 1852.

247 Drayton joined a celebration: *New York Tribune* (by telegraphic communication) in *Frederick Douglass' Paper*, October 8, 1852.

247 he introduced himself to Mary Mann: Tharp, *The Peabody Sisters*, 205.

248 "To the Friends of Humanity": *Frederick Douglass' Paper*, October 8, 1852.

249 Blacks already living in Ohio: *Oberlin Evangelist*, cited in *Frederick Douglass' Paper*, January 7, 1853.

250 His father, John B. Vashon: Benjamin Quarles, *Black Abolitionists* (New York: Da Capo Press, 1991), 20.

250 Sarah Margru Kinson, a native of Bendembu: Marlene D. Merrill, *Sarah Margru Kinson: The Two Worlds of an Amistad Captive* (Oberlin, Ohio: Oberlin Historical and Improvement Organization, 2003).

251 "are of a *noble* family": Harriet Beecher Stowe to Minerva Cowles, Cowles Papers, Oberlin College. The letter is undated but, it was meant as an introduction for the Edmonson sisters, so was likely written in early July 1852.

251 under the influence of questionable "advisors": Harriet Beecher Stowe to Minerva Cowles, Cowles Papers, Oberlin College.

252 "yet abide in bonds": Harriet Beecher Stowe to Minerva Cowles, 8 July [1852]. Cowles Papers, Oberlin College. The year is not on the letter, but it is likely 1852.

252 "for a few days . . .": Mary Cowles to Aunt, 9 August 1852. Cowles Papers, Oberlin College.

252 "Mr. Valdenar says that sickness . . .": Harrier Beecher Stowe to Mary Edmonson 2 October 1852. Cowles Papers, Oberlin College.

253 "the girls could write . . .": Harrier Beecher Stowe to Minerva Cowles, 13 November 1852. Cowles Papers, Oberlin College.

253 she "thought she would be suffocated . . .": John White Chadwick, ed., *A Life for Liberty: Anti-Slavery and Other Letters of Sallie Holley* (New York: Negro Universities Press, 1969), 147.

254 "I am pained to hear . . .": Harrier Beecher Stowe to Minerva Cowles, 24 March 1853. Cowles Papers, Oberlin College.

254 "now lies dangerously ill . . .": *Frederick Douglass' Paper*, April 29, 1853.

255 "the watchings here . . .": Mary Cowles Diary. Cowles Papers, Oberlin College.

255 "in the hope, as she expressed herself . . .": *The Oberlin Evangelist*, May 25, 1853.

255 "to see her off to heaven": *Cleveland True Democrat in Frederick Douglass' Paper*, June 3, 1853.

256 her "heart still lingers around Oberlin . . .": Emily Edmonson to the Cowles family, 1 June 1853. Cowles Papers, Oberlin College.

256 "dear child in her last moments . . .": Amelia Edmonson (dictated) to Minerva Cowles, 1 June 1853. Cowles Papers, Oberlin College.

257 "That you should have met . . .": Harriet Beecher Stowe to Minerva Cowles, 12 December 1853. Cowles Papers, Oberlin College.

TEN

Emily Comes Home; Samuel Edmonson Escapes Again

258 "now the disgust and disgrace . . .": *Washington Evening Star*, May 30, 1853.

259 "comply with a barbarous law . . .": Daniel A. Payne, *Recollections of Seventy Years* (1888; New York: Arno Press, 1968), 75.

259 "only 8 of the 603 persons . . .": Constance McLaughlin Green, *The Secret City: A History of Race Relations in the Nation's Capital* (Princeton, N.J.: Princeton University Press, 1967), 181.

260 Northup instituted a criminal prosecution: Northup, *Twelve Years a Slave*, 245–51.

260 public gardener was planting three hundred trees: *Baltimore Sun*, December 1, 1853.

261 a fifteen-foot shark: *Washington Evening Star*, June 1 and 9, 1853.

262 "Gumballs, Peelers, Lemons . . .": *Washington Evening Star*, May 30, 1853.

262 "colored population died in greater numbers . . .": 1853 City Directory Alfred Hunter, comp., *Washington and Georgetown Directory, Strangers' Guide-Book for Washington and Congressional and Clerk's Register* (Washington, D.C.: Printed by Kirkwood & McGill, 1853), 125.

262 engaging in outdoor "demoralizing games": *Washington Evening Star*, May 31, 1853.

263 estate sale for Jesse Brown: *Washington National Era*, January 6, 1853.

263 "genteel colored men": *Frederick Douglass' Paper*, April 13, 1855.

265 "Mr. Brent and the other parties": Jacob Bigelow to Myrtilla Miner, 21 October 1851. Myrtilla Miner Papers, Manuscript Division, Library of Congress.

265 "he became alarmed . . .": undated typed paper. Myrtilla Miner Papers, Manuscript Division, Library of Congress.

265 their schools would not be in conflict: John Cook to Myrtilla Miner, 31 July 1851. Myrtilla Miner Papers, Manuscript Division, Library of Congress.

266 black man named Edward Younger: Gerrit Smith Wormley, "Myrtilla Miner," *Journal of Negro History* 5, no. 4 (October 1920), 452.

266 Miner approached the Rev. John W. Bull: Ibid.

266 she had "by some magic . . .": Myrtilla Miner to Millard Fillmore, undated draft. Myrtilla Miner Papers, Manuscript Division Library of Congress.

267 "much native power": Myrtilla Miner to Harriet Beecher Stowe, 1 October 1853. Myrtilla Miner Papers, Manuscript Division, Library of Congress.

268 "Emily and I live here alone": Myrtilla Miner to anonymous, May 3, 1854, in Ellen M. O'Connor, *Myrtilla Miner: A Memoir* (1885; New York: Arno Press and the *New York Times*, 1969), 51.

269 he was the New Orleans commissioner: Tennessee State Library and Archives Website, State Records, Acts of Tennessee, 1831–1850, C (Part 1): Cage-Cantrell.

270 "a lady of much beauty and refinement": Paynter, *Fugitives*, 164.

270 inventory of the assets Cammack left: Obituary records, New Orleans Public Library.

270 his brother Hamilton: Paynter, *Fugitives*, 170. The details of Samuel's life in New Orleans and his subsequent escape are based on both Paynter sources supplemented by census records, obituaries, and city directories that have confirmed important parts of his story.

272 "either labouring under some delusion . . .": Charles Cleveland to Daniel Drayton, 14 November 1853. Lysander Spooner Letters, New-York Historical Society. The letters of Lysander Spooner at the New-York Historical Society reveal the only known account of the meeting and discussions of Charles Cleveland and Daniel Drayton. They also chart the ongoing hostility between the men and subsequent involvement of a number of leading abolitionists. Daniel Drayton's *Personal Memoir*, written in the main by Richard Hildreth, makes no mention of this friction within the abolitionist community.

272 Cleveland wrote to the *Commonwealth*: Copy of Charles Cleveland's letter to the Commonwealth, 2 January 1854. Lysander Spooner Letters, New-York Historical Society.

273 "will not be ended so long . . .": Wendell Phillips, Francis Jackson, and Lysander Spooner to Charles Cleveland, 11 February 1854. Lysander Spooner Letters, New-York Historical Society.

273 "knew enough about my character . . .": Charles Cleveland to Wendell Phillips, Francis Jackson, and Lysander Spooner, 18 February 1854. Lysander Spooner Letters, New-York Historical Society.

274 "bound in honor and conscience . . .": Wendell Phillips, Francis Jackson, and Lysander Spooner to Charles Cleveland, 23 March 1854. Lysander Spooner Letters, New-York Historical Society.

274 "[d]o not despond Captain . . .": Grover, *The Fugitive's Gibraltar*, 258–59.

274 "have survived the storm of public indignation": Speech of Joshua Giddings on March 17, 1852, in *Washington National Era*, April 1, 1852.

275 "colored residents of Circleville, Ohio . . .": *Washington Evening Star*, June 8, 1853.

276 The Edmonson family had learned: *Frederick Douglass' Paper*, January 4, 1855.

276 Donations for the fair: *Frederick Douglass' Paper*, January 19, 1855.

277 "a new and more thrilling" account: *Frederick Douglass' Paper*, January 4, 1855.

277 close to their goal of $800: *Frederick Douglass' Paper*, July 27, 1855.

277 George T. Downing accused Miner: Philip S. Foner and Josephine Pacheco, *Three Who Dared: Prudence Crandall, Margaret Douglass, Myrtilla Miner— Champions of Antebellum Black Education* (Westport, Conn.: Greenwood Press, 1984), 153–55.

278 "beautiful—tho' dark . . .": Myrtilla Miner to her brother, 15 March 1852. Myrtilla Miner Papers, Manuscript Division, Library of Congress.

278 "We have just had a call . . .": *Frederick Douglass' Paper*, September 1, 1854.

278 the positive side of Miner's work: *Washington National Era*, February 1, 1855.

279 "there was no 'appeal' . . .": Myrtilla Miner to Elton and Jane Brent, 8 May 1853. Myrtilla Miner Papers, Manuscript Division, Library of Congress.

279 Emily Brent, Emily Edmonson's niece: Letter written by Matilda A. Jones, a student at the Miner School, in Dorothy Sterling, ed., *We Are Your Sisters: Black Women in the Nineteenth Century* (New York: W.W. Norton, 1984), 191.

279 A deed of trust for part of Lot 4: J. A. S. 190, 382, Recorder of Deeds, Washington, D.C., February 25, 1860.

280 "I want your name associated . . .": Emily Fisher to Myrtilla Miner, 26 November 1855. Myrtilla Miner Papers, Manuscript Division, Library of Congress. The fact that Emily Fisher was still involved with Miner's school tends to support the theory that she was not married at the time she wrote this letter. It was rare

for young married women to be allowed to continue to study or teach. Nor was it the voice of a young student named "Emily Fisher." It was the voice of a mature young woman well versed in the politics of the day.

281 Johnson traveled with a note: *Frederick Douglass' Paper*, July 27, 1855; William Still, *Underground Railroad* (1872; Chicago: Johnson Publishing Company, Inc., 1970), 73–84. Bigelow stated that he had not been sure the note had ever reached Still as was intended. Because there was some discussion in court as to whether Johnson had been enticed to leave the boat, Bigelow informed Still that he had personal knowledge that it had been her plan all along to leave her owner.

281 "all men are born free and equal . . .": Emily Fisher to Myrtilla Miner, 26 November 1855. Myrtilla Miner Papers, Manuscript Division, Library of Congress.

282 a small farm of about forty acres . . . : *Montgomery County Sentinel*, December 8, 1855.

282 "a very likely young Negro . . .": Ibid.

283 "my NEGRO GIRL 'Ann Maria Weems,' . . .": *Montgomery County Sentinel*, January 26, 1856.

283 *only one* SMALL package to your city": Still, *Underground Railroad*, 22.

283 Ann Maria's father, John Weems: C. Peter Ripley, ed., *The Black Abolitionist Papers*, vol. 1 (Chapel Hill: University of North Carolina Press, 1985), 327–29. In 1852 the Garnets traveled to Jamaica, where Stella Weems died of a "bilious fever" (329*n*).

284 they paid $1,000: Still, *Underground Railroad*, 174.

284 "any colored citizen is liable . . .": Ibid., 177.

284 he had purchased Kephart's establishment: *Montgomery County Sentinel*, February 24, 1860.

285 an operative in Canada wrote to Still: Still, *Underground Railroad*, 66–67.

286 the Montgomery County Agricultural Society: MacMaster and Hiebert, *A Grateful Remembrance*, 160.

286 a strong hand in the new party: Thomas B. Thayer, ed., "Gamaliel Bailey," *The Universalist Quarterly and General Review* (Boston: The Universalist Publishing House, 1868).

286 "newly baptised and freshly born": Paul M. Angle, ed., *The Lincoln Reader* (1947; New York: Da Capo Press, 1990), 215–17.

286 Elect Fremont, they threatened, and free blacks: James McPherson, *Battle Cry of Freedom: The Civil War Era* (New York: Ballantine Books, 1988), 158.

287 Edmonson had sold his farm: Montgomery County Deed Records, J. G. H. 6, 263.

287 Jennings had purchased a nearby lot: Record of Deeds, J. A. S. 116, 372, May 15, 1856.

287 John Wesley A.M.E. congregation: Harold T. Pinkett, *National Church of Zion Methodism: A History of John Wesley A.M.E. Zion Church, Washington, D.C.* (Baltimore: Gateway Press, 1989), 7–8. See also *The Washington and Georgetown Directory, Strangers' Guidebook for Washington, and Congressional and Clerks' Register, 1853,* compiled and published by Alfred Hunter, which states that "a new brick church for colored people has been erected" in Ward 1 of the city.

288 "and wished to be properly interred": Grover, *Fugitive's Gibraltar,* 259. See also, Brian Murphy, *A Martyr for Freedom: The Story of Daniel Drayton and the Schooner Pearl,* unpublished manuscript, 44–46.

288 "Capt. Drayton's health was completely shattered . . .": *Washington National Era,* July 9, 1857, quoting the *New Bedford Standard.*

288 "Captain Drayton, Commander of the Schooner *Pearl*": Pacheco, *The Pearl,* 238–39.

289 "from every section of the union": *Washington National Daily Intelligencer,* May 6, 1857.

290 mounted a strong defense of Miner: *Washington National Era,* May 14, 1857.

290 "marvellously [*sic*] large business": Still, *Underground Railroad,* 477 (first quote), 41 (second quote). Summary of cases from Washington area are from throughout the volume.

ELEVEN
DRED SCOTT *and the Rise of Lincoln*

293 "resolutions amount to nothing": *Chatham Provincial Freeman,* April 18, 1857.

293 substitute "native" for "citizen": *Chatham Provincial Freeman,* July 4, 1857.

294 "[r]iot and bloodshed . . .": Constance McLaughlin Green, *Washington: A History of the Capital, 1800–1950* (Princeton, N.J.: Princeton University Press, 1962–63), vol. 1, 215.

295 "dingy little room in the City Hall": *New York Times,* April 5, 1859.

295 "the vulgar monotony . . .": *New York Times,* February 28, 1859.

296 Brown "had never consulted me . . .": *Washington National Era,* October 24, 1859.

296 the "benighted" Africans: *New York Times,* November 29, 1859.

297 "for the protection of their homes . . .": MacMaster and Hiebert, *A Grateful Remembrance* 162.

297 U.S. Census of 1860 showed: Green, *Washington,* vol. 1, 221 (Table 1, Population of the District of Columbia).

298 "even in those days . . .": Louise Wigfall Wright, *A Southern Girl in '61: The War-Time Memories of a Confederate Senator's Daughter* (New York: Doubleday, 1905), 23.

298 Wormley's may have been the site: Ernest B. Furgurson, *Freedom Rising: Washington in the Civil War* (New York: Alfred A. Knopf, 2004), 22.

299 April 5, 1860: Marriage Records of the District of Columbia, Paul E. Sluby and Stanton Wormley, *Blacks in the Marriage Records of the District of Columbia, Dec. 23, 1811–Jan. 16, 1870* (Washington D.C.: Columbia Harmony Society, 1988), vol. 1, 299.

299 "hereby release from slavery . . .": Microfilmed manumission records, Montgomery County Historical Society, Rockville, Maryland.

299 Maryland Colonization Society Manumission Book: Partial listings of Maryland Colonization Society Records, Sandy Spring Museum, Sandy Spring, Maryland.

299 Larkin Johnson purchased ten acres: Microfilmed Deed Records, Montgomery County Historical Society.

300 fifty-one black landholders: MacMaster and Hiebert, *Grateful Remembrance,* 156.

300 "a very pointed discourse . . .": Ibid., 159.

300 some Friends are believed: Anthony Cohen, *The Underground Railroad in Montgomery County, Maryland* (Mongtomery County Historical Society, 1994), 21–27.

301 the Montgomery County Slaveholders' Association: MacMaster and Hiebert, *Grateful Remembrance,* 160.

301 the "day a sectional party . . .": *New York Herald,* March 4, 1861.

302 "the remaining Southern States . . .": *Charleston Mercury,* January 21, 1861.

302 "The attendance upon this meeting . . .": *Montgomery County Sentinel,* January 4, 1861.

303 Henry Stabler, objected strongly: *Montgomery County Sentinel,* January 11, 1861.

303 "while we oppose secession . . .": *Washington Evening Star,* February 1, 1861.

304 "I have seen today such a sight . . .": *Baltimore Sun,* cited in *Charleston Mercury* of March 7, 1861.

304 "no purpose, directly or indirectly . . .": Abraham Lincoln, "First Inaugural Address," March 4, 1861, *Collected Works*, vol. 4.

305 "[t]he City is again threatened . . .": *The Diary of Horatio Nelson Taft, 1861–1865*, April 6, 1861, Library of Congress, Manuscript Division, Library of Congress. Available online at http://rs6.loc.gov/ammem/tafthtml/caption.html.

306 Jacob Dodson: Gibbs, *Black, Copper & Bright: The District of Columbia's Black Civil War Regiment* (Silver Spring, Md.: Three Dimensional Publishing, 2002), 3–5.

306 "a free young colored man . . .": http://www.longcamp.com/jacob_dodson. html.

306 the "strong oath": *Taft Diary*, April 22, 1861.

306 "administered the oath of allegiance . . .": *Diary of Michael Shiner*, Manuscript Division, LOC.

307 "gymnastic exercises equal to a circus performance": *Taft Diary*, May 21, 1861.

308 Lincoln's election proved a boon: *Christian Recorder*, May 21, 1864.

308 "brilliant wedding" in the Brent home: *Christian Recorder*, May 25, 1861.

310 "a solemn oath to obey . . .": *New York Herald*, May 28, 1861.

311 "the French cooks and hotel-keepers . . .": Margaret Leech, *Reveille in Washington* (New York: Harper & Brothers, 1941), 123.

312 ". . . nothing to do with Slavery . . .": *New York Times*, July 29, 1861.

313 William Wormley, son of James Wormley: Wormley Family Papers.

314 "What in the world is the matter . . ." Harry J. Maihafer, *The General and the Journalists: Ulysses S. Grant, Horace Greeley, and Charles Dana* (Washington, D.C.: Brassey's, 1998), 129.

314 the greatest antislavery orator: Mayer, *All on Fire*, 532–33.

314 "meet, fight, dislodge, drive back . . ." *Christian Recorder*, January 18, 1862.

314 Senator Henry Wilson of Massachusetts: *Congressional Globe*, 37th Cong., 2nd sess., Pt. 1, December 4, 1861, 10–12.

315 Senator Sumner raised the issue: *Congressional Globe*, 37th Cong., 2nd sess., Pt. 1, December 16, 1861, 89.

TWELVE

Freedom in the District of Columbia

316 "stubborn mules refusing to go . . .": Haft Diary, March 22, 1862. Manuscript Division, Library of Congress.

316 "immediate, preemptory, and absolute": *Congressional Globe*, 37th Cong., 2nd Sess., Pt. 1, December 16, 1861, 89–90.

317 he "was better acquainted . . .": Ibid., March 12, 1862, 1191–92.

318 instead of a gradual program, "mischievous": *New York Times*, April 4, 1862.

318 "produced irreparable domestic confusion . . .": *New York Herald*, April 13, 1862.

318 "to purchase a few . . .": *National Republican*, March 19, 1862.

319 in August 1861, he wrote a tract: Mary Mitchell, *Divided Town: A Study of Georgetown, D.C., During the Civil War* (Barre, Mass.: Barre Publishers, 1968), 74; advertised in the *New York Times* on November 24, 1862.

319 Some slave owners did not file: Ibid., 60.

320 a more objective estimate: "Report of the Commissioners on Emancipation in the District of Columbia," sent to the United States Congress by Secretary of the Treasury Salmon P. Chase, January 14, 1863.

320 "sticks, pieces of iron . . .": *American and Commercial Advertiser*, June 2, 1862.

321 "in consideration of love and affection . . .": Recorder of Deeds of the District of Columbia 215 JAS 389. Armistead gave a second enslaved woman, named "Caroline," to another daughter, again for love and affection and $1. This may have been Eleanora's sister Caroline, but she does not appear in the emancipation lists; she may have been taken out of the jurisdiction. See 215 JAS 390.

323 "late of Arlington Heights": "Report of the Commissioners," 72.

324 Harriet A. Jacobs, a former slave: *Liberator*, September 5, 1862.

325 The *Montgomery County Sentinel* reported: *Montgomery County Sentinel*, March 7, 1862.

325 A Confederate flag was hoisted: Ibid., March 14, 1862.

326 log of the Library of Congress: Confirmation by Dr. John R. Sellers, Manuscript Division, Library of Congress.

326 "all persons held as slaves . . .": Allen C. Guelzo, *Lincoln's Emancipation Proclamation: The End of Slavery in America* (New York: Simon & Schuster, 2004), 119–21.

326 "Wormley and I went . . .": Peter Wisbey, Vice Executive Director and Executive Director of Seward House, "In the 'Emancipation business': William and Frances Seward's Abolition Activism." http://www.rootsweb.com/~nycayuga/ugrr/seward.html.

327 "tolerably intelligent" black men: Guelzo, *Emancipation*, 143.

327 "both a perverse way of recognizing . . .": Mayer, *All on Fire*, 538.

327 "President of African Colonization": Ibid.

328 "well-known among all the negroes": *Washington, D.C., National Republican* in *Philadelphia Christian Recorder*, October 25, 1862.

328 emancipation "will be pushed . . .": Guelzo, *Emancipation*, 156.

329 a column of some forty carts: Louisa May Alcott, *Hospital Sketches* (1863; Bedford, Mass.: Applewood Books, n.d.), 26.

329 help of the "colored sisters": Ibid., 27.

331 "had come from midnight darkness to . . .": Mayer, *All on Fire*, p. 546.

331 The *New York Herald* derided Lincoln: *New York Herald*, January 3, 1863.

331 likely freed two hundred thousand: Guelzo. *Emancipation*, 222.

331 "had there been a defeat instead . . .": McPherson, *Battle Cry of Freedom*, 424.

332 "the wants of those destitute people . . .": *Philadelphia Christian Recorder*, March 14, 1863.

332 Paul Edmonson's seventeen-year-old grandson: Notebook privately held by the Taard family, descendants of Edward Young.

332 "Amelia Edmondson [*sic*], (col'd), wid Paul": Andrew Boyd, compiler, *Boyd's Washington and Georgetown Directory* (Washington, D.C.: Hudon Taylor, 1864), 146.

333 she had nursed "two cousins . . .": Grover, *Fugitive's Gibraltar*, 65.

333 "a meeting will be held in Asbury Chapel . . .": Gibbs, *Black, Copper, & Bright*, 28.

335 "beautifully wrought banner" *Philadelphia Christian Recorder*, August 1, 1863.

335 Amelia Edmonson purchased Lot 7: 9 NCT 262, Land Records, Recorder of Deeds, District of Columbia.

336 In 1864, to help finance: 28 NCT 300, Land Records, Recorder of Deeds, District of Columbia.

336 working in a hotel in Chicago: Pension Records, National Archives.

338 "could hardly reply": Doris Kearns Goodwin, *Team of Rivals: The Political Genius of Abraham Lincoln* (New York: Simon & Schuster, 2005), 630.

339 "The Negroes, under proper circumstances . . .": McPherson, *Battle Cry*, 836, citing correspondence from Robert E. Lee to Andrew Hunter, 11 January 1865, in O.R., Ser. IV, Vol. 3: 1012–13.

340 Cobb hired out: Misc. Mss. C, New-York Historical Society.

340 "grand, triumphal march." Noah Andre Trudeau, *Like Men of War: Black Troops in the Civil War 1862–1865* (Boston: Little, Brown and Company, 1998), 423.

340 An older black woman approached: Ibid., 424.

340n "was at the fall of Richmond . . .": Memorial prepared by John Brent's widow on March 25, 1917, the day after his death. From private papers of his descendant Marion Scott.

THIRTEEN
Emily and Samuel Return to Washington; John Is Found

343 "The rents are high . . .": *New York Tribune*, July 13, 1865.

344 she prepared the first of two wills: Wills at District of Columbia Archives.

346 employed as a coach driver: *Washington Eagle*, March 31, 1917.

346 "The Log Book . . .": Privately held by the Taard Family.

346 Brent took on his cousin Edward Young: Interview with Nancy Swartz, author of unpublished mss. on Calvin Brent, *Calvin Brent: Washington's First African American Architect*.

347 their six-and-a-quarter-acre farm: Montgomery County Land Records, EBP 8,64 Montgomery Country Courthouse, Rockville, Maryland.

347 two large contiguous lots of land: Liber 683, folio 22, Recorder of Deeds for the District of Columbia.

347 Larkin and Emily took out a loan: Liber 724, folio 260, Recorder of Deeds for the District of Columbia.

348 At a Hillsdale Civic Association meeting: Anacostia History file, Washingtoniana Room, Martin Luther King Public Library, Washington, D.C.

348 "Grandma & Frederick Douglass . . .": Private collection of Dr. Marion Holmes, a descendant of Emily Edmonson Johnson.

348 Amelia Edmonson revoked her earlier will: Wills at District of Columbia Archives.

348 Amelia Edmonson died on November 4, 1874: Ibid.

349 Larkin Johnson died: Death Certificate, Archives of the District of Columbia.

349 September 15, 1895: Death Certificate, Archives of the District of Columbia.

350 Lot 6 and Lot 20: Wills at District of Columbia Archives.

Epilogue

352 Daniel Bell died in 1877: Wills at District of Columbia Archives.

352 in 1883, Mary Bell wrote a letter: Probate Records of the Orphans Court of the District of Columbia Circuit Court. RG 21, National Archives, Washington, D.C.

353 *Pearl* veteran Alfred Pope, of Georgetown: Wills at District of Columbia Archives.

353 she had sold Hannah to Carter: Records of Tudor Place Historic House and Mansions.

353 Professor Kathleen M. Lesko: Telephone interview with Lesko.

354 the two slave pens on: Miller, "Overview of Bruin's Slave Pen."

Index

Entries followed by *(f)* indicate the fugitives on the *Pearl*.

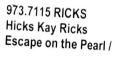